# Fuchsias
## ~A COLOUR GUIDE~

### George Bartlett

The Crowood Press

First Published in 1996 by
The Crowood Press Ltd
Ramsbury, Marlborough
Wiltshire SN8 2HR

This Impression 1998
© The Crowood Press, 1996

**British Library Cataloguing-in-Publication Data**

A catalogue reference for this book is available from the British Library

ISBN 1 85223 927 1 HB

**Acknowledgements**
The author would like to thank most sincerely the following specialist fuchsia nurseries for allowing the use of their catalogues in researching the names and descriptions of fuchsias available today:
Arcadia Nurseries, Brasscastle Lane, Nunthorpe, Middlesborough, Cleveland TS8 9EB
Blaenporth Nurseries, West Wales Fuchsia Centre, Cardigan, Dyfed SA43 2AU
Fuchsiavale Nurseries, Worcester Road, Torton, Kidderminster, Worcestershire DY11 7SB
Goulding's Fuchsias, West View, Link Lane, Bentley, Nr. Ipswich, Suffolk IP9 2DP
Jackson's Nurseries, Clifton Campville, Tamworth, Staffordshire, B79 0AP
J.V. Porter. 12 Hazel Grove, Southport PR8 6AX.
Kathleen Muncaster Fuchsias, 18 Field Lane, Morton, Gainsborough, Lincolnshire DN21 3BY
Littlebrook Fuchsias, Ash Green Lane West, Ash Green, Nr Aldershot, Hampshire GU12 6HL
Mike Oxtoby Fuchsias, 74 Westgate, North Cave, Brough, North Humberside HU15 2NJ.
Oldbury Fuchsias, Brissenden Green, Bethersden, Ashford, Kent TN26 3BJ
Silver Dale Nurseries, Shute Lane, Coombe Martin, North Devon EX34 0HT

The author would also like to thank, even more sincerely, the following nurseries who permitted their routines to be disrupted during the photography of their superb plants:
Arcadia Nurseries, Brasscastle Lane, Nunthorpe, Middlesborough, Cleveland TS8 9EB
Fisher Fuchsias, Brynawel Garden Centre, Sully Road, Penarth, South Glamorgan CF64 3UU
Fuchsiavale Nurseries, Worcester Road, Torton, Kidderminster, Worcestershire DY11 7SB
Kathleen Muncaster Fuchsias, 18 Field Lane, Morton, Gainsborough, Lincolnshire DN21 3BY
Littlebrook Fuchsias, Ash Green Lane West, Ash Green, Nr. Aldershot, Hampshire GU12 6HL
P & B Fuchsias, 30 Abingdon Road, Dorchester-on-Thames, Wallingford, Oxfordshire OX10 7LE
Warrenorth Fuchsias, East Grinstead Road, North Chailey, Lewes, East Sussex BN8 4JD

Typeset and designed by:
D & N Publishing
Ramsbury, Marlborough
Wiltshire SN8 2HR.

Typeface used: Sabon, main text; Helvetica, captions.

Phototypeset by Dorwyn Ltd, Chichester.
Printed and bound by Times Offset, Malaysia.

# Contents

# Introduction

The versatility of the fuchsia, allied to its enormous range of colour and form, makes it one of the most well-loved garden plants. And despite its rather exotic appearance, the fuchsia is easy to grow and to propagate, making it an especially good choice for the gardener with limited tine or experience. No special facilities are necessary and there is no magic formula or set of rules that you have to obey in order to produce superb specimen plants: fuchsias do well in spite of what we might do to them.

Grown in the garden or on the patio in containers, fuchsias will give a generous display of flowers from early summer to the first frosts; and in hanging baskets, the pendulous flowers of the trailing varieties will make a diverse and stunning display of their own, as well as an interesting complement to other plants. They are easy to train, and the numerous varieties that are available provide the more creative or ambitious gardener with endless opportunities for experiment. The protection of the greenhouse offers yet more possibilities: earlier flowers and larger plants, and also the chance to train plants into exotic shapes.

This book describes more than 2,000 of the cultivars and species that are available from specialist nurseries. The text gives a concise profile of each listed cultivar or species, and a good proportion of these are illustrated on the opposite page for easy reference. There are notes on the plant's size, habit and hardiness, and, where appropriate, suggestions on the best way to cultivate and display it. Thus, the description will serve not only to facilitate identification of a plant that you may already possess, but to enable you to determine whether a particular plant that you would like to obtain will really suit your requirements.

While the book is intended to be primarily a source of reference and useful information, it is hoped that it will also serve to inspire the reader to try new and unusual varieties, and to realize to the full the vast potential of the fuchsia.

## History

It seems almost impossible to believe that fuchsias have only been known to the modern world since 1703; and it was not until the 1820s that the nurserymen and hybridists realized the potential of these plants and started to breed new plants from the available species. It is quite amazing that such a vast quantity of cultivars, of so many differing colours and form, has become available to us in so short a time.

Some 104 different species have been identified to date. All are native to the southern hemisphere, most growing in the countries of South America although one group is native to New Zealand. As it is from these species that all our modern cultivars have emanated, I feel that it is important to tabulate them giving the areas within which they are found (see table opposite).

## Composts

There are many different brands of compost on the market and beginners to the art of growing fuchsias are very often confused as to the best type of compost to use. However, there is no need to let this worry you at all since fuchsias will grow well in virtually any type of compost. The important factor is that the compost should be well drained and open.

Composts basically are either loam-based, peat-based or peat free. The loam-based composts (such as the John Innes type mixes) are much heavier than their peat-based counterparts and, because of their ability to retain more moisture, are best suited for use in clay pots. Even when using loam-based composts it is advisable to add further quantities of grit, Perlite or Vermiculite to aid the drainage properties. Peat-based composts are much lighter and are best used in plastic containers. They, too, need to be given additional drainage material so that the compost does not become waterlogged. Peat-based composts will also need the addition of fertilizers more frequently as the seasons progress.

Other types of compost are now being mixed using coir, which is the waste fibre product from coconuts. Additional feeding at a very early stage will be necessary when using coir composts as the openness encourages excessive drainage and the leaching of the nutrients.

Mixing one's own compost is often recommended by some growers and is a very satisfactory and easy method of obtaining a good compost. It is possible to purchase bags of compost mixes which are simply added to the required quantities of peat and grit or Perlite. One very important factor is that

# All the Species of Fuchsias

## Section 1. *Quelusia* (Argentina, Brazil and Chile)

F. bracelinae
F. campus-portoi
F. magellanica var. macrostema
F. coccinea
F. magellanica
F. regia var. regia
F. magellanica var. alba
F. regia
F. regia var. alpestris

## Section 2. *Fuchsia* (Andes and Central America)

F. abrupta
F. andrei
F. ayavacensis
F. canescens
F. ceracea
F. concertifolia
F. collata
F. crassistipula
F. decussata
F. dependens
F. fontinalis
F. gehrigeri
F. harlingii
F. hirtella
F. llewelynii
F. macropetala
F. macrostigma
F. mathewsii
F. orientalis
F. pallescens
F. pilosa
F. pringsheimii
F. rivularis
F. sammartina
F. scherffiana
F. simplicaulis
F. sylvatica
F. triphylla
F. venusta
F. vulcanica
F. ampliata
F. austromontana
F. boliviana
F. caucana
F. cohabambana
F. coriacifolia
F. corymbifolia
F. cautrecasii
F. denticulata
F. ferreyrae
F. furfuracea
F. glaberrima
F. hartwegii
F. lechmanii
F. loxensis
F. macrophylla
F. magdalenae
F. nigricans
F. ovalis
F. petiolaris
F. polyantha
F. putamayensis
F. sanctae-rosa
F. scabriuscula
F. sessilifolia
F. steyermarkii
F. tincta
F. vargasiana
F. verrucosa
F. wurdackii

## Section 3 *Kierschlegeria* (Chile)
F. lycioides

## Section 4 *Skinnera* (New Zealand and Tahiti)
F. colensoi
F. exorticata
F. procumbens
F. cyrtandroides
F. perscandens

## Section 5 *Hemsleyella* (Bolivia and Venezuela)
F. apetala
F. chloroloba
F. huanucoensis
F. insignis
F. membranacea
F. pitaloensis
F. tilletiana
F. cestroides
F. garleppiana
F. inflata
F. juntasensis
F. nana
F. salcifolia
F. tunariensis

## Section 6 *Schuffia* (Central America and Mexico)
F. arborescens
F. paniculata

## Section 7 *Encliandra* (Central America and Mexico)
F. × bacillaris
F. encliandra ssp encliandra
F. encliandra ssp tetradactyla
F. microphylla ssp hemsleyana
F. microphylla ssp microphylla
F. microphylla ssp mintiflora
F. parviflora
F. thymifolia ssp minimiflora
F. thymifolia ssp thymifolia

## Section 8 *Jimenezia* (Costa Rica and Panama)
F. jimenezia

## Section 9 *Ellobium* (Central America and Mexico)
F. fulgens
F. splendens
F. decidua

when mixing your own you can be sure that the compost you are using is fresh.

A good start for the root system is essential to obtain excellent plants, and a well-balanced compost will give you that good start. However, the compost is only the medium into which the plant will anchor its roots; the nutrient which is present at the beginning will rapidly become exhausted and will need to be replenished on a regular basis.

It is possible to replace these essential nutrients by using liquid fertilizers, which are purchased in granular form and added to water. There are a number of suitable fertilizers on the market but it will be necessary to look carefully at the analysis to determine

the right type to use in any given season. At the beginning of the growing, season a higher nitrogen (N) content will boost the growth and development of the foliage. Phosphorous (P) is essential for the growth of a sturdy root system. Potash (K) is necessary later in the season to assist in the ripening of the wood, the formation of buds and in increasing the depth of colour in the flowers. So a fertilizer high in nitrogen would be used at the beginning of the season; a good balanced fertilizer (equal proportions of nitrogen, phosphorous and potash) can be used during the major part of the growing season, and a high potash fertilizer would be used as the plants start to produce their buds. However,

5

if you wish, it is possible to grow superb plants using just a balanced liquid fertilizer throughout the season.

To sum up, a good compost must be able to absorb and hold moisture and nutrients, but it must also be sufficiently open and well drained to prevent stagnation and the drowning of the roots. It should also be pointed out that the most expensive compost is not always the best; if you are happy with the results you are getting then your fuchsias will be happy growing in it.

# Watering

In describing the types of compost available today, mention was made of the need to ensure that the compost is 'well drained'. As all plants need quite large quantities of water in order to be able to live and grow, the question is often asked, 'How often and how much?'

The first part of the question is very difficult to answer. It would be very easy to say 'whenever they need it' but that really begs the question. Plants will show you when there is a dire need for moisture as the leaves will become very flaccid and the sepals of any flowers will start to droop. Get to know the weight of each pot by constantly handling them. If the symptoms described above are evident, then lifting the pot up will indicate if it is short of water as it will feel very light in weight. The remedy will be to give the compost a thorough soaking: this can be achieved either by pouring water into the top of the pot and allowing it to seep through the compost, by pouring water into a saucer in which the pot is standing; or by immersing the whole pot in a bucket of water until all air bubbles cease to rise from the compost.

Unfortunately many of the peat-based composts tend to shrink away from the sides of the pot as they dry out, and water poured into the top will find the easy route out and escape down the sides without moistening the compost to any great extent. Filling a saucer with water will have the desired effect of moistening all the compost by capillary action, but this takes time. There is also the possibility that the plant will be left standing in water so the compost becomes saturated and the air spaces disappear. After a period of time this will result in the root system being starved of air, and cause the plant to die by drowning. Immersing the pot in a bucket is perhaps the safest and quickest way of ensuring that the compost is thoroughly moistened.

There is also considerable debate as to whether tap water or rainwater should be used. Rainwater contains many minerals collected from the air and so is undoubtedly the best, but when supplies run out, as they invariably do during hot summer weather, then we will need to use water from the tap. If possible such water should be allowed to stand for a couple of hours before use to allow the chlorine content to disperse; if it is not, however, and watering is carried out directly with the use of a hosepipe, no harm will come to the plants. Watering overhead with a hosepipe does mean that the leaves will have a residue of chalk on them in hard water areas of the country.

When large numbers of plants have to be watered in a relatively short space of time then a hosepipe is the only real solution. However, bearing in mind that our plants sometimes also need feeding, it may be necessary to carry out this task by using a watering can. It is so easy to forget that during a long spell of hot weather, the plants will suffer with the continual leaching out of the nutrients when the watering takes place.

Plants indoors on windowsills will probably be standing in saucers to protect the woodwork. Watering of these plants should be carried out either by taking them to a sink where the water can be allowed to drain through the compost, or by watering into the saucer. If this is done, the recommendation is that the plant should be allowed to take up as much moisture as possible in about a quarter of an hour and then any excess water should be removed from the saucer.

Bear in mind that a damp sponge will always pick up more moisture than a dry one, and that very dry compost will take a great deal of patience before it contains the requisite quantity of moisture.

## Overwatering
The symptoms which are present when the plant is dry and needs watering are unfortunately the same as when the plant is too wet and is 'drowning'. However, by lifting the pot you can quickly determine if the pot is too light or too heavy, and if it is very heavy then it is important to take immediate action to reduce the quantity of moisture in the compost.

Remove the whole of the rootball from the pot: if it is very heavy the compost will look dark and soggy; there might also be a rather unpleasant smell coming from it. Stand the rootball on an upturned flowerpot and allow it to drain for several hours. If there is still no improvement to the look of the plant then more drastic action might be necessary, and as much of the old compost must be removed from the root system as is possible. The state of the roots can then be determined: white roots are alive and active, whilst brown gnarled roots are probably dead. If repotting is necessary then the plant, when repotted, should be placed in a shaded position until recovery is complete.

### Treatment in Hot Weather

Often during periods of extremely hot weather, plants will give the impression of wilting even when there is sufficient water in the compost, the roots being unable to take up water in sufficient quantities to maintain the turgidity of the leaves. This excessive transpiration can be rectified by spraying the foliage at intervals during the day. Fuchsias are happier in shaded conditions so we must endeavour to give them this type of situation.

## Propagation

It is very satisfying to be able to increase the number of your favourite plants. Cuttings taken from the shoots of branches will root very easily if given the right sort of conditions. Surprisingly, though, many growers of long standing complain that a fairly high proportion of their cuttings fail to root. What, then, are the conditions required to assist the cuttings in the formation of roots?

It is important to take cuttings from plants which are in excellent condition. They should preferably have been watered well a few hours before the operation takes place; having removed the piece from the plant it should be inserted into its rooting medium as quickly as possible, and should not be allowed to wilt. The cuttings should be kept as turgid as possible by keeping them in an area of high humidity. They should be shaded from the sun. The use of hormone powders is not really necessary for fuchsia cuttings especially if the piece has been removed from the very tip of the plant; this sort can be described as a soft green-tip cutting. In actual fact a fuchsia cutting will root very easily provided it is given warmth and moisture.

It is possible to purchase electric propagators which give the very necessary gentle bottom warmth necessary for rooting; a temperature of 60–65°F (15–18°C) is all that is required. However, I have found that the most perfect of all propagators is perhaps one of the cheapest: a sweet jar. Cuttings placed within a sweet jar and away from the direct rays of the sun will have their own mini-climate of high humidity around them. Let us go through the process step by step.

### Procedure

The equipment you require will be a sweet jar (propagator); a strip taken from a preformed fifty or sixty tray; compost (your own ordinary potting compost mixed with an equal quantity of Vermiculite); a sharp knife, razor blade or scalpel; labels; a waterproof marking pen; a watering can with a fine rose; and of course a healthy, well watered parent plant.

Mix the compost and Vermiculite well, keeping it as light and airy as possible. Place some of the compost in the tray, tapping it gently on the bench to settle the compost; do not insert your fingers to firm the compost. Using the sharp knife, remove a piece from the end of a branch by cutting just above a leaf node. The cutting will be quite small, soft and green; it will have a pair of mature leaves, a pair of immature leaves and a growing tip, and there will be about ½in (1cm) of stem from the lowest leaves to the end. Push the cutting gently into the compost so that the lowest set of leaves is just about resting on the surface of the compost. Do not firm the compost around the cutting because the water will do that later. When the strip has been completely filled with cuttings – you can have a strip of just one type or have ten or twelve different ones – make sure that each cutting has its own label.

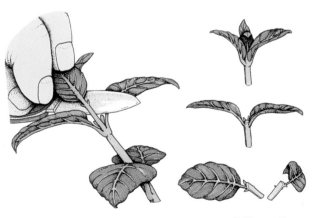

Taking cuttings.

coffee jar       jam jar       sweet jar

Types of Propagator.

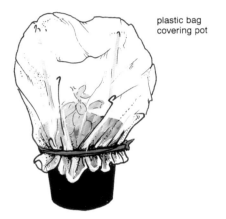

plastic bag covering pot

pot on rooted cuttings to individual pots

Potting on.

With the sweet jar lying on its side, push the strip of cuttings into the jar. A word of warning: many labels are about 4in (10cm) in length, and the opening to the sweet jar is usually a little less than that, so it is important to reduce the length of the label before insertion. Using the fine rose on the end of the watering can, give the strip of cuttings a good watering. This will settle the compost around the cuttings and will be the only watering that they will have until they have rooted. Screw on the lid of the sweet jar.

The jar containing the cuttings should now be placed in a position which has plenty of light but which will never receive the full rays of the sun. Under the staging of a greenhouse is ideal, or on the windowsill of a north-facing window.

After a few days you will notice that there is condensation inside the jar. However, do not be tempted to open the jar to remove this, because a high humidity is necessary for rooting. There will be no loss of turgidity on the cuttings, and after approximately three weeks it might be possible to see signs of new growth in the tips. Keep them as cool as possible as we are not looking for rapid growth at this stage.

When it is obvious that there is new growth, it is time to wean the new young plants gently from their cloistered, humid conditions. Unscrew the lid of the sweet jar and leave it off for a few minutes several times a day. Gradually increase the length of time the lid is off until it is obvious that it can be left off permanently. Remove the strip of rooted cuttings from the sweet jar and place them on the staging, but still keeping them shaded from direct sunshine.

8

It will now be possible to remove each rooted cutting from the tray and the root system can be examined. The cuttings can now be given their first individual pots and I would suggest placing them in the same type of compost as that in which rooting took place, ie fifty-fifty your normal compost and Vermiculite. Do not be tempted to give them too large a pot; a 3in (7½cm) or a 2¼in (6cm) square pot will be ideal at this stage.

From now onwards the cuttings are young plants and can be treated as such, and the process of training them into the shapes that you require can now start.

I have gone into some detail to describe this method of taking cuttings; it is one I use and have found very satisfactory. However, many other mediums and means of maintaining a high humidity around the cuttings can be used; recently I have been rooting cuttings in blocks of flower arrangers' oasis. Cuttings root easily in this medium; after all, they have moisture and will be given warmth. Insert them by pushing them gently into the oasis if it is sufficiently wet and soft, or by making a small hole with a flower-stick. I find it is advisable to keep these oasis blocks moist by standing them in water in a container such as an ice cream box. There does not appear to be any need to enclose the container in polythene, as the humidity from the water surrounding the oasis will keep the cuttings turgid.

When such cuttings have rooted, cut out the small cube of the oasis containing the roots of the cutting, and plant it into your pot of compost. Ensure that no part of the oasis is above the surface of the compost or you will find that moisture will be leached away from the roots and the oasis will become very hard.

Larger quantities of cuttings can be taken at any one time by using an electrically heated propagator or a greenhouse bench with undersoil heating. The method of taking cuttings and inserting them into their growing medium is exactly the same. The major problem is caused by the need to maintain humidity around the plants: this can be achieved by spraying them regularly with water or by using a misting system. It is also important to shade such cuttings from the rays of the sun to prevent them rapidly drying out and subsequently wilting. Yes – fuchsia cuttings will root very easily in any type of medium, *provided* that they have moisture and warmth.

I have described the method used for soft green-tip cuttings; I did not use hormonal rooting powder because cuttings of this type root very easily without it. There are other types of cutting that can also be used, and it is possible from one fairly short stem to secure as many as a dozen cuttings of various types, all of which will root easily. If you are using harder wood cuttings from ripe stems, perhaps in the colder months, then hormonal rooting powders or liquids might be of benefit. However, once open, rooting

Electric seed tray propagator.

foliar feeding should not be done when the plant is in flower

Foliar feeding.

powders are thought to lose their viability after a couple of months; the powder must be fresh. Rooting liquids have a much longer lifespan and may therefore be more useful.

You will have noticed that I remove my soft-tip cutting by severing above the leaf node. Many growers, particularly those who grow other plant types from which they take cuttings, will always remove a piece by cutting below the leaf node and then removing the lower set of leaves. I feel that this is a waste of the plant's energy, growing the leaves only for them to be removed, especially as the next set of leaves, together with the buds growing in the leaf axils, will in itself be available as another cutting.

# New Plants from 'Sports'

Occasionally plants do rather strange things and produce branches which exhibit flowers which are different, or foliage which is a variation from the normal. This phenomenon is known as 'sporting' and can occur in any genus of plant. It is strange that occasionally plants of the same cultivar will produce sports in many widespread parts of the country in the same season. When this happens the confusing situation arises of similar sports being introduced with different names.

If you should be fortunate enough to discover that one of your plants is 'throwing' a sport you should first determine that there is sufficient variation from the norm to make it worth 'saving'. Variegated foliage can be very attractive, as can a completely different coloured flower. To 'save' the sport, cuttings must be taken from the branch which is producing the variation, in the hope that when each of these cuttings reaches maturity it will still be exhibiting the new variation. It is possible that the new plant will revert to its original coloured leaf or flower, so a lengthy trial period is essential to ensure that the variation has been 'fixed'.

# Shaping your Plants

Once your cuttings have rooted and have been transferred into their own individual pots, it will be necessary to consider the type of plant you require. Plants can be grown as bushes, in baskets, as standards, or as fans, pillars or conicals. It is also possible, going from one extreme to the other, to train fuchsias as bonsai plants. You should start training your plant as soon as rooting has taken place.

**Bushes**
The most basic of all shapes is the bush; it is also the one that is required for practically all other types of training, at some time. When the rooted cutting has developed two or three sets of leaves, it can be encouraged to send out side shoots from each of the leaf axils by discouraging any further upward growth. The growing tip can be gently removed by bending it at right angles to the leaves. It will snap off very cleanly if the young plant is well charged with moisture. Otherwise, scissors can be used. This removal of the growing tip, usually described as 'stopping', will prevent any further upward growth of the main stem but will encourage the growth of laterals from the leaf axils; thus if there were three sets of leaves on the stem (each set having two leaves) then six branches will grow as a result of this 'stopping'. Occasionally cuttings will have their leaves growing in groups of three, so nine branches will be the result of 'stopping' this type of plant.

The young plant will be encouraged to grow fairly rapidly, and each branch will develop further sets of leaves. After about three to four weeks, another 'stopping' can

Pruning for new growth.

10

Stopping to promote bushy growth.

and 10in (15 and 25cm) in length. A quarter standard has a clear stem between 10 and 18in (25 and 45cm). A half standard has a clear stem between 18 and 30in (45 and 75cm) and a full standard has a clear stem between 30 and 42in (75 and 101cm).

The training of a standard fuchsia is similar to that of a bush. However, as our initial intention will be to grow the stem strong and straight we should do all we can to encourage that upward growth: all the energy of the plant should be directed up the central stem, and any sideshoots which develop in the leaf axils should be removed. At an early stage a short flower stick should be placed alongside the stem and the plant tied to it loosely so that a straight stem is developed.

Straightness of the stem is encouraged by turning the plant regularly so that all parts share the available light equally. When a

be undertaken when each branch has two or three sets of leaves, removing the growing tip of each of the branches. This will now give us 6 × 6 (36); or 9 × 9 (81) branches. Always remove the growing tips of *all* the branches on the plant during the same session, otherwise the strength and vigour of the plant will be concentrated on any shoots which have inadvertently been left thus creating a very unevenly shaped bush. We will be aiming for as much symmetry as possible during this training process.

In many cases this could be considered sufficient 'stopping' as a very attractive bushy plant will have resulted.

### Standards

The training of a plant into a standard takes several months so it is advisable, if possible, to start this process in the autumn of one year so that the necessary amount of growth is achieved for flowering during the following season. With some strong-growing cultivars, a cutting taken in late winter will produce the desired result. A cutting which has a set of three leaves growing at each axil would be an excellent choice for training as a standard, because the resultant head, producing 50 per cent more branches, will be much thicker and more floriferous. However, excellent standards can be grown using the more usual two leaved cuttings.

Standards, within the definitions given by the British Fuchsia Society for show purposes, come in numerous sizes, the length of the stem deciding the type of standard. A 'mini-standard' is one that has a clear stem from compost level to the first branch, between 6

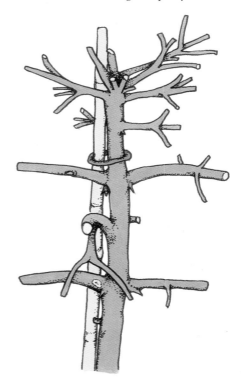

Hard pruning of the top growth of a standard head in order to encourage fresh shoots.

Training to produce a standard.

height of 15–18in (38–45cm) has been reached, I then allow the sideshoots to develop in the next four sets of leaf axils. As further sideshoots develop I remove the lowest set so that I always have four sets at the top of my developing standard; then should an accident occur and the tip of the plant become damaged preventing any further upward growth, I will have sufficient branches already forming to make the head of the plant.

Continue to grow the stem of your standard until it reaches the height you require. If you are aiming for a half standard, for example, allow it to grow until the bottom laterals are about 24in (60cm) from the soil. You will notice that this height is half way between the maximum and minimum permitted for this type of growth.

When the height you require has been reached it is time to start building up the 'head' of the standard. To do this, remove the growing tip of the plant: upward growth will now stop, and the laterals in the top four sets of leaf axils will grow strongly. From now onwards you can treat the development of

the head in exactly the same way as you would treat the development of a bush plant.

At no stage during the growing of a standard should the plant feel threatened. Thus if the pot becomes full of roots so that the plant has difficulty in finding nutrient, then upward growth will stop and the plant will start to produce flower buds. Regular inspection of the compost in the pot is therefore necessary, and when a good supply of roots can be seen on the surface of the compost the plant should be transferred into a larger pot with fresh compost. Also, you need to feed with either a balanced or a high nitrogen-content liquid fertilizer throughout this growing period to ensure uninterrupted growth.

Standards can be used in the open garden to give added height to flower borders, but under no circumstances should a standard fuchsia be left outside during the winter because the first severe frost will kill the stem that has taken so long to develop. Any type of fuchsia can be used for training into standards; you need not limit yourself to growing only the strong, upright-growing ones, and in my opinion the most attractive standards are those devel-

12

oped from plants which have a trailing habit. For example, fuchsias usually recommended for baskets will make excellent 'weeping' standards; they may require a little longer or a little more patience to achieve the required height, but the result is usually breathtaking.

If you are keen to try your hand at growing a standard start by experimenting with the mini-standards which can be developed easily in a season and are very satisfying. Preferably for this type of standard use the smaller-leaved and smaller flowering cultivars; to ensure, too, that the pot in which the plant is being grown is in proportion to the eventual size of the plant. With a mini-standard, show regulations permit a pot no larger than 5in (13cm). The others are normally permitted in any sized pots.

## Baskets

The most attractive baskets of fuchsias will contain a number of plants all of the same cultivar. It is a mistake to think that different cultivars will produce an exciting kaleidoscope of colour because they grow and develop at different rates; so when one plant is ready to burst into bloom, another will be just about forming its buds and consequently a very uneven basket will result. Our objective is to produce a complete ball of flower.

A 12in (30cm) diameter basket will require four or five well developed plants, and I would suggest that plants grown from cuttings rooted in the Autumn will be the best ones to choose. The plants should have been grown in exactly the same way as has been recommended for bush plants, except that I would recommend allowing the laterals to develop three sets of leaves before removing the growing tips; by allowing the extra growth of the stem the plant will be encouraged to trail. Some cultivars are far too stiff and upright in their growths to make good baskets so it is better to select those which are laxer in their growth habit. Most nurserymen list fuchsias which are specially recommended for baskets.

The earlier a basket can be made up, the better it is. Early spring would be an ideal time, although no attempt should be made to place such baskets in their final flowering positions until early to midsummer (and even then it will be necessary to keep an eye on the weather forecast and give protection if frost is forecast).

A quantity of your usual compost to which a long-lasting fertilizer has been added, should be placed in the base of the basket; the preformed shapes or moss will prevent the compost falling through the wires of the basket. Using five plants, I always place one in the centre and four around the edge of the basket. If you place in position empty pots of the same size as that in which the plants are growing, the whole container, including the pots, can be filled with the compost. A tap on the bench will settle the compost, and the pots can then be removed from the compost, one at a time, leaving the perfect shape of the pot into which the plant can be placed.

When all plants have been put into position the whole basket should be given a good watering, using the fine rose on a watering can, in order to settle the compost around the plants. Within the protection of a greenhouse the plants will grow rapidly and fill the top of the basket. Each time the laterals on the plants develop three or four sets of leaves then the growing tips should be removed, as this will encourage even more bushiness of the plants. It will be appreciated that as the season progresses it will become quite a task to ensure that all growing tips are removed at the same time. Turn the basket regularly so that all sides get an equal share of the light.

From early summer it will be possible to hang each basket in its final position. However, it must be remembered that frosts are still possible, and a careful watch will have to be kept on the baskets so they are not left short of water; the additional movement of the air outside causes the compost to dry out more quickly. Moreover additional watering will

When planting a basket, support it by resting it on a bucket or something similar.

mean that nutrients are being leached more rapidly from the compost, so a regular feeding pattern, preferably with a balanced fertilizer, is essential to maintain steady growth. You will have to stop pinching out the growing tips as flowering time approaches: single-flowered cultivars need eight to ten weeks to develop sufficiently for flowers to be produced, and those carrying double flowers need an additional two to three weeks.

Half or wall baskets are trained in the same sort of way, and look very attractive as they break up the bareness of a blank wall. The number of plants required in a half basket will be determined by its size and the strength of the plants growth.

Training for a fan shape.

Training an espalier: remove growing tip to leave eight lateral shoots.

Hanging pots of fuchsias can be very useful and there are many proprietary brands available at the moment. Pots in the region of 6in (15cm) in diameter can contain just one well grown plant, whilst 8in (20cm) diameter pots will look better with three.

**Large Structures**

The sight of a well grown fuchsia fan always attracts considerable attention. The growing and training of structures such as this and other large plants (pillars, conicals, pyramids and so on) demands a great deal of patience and expertise. Patience is required because the training will take three or four years. Using a 'fan' as an example, it is better to use one of the well tried, strong-growing plants such as 'Phyllis', 'Display', 'Checkerboard' or 'Koldings Perle'. A framework of the desired shape needs to be placed in a 5in (13cm) pot containing the upward-growing plant. Both the upward shoot and the laterals should be encouraged to grow. As the laterals of most twin-leaved plants grow in a 'cruciform' manner, only the alternate laterals should be retained. These laterals can be trained along the framework. It is now a question of encouraging rapid growth and tying in the shoots to form the shape you require.

Bearing in mind the comments made when training bushes and standards – if upward growth is required the laterals should be 'stopped', and if lateral growth is required the upward shoot should be 'stopped' – it should be possible to fill in the framework. At the end of the first season a height of 2 to 3ft (60–90cm) should be achieved. The plants will require a short period of rest so in early autumn it will be necessary to prune back gently the tips of all shoots, and to defoliate the plant completely. Remove the risk of overwintering any pests or diseases by using a good combined insecticide/fungicide, and then encourage the development of the young buds in each leaf axil. 'Ticking over' growth will be maintained during the winter months by giving sufficient artificial heat to keep the plants frost free.

With the rise in temperature and light intensity in the spring, the amount of root growth space will have to be increased by moving the

Training for a pyramid shape: remove the growing tip leaving six lateral shoots. The plant will form a new tip and new lateral shoots, from which the tip should again be removed. Continue stopping out in this way as the plant matures.

Training for pillar formation: remove the growing tip from the young plant, leaving two lateral shoots. As the plant matures, maintain the shape by removing side shoots as shown.

plant into a larger pot. Some of the old compost should be teased away and any diseased roots should be removed. The rapid growth of the plant will also now necessitate increasing the size of the framework; as we should hope to achieve something like a 4ft (120cm) height and spread in the second year, the size of the new structure should reflect this. There is no need to prevent the plant from flowering; with this type of training it is possible still to appreciate the flowers whilst the plant is being developed. However, it might be advisable not to allow the plant to set seeds during this process.

The training in subsequent years is a continuation of that already described: thus the framework will be getting bigger each year and the space required will probably rapidly exceed the space available; a major problem will therefore be to contain the plant within the limits that we have set.

When training upright structures the same advice can be given, although height is the major concern. There is always one shoot at the apex of the plant which is the 'leader'; when the top shoot is 'stopped' to encourage thickening of the side branches, then one of the upward growing shoots should be allowed to develop to take over the duties of the 'leader'. This shoot will grow rapidly when the tips of all the laterals are 'stopped'.

Once maximum-sized pot possible has been achieved and a fresh supply of nutritious compost needs to be given, some growers use the 'Christmas Cake' method. This entails removing the plant from its pot and cutting a wedge out of the rootball; the plant is then replaced in the pot and this wedge is filled with the new compost. A record needs to be kept as to where the wedge has been situated (usually by using plant labels) so that when the operation is next carried out the wedge can be removed from a different part. Other growers simply cut away the bottom portion of the rootball and place fresh compost in the bottom of the pot. All, however, are working on the known principle that there can only be top growth in any plant if there is root growth, and removing some of the rootball gives the plant room to grow fresh roots either within the wedges or at the base of the pot.

**Bonsai Fuchsias**

At the other extreme it is possible to grow fuchsias 'in miniature'. I hesitate to use the word 'bonsai', although we are growing our plants in small pots, because most people think of bonsai plants as being miniatures of larger plants. However, fuchsia flowers and foliage when grown in smaller pots still retain their original sizes. Nevertheless it is possible to use the bonsai style of growing and form with some considerable effect: the resultant plants can look extremely attractive, and can remain growing in their specialized containers over many years. Obviously it is advisable to use types of plants which have smaller leaves and smaller flowers because they will then be in proportion to the size of the pot being used.

Young rooted cuttings can be used and placed in very small pots. Some growers recommend using pots which have lattice type holes around the sides, as the roots will then grow through these holes and can be trimmed back to encourage the dwarfing effect.

Shaping the framework of the plant into true bonsai patterns can be accomplished either by using wires to place the branches in the positions required, or by lying the pot and plant on its side to get the growing shoot, which will always try to grow perpendicularly, to move in the direction you want. Judicious pruning of top growth and roots will be necessary to achieve the desired attractive results. The beauty of any bonsai plant is very much in the eye of the beholder, but the appearance of age can be accentuated with fuchsias by the careful positioning of branches and by encouraging roots to grow over strategically placed rocks. Small, flat containers will complete the picture and if the whole of the surface of the compost is covered with a blanket of moss, then the resultant plant will be much admired.

Displays of plants grown by the bonsai method should become features of major fuchsia shows in future years.

# Overwintering your Plants

Fuchsia plants are really deciduous, losing their leaves and going into a state of dormancy during the winter months, then breaking into fresh growth when temperatures rise. However, it is possible to keep them growing through the winter, in green leaf, provided that the temperature is maintained at around the 40°F (4°C) mark.

Fuchsias growing in pots or baskets should not be left outside during the winter months but should be given protection to ensure that the root system is not killed. If plants can be kept in a frost-free environment and as long as the root system is not allowed to dry out completely then all should come safely through the winter. Equally, larger structures such as standards should not be left outside during the winter, even when planted in the open ground. They should always be dug up and taken under cover, and this applies even to those plants which are normally considered to be 'hardy' cultivars.

Plants established in the garden will come safely through the winter provided they have been planted sufficiently deeply and have been given enough time to develop a strong root system. Ideally they should have been planted in early summer, and with the top of the compost some 2 or 3in (6–8cm) beneath the surface of the soil. When the first severe frost has defoliated the plants do not be tempted to cut away all the apparently dead branches, but leave them where they are because they serve two purposes: they remind you as to their position, and they will also give a slight protection from frosts later in the season. In the spring, when fresh growth starts to come from the base of the plants, all this old wood can then be trimmed back. Additional protection can be provided by placing peat or bracken around the plants to insulate them. A true 'hardy' fuchsia will come through the winter successfully and will produce its young shoots from below soil level sufficiently early for the new branches to produce their first flowers from about the beginning of July.

The means by which plants are kept frost free will depend entirely upon the facilities available. A small number of plants can be placed in a large box in a cold greenhouse and given the protection of polystyrene chips or some other form of insulation. If you have a slightly heated greenhouse then additional protection can be given, when severe frost threatens, by covering with newspaper or horticultural fleece.

Some zealous growers go to the trouble of burying their plants in the garden. A 'grave' is lined with straw and the trimmed-back plants placed on it, and these are then covered with more straw; this method will give excellent protection. It is necessary, though, to have a deep 'grave', and one which will not also act as a reservoir for water. In the spring the plants taken from such 'graves' often have long, thin white growths; these do at least indicate that the plant is still alive, but they should be trimmed back hard to encourage new, sturdy growth.

Winter and the overwintering of your plants can be rather a worrying time but there is no real reason why the majority of your plants should not come safely through.

## Pests and Diseases

Fortunately fuchsias do not suffer very greatly from many pests and diseases, and with a little extra care those that do attack can be kept under control.

### Pests

WHITEFLY
Whitefly is probably the biggest menace as far as fuchsias are concerned. They have the ability to multiply very rapidly indeed and a minor infestation one day can develop rapidly into a major problem. The main difficulty is that the chemical sprays at our disposal will only kill the adult flies, so when an attack is discovered it is necessary to spray at intervals of about four days to kill the adults as they emerge. After four or five such sprayings the problem should have been solved. Any good insecticide specifically designed for the eradication of whitefly, diluted to the correct strength as marked on the bottle, will be satisfactory – though always ensure that the bottle does not indicate that the contents are unsuitable for using with fuchsias.

Unfortunately wet sprays cannot be used when the plants are heavily in bud or in flower, and at this stage in the season it will be necessary to use fumigating smokes; these are very effective, however, and do not mark the flowers. A regular course of 'smoke cones' will still be necessary in order to kill the whitefly as they emerge.

It is possible to use natural predators throughout the season. The chalcid wasp *Encarsia formosa* can be used to great effect, but the conditions need to be correct for them to work satisfactorily. The 'wasp' lays its eggs in the 'scales' of the whitefly thus preventing adult whitefly from emerging. Remember also that predators will not kill *all* the whitefly because to do so would rob them of their source of food – the honeydew produced by the whitefly.

GREENFLY
Greenfly can usually be seen in clusters around the light green tip of each shoot, and are unmistakable in appearance. They are sap-sucking insects, and this habit causes distortion and curling of the young leaves. They are very prolific in their reproductive habits, so quick action is advisable; regular spraying with any good proprietary insecticide will keep them at bay – *regularity* in a spraying programme is essential to keep these pests under control. Many of the 'old-fashioned' methods of controlling greenfly are still being used; if you have one and you find it satisfactory, then continue to use it.

RED SPIDER MITE
Not really a 'spider' but it is certainly one of the worst pests for fuchsias. They are very difficult to detect in the early stages as they are virtually invisible to the naked eye. Plants which have been attacked by 'red spider' can be recognized because the foliage turns to a bronzy colour and becomes extremely brittle. In the later stages of severe attack, very fine webs can be seen spreading from leaf to leaf. The pest will spread rapidly from plant to plant in a greenhouse.

It is often considered that an attack of red spider results from poor growing conditions. However, the mite thrives in a hot dry atmosphere, so if your plants are growing in their ideal environment of warm and moist conditions they are in fact *less* likely to suffer severe attacks. Plants which are affected should be isolated and thoroughly sprayed with a good systemic insecticide. After an attack, all plants in the greenhouse should be sprayed regularly.

CAPSID BUGS
Plants growing outside are often attacked by another pest which causes disfiguration and blindness of the growing tips, the capsid bug. This is another sap sucking insect which punctures the young leaves in the growing tips, causing them to turn red and to blister. Spraying with an insecticide will keep the pests under control. Unfortunately it is easy to forget that plants growing in the hardy border are likely to be the subject of an attack, but it happens quite frequently especially if there are larger trees in close proximity.

VINE WEEVIL
A pest which seems to have become far more prevalent in recent years – which seems to coin-

cide with the advent of peat-based composts – is the vine weevil larva. The adult is a black beetle-like insect and is nocturnal in its habits. The first sign of the presence of vine weevils is when notches are seen to have been eaten from the edges of the leaves; the eggs are laid in the surface of the compost and when hatched they produce a grub which is about ½in (1cm) in length, whitish with a brownish head. These grubs burrow down into the compost and feed off the young white roots, an action which can do untold damage to a young plant.

Many cures have been tried but none seems to be completely successful, although a liquid disinfectant soaked into the compost appears to give some protection. Prevention is perhaps better than cure, so dissuading the adults to lay their eggs in the first place is possibly the best method of control. Being nocturnal, vine weevils will seek out places to hide during the day. Ensuring that no hiding places are available would be difficult but is an ideal well worth seeking; however, if you *provide* daily hiding places, such as rolled-up corrugated cardboard on the greenhouse staging, it means the adults can be captured and destroyed.

OTHER PESTS
There are several other pests which you may discover during the course of a season, including thrips, sciarid flies and caterpillars. A systemic insecticide will usually destroy all these. Slugs can also be a bit of a problem and it will be necessary to use metaldehyde (slug pellets) to keep these under control.

## Diseases

BOTRYTIS
Sometimes called 'damping off', this disease usually occurs when the growing conditions are less than perfect. Overcrowding, overwatering, insufficient ventilation and poor hygiene (leaving rotting leaves on or around the plants) can all be contributory factors. General cleanliness, care when watering and good ventilation will prevent the problem, as will regular use of a fungicide.

RUST
One of the major diseases experienced in recent years is 'rust'. Pale yellowish spots appear on the upper surface of affected leaves and an examination of the undersurface will reveal orange postules, the appearance of which makes one instantly think of rust. At one stage it was considered that the complete destruction of the plant by burning was the only remedy.

However, careful removal of any affected leaves (the spores are airborne so great care will be needed in their removal) and destroying them, followed by regular spraying with a fungicide will keep the disease under control.

YELLOWING OF LEAVES
Old age is the major cause for premature yellowing although there *are* other factors that might also cause it such as overwatering, underwatering, severe attacks by aphids, misuse or excessive feeding, magnesium deficiency, iron deficiency.

Excessive use of the watering can probably causes more problems than any other factor. Err on the side of underwatering. If there is magnesium deficiency then a regular watering with a solution made up of one tablespoon of epsom salts (magnesium sulphate) in a gallon of water will remedy the situation. If such a watering takes place two or three times during the course of a season then there should be no problem. Iron deficiency can be remedied by using a seaweed extract plus sequestrated iron occasionally within your feeding programme.

# Understanding the Descriptions

The descriptions of species and cultivars which follow are, of necessity, very brief. In order to achieve some degree of uniformity a certain format and various abbreviations have been used, an explanation of which is given here.

'**Tom Thumb**' This is the name of the plant. The name in normal print (as here) indicates that the plant is a 'cultivar' (a cultivated variety). If the name is printed in *italics* then the plant being described is one of the species e.g. *F. arborescens*.

**Single H3 Bush** This line of information is quite important, not only to aid identification but to give you an indication of whether the plant will suit your purposes.

**Single, semi-double** or **double** indicates the type of flower that is produced by this plant. **Single** means that the flower has four petals. **Semi-double** means that the flower has five, six or seven petals.

**Double** means that the flower has eight or more petals. Some plants produce very small petals called petaloids which increase the size of the flower and are taken into account in determining the type of flower.

**H1 H2 H3** These letters and figures indicate the hardiness of the plant. Such indications can only be a guide, however, as the hardiness of a plant can vary considerably according to the locality in which it is grown.

**H1** indicates that the plant is rather tender and can be described as frost shy. To grow to perfection, the protection of a heated greenhouse will be necessary and it is advisable to maintain a temperature in excess of 7°C (45°F) throughout the year. Plants of the **Triphylla types** are particularly frost shy and require this level of protection.

**H2** indicates that the plant requires protection during the winter but can be safely grown in a cold greenhouse during the rest of the year or used as a temporary plant in the outside border. Probably it is best to describe them as half-hardy.

**H3** indicates that the plants are hardy and can be planted permanently in the garden,

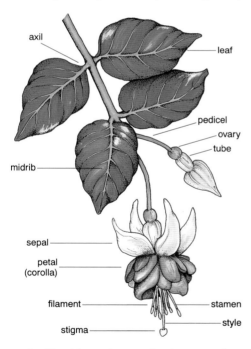

and will withstand normal winter weather without lifting. Such plants should be planted, initially, fairly deeply so that there is ample insulation around the root system. The top growths of such plants are usually killed by severe frosts, but fresh growths emerge from the root systems in the spring.
**Bush** or **Trailer** This indicates the type of growth normally associated with each cultivar or species.

**Bush** indicates a very strong and upright growth, readily forming branches. These plants will be useful when growing bushes for pots, patio tubs or borders.
**Trailer** indicates a lax, trailing growth. Such plants are best suited to being grown pendulously from hanging containers.

Some plants fall somewhere between these two types, and are described as either a lax bush or a stiff trailer, depending on which is the dominant tendency.

The main part of the description will give an indication of the colour of the flowers and of the foliage. Throughout the descriptions references are made to *tubes*, *sepals*, and *corollas*. The *corolla* is the term used for the petals of the flower irrespective of the number involved; a better indication of the parts of the flowers being described can be obtained from the diagram (left). It is very difficult to give exact references to sizes of flowers or foliage as these measurements vary considerably according to the type of cultivation given and the size of the pot in which the plant is grown.

**Height and Spread (H. & S.)**
If a plant has been shown as H3 – that is, a hardy plant for use in the garden – then an indication has been given as to the Height and Spread which would be expected. Such measurements can be only a very rough guide, as the positioning of the plant and the fertility of the soil can make a considerable difference. When established for a number of years, greater height and width would normally be expected.

**('Jackie Bull' × 'Annabel')** Where possible, the names of the plant's parents are given and appear in parentheses (as here) before the raiser's name.

**(Kennett, USA, 1965)** The name of the raiser of the cultivar, or the name of the person who first described the species, is always given in parentheses (as here). The nationality of the raiser or finder is given next, together with the date when this event occurred. Many growers find this information very useful especially when a decision has been made to make a collection of plants raised by a certain hybridist or to collect plants which are over a certain age. There are a number of instances however where such information is not available or cannot be guaranteed. The plant's parents are given where possible, and appear in parentheses before the hybridist's name.

19

# A–Z of Species and Cultivars

## A

**'Aad Franck'**
Single H1 Basket
Very vigorous trailing cultivar.
*Tube* light red. *Sepals* white
flushed rose. *Corolla* purplish-
red. Medium-sized blooms.
*Foliage* pale bronze-green.
(Franck, Holland, 1989)

**'Aaltje'**
Single H1 Bush
Medium upright cultivar. *Tube*
yellow/green flushed pink.
*Sepals* rose. *Corolla* deep violet.
(Breemer, Holland, 1991)

**'Abbe Farges'**
Semi-double H3 Quarter
standard, bush
Very vigorous, self-branching,
free-flowering plant. *Tube* and
*sepals* light cerise. *Corolla* rosy
lilac. Flowers medium to small.
*Foliage* slightly serrated, small
shiny leaves. H: 18–24in
(45–60cm); S: 12–18in
(30–45cm).
(Lemoine, France, 1901)

**'Abigail'**
Single H1 Basket, bush
Good semi-trailing cultivar.
*Tube* and *sepals* white to pale
pink. *Corolla* opens flat with
four petals of cyclamen purple
and a centre circle of white.
*Foliage* medium green.
(Springer, Germany, 1988)

**'Achievement'**
Single H3 Bush
Excellent plant for the border
giving a continuous show of
flowers from early in the
season. Upright, self-branching
growth. *Tube* and recurving
*sepals* reddish-cerise. *Corolla*
reddish-purple turning to
scarlet at the base of the petals.
Medium-sized flowers. *Foliage*
yellowish-green. H: 24–30in
(60–75cm); S: 24–30in
(60–75cm).
(Melville, UK, 1886)

**'Ada Perry'**
Double H1 Basket, bush
Large double flowers held on

fairly stiff trailing branches.
Will make a good basket, with
assistance. *Tube* scarlet. *Sepals*
scarlet on top with a deepening
of the colour underneath.
*Corolla* blue-purple streaked
with cardinal red. *Foliage* dark
green and fairly large. ('Seventh
Heaven' × 'Hula Girl')
(Stubbs, USA, 1983)

**'Adrian Young'**
Semi-double H2 Bush
Medium-sized, semi-double
flowers. *Tube* and *sepals* light
pink. *Corolla* medium pink.
*Foliage* light green.
(Young, UK, 1986)

**'Aintree'**
Single H2 Bush, basket
Vigorous upright, free-
flowering, self-branching plant
with a tendency to horizontal
growth. *Tube* ivory white.
*Sepals* ivory white with slight
rose tint, green tips. *Corolla*
rose madder with traces of
white at the base. *Foliage*
medium green. H: 18–24in
(45–60cm); S: 18–24in
(45–60cm).
(Need, UK, 1964)

**'Airball'**
Single H2 Bush
*Tube* white. *Sepals* magenta on
top and slightly darker
underneath. *Corolla* opens
magenta and matures to fuchsia
purple. Flowers medium size.
*Foliage* light green. Growth is
upright and bushy.
(L. Hobbs, UK, 1984)

**'Airedale'**
Single H2 Bush
Upright growth. Early and free-
flowering. *Tube* and *sepals* pale
rose. *Corolla* dark reddish-
purple. Medium-sized flowers.
*Foliage* medium green.
(Hanson, UK, 1991)

**'Ajax'**
Double H2 Basket
Strong, arching growth ideal
for mixed basket, planting.
*Tube* ivory. *Sepals* pale pink
with upturned tips. *Corolla*
fully double and heavily pleated

with pink and rose marbling.
*Foliage* medium green.
(Goulding, UK, 1989)

**'Aladna'**
Single H2 Bush
Medium-sized flowers carried
on upright growth. *Tube* and
*sepals* rose. *Corolla* purple
with red and orange fleck.
*Foliage* mid-green.
(Kempinck, Holland, 1989)

**'Aladna's Sanders'**
Double H2 Bush, basket
Medium-sized flowers carried
on fairly stiff trailing branches.
*Tube* and *sepals* white with
rosy flush. *Corolla* deep
reddish-purple. *Foliage* medium
green.
(Kempinck, Holland, 1989)

**'Alan Ayckbourn'**
Single H2 Bush, standard
Medium-sized flowers borne
profusely on self-branching
plants. Upright growth rather
lax. *Tube* and *sepals* baby pink.
*Corolla* white and bell-shaped.
*Foliage* medium green.
(D. Clark, UK, 1985)

**'Alan Stilwell'**
Double H2 Basket
Medium to large flowers on
good trailing branches. *Tube*
white. *Sepals* white, long,
narrow and twisted. *Corolla*
Wedgwood blue. *Foliage*
medium green.
(A. Dyos, UK, 1993.)

**'Alaska'**
Double H2 Bush
One of the purest white
doubles. Large flowers carried
on strong, upright, slow-
growing stems. *Tube* and
*sepals* pure white, slightly
tipped with green. *Corolla*
white, large and fluffy. *Foliage*
dark green.
(Schnabel, USA, 1963)

**'Albert H'**
Single H2 Bush
*Tube* and *sepals* deep rose-red.
*Corolla* carmine red. Medium-
sized flowers. *Foliage* mid-green.
(Marsman, Holland, 1988)

'ABBE FARGES'

'ABIGAIL'

'ALADNA'S SANDERS'

'ADA PERRY'

'ALASKA'

**'Albertina'**
Single H2 Bush
*Tube* and *sepals* white-flushed and striped with rose. *Sepals* white. *Corolla* lavender rose. Medium-sized flowers. *Foliage* medium green.
(Netjes, Holland, 1988)

**'Albion'**
Single H2 Bush, standard
Perfectly shaped flowers freely produced as befits the pollen parent, Lady Isobel Barnett. *Tube* long, neyron-rose. *Sepals* neyron-rose, pointed and held back against the tube. *Corolla* medium-sized, starts as hyacinth blue, passing through spectrum-violet and maturing to mallow purple. Petals open into a saucer shape. *Foliage* medium green.
(Gadsby, UK, 1972)

**'Alde'**
Single H2 Bush, basket
Strong, sturdy growth makes this plant ideal for temporary outside bedding. *Tube* and *sepals* pale orange. *Corolla*, with pleated petals, apricot. Smallish, plum flowers. *Foliage* medium to dark green. **H:** 12–18in (30–45cm); **S:** 18–24in (45–60cm).
(Goulding, UK, 1988)

**'Alexandra Dyos'**
Double H2 Basket, lax bush
The plant is a natural trailer with arching growth. *Tube* long, dark pink. *Sepals* pale pink, reflexing. *Corolla* creamy white.
(Dyos, UK, 1988)

**'Alfie'**
Double H2 Basket
Naturally trailing in growth and will make a good full or half basket. *Tube* and *sepals* red. *Corolla* deep purple. *Foliage* medium green.
(Tiret, USA, 1968)

**'Alfred Rambold'**
Double H2 Bush, standard
Strong, upright, bushy growth which produces large double flowers late in the season. *Tube* and *sepals* rich scarlet. The broad sepals reflex to hide the tube completely. *Corolla* violet-

purple ageing to rosy purple. *Foliage* dark green.
(Lemoine, France, 1896)

**'Alf Thornley'**
Double H2 Bush, standard
Strong-growing, upright, bushy and self-branching plant. *Tube* pink. *Sepals* neyron rose. *Corolla* creamy white, near perfect. Flowers medium-sized. *Foliage* mid-green. ('Lilac Lustre' ×)
(D. Clark, UK, 1981)

**'Alice Ashton'**
Double H2 Basket
Medium-sized blooms produced on good trailing growth. *Tube* and *sepals* pink. *Corolla* porcelain blue. *Foliage* medium green.
(Tiret, USA, 1971)

**'Alice Hoffman'**
Semi-double H3 Bush
Small flowers are freely produced on compact upright bushes. *Tube* and *sepals* rose. *Corolla* white veined with rose. *Foliage* bronzy green in colour. **H:** 18–24in (45–60cm); **S:** 12–18in (30–45cm).
(Klese, Germany, 1911)

**'Alice Mary'**
Semi-double H2 Basket
*Tubes* peach. *Sepals* pink. *Corolla* deep pink, attractive. Medium-sized flowers. *Foliage* medium green. A natural trailer.
(Stiff, UK, 1992)

**'Alice Rowell'**
Double H2 Bush, basket
The medium to large flowers are profusely produced. *Tube* and *sepals* orange streaked with dark pink. *Corolla* opens purplish pink and matures to dark rose. *Foliage* medium green with serrated edges.
(Rowell, UK, 1988)

**'Alice Topliss'**
Single H2 Bush
A small but very beautiful fuchsia. *Tube* and *sepals* white. *Corolla* baby pink. *Foliage* medium to dark green. Sport from 'Lady Ramsey'.
(Orton, UK, 1987)

**'Alice Travis'**
Semi double to double H2 Bush
*Tube* and *sepals* carmine cerise. Sepals are held horizontally when fully open. *Corolla* deep violet-blue. *Foliage* medium green. The large blooms are freely produced.
(Travis, UK, 1956)

**'Alison Ewart'**
Single H2 Bush or miniature standard
Very floriferous, small-flowered fuchsia. *Tube* short, light carmine. *Sepals* light carmine on the upperside, slightly deeper mauve flushed with pink on the undersurface. *Corolla* mauve, flushed pink. *Foliage* dark green with distinct serrated edging.
(Roe, UK, 1977)

**'Alison Patricia'**
Semi-double H2 Bush, standard
An attractive upright flowering plant with good compact growth. *Tube* red. *Sepals* pale pink. *Corolla* violet-rose with red veining. *Foliage* medium to dark green.
(Johns, UK, 1990)

**'Alison Reynolds'**
Double H2 Bush, standard
Strong, upright-growing plant which produces an abundance of flowers. *Tube* and *sepals* rose bengal. *Corolla* orchid blue. *Foliage* small to medium mid-green leaves. The best colour of the flower develops in the shade.
(Reynolds, UK, 1982)

**'Alison Ryle'**
Semi-double H2–H3 Bush, standard
Upright grower suitable for summer bedding in full sun. *Tube* short and fuchsia pink. *Sepals* brilliant fuchsia pink paling at the tips. *Corolla* deep lavender blue flushed with pale mauve with rose veins. There is deeper colour around the edge of the petals. *Foliage* dark green, oval, with serrated edges. ('Lena Dalton' × 'Tennessee Waltz')
(Ryle/Atkinson, UK, 1968)

'ALICE ASHTON'

'ALICE HOFFMAN'

'ALICE MARY'

'ALISON REYNOLDS'

'ALISON PATRICIA'

**'Alison Sweetman'**
Single H3 Bush, standard
*Tube* longish, crimson. *Sepals*
long and narrow, bright crimson,
and held horizontally. *Corolla*
deep beetroot purple. Medium-
sized flowers freely produced.
*Foliage* dark green, serrated
edges to the ovate leaves. Very
strong upright growth, better
served in the open garden.
('Herald' × 'Celia Smedley')
(Roe, UK, 1984)

**'All Square'**
Single H2 Bush
*Tube* and *sepals* pink. *Corolla*
red flushed with pink at base
when young, maturing to pink-
edged red. The flower is very
'square-shaped' when first
opening. *Foliage* medium
green. The best colour is
achieved in bright light.
(Adams, UK, 1988)

**'Allure'**
Double H2 Basket
The lax growth of this cultivar
makes it very suitable for use
in baskets. *Tubes* long and
thin, ivory white. *Sepals*
spreading, white flushed pink.
*Corollas* clear pink. Preferable
to grow in semi-shade.
(Moerman, Holland, date
unknown)

**'Alma Hulscher'**
Large double H2 Basket
*Tube* and fully recurved *sepals*
bright red. *Corolla* pink with
red veins. Excellent in full
baskets for garden display.
(Stoel, Holland, 1988)

*F. alpestris*
Species H2 Bush
Often described as *F. Regia* var
*Alpestris*. *Tube* deep red. *Sepals*
long, narrow and well held out,
red. *Corolla* purple, short and
compact. *Foliage* dark green
with red veins and usually
hairy.
(Brazil, 1843)

**'Altmark'**
Semi-double to double H2 Bush
A free-branching cultivar which
is extremely floriferous for a

semi-double or double. The
growth is upright and free
branching. The flowers are
borne at the ends of the laterals.
*Tube* and *sepals* white. *Corolla*
medium-sized, pale lilac turning
to pink. *Foliage* medium green.
(Goulding, UK, 1989)

**'Alton Water'**
Semi-double or double H2
Basket
A sport from Thames Valley.
*Tube* and *Sepals* pale pink.
*Corolla* mauve. Growth is
spreading, short-jointed and
free-branching. *Foliage*
variegated. A very attractive
plant for baskets or window
boxes.
(Ransby, UK, 1992)

**'Alwin'**
Semi-double H2 Bush
A good bushy plant producing
many medium sized flowers.
*Tube* thick, short and *sepals*
neyron rose. *Corolla* tightly
fluted, white with red veins.
Short-jointed growth makes
this an ideal type of plant for
the show bench, especially in
the smaller pot classes. *Foliage*
medium green. ('La
Campanella' × 'Liebriez')
(Clyne, UK, 1976)

**'Alyce Larson'**
Double H2 Basket
A natural trailer with medium to
large flowers. *Tube* and *sepals*
white, tipped pink. *Corolla*
white with pale pink veining.
*Foliage* medium green.
(Tiret, USA, 1972)

**'Amanda Bridgland'**
Double H2 Bush
The medium-sized blooms are
tightly formed with fluted
petals. *Tube* short and thick,
green streaked with rosy red.
*Sepals* horizontally held,
greenish-white on top with a
rosy-red sheen underneath.
*Corolla* opens deep blue and
matures to mauve-blue with
pink shading. *Foliage* lightish
green. ('Speedbird' × 'Preston
Guild')
(Bridgland, UK, 1985)

**'Amanda Jones'**
Single H2 Bush
A sister seedling to 'Micky
Goult', but not quite so prolific
in its flowering. *Tube* bulbous,
white with a shade of pink.
*Sepals* white, with soft pink on
top and rose beneath. *Corolla*
soft mauve-pink with minimal
veining. *Foliage* small to medium
and mid-green. Short-jointed and
bushy growth. ('Bobby Shaftoe'
× 'Santa Barbara')
(Roe, UK, 1981)

**'Amelie Aubin'**
Single H2 Trailer
*Tube* very long and thick, waxy
white. *Sepals* waxy white and
tipped with green. *Corolla*
rosy-cerise, white at the base.
*Foliage* medium, medium
green. A natural trailer but
could be used as a bush with
frequent stopping and staking.
One of the 'good old cultivars'.
(Eggbrecht, Germany, 1884)

**'America'**
Single H2 Trailer
*Tube* very thin and long, white
gradually changing to rose-
madder as it nears the sepals.
*Sepals* crimson inside with
greenish-white tips. *Corolla*
deep crimson. *Foliage* mid-
green. Flowers large and freely
produced. The very lax growth
makes it a natural for use in
baskets. ('Golondrina' ×
'Rundle')
(Niederholzer, USA, 1941)

**'American Flaming Glory'**
Double H2 Trailer, bush
*Tube* and *sepals* pink. *Corolla*
purple toning to flame red.
*Foliage* fairly large and
medium green in colour.
Largish blooms produced quite
freely. Although a trailer, will
require the assistance of
weights to cover a basket.
Upright growth can be
maintained with staking.
(Martin, USA, 1958)

'ALISON SWEETMAN'    'ALTON WATER'

'ALWIN'    'ALYCE LARSON'

'AMANDA JONES'    'AMELIE AUBIN'

**'Amethyst Fire'**
Double H3 (in south of England) Bush
*Tube* and *sepals* red. *Corolla* amethyst blue, heavily splashed with pink. Large blooms continuously produced. *Foliage* dark green. Growth strong, upright and bushy. H. and S. 18–24in (45–60cm).
(Tabraham, UK, 1975)

**'Amigo'**
Single/semi-double H2 Bush
*Tube* and *sepals* salmon. *Corolla* dark purple with deep salmon and light patches of coral. *Foliage* medium green. Flowers of medium size on good upright growth.
(Kennett, USA, 1969)

**'Amy Lye'**
Single H2 Lax bush
Typical 'Lye' with *tube* waxy cream. *Sepals* white tipped with green. *Corolla* coral orange. Medium-sized blooms freely produced. *Foliage* dark green with crimson mid-rib. Frequent pinching is necessary to give a compact bush. Suitable for trailing-type standards.
(Lye, UK, 1885)

**'Andenken an Heinrich Henkel'**
Single (triphylla type) H1 Upright
*Tube* very long; *tube, sepals* and *corolla* delightful rosy crimson. One of the nicest of the triphylla-type fuchsias. Extremely frost shy and requires winter protection. Growth rather lax. Try it as a standard.
(Berger, Germany, 1896)

*F. andrei*
Species single H1 Bush
The numerous flowers are carried in terminal and sub terminal racemes. *Tube* (approx 1½–2in (3–4cm) long, orange to coral-red. *Sepals* coral-red. *Corolla* orange-red with light red filaments and stile. *Foliage* mid-green.
(Equador and Peru, 1925)

**'Andre le Nostre'**
Double H2 Bush
*Tube* and *Sepals* fairly long, cerise. *Corolla* violet-purple. Fairly large blooms freely produced. *Foliage* dark green, broad with reddish veining. Strong upright growth. Old but still good.
(Lemoine, France, 1909)

**'Andrew George'**
Semi-double H2 Trailer
*Tube* red. *Sepals* long, pointed, slightly twisted, red. *Corolla* violet but base of petals bright red. *Foliage* mid-green tinged with bronze. A natural trailer so will make a good basket, or half basket.
(Hooper, UK, 1990)

**'Andrew Hadfield'**
Single H2 Bush
One frequently seen on the show bench because of its floriferousness. *Tube* and *sepals* carmine. *Corolla* blue. The petals flare as the flower matures. Flowers held upright from the foliage. *Foliage* medium green on the upper surface, lighter on the lower. Shown most frequently in small pots but is considered by some to be better in larger pots.
('Estelle Marie' ×)
(Rowell, UK, 1987)

**'Andrew Ryle'**
Single H2 Bush
A dainty flower. *Tube* short, crimson. *Sepals* crimson, well curved, held horizontally, shiny on the upperside. *Corolla* white has a central crimson vein. *Foliage* small, mid-green. The best colouring of the flowers appears in full sun. Upright and self-branching, should be seen more on the show bench.
('Pinky' × 'Pink Cloud' seedling × 'Strawberry Delight')
(Ryle, UK, 1975)

**'Angela'**
Double H2 Trailing
*Tube* and *sepals* deep pink. *Corolla* pale pink. Large blooms with a delightful colour combination. Lax growth

makes this plant ideal for growing in baskets. *Foliage* fairly large and mid green.
(Raiser and date unknown)

**'Angela Leslie'**
Double H2 Bush
This medium- to large-flowered cultivar has strong, upright and bushy growth. The heavy blooms will necessitate supporting the branches. *Tube* pink. *Sepals*, which recurve, pink tipped with green and with darker pink on the undersurface. *Corolla* deep pink with veins of rose. *Foliage* fairly large mid green.
(Tiret, USA, 1959)

**'Angela Rippon'**
Single H2 Bush
A good, strong upright, self-branching plant which carries its medium-sized flowers freely. *Tube* china rose. *Sepals* waxy china rose with green tips. *Corolla* attractive wisteria blue maturing to imperial purple. Flowers held horizontally. *Foliage* mid green. ('Christine Clements' × 'Forward Look')
(Gadsby, UK, 1977)

**'Angeline'**
Double H2 Trailing
*Tube* long, thin, white. *Sepals* white. *Corolla* violet with pink flecks. Extremely multi-flowering on self-branching plants. *Foliage* medium green. Excellent for basket, and half basket, display work. ('Shelley Lynn' × self)
(Dunnett, UK, 1979)

**'Angels Dream'**
Double H2 Trailer
*Tube* short, fuchsia pink. *Sepals* brilliant fuchsia pink flaring from tube. *Corolla* pure white with pink markings and serrated edges. *Foliage* medium dark green veined with red. A natural trailer, it makes an excellent basket. Best colour develops in the shade.
(Stubbs, USA, 1973)

'ANDREW HADFIELD'                    'ANDRE LE NOSTRE'

'ANDREW RYLE                              'ANGELA'

**'Angel's Flight'**
Double H2 Trailer
*Tube* long, white. *Sepals* pink, slightly deeper colour at the base and curling right back against the tube. *Corolla* white with pale pink veining. *Foliage* medium green. A natural trailer which is self-branching and very vigorous. Grows best in cool conditions. Could be used as a bush but will require heavy staking. Nice basket.
(Martin, USA, 1957)

**'Anita'**
Double H2 Bush
Strong upright growth, almost impossible to control in pots. Might be better suited for greenhouse border. *Tube* and *sepals* red. *Corolla* is violet splashed with red. Large flowers. *Foliage* strong medium green.
(Niederholzer, USA, 1946)

**'Anjo'**
Single H2 Bush
Plant grown mainly for its superb foliage. *Tube* and *sepals* white. *Corolla* mauve-pink. *Foliage* has delightful yellow and green variegation.
(Heesen, Holland, 1989)

**'Anna'**
Double H2 Trailer
*Tube* and *sepals* carmine. *Corolla* magenta, carmine at base, almost self-coloured. Blooms are very large and long. *Foliage* dark green and large. A natural trailer so will be excellent for use in basket.
(Reiter, USA, 1945)

**'Annabel'**
Double H2 Lax bush
*Tube* white flushed with neyron rose. *Sepals* slightly curved down from the horizontal, white flushed with neyron rose. *Corolla* fully double, white slightly flushed with rose. *Foliage* light green. Although the growth is bushy and the plant self-branching this very versatile cultivar can be used in almost any type of growth.

Very free-flowering especially for the size of the flower.
('Indian Maid' × 'Nancy Lou')
(Ryle, UK, 1977)

**'Annabelle Stubbs'**
Double H2 Trailing
Large double. *Tube* light pink. *Sepals* with coral pink. *Corolla* fully double, is reddish purple. *Foliage* medium green. The natural habit is trailing.
(Riley, USA, 1991)

**'Ann Adams'**
Single H2 Bush
*Tube* and *sepals* white flushed with pink and tipped green. *Corolla* almost white with cerise hue and deeper cerise veining at base of petals. *Foliage* medium sized with sage green colouring. Fairly strong upright grower.
(Redfern, UK, 1987)

**'Anna of Longleat'**
Semi-double H2 Trailing or lax bush
A very floriferous plant which produces four or more flowers from each node. *Tube* thin shell pink. *Sepals* held horizontally, shell pink on upper surface, bright pink underneath. *Corolla* opens bright lavender maturing to pale lavender. *Foliage* small, dark green. Will need constant pinching and staking if grown as a bush. ('La Campanella' × 'Cliff's Own')
(Robertson, UK, 1985)

**'Anna Pauline'**
Semi-double H2 Trailing
*Tube* and *sepals* crimson flushed orange. *Corolla* light violet. *Foliage* medium green. A good trailing cultivar, very floriferous.
(Krom, Germany, 1990)

**'Ann H. Tripp'**
Single/semi-double H2 Bush
A very floriferous plant extremely popular with exhibitors. *Tube* short and thick, white with faint stripe. *Sepals* white, held at the horizontal and the *Corolla* also white with light pink veins.

*Foliage* light green, starting almost as yellow at the growing tips. Growth vigorous, upright and self-branching. Requires rather longer than usual from the final stop to produce mature flowers. Rain or spray will mark the blooms.
('Lady Isobel Barnett' × 'Joy Patmore')
(Clark, UK, 1982)

**'Annie Earle'**
Single H2 Bush
Another of 'Lye's' raisings, therefore *tube* and *sepals* waxy cream with green tips. *Corolla* carmine scarlet. Medium-sized blooms produced freely and early in the season. *Foliage* medium green. Upright strong growth for bush or standard. One worth looking for.
(Lye, UK, 1887)

**'Anniek Geerlings'**
Single H2 Bush
Medium-sized single. *Tube* carmine rose. *Sepals* light rose flushed with lilac. *Corolla* carmine rose. The upright growth will make a good bush with support. *Foliage* medium green.
(Franck, Holland, 1988)

**'Ann Pacey'**
Double H2 Bush
*Tube* short, thick, white. *Sepals* broad pink tipped with green with neyron rose underneath. *Corolla* phlox pink at base shading to neyron rose. Self-branching medium upright. Medium to large blooms freely produced. *Foliage* medium green. The best colour of flower is produced in the shade. ('Joan Pacey' ×)
(Gadsby, UK, 1978)

**'Ann Porter'**
Single H2 Bush
*Tube* white. *Sepals* white veined with red. *Corolla* aster violet. Medium-sized flowers produced on good, bushy, self-branching plant. *Foliage* mid green.
(Porter, UK, 1978)

'ANITA'

'ANNABEL'

'ANNA OF LONGLEAT'

'ANNA PAULINE'

'ANN H. TRIPP'

**'Ann Roots'**
Single  H2  Trailing
*Tubes* and *sepals* cream with
red stripes. *Corolla* large, bell-
shaped with wavy edges, pale
lavender. Spreading and bushy
growth best grown in wall or
hanging baskets. *Foliage* mid-
green.
(Goulding, UK, 1991)

**'Anthea Bond'**
Single  H2  Lax bush
*Tube* short, medium thick,
spiraea red. *Sepals* long and
slender, also spiraea red.
*Corolla* of long, tapering rolled
petals of wisteria blue
lightening at the base. *Foliage*
dark green. The rather lax
growth is self-branching but
will need supporting to make a
good bush. Used as a trailer it
will be necessary to assist the
cascading habit with weights.
('Upward Look' ×)
(Gadsby, UK, 1975)

**'Anthonetta'**
Single  H2  Lax bush or trailer
Very small-flowered cultivar
similar to the *Encliandra* type
miniatures. *Tube* and *sepals*
small carmine. *Corolla* opens
violet,blue, matures to light
violet. Very small *foliage*
which is dark green with red
veining.
(Netjes, Holland, 1987)

**'Antigone'**
Single  H2  Bush
An old but still popular cultivar.
*Tube* and *sepals* white with a
pink blush. *Corolla* pinkish-
orange. Medium-sized blooms
freely produced and very eye-
catching. *Foliage* dark green
acts as an excellent backcloth
for the colour of the flowers.
(Banks, UK, 1887)

**'Apart'**
Single  H2  Lax bush
Medium-sized flower. *Tube* and
*sepals* waxy white. *Corolla*
pinkish-orange. Each petal
formed on a right-angle, and
when viewed from below
impression is of a square
corolla. The lax growth makes

it suitable for bush work with
supports or as a trailer with
weights. *Foliage* mid-green.
(Moerman, Holland, 1991)

**'Aphrodite'**
Double  H2  Bush
Large blooms. *Tube* and *sepals*
pink. *Corolla* long and full,
white. Very prolific for the size
of the blooms. Strong upright
growth, suitable for training as
a standard. *Foliage* fairly large
medium green.
(Colville, UK, 1964)

**'Applause'**
Double  H2  Lax bush or
trailer
*Tube* short, thick pale carmine.
*Sepals* very broad (some up to
1in (2.5cm) across), carmine
with a pale streak down the
centre. *Corolla* deep orange-red.
The very large blooms will need
supporting when grown as a
bush. *Foliage* large, dark green.
Vigorous growth demands early
training to keep within bounds.
(Stubbs, USA, 1978)

**'Appollo'**
Single  H2  Trailing
*Tube* and *sepals* salmon
orange. *Corolla* rather unusual
colour combination, being pink
on the upper half and magenta
on the lower. *Foliage* medium
green. A natural trailer, so will
make an excellent basket.
(Dresman, UK, 1987)

**'Apricot Slice'**
Single  H2  Upright Bush
*Tube* light coral pink. *Sepals*
coral pink tipped with green.
*Corolla* light coral pink. *Foliage*
medium green. Medium-sized
flowers borne on very strong,
upright-growing branches.
(Sharpe/Profitt, 1990)

**'Arabella'**
Single  H2  Lax bush
*Tube* and *sepals* white. *Corolla*
dark rose. *Foliage* medium
green. Medium-sized flowers
fairly freely produced. A very
old cultivar not generally
available today.
(Banks, UK, 1866)

**'Arabella Improved'**
Single  H2  Bush
*Tube* and reflexed *sepals* waxy
cream. *Corolla* rosy cerise.
Medium-sized blooms very
freely produced. *Foliage*
medium green. No real
resemblance to the plant after
which it was named.
(Lye, UK, 1871)

*F. arborescens*
Species  H1  Bush
*Tube*, recurving *sepals* and
*corolla* very small. Blooms held in large terminal
panicles. *Foliage* large, lustrous
green, slightly roughened. Very
strong upright growth. Often
referred to as the 'Lilac
Fuchsia' as the large panicles of
flowers are similar to a lilac
spray. A free root-run should
be given where possible.
(Sims, 1826)

**'Arcadia Aubergine'**
Single  H2  Bush
*Tube*, *sepals*, *corolla* rich dark
aubergine. A chance seedling.
Masses of medium-sized
flowers produced over a long
period. *Foliage* dark green.
(Birch (Arcadia Nurseries), UK,
1994)

**'Arcadia Gold'**
Double  H2  Lax bush
A sport of 'Swingtime'. *Tube*
and *sepals* short, a rich, shiny
red of crêpe texture. *Corolla*
fully double milky white faintly
veined with pink. *Foliage*
variegated. Rather stiff in its
growth but will make an
excellent basket, with the
assistance of weights.
(Birch (Arcadia Nurseries), UK,
1985)

**'Arcadia Lady'**
Single  H2  Bush
Very floriferous. *Tubes* and
*sepals* pale pink. Darker edge
to each *sepal*. *Corolla* very
deep magenta at outer edges
fading to white. Medium-sized
flowers are held erect. *Foliage*
pale lime green. ('Estelle Marie'
× 'Linda Goulding')
(Webb, UK, 1988)

'ANTHONETTA'

'APHRODITE'

'APPLAUSE'

*F. ARBORESCENS*

'ARCADIA AUBERGINE'

'ARCADIA LADY'

# 'Arc en Ciel'

**'Arc en Ciel'**
Single H2 Bush
Large single flower. *Tube* and
*sepals* deep cerise. *Corolla*
metallic blue. *Foliage* medium
green. Upright grower.
(Rozaine, France, 1892)

**'Archie Owen'**
Double H2 Trailer
*Tube* soft pink. *Sepals* soft pink
medium long with an average
taper. *Corolla* fully double also
soft pink. *Foliage* small, dark
green with a reddish tinge. A
natural trailer so will make a
good basket.
(Stubbs, USA, 1977)

**'Arels Avendzon'**
Double H2 Lax bush
*Tube* and *sepals* white flushed
rose. *Corolla* deep robin red.
*Foliage* medium green. Lax
upright so will need support if
used as a bush, but should be
useful in a basket.
(Elsman, Holland, 1991)

**'Arels Fleur'**
Double H2 Trailer
*Tube* and *sepals* light rose.
*Corolla* violet. *Foliage* medium
to dark green. It is a natural
trailer so will make a good
basket.
(Elsman, Holland, 1989)

**'Ariel'**
*Encliandra Hybrid*
Single H2 Bush
Very small *tube* and *sepals*
magenta. *Corolla* small deep
pink. Tiny flowers freely
produced in leaf axils. *Foliage*,
glossy darkish-green. Although
growth is rather lax, will give a
very presentable bush if
'stopped' frequently.
(Travis, UK, 1973)

**'Army Nurse'**
Semi-double H3 Bush
*Tube* and s*epals* carmine.
*Corolla* bluish-violet. *Foliage*
medium green. Growth very
upright and strong. Small to
medium flowers produced in
profusion. Will make an
excellent pot or border plant.
(Hodges, USA, 1947)

**'Art Deco'**
Double H2 Trailer
*Tube* and *sepals* aubergine with
delightful red cast. *Corollas*
open white with aubergine
veining. *Foliage* medium green.
Natural spreading habit so will
make a good basket. Does best
in cool conditions.
(de Graaff, Holland, 1989)

**'Arthur Cope'**
Semi-double H2/H3 Bush
*Tube* long, white. *Sepals* waxy
white. *Corolla* spiraea red
flushed with rose red and
splashed with white. Free-
flowering with large blooms.
*Foliage* mid- to dark green. Its
vigorous spreading habit makes
it excellent for the border. Best
in semi-shade.
(Gadsby, UK, 1968)

**'Art Nouveau'**
Single H2 Trailer
*Tube* and *sepals* red. *Corolla*
rose purple with a bluish-
purple edge. *Foliage* medium
green. A natural trailer.
(de Graaff, Holland, 1989)

**'Athela'**
Single H2 Bush
*Tube* creamy pink. *Sepals* pink.
*Corolla* salmon pink deepening
in colour at base. *Foliage*
medium green. Medium to
large flowers produced in
profusion early in the season.
('Rolla' × 'Mrs. Rundle')
(Whiteman, UK, 1942)

**'Athene'**
Single H2 Trailer
Medium-sized single flower.
*Tubes* and *sepals* white flushed
tyrian rose. *Corolla* rose.
*Foliage* medium green. A
natural trailer. Good in hot
conditions.
(Warren, USA, 1947)

**'Atlantic Star'**
Single H2 Bush
*Tube* cream striped with pink.
*Sepals* white with slight hint of
pink. *Corolla* white base
striped with pink. *Foliage* green
with red veining. Short, jointed
growth makes it an excellent

plant for pot work on the show
bench. Flowers medium sized.
('Norman Mitchinson' ×
'Seedling' ('Estelle Marie' ×
'Mieke Meursing'))
(Redfern, UK, 1986)

**'Atlantis'**
Semi-double H2 Lax bush
Medium-sized flowers. *Tubes*
white. *Sepals* white flushed
with pink on the inside. *corolla*
clear lilac. *Foliage* dark green.
Lax growth which makes it
suitable as a bush with
supports or as a hanging
basket.
(Handley, UK, 1974)

**'Atomic Glow'**
Double H2 Lax bush
*Tube* pale pink. *Sepals* pale
orange, tipped with green.
*Corolla* glowing pink with
orange tint. *Foliage* medium
green. Medium sized flowers
appear in flushes through the
season from an early start. The
lax growth can be used as a
bush or a basket, with training.
(Machado, USA, 1963)

**'Aubergine'**
Single H2 Bush
*Tube, sepals, corolla* of this
attractive plant dark aubergine.
*Foliage* medium to dark green.
Growth is rather lax so might
be used, with training, as a
basket.
(de Graaff, Holland, 1989)

**'Audrey Hepburn'**
Single H2 Trailer
*Tube* and *sepals* carmine.
*Corolla* white, long barrel
shape. *Foliage* medium green.
A natural trailer, will make an
excellent basket. ('Iceberg' ×
'Cascade')
(Jonker, Holland, 1987)

**'August Siebert'**
Single (triphylla type) H1
Bush
*Tube* long; *tube, sepals* and
*corolla* dark cerise. A very
floriferous cultivar with flowers
hanging in clusters at the ends
of branches. *Foliage* dark.
(Bonstedt, Germany, 1915)

'ARELS AVENDZON'

'ARMY NURSE'

'ATLANTIC STAR'

'AUDREY HEPBURN'

**'Auntie Jinks'**
Single H2 Trailing
Medium to small flowers
produced in profusion over
very long season. An excellent
cultivar to use in hanging
receptacles of all sizes. *Tube*
pink-red. *Sepals* white edged
with cerise. *Corolla* purple with
white shading. *Foliage* small,
mid green.
(Wilson, UK, 1970)

**'Auntie Maggie'**
Single H2 Bush
*Tube* flesh pink. *Sepals* pink on
the topside, pale geranium pink
on the underside. *Corolla*
Indian red, distinct barrel
shape. *Foliage* pale green.
Medium-sized blooms freely
produced. Good upward
growth makes a good bush or
small standard. ('Mrs Marshall'
seedling)
(Tolley, UK, 1974)

**'Aunt Juliana'**
Double H2 Lax bush or
trailer
*Tube* short, red. *Sepals*
upturned, red. *Corolla* a deep
lavender blue. Stamens and
pistil red. Fairly large blooms
freely produced. *Foliage* mid-
green. Needs support as a bush,
but would make a good basket.
(Sport from Uncle Jules)
(Hanson, USA, 1950)

**'Aurora Superba'**
Single H1 Lax bush
Fairly large single. *Tube* and
*sepals* light apricot. *Corolla* deep
orange. *Foliage* soft light green.
Rather temperamental cultivar
requiring more warmth than
most.
(Name of raiser unknown,
USA)

**'Australia 200'**
Double H2 Bush
*Tube* and *sepals* brilliant red,
sepals fully reflex to the stem.
*Corolla* burgundy red fading to
brilliant red with maturity. The
medium-sized flowers are
carried on self-branching
plants. *Foliage* dark green.
(Scrase, Australia, 1988)

**'Australia Fair'**
Double H2 Trailing
*Tube* and *sepals* bright red.
*Corolla* white flushed and
veined red. Large flowers
produced fairly freely. *Foliage*
medium green. Care must be
taken when young not to
overwater.
(Raiser not known)

**F. austromontana**
Species H1 Bush
*Tube* and *sepals* scarlet.
*Corolla* deep red. The very few
flowers are pendant from upper
leaf axils. An upright grower
occasionally climbing.
(Johnston, Southern Peru and
Bolivia, 1939)

**'Autumnale'**
Single H2 Horizontal bush
A plant grown mainly for its
very attractive foliage. *Tube*
and *sepals* scarlet rose. *Corolla*
purple. Medium sized flowers
produced quite freely later in
the season. *Foliage* quite small
and shiny. Young leaves start as
green and yellow but mature to
dark red and salmon with
splashes of yellow. Growth is
stiff. Habit lax, and can be
described as more horizontal
than vertical. The best colour of
the leaves is in the young
growth, so regular 'pinching
out' will give the required
result.
(Hybridist and year unknown)

**'Avalanche' (1)**
Double H3 Lax bush
*Tube* and *sepals* scarlet.
*Corolla* purplish-violet shaded
with splashes of carmine.
*Foliage* yellowish green. Size
and weight of blooms require
them to be supported when
growing as a bush.
(Henderson, UK, 1869)

**'Avalanche' (2)**
Double H2 Lax bush
*Tube* white. *Sepals* white
edged with rose. *Corolla*
white, star-shaped. Blooms
produced in clusters at the
ends of branches. *Foliage* a
very lax bush which is

probably better grown as a
basket.
(Schnabel, USA, 1954)

**'Avocet'**
Single H2 Bush
*Tube* short, crimson. *Sepals*
crimson and crêpe-like, long,
pointed and reflexing. *Corolla*
white with red veining, tight
barrel shape. *Foliage* dark
green with red veins. Strong
upright growth might make it
suitable for growing as
standards or pillars. ('Jules
Daloges' × 'Elizabeth Travis')
(Travis, UK, 1958)

**'Avon Gem'**
Single H2 Bush
*Tube* and *sepals* red. *Corolla*
purple to magenta. Medium
sized flowers freely produced.
*Foliage* medium green. Strong
upright grower, will make good
standard.
(Lockyer, UK, 1978)

**F. ayavacensis**
Species H1 Upright
*Tube* long, orange-red. *Foliage*
fairly large, medium green,
slightly hairy on the upper
surface. Needs plenty of root
room and space as it can climb
to 4 or 5m (13–16ft).
(Humboldt, Bonpland and
Kunth, Peru, 1823)

**'Aztec'**
Double H2 Bush
*Tube* and *sepals* rich red.
*Corolla* vivid violet. *Foliage*
deep green with a faint touch
of red. Growth tall and
vigorous.
(Evans and Reeves, USA, 1937)

**'Azure Sky'**
Semi-double H2 Bush
Medium-sized flowers. *Tubes*
white. *Sepals* horizontal.
*Corolla* deep lilac blue fading
very slightly with age. *Foliage*
medium green.
(Johns, UK, 1990)

'AUNTIE JINKS'

'AUNT JULIANA'

'AUTUMNALE'

'AVALANCHE' (1)

# B

**'Baby Blue Eyes'**
Single H3 Bush
*Tube* and *sepals* red. *Corolla*
dark lavender. A very strong
and floriferous plant which will
give good service in the hardy
border for many years. *Foliage*
medium-sized, dark green. H:
4ft (120cm); S: 3ft (90cm).
('Erecta' × 'Wood Violet')
(Plummer, UK, 1952)

**'Baby Bright'**
Single H2 Bush
*Tube* and *sepals* white blushed
pink. Green tips on sepals and
phlox pink on the underside.
*Corolla* white blushed pink.
*Foliage* small, med- to light
green. Very floriferous, medium
to small flowers. Excellent for
small pot work.
(Bright, UK, 1992)

**'Baby Chang'**
Single H2 Lax bush
Tiny flowers, are produced
profusely. *Tube* and *sepals*
orange red . *Corolla* brilliant
orange. *Foliage* very small,
mid-green. An untidy grower
which requires frequent
pinching to keep in shape.
(Hazard and Hazard, USA,
1950)

**'Baby Face'**
Double H2 Bush
Large blooms. *Tube* and *sepals*
baby pink. *Corolla* creamy
white. *Foliage* light to medium
green, slightly crimped. Self-
branching. Colours best in the
shade.
(Tolley, UK, 1973)

**'Baby Love'**
Single H2 Bush
Medium-sized flowers. *Tubes*
carmine rose. *Sepals* neyron
rose. *Corolla* carmine rose.
*Foliage* medium green. Growth
is vigorously upright.
(Kempinck, Holland, 1989)

**'Baby Pink'**
Double H2 Trailer
*Tube* and *sepals* light pink.

*Corolla* very light pink. *Foliage*
dark green, light green veins
and red stems. Combined with
the colour of the flower this
presents a very attractive plant
suitable for use in baskets.
(Soo Yun, USA, 1976)

**'Baby Thumb'**
Single H3 Bush
This sport from 'Lady Thumb'
has the same colouring of
flower as its parent. *Tube* and
*sepals*. *Corolla* white. Growth is
dwarf. *Foliage* green and cream.
('Lady Thumb' sport, 1992)

**'Baby Veerman'**
Single H2 Bush
Unusual small branching
growth. Flowers are almost
cone-shaped with a very short
tube. *Tube*, *sepals*, *corolla*
white flushed pink.
(Franck, Holland, 1991)

**F. x bacillaris**
*Encliandra* species H2 Bush
As one of the Encliandra group
from which there are many
hybrids, the foliage and flowers
are typically very small and
usually about ⅓in (1cm) in
length. *Tube*, *sepals*, *corolla*
rose. *Foliage* medium green.
(Lindley, 1832)

**'Balkonkoningen'**
Single H2 Trailer
Vigorous free-flowering plant
with small flowers. *Tube* and
*sepals* deep pink.*Corolla* very
deep pink, almost crimson.
*Foliage* fairly small and
medium green, with crimson
mid-rib and veins. Responds to
training to make a good
basket. Beware of
overwatering.
(Neubronner, Germany, 1896)

**'Ballet Girl'**
Double H2 Bush
*Tube* and *sepals* bright cerise.
*Corolla* white. Large flowers
freely produced. *Foliage* fairly
large, mid- to dark green. The
plant is vigorous and naturally
bushy. Will make an excellent
standard.
(Veitch, UK, 1894)

**'Bambini'**
Single H2 Bush
Small *tube* and *sepals* rich
crimson. *Corolla* mallow
purple, heavily veined at the
base. The extremely small
flowers are very freely
produced. Small upright
growth, short-jointed and
vigorous.
(Pacey, UK, 1985)

**'Banstead Bell'**
Single H2 Bush
*Tube* and *sepals* deep rose.
*Corolla* white. Large flowers
freely produced. *Foliage*
medium green. ('Steve Wright'
× 'Royal Treasure')
(Hobson, UK, 1987)

**'Banzai'**
Single H2 Bush
*Tubes*, *sepals*, *corolla* purplish-
red. The tube can be described
as 'fat' and the corolla small.
*Foliage* medium green.
(Bogemann, Germany, 1992)

**'Barbara'**
Single H2 Bush
*Tube* short, medium thick, pale
pink. *Sepals* pale pink, slightly
turned up. *Corolla* tangerine
pink, semi-flared. *Foliage*
medium-sized, pale dull green.
Strong upright growth, self-
branching. Will make a good
bush or standard. ('Display' ×)
(Tolley, UK, 1971)

**'Barbara Pountain'**
Double H2 Bush
*Tube* white. *Sepals* white,
tipped with green. *Corolla*
violet on outer petals, pink at
the base. Very free-flowering
for a full double. *Foliage*
medium green. Good strong
upright growth.
(Redfern, UK, 1990)

**'Baron de Ketteler'**
Double H2 Bush
*Tube* and *sepals* rich crimson.
*Corolla* intense purple, light
pink centre. *Foliage* mid- to
dark green. Very large blooms,
are freely produced. Strong
upright sturdy growth.
(Lemoine, France, 1901)

'BABY BLUE EYES'

'BABY BRIGHT'

'BABY PINK'

'BABY THUMB'

'BALLET GIRL

'BARON DE KETTELER'

**'Baroness van Dedem'**
Single H2 Lax bush
*Tube* red. *Sepals* red, short, folding back to the tube. *Corolla* aster violet, saucer shaped with maturity. Small to medium-sized flowers. *Foliage* small mid-green. Excellent for small pots or hanging pots.
(de Groot, Holland, 1980)

**'Baroque Pearl'**
Double H2 Bush
*Tube* greenish-white. *Sepals* white blushed with pink. *Corolla* lavender with pink base. *Foliage* light fuchsia green with serrated edges. The smallish flowers are produced in quantity. Vigorous growth, self-branching. Prefers cool conditions.
(de Graaff, Holland, 1985)

**'Barry M. Cox'**
Single H2 Trailing
*Tube* and fully recurving *sepals* white. *Corolla* bright red. *Foliage* medium green. Flowers are freely produced on strong pendulous growth. Excellent show potential for baskets and hanging pots.
(Gouldings Fuchsias, UK, 1994)

**'Barry's Queen'**
Single H2/3 Bush
This sport from 'Border Queen' has identical flowers to its parent but yellow *foliage*. Short thin *tube* and *sepals* are rhodamine pink with green tips. *Corolla* is amethyst violet, flushed with pale pink and dark pink veining. Growth upright, vigorous. Needs regular pinching to make a plant of substance.
(Sheppard, UK, 1980)

**'Bashful'**
Double H3 Bush
*Tube* and *sepals* deep pink. *Corolla* white veined with red. Small blooms are freely produced. *foliage* deep green. Upright growth, quite strong. H. and S. 9–15in (23–38cm).
(Tabraham, UK, 1974)

**'Basketful'**
Double H2 Trailer
*Tube* and *sepals* pink. *Corolla* white and pink. *Foliage* medium-sized blooms produced quite freely. A natural trailer.
(Raiser not known)

**'Beacon'**
Single H3 Bush
A very easy and floriferous fuchsia. *Tube* and *Sepals* deep pink. *Corolla* bright mauvish-pink. Blooms medium-sized. *Foliage* darkish-green with wavy edges. H. and S. 24in (60cm).
(Bull, UK, 1871)

**'Beacon Rosa'**
Single H3 Bush
*Tube* rose red. *Sepals* red. *Corolla* pink, lightly veined red. The medium-sized blooms are carried on strong, upright-growing branches. *Foliage* similar to 'Beacon': dark green with wavy edges. H. and S. 24in (60cm).
(Burgi-Ott, Switzerland, 1972)

**'Bealings'**
Double H2 Bush
An excellent medium-sized double for the show bench. *Tube* and *sepals* are white. *Corolla* bright violet turning to pink. The colour combination is very eye-catching. Growth strong, upright and free-branching. *Foliage* mid-green, with smaller than average leaves.
(Goulding, UK, 1983)

**'Beatrice Burtoft'**
Single H2 Bush
*Tube* and *sepals* red. *Corolla* deep rose. Flowers semi-erect, produced on stiff bushy growth. *Foliage* medium green.
(Bielby/Oxtoby, UK, 1992)

**'Beatrice Ellen'**
Single H3 Bush
Medium-sized flower. *Tube* pale rose. *Sepals* rose-coloured. *Corolla* dark rose. *Foliage* medium green with white veining and rose stems. Good upright grower. H. and S. 24–30in (60–75cm).
(Adams, UK, 1988)

**'Beauty of Bath'**
Double H1 Bush
*Tube* pale pink. *Sepals* pale pink, deepening at base, edged with bright pink and green tips. *Corolla* pure white. Flowers are large and hold their shape well. *Foliage* medium green and fairly large. Very free-flowering.
(Colville, UK, 1965)

**'Beauty of Cliff Hall'**
Single H2 Bush
Typical of Lye's raisings, *tube* and *sepals* waxy cream. *Corolla* is pink. Growth is rather lax but makes a good bush plant with supports. *Foliage* medium green.
(Lye, UK, 1881)

**'Beauty of Exeter'**
Semi-double H2 Lax bush
*Tube* and *sepals* light rosy salmon. *Corolla* a deeper shade of salmon (almost self-colouring). Flowers are large and freely produced. *Foliage* yellowish-green.
(Letheren, France, 1890)

**'Beauty of Purbeck'**
Semi-double H2 Bush
Medium-sized flowers. *Tube* white, striped pink. *Sepals* white, striped and flushed rose. *Corolla* white. *Foliage* medium green.
(Swinbank, UK, 1991)

**'Beauty of Swanley'**
Single H2 Lax bush
The Lye hallmark of *tube* long, waxy white. *Sepals* waxy white and recurving. *Corolla* is soft rose pink. The medium-sized flowers are freely produced early in the season. Growth 'spreading' rather than 'upright'. *Foliage* medium green.
(Lye, UK, 1875)

**'Beauty of Trowbridge'**
Single H2 Bush
*Tube* thick, waxy creamy white. *Sepals* recurved, waxy white. *Corolla* rosy cerise. *Leaves* long, medium green, with serrated edges. The fairly strong upright growth makes this cultivar suitable for larger structures.
(Lye, UK, 1881)

'BASHFUL'

'BASKETFUL'

'BEACON'

'BEACON ROSA'

'BEALINGS'

'BEAUTY OF BATH'

**'Becky'**
Single H2 Bush
*Tube* short, dark red. *Sepals*
upswept, dark glossy red.
*Corolla* bell-shaped dark
aubergine to red. Show-quality
plants which are upright and
bushy in growth. *Foliage*
medium green.
(Goulding, UK, 1994)

**'Begame Kiekeboe'**
Single H2 Bush
Small erect single.*Tube* and
*Sepals* red. *Corolla* red-purple.
*Foliage* The growth is similar to
F. *Lycioides*.
(de Graaff, Holland, 1989)

**'Bella Forbes'**
Double H2 Bush
*Tube* and *sepals* cerise. The
sepals are held back against the
tube. *Corolla* creamy white
veined with cerise. Very full and
fluffy. *Foliage* medium green.
The growth is upright and very
strong. Dislikes 'pinching' but
is self-branching.
(Forbes, UK, 1890)

**'Bella Rosella'**
Double H2 Trailer
Very large attractive flowers.
*Tube* and *sepals* whitish-pink.
*Corolla* very full mauvish edged
magenta. *Foliage* medium green
on the upper surface, lighter on
the underside. ('Quasar' ×
'Applause')
(Garrett, USA, 1989)

**'Bella van Cappelen'**
Single H2 Bush
*Tube* carmine. *Sepals* cherry
pink. *Corolla* fuchsia violet.
*Foliage* medium green.
Medium-sized flowers pro-
duced on an upright-growing
plant.
(van den Bergh, Holland, 1991)

**'Belle de Lisse'**
Double H2 Lax bush
*Tube* and *sepals* cream. *Corolla*
pink. *Foliage* medium green.
The lax upright growth makes
it a possibility for training as a
bush with supports or within a
hanging basket.
(de Graaff, Holland, 1979)

**'Belsay Beauty'**
Semi-double H2 Lax bush
*Tube* short, rhodamine pink.
*Sepals* rhodamine pink on the
undersurface, whitish with
rhodamine pink shading on the
upper. *Corolla* is violet fading to
cyclamen purple. Medium-sized
flowers. *Foliage* mid- to light
green. Natural trailer but can be
encouraged to grow as a bush.
(Ryle, UK, 1975)

**'Belvoir Beauty'**
Semi-double H2 Bush
Medium-sized flowers freely
produced. *Tube* short, white
flushed with green. *Sepals* white
with green tips. *Corolla* white
at the base shading through
pale wisteria with a distinct blue
edge to each petal. *Foliage* light
green. A very attractive plant.
(Gadsby, UK, 1975)

**'Ben Jammin'**
Single H2 Bush
*Tube* pale pink. *Sepals* pink
flushed with pale aubergine.
*Corolla* dark aubergine. *Foliage*
medium to dark green. Medium-
sized flowers freely produced on
short jointed plants. Very distinctive colouring.
(Carless, UK, 1993)

**'Ben's Ruby'**
Double H2 Bush
This sport from 'Royal Velvet'
has large double flowers. *Tube*
and *sepals* red. *Corolla* turkey
red. *Foliage* medium-green.
(Finder and date unknown)

**'Berba'**
Semi-double H2 Stiff trailer
Large semi-double flowers. *Tube*
white. *Sepals* white blushed
rose. *Corolla* pale red-purple.
The natural growth is as a stiff
trailer so will make a good basket with the assistance of
weights. *Foliage* mid-green with
lighter colouring underneath.
The leaves are quite large.
(Bats, Holland, 1986)

**'Berbanella'**
Semi-double H2 Bush
*Tube* short, pink. *Sepals* pink
on the upper surface and much

darker pink beneath. *Corolla*
pink with smooth petal edges.
*Foliage* mid-green with lighter
colouring on undersurface. The
flowers are fairly large and are
freely produced.
(Bats, Holland, 1986)

**'Berba's Coronation'**
Double H2 Trailing
Large double flowers. *Tube*
white, flushed rose. *Sepals* light
coral rose. *Corolla* dark mauve
with light orange petaloids.
*Foliage* medium green.
(Bats, Holland, 1985)

**'Berba's Delight'**
Semi-double H2 Bush
*Tube* and *Sepals* rose red.
*Corolla* aubergine purple.
*Foliage* mid-green. Medium-
sized flowers on upright
growth.
(Bats, Holland, 1988)

**'Berba's Fleur'**
Double H2 Bush
Large double flowers. *Tube* and
*Sepals* rose red. *Corolla* light
violet. *Foliage* medium green.
('First Kiss' × 'Tropicana')
(Bats, Holland, 1986)

**'Berba's Frances Femke'**
Semi-double H2 Trailer
Large semi-double flowers.
*Tube* and *sepals* rose. *Corolla*
white flushed with rose. *Foliage*
mid-green. Perhaps the growth
should be described as lax
trailer as it can be encouraged
to bush and may be used in
baskets. ('La Campanella' × 'La
Neige')
(Bats, Holland, 1986)

**'Berba's Happiness'**
Double H2 Trailer
Large double flowers. *Tube*
greenish-white. *Sepals* white
flushed pink. *Corolla* cyclamen
purple. Natural trailing cultivar
suitable for baskets. *Foliage*
fairly large and mid-green.
(Bats, Holland, 1988)

'BEAUTY OF EXETER'

'BELLA FORBES'

'BELLA ROSELLA'

'BERBA'S CORONATION'

**'Berba's Impossible'**
Semi-double H2 Bush
*Tube* and *Sepals* light pink.
*Corolla* violet. *Foliage* mid-
green and lighter on the under-
surface. Upright grower.
('Barbanella' × 'Golden Glow')
(Bats, Holland, 1986)

**'Berba's Inge Mariel'**
Semi-double or double H2
Trailer
*Tube* and *sepals* ivory white.
*Corolla* two-tiered, lilac with
light streaks. *Foliage* mid- to
light green. Strong growth
which needs assistance to trail.
('La Campanella' × 'La Neige')
(Bats, Holland, 1986)

**'Berba's Ingrid'**
Single H2 Stiff trailer
Single or occasionally semi-
double medium-sized blooms.
*Tubes* striped cream. *Sepals*
white tipped with green.
*Corolla* violet-purple. *Foliage*
medium green. ('Sincerity' ×
'Bicentennial')
(Bats, Holland, 1986).

**'Berba's Love'**
Large double H2 Lax bush
*Tube* greenish-white. *Sepals*
white with an undersurface of
rose. *Corolla* is violet-purple.
*Foliage* mid-green. Rather stiff
trailing growth.
(Bats, Holland, 1988)

***F. bergnimf***
Species × Single H1 Bush
Medium-sized flower. *Tube*
long and slender, rose red.
*Sepals* short, recurved, deep
rose tipped with green. *Corolla*
deep rose red. *Foliage* dark
green, similar to *F. sessilifolia*
but longer. Upright growth. (*F.
sessilifolia* × *F. fulgens)*
(Appel, Holland, 1981)

**'Bermuda'**
Double H2 Bush
Very large striking flowers.
*Tube* and *sepals* velvety red.
*Corolla* dark purple with red
flecks. *Foliage* large, mid- to
dark green. Upright bushy
growth.
(Lockerbie, Australia, 1960(s))

**'Bernard Rawdin'**
Single H2 Bush
*Tube* and *sepals* rose red.
*Corolla* cyclamen purple. Wide,
bell-shaped blooms freely
produced. *Foliage* medium
green. Prefers to grow in partial
shade. ('Upward Look' ×
'Caroline')
(Gadsby, UK, 1968.

**'Bernisser Molen'**
Single H2 Bush
*Tubes* deep rose. *Sepals* cherry
pink. *Corolla* deep mauve-purple. *Foliage* medium green.
Medium-sized, upward-looking
flowers produced on an
upright-growing plant.
(Weeda, Holland, 1991)

**'Bernisser Stein'**
Semi-double H2 Bush
*Tube* and *sepals* neyron rose.
*Corolla* cyclamen purple.
*Foliage* medium to dark green.
Growth upright and bushy.
(Weeda, Holland, 1989)

**'Bertha Gadsby'**
Single H2 Trailer
*Tube* long, pale pink. *Sepals* are
pale pink. *Corolla* bright
orange-pink. Medium-sized
flowers produced very freely.
*Foliage* medium to light green.
(Bielby/Oxtoby, UK, 1991)

**'Bertha Timmer'**
Single H2 Bush
Flowers small. *Tubes* and *sepals*
deep reddish purple. *Corolla*
dark aubergine purple. *Foliage*
medium to dark green. Self-
branching, upright-growing
plant.
(Beije, Holland, 1991)

**'Beryl's Choice'**
Double H2 Bush
Flowers large. *Tube* pink.
*Sepals* medium length, reflexing, pink tipped with green.
*Corolla* light magenta pink
with deep rose blotches at the
bases of petals. *Foliage*
light green, medium size, serrated edges. Fairly strong
upright grower.
(Sport from 'Georgana')
(Richardson (Australia, 1980)

**'Beth Robley'**
Double H2 Trailer
*Tube* and *sepals* salmon. Flowers
fairly large. *Corolla* salmon
orange. A natural trailer so will
make a good plant for a hanging
container. *Foliage* medium green.
(Tiret, USA, 1971)

**'Betsy Ross'**
Double H2 Lax bush
*Tube* red. *Sepals* long and
upturned, white. *Corolla* blue
spectrum-violet. Blooms
medium-sized and freely produced. Natural growth is as a
lax bush but can be encouraged
to trail with weights. *Foliage*
medium green.
(Walker and Jones, USA, 1954)

**'Bette Sibley'**
Semi-double H2 Bush
*Tube* short, carmine. *Sepals*
upswept, carmine. *Corolla* lilac
pink veined with deep pink.
Flowers freely produced and
bell-shaped. *Foliage* mid-green
on upright, short jointed
growth. ('Katherine Maidment'
× 'Miss California')
(Dyos, UK, 1987)

**'Beverley'**
Single H2 Bush
*Tube* short, medium thick,
empire rose. *Sepals* striped with
empire rose and neyron rose
and have green tips. *Corolla*
fuchsia purple with neyron rose
at the base. The bell-shaped
flowers are medium-sized.
*Foliage* mid-green on upper
surface and lighter on the lower
with serrated edges. ('Percy
Holmes' ×)
(Holmes, R., UK, 1976)

**'Bewitched'**
Semi-double H2 Lax bush
*Tube* and long *sepals* white outside, flushed pale pink on the
inner surface. *Corolla* dubon-
net-purple, flushed white at the
base. Large blooms freely produced. *Foliage* medium green.
Growth very vigorous, and
staking will be required to produce a good bush. With assistance will make a good basket.
(Tiret, USA, 1951)

'BERMUDA'

'BERTHA GADSBY'

'BERYL'S CHOICE'

'BETSY ROSS'

**'Bianca'**
Double H2 Trailer
*Tube* short, white. *Sepals* white.
*Corolla* very large also white. A
natural trailer so will make an
excellent basket. *Foliage*
medium green.
(Pennisi, USA, 1967)

**'Bicentennial'**
Double H2 Trailer
Medium-sized double. *Tube*
white. *Sepals* Indian orange.
*Corolla* magenta in the centre
surrounded by indian orange.
*Foliage* light to medium green.
This self-branching cultivar will
make a good basket with its
natural trailing ability. With
supports will also make a lax
bush. Used as a standard the
trailing habit will give a very
impressive weeping plant.
Colours best in the sun.
(Paskesen, USA, 1976)

**'Big Blue Boy'**
Double H2 Bush
*Tube* white. *Sepals* white on
top, pale pink on the undersurface, green tips. *Corolla* deep
purple fading to burgundy purple. Large blooms freely produced. *Foliage* large, dark
medium green.
(Gorman, USA, 1970)

**'Big Charles'**
Double H2 Trailer
*Tubes* immensely long, thin,
white. *Sepals* shorter, arched,
white above pink reverse.
*Corolla* frilly with mixed
mauves and pinks. Growth
rather sparse. *Foliage* medium
green. Looks best in hanging
pots.
(Moerman, Holland, 1988)

**'Bill Gilbert'**
Single H2 Bush
*Tube* short, rose. *Sepals* rose
with green recurved tips.
*Corolla* opens dark violet, and
matures to violet. *Foliage*
medium green with fairly wide
leaves. Medium-sized blooms
produced in profusion.
('Lady Isobel Barnet' × 'Brookwood Belle')
(Gilbert, UK, 1989)

**'Bill Hill'**
Double H3 Bush
Medium-sized double. *Tube*
and *sepals* deep pink. *Corolla*
white veined with pink. *Foliage*
mid-green. H. and S. 18–24in
(45–60cm).
(Weeks, UK, 1991)

**'Bill Kennedy'**
Single H2 Trailer
*Tube* and *sepals* red. *Corolla*
purple veined with red. *Foliage*
medium green on the upper
surface with a lighter shade on
the lower. Good strong grower
which produces many flowers.
A natural trailer, will make an
excellent basket ('Flying Saucer'
× 'Bianca')
(Drapkin, USA, 1988)

**'Bill Stevens'**
Double H2 Trailer
Large double flowers on very
strong branches capable of supporting the flowers when grown
outside, even when the wind is a
problem. *Tube* deep red. *Sepals*
horizontal, recurved, shiny red.
*Corolla* very full, deep red with
scarlet base. *Foliage* medium
green. Makes a large basket and
needs a couple of pinches to
encourage branching.
(Elliot, UK, 1994)

**'Billy Green'**
Single H2 Bush
Considered to be a Triphylla
Type, as tube, long, tapering
2in (5cm). Not now eligible for
showing in triphylla classes as
it produces its flowers from the
axils along each stem. *Tube*,
*sepals*, *corolla* all salmon.
*Foliage* olive green a perfect
backcloth to the flowers which
are produced throughout the
season in profusion. A superb
fuchsia. Parentage unknown.
(Raiser unknown, UK, 1962)

**'Birgit Heinke'**
Double H2 Trailer
*Tube* and *sepals* cerise. *Corolla*
lavender marbled with pink.
*Foliage* large, medium green.
An excellent large-flowered
double for hanging baskets.
(Raiser and date unknown)

**'Bishops Bells'**
Semi-double H2 Bush
A delightful, large flowered cultivar. *Tube* rosy red. *Sepals* very
long, rosy red with lighter
colouring towards the tips
which are green. *Corolla*
bishop's violet ageing to reddish-purple. Flowers often measure 5in (13cm) across. Strong
upright bushy growth. Prefers
partial shade. ('Caroline' ×)
(Gadsby, UK, 1970)

**'Bits'**
Double H2 Trailer
*Tube* short thin magenta and
green. *Sepals* upswept, reflexing, white with green tips,
heavily veined with magenta.
*Corolla* opens violet-blue
maturing to violet-purple.
Medium-sized blooms pro-
duced in flushes. Mid-green serrated edges. Natural trailer so
will produce a good basket.
('White King' × 'Little Bit')
(Wilkins/Higginbottom, Australia, 1986)

**'Bittersweet'**
Double H2 Lax bush or trailer
*Tube* and *sepals* pale pink and
white. *Corolla* rose with
salmon to orange marbling.
Flowers are large. *Foliage*
medium green. Will make a
good bush with supports but
better in a hanging container
where it will naturally trail.
(Kennett, USA, 1971)

**'Black Prince'**
Single H2 Bush
Synonymous with 'Gruss aus
dem Bodethal'. *Tube* and *sepals*
red. *Corolla* very deep (almost
black) purple. *Foliage* medium
green. An excellent cultivar for
the show bench. Can be trained
with weights in a basket.
('Cupido' × 'Creusa')
(Sattler and Bethga, Germany,
1893)

'BICENTENNIAL'

'BILL GILBERT'

'BILLY GREEN'

'BIRGIT HEINKE'

'BITTERSWEET'

**'Blanch Regina'**
Double H2 Trailer
*Tube* white, medium length.
*Sepals* reflexing, white, crêpe
inside. *Corolla* amethyst violet
changing to rhodamine purple
with maturity, petals flared and
fluted. Medium-sized blooms
freely and continuously produced. *Foliage* medium green
with serrated edging. Natural
trailer and self-branching, with
pinching will form a bush. Best
colour in shade. ('La Campanella' × 'Flirtation Waltz')
(Clyne, UK, 1974)

**'Bland's New Striped'**
Single H2 Bush
*Tube* cerise, medium length.
*Sepals* recurved, cerise. *Corolla*
rich purple with streaks of pink
down the centre of each petal.
Flowers medium to large, freely
produced. *Foliage* mid-green,
longish. Upright and bushy
growth, self-branching. One of
the best of the 'striped' cultivars. A very good bush, standard or pot plant.
(Bland, UK, 1872)

**'Blowick'**
Double H2 Trailer
*Tube* and *sepals* flesh pink.
*Corolla* violet maturing to
plum. *Foliage* medium green.
Growth free branching, sturdy
and weather resistant. Makes a
large show basket very easily
but can be used for practically
any shape.
(Porter, UK, 1984)

**'Blue Anchor'**
Semi-double H2 Bush
*Tube* and *sepals* bright red.
*Corolla* whitish blue. Medium-
sized blooms have deep pink
filaments and anthers. The
growth is fairly strong and
upright. *Foliage* mid-green.
('Grace Groom' × 'John Baker')
(Weeks, UK, 1987)

**'Blue Beauty'**
Double H2 Bush
*Tube* short, red. *Sepals* red,
held moderately erect. *Corolla*
is bluish violet. Flowers full and
freely produced. Strong growth

makes a good bush and might
be considered for standards.
(Bull, UK, 1854)

**'Blue Bonnet'**
Double H3 Bush
*Tube* and *sepals* red. *Corolla*
deep blue. The medium-sized
blooms are produced in profu-
sion for a hardy cultivar.
*Foliage* medium green. H. and
S. 18–24in (45–60cm).
(Tabraham, UK, 1974)

**'Blue Bush'**
Single H3 Bush
*Tube* and *sepals* rosy red.
*Corolla* bluebird blue, fading to
bishop's violet with rose veins.
Medium sized blooms. *Foliage*
mid- to dark green. Very vigor-
ous upright growth. May be
considered for hedges. H. and
S. 3–4ft (90–120cm).
(Gadsby, UK, 1973)

**'Blue Butterfly'**
Semi-double H1 Trailer
*Tube* short, white. *Sepals* white.
*Corolla* deep violet-blue,
splashed with white. Blooms are
medium to large. With maturity,
inner petals open wide, orchid
with blue undertones. *Foliage*
dark green. A natural trailer so
will make a good basket.
(Waltz, USA, 1960)

**'Blue Gown'**
Double H2 Bush or standard
*Tube* and *sepals* cerise. *Corolla*
bluish purple, splashed with
pink and carmine. Large
blooms freely produced early in
the season. *Foliage* medium
green, slightly serrated. Good
strong upright growth. Will
need staking in greenhouse
because of weight of blooms.
Try as a standard to give height
in the border. H. and S.
30–36in (75–90cm).
(Milne, UK)

**'Blue Halo'**
Double H2 Trailer
*Tube* short, thin, pinkish ivory.
*Sepals* long, curving, white with
pink markings at the base.
*Corolla* white to pale pink with
petals edged with blue to

purple shading. *Foliage* dark
green with red veining.
(Stubbs, USA, 1981)

**'Blue Hawaii'**
Double H2 Trailer
*Tubes* greenish-white. *Sepals*
white. *Corolla* violet. Medium-
sized flowers produced on trailing branches so will make a
good basket. *Foliage* mid-green.
(McDonald, USA, 1989)

**'Blue Ice'**
Single H2 Bush
*Tube* small, thin, rose pink.
*Sepals* held well up, tips
recurved and twisting rose
pink. *Corolla* pale lavender
blue, with rose veining, white
at the base of the petals. An
easy cultivar recommended for
beginners. *Foliage* yellow-
green. Upright, vigorous
growth, short jointed and free-
flowering. Good as small pot
plant or miniature standard.
(Hall, UK, 1984)

**'Blue Jacket'**
Semi-double H2 Bush
*Tube* crimson. *Sepals* curl right
back to the tube, crimson.
*Corolla* dark blue ageing to
purple with maturity. Medium-
sized blooms freely produced.
*Foliage* medium green. Upright,
bushy, self-branching growth.
('Joy Patmore' × 'Madame Cor-
nelissen')
(Dyos, UK, 1980)

**'Blue Lace'**
Double H3 Bush
*Tube* and *sepals* red. *Corolla*
blue. Large blooms continuously produced. *Foliage* dark
green. Upright bushy growth
(see photo overleaf). H. and S.
24–30in (60–75cm).
(Tabraham, UK, 1974)

**'Blue Lagoon'**
Double H2 Bush
*Tube* short, bright red. *Sepals*
bright red. *Corolla* blue with
deep purple cast on the petals.
Blooms large, with a spreading
habit as they open. *Foliage*
mid-green.
(Travis, UK, 1958)

'BLOWICK'

'BLUE BUSH'

'BLUE BUTTERFLY'

'BLUE GOWN'

'BLUE HALO'

'BLUE ICE'

**'Blue Lagoon'**
Double H1 Bush
*Tube* and *sepals* rosy-red.
*Corolla* large, medium blue.
Growth upright and bushy.
Responds to careful pinching to
form the best shape. *Foliage*
medium to dark green.
(Tiret, USA, 1961)

**'Blue Lake'**
Double H2 Bush
*Tube* medium-sized greenish-
white. *Sepals* white, curl
upwards. *Corolla* rich aster violet shading to magnolia purple
at base of petals. Medium-sized
blooms. *Foliage* mid-green,
medium size, slight serrations.
Early and continuous flowering. A good pot plant.
(Pacey, UK, 1985)

**'Blue Mink'**
Single H2 Bush
*Tube* short, thick, crimson.
*Sepals* reflex and twist around
the tube, crimson. *Corolla* dark
violet veined with crimson.
Flowers of medium size.
*Foliage* medium to dark green
with red veins. Self-branching,
short-jointed habit, very florif-
erous and bushy. Good plant
for bedding out or for pots.
('Gruss aus dem Bodethal' ×
'Dutch Mill')
(Holmes, UK, 1976)

**'Blue Mirage'**
Double H2 Trailer
*Tube* and *sepals* white and pink
flush. *Corolla* pink through to
blue full and compact. Growth
is strong, upright and self-
branching. *Foliage* dark green.
Suitable for hanging pots or
baskets.
(Bellamy, UK, 1984)

**'Blue Pearl'**
Double H2 Lax bush
*Tube* pink. *Sepals* heavy, broad
arching, pink tipped with
green. *Corolla* violet blue.
*Foliage* mid-green. Free flowering plants mid-green, large
blooms, flower opens flat. Vigorous upright growth, can be
made to trail.
(Martin, USA, 1955)

**'Blue Peter'**
Double H2 Bush
*Tube* and *sepals* of these large-
flowered plants are pinkish-
white. *Corolla* imperial purple.
Very attractive and eye-catching
flowers. *Foliage* mid-green.
(M. Porter, UK, 1985)

**'Blue Pinwheel'**
Single H2 Trailer
*Tube* red. *Sepals* red, curl to
form a pinwheel. *Corolla*
orchid blue, pale pink at base.
Flowers medium size. *Foliage*
small and dark. A natural
trailer, free-flowering, self-
branching. Makes a good half
basket.
(Stubbs, USA, 1970)

**'Blue Ranger'**
Semi-double H2 Bush
*Tube* long, thick, crimson.
*Sepals* broad, waxy crimson.
*Corolla* blue-bird blue shading
to hyacinth blue, and fading to
violet. Flowers medium to
large, plant is free-flowering.
*Foliage* medium-sized mid-
green. Self-branching, upright
growth, will trail with weights.
(Gadsby, UK, 1974)

**'Blue Sails'**
Single H2 Bush
*Tube* neyron rose. *Sepals* neyron rose, deeper on the undersurface. *Corolla* dark
violet-blue fading to fuchsia
purple. White at the base of the
petals. Short-jointed and vigorous upright growth. *Foliage*
medium green.
(Pacey, UK, 1982)

**'Blue Satin'**
Double H1 Trailer
*Tube* and *sepals* glistening
white. *Corolla* indigo blue
shading to white at the base of
the petals. *Foliage* dark green.
Best grown as lax bush with
supports, or a trailer in a
basket.
(Walker, USA, 1969)

**'Blue Tit'**
Single H3 Bush
*Tube* red, small, thin. *Sepals*
reflexing, red. *Corolla* violet

veined red with pale pink splash
at base of petals. The small flowers are prolifically produced.
*Foliage* mid green on sturdy
upright, bushy growth. Plant
suitable for the small pot classes.
(Hobson, UK, 1982)

**'Blue Veil'**
Double H2 Trailer
*Tube* and *sepals* pure white.
*Corolla* lobelia blue, full and
compact. Large flowers, full and
well shaped. *Foliage* medium
green. A natural trailer so will
make an excellent basket.
(Pacey, UK, 1980)

**'Blue Waves'**
Double H2 Bush
*Tube* short, very pale pink.
*Sepals* upturned, neyron rose.
*Corolla* deep campanula violet
with decided blue overtone on
wavy petals. Blooms fairly large
and freely produced. *Foliage*
mid- to dark green. Growth
upright and bushy, easy to
grow, a lovely exhibition plant.
(Waltz, USA, 1954)

**'Blush of Dawn'**
Double H2 Trailer
An excellent cultivar in every
respect. Large flowers. *Tube*
white. *Sepals* white waxy with
green tips. *Corolla* is silver
grey/lavender. Not the earliest
to flower but the flowers are
freely produced and long-lasting. *Foliage* is medium green.
Growth is naturally bushy and
trailing responding well to frequent pinching.
(Martin, USA, 1962)

**'Blythe'**
Semi-double H2 Bush
*Tube* rose pink. *Sepals* long,
recurving, rose pink. *Corolla*
lavender blue changing to lilac.
The flower is bell-shaped.
*Foliage* medium green. Growth
strong and upright. Good for
bush or standard growth.
(Goulding, UK, 1988)

'BLUE LACE'

'BLUE PEARL'

'BLUE VEIL'

'BLUSH OF DAWN'

**'Bob Brown'**
Single/semi-double H2 Bush
*Tube* and *sepals* red. *Corolla*
palest pink with red veining.
*Foliage* medium green. Good
floriferous bushy plant.
(Fleming, UK, 1991)

**'Bobby Boy'**
Double H2 Lax bush
*Tube* and *sepals* reddish-rose.
*Corolla* bluish-rose which fades
to rose, with touches of orange
on outer petals. The small
blooms are profuse and have
the appearance of a small rose.
*Foliage* mid-green.
(Fuchsia Forest, USA, 1965)

**'Bobby Dazzler'**
Double H2 Bush
*Tube* and *sepals* claret rose.
*Corolla* Indian lake which
matures to crimson. *Foliage*
medium green. Early to flower
on strong upright branches. A
very eye-catching cultivar.
('Eusebia' × 'Orange Flair')
(Bielby/Oxtoby, UK, 1987)

**'Bobby Shaftoe'**
Semi-double H2 Bush
*Tube* short, clear frosty white
with a pale pink flush. *Sepals*
clear frosty white with the
palest of pink flushes and lemon
tips. The *corolla* is frosty white
with pink flush and pink veins.
*Foliage* medium to light green.
The blooms are produced prolifically throughout a long season and are medium in size. A
very eye-catching cultivar.
(Ryle/Atkinson, UK, 1973)

**'Bobby Wingrove'**
Single H2 Bush
A very floriferous, small flowered cultivar which blooms per-
petually. *Tube* short, red. *Sepals*
red, tipped with green. *Corolla*
turkey red. Growth upright and
bushy. *Foliage* mid- to dark
green.
(Wingrove, UK, 1966)

**'Bobolink'**
Double H2 Bush
*Tube* and upturned *sepals* flesh
pink. *Corolla* an intense blue-
violet. Blooms large, freely

produced, but rather loose.
*Foliage* fairly large and mid-
green. Vigorous upright, bushy
plant.
(Evans and Reeves, USA, 1953)

**'Bob Pacey'**
Single H2 Bush
*Tube* and *sepals* white, tipped
green. *Corolla* pale violet-
purple, changing to a delicate
lavender. Flowers are held erect
and are produced in quantity.
Short-jointed compact bush.
*Foliage* mid green.
(Pacey, UK, 1991)

**'Bob Paisley'**
Double H2 Bush
Medium-sized flowers. *Tube*
rose red, short, narrow. *Sepals*
rose red top, crimson underneath, long tips recurving.
*Corolla* mallow purple, ageing
to rose purple. *Foliage* medium
green. Upright, free-flowering A
sport from 'Spion Kop' and well
named for a former Manager of
Liverpool Football Club. Needs
regular pinching and will make
good standard or bush.
(Sinton, 1984)

**'Bob's Best'**
Double H2 Bush
*Tube* and *sepals* white. *Corolla*
cardinal red striped with pink.
The large full double flowers
are very striking and free-flowering. *Foliage* medium green on
upright growing bushes. Worth
trying as a standard.
(Pacey, UK, 1988)

**'Boerhaave'**
Single H2 Bush
*Tube* very long, red. *Sepals* deep
red. The reflexed sepals are held
well away from the tube. Buds
are very long, thin and tapering.
*Corolla* deep rose to rosy purple. *Foliage* medium to darkish
green. Upright and bushy
growth. Flowers profusely.
(Van Wieringen, Holland,
1970)

**'Bohemienne'**
Single H2 Bush
Most unusual-shaped flower,
with four distinct triangular-

shaped petals. *Tube* medium
pink. *Sepals* pink, recurved,
with green tips. *Corolla* white
with red base to each petal.
*Foliage* dark olive-green on the
upper surface and slightly
lighter on the lower. A good
self-branching bush, or could
be used for larger structures.
('Loecky' × 'U.F.O.')
(de Graaff, Holland, 1987)

**F. boliviana**
Species H1 Climbing bush
Tube long, funnel-shaped.
*Sepals* and *corolla* light red to
deep crimson. *Foliage* very
large medium to dark green
with reddish veins. The hairy
leaves measure up to 8–4in
(20–10cm). Classified as a
climber and is best grown with
as much root room as possible
in a conservatory or greenhouse
border.
(Carr, South America, 1882)

**F. boliviana var luxurians alba**
Species H1 Climbing bush
The description of this species
is precisely the same as that
given for *F. Boliviana*, except
that the *tube* and *sepals* are
white.
(Lamark, South America, 1768)

**'Bon Accorde'**
Single H2 Bush
*Tube* short, medium thickness,
white. *Sepals* pale pink, almost
a waxy white. *Corolla* pale purple. Flowers of this upward
looking flower are small, but
freely produced. *Foliage*
medium green. Stiff upright
growth. Requires frequent
pinching to make a bushy
plant. Could be useful as pot
plants grown as quarter or half-
standard.
(Crousse, France, 1861)

**'Bonanza'**
Double H2 Lax bush
*Tube* and *sepals* spinel pink.
*Corolla* spectrum violet, fading
to petunia-purple with maturity. Medium-sized blooms produced fairly freely. *Foliage*
medium green.
(Fuchsia, La, USA, 1963)

'BOBBY DAZZLER'

'BOB PACEY'

'BOBBY WINGROVE'

*F. BOLIVIANA* VAR *LUXURIANS ALBA*

'BOB'S BEST'

### 'Bon Bon'
Double H2 Lax bush
*Tube* greenish-white. *Sepals* pale pink, deeper pink underneath, short, broad. *Corolla* very pale pink. The flowers are medium-sized, freely produced. When growing under shade can almost be described as a self-white. Small glossy *foliage* medium to dark green, slightly serrated. Self-branching, long-arching stems, prolific bloomer. Needs careful pinching, does well in half basket.
(Kennett, USA, 1963)

### 'Bonita'
Double H2 Trailer
*Tube* and *sepals* light pink, sepals shading to white on top side and china rose underneath. *Corolla* orchid purple. *Foliage* dark green. Blooms medium-sized and freely produced. Excellent cultivar for basket work.
(Fuchsia La, USA, 1972)

### 'Bonnie Berrycloth'
Double H2 Bush
*Tube* red. *Sepals* red on upper surface, crêped red on the lower. *Corolla* opens dark purple with red base, matures to reddish purple. *Foliage* medium green. ('General Monk' × 'Gruss aus dem Bodethal')
(Holmes, UK, 1989)

### 'Bonnie Doan'
Single H2 Trailer
*Tube* pale pink striped with deep pink. *Sepals* pale pink, as also is the *Corolla*. *Foliage* yellowish-green. A natural trailer so will make a good basket. ('Pink Marshmallow' × 'Los Angeles')
(Drapkin, USA, 1987)

### 'Bonnie Lass'
Double H2 Bush
*Tube* clear, frosty white. *Sepals* frosty white on the outer surface and palest pink on the inner, reflexed. *Corolla* clear lilac fading to pleasing shade of rose. The medium-sized flowers are freely produced. *Foliage* small and dark green. Growth is naturally upright and bushy, self-branching, good pot plant.
(Waltz, USA, 1962)

### 'Bonnie's Pride'
Single H2 Bush
*Tube* light pink. *Sepals* dark pink. *Corolla* is dark rose, edged reddish purple. *Foliage* medium green on the upper surface with lighter colouring on the underneath. ('Pink Marshmallow' × 'Ocean Beach')
(Drapkin, USA, 1989)

### 'Bora Bora'
Double H2 Trailer
*Tube* white, faintly pink. *Sepals* white. *Corolla* purplish-blue, fading to pinkish purple with small green petaloids. *Foliage* light green, excellent for basket work given suitably ventilated conditions. Very bushy trailer, self-branching, free-flowering, prefers shade.
(Tiret, USA, 1966)

### 'Border Queen'
Single H2 Bush
*Tube* short, thin, pale pink. *Sepals* rhodamine pink, tipped with green. *Corolla* amethyst violet flushed pale pink with dark pink veins, fading to white at the base. *Foliage* medium green with reddish stems. Vigorous, free-flowering upright. ('Leonora' × 'Lena Dalton')
(Ryle/Atkinson, UK, 1974)

### 'Border Reiver'
Single H2 Bush
*Tube* neyron rose. *Sepals* semi-reflexed neyron rose on the upper surface, vermilion beneath. *Corolla* cardinal red. Medium-sized flowers produced very freely. *Foliage* dark green medium-sized with serrated edges. Needs careful pinching for good shape; growth vigorous, upright.
(Ryle, UK, 1980)

### 'Bornemann's Beste'
Triphylla type. H1 Bush
A very strong-growing plant.
*Tube*, *sepals*, *corolla* orange red. Flowers produced in clusters terminally. *Foliage* dark green.
(Bonstedt, Germany, 1904)

### 'Bossanova'
Semi-double H2 Bush
Flowers of this cultivar grow erect. *Tube* yellow/green flushed vermilion. *Sepals* rose. *Corolla* deep purple. Flowers medium-sized, produced quite freely. *Foliage* mid-green.
(Brouwer, Holland, 1991)

### 'Bouffant'
Single H2 Trailer
*Tube* and *sepals* red. *Corolla* white-veined, rosy red. *Foliage* medium green. The large flowers are freely produced on a naturally trailing plant.
(Tiret, USA, 1949)

### 'Bountiful'
Double H2 Bush
*Tube* white, long. *Sepals* palest pink, green tips upturned. *Corolla* milky white, veined pink. The full globular blooms are produced early in the season and very freely. Needs support to counteract the weight of the flowers. *Foliage* mid-green, slightly serrated.
(Munkner, USA, 1983)

### 'Bouquet'
Double H3 Bush
*Tube* and *sepals* red. *Corolla* violet, ageing to reddish-purple. The small flowers are produced in quantity. *Foliage* small, medium green. Self-branching, excellent for the front of a hardy border. H. and S. 18–24in (45–60cm). ('Myrtifolia' ×)
(Lemoine, France, 1893)

### 'Bouvigne 91'
Semi-double H2 Lax bush
*Tube* and *sepals* red. *Corolla* bluish purple. *Foliage* medium to dark green. Growth rather lax, so will need supporting to make a bush or could be used in hanging containers.
(de Leeuw, Holland, 1991)

'BONITA'

'BONNIE DOAN'

'BONNIE LASS'

'BOUQUET'

**'Bow Bells'**
Single to semi-double  H2
Bush
*Tube* short, white. *Sepals* long,
white, tipped with green.
*Corolla* magenta, white at base
of the petals. Early and prolific
bloomer. *Foliage* medium
green. The weight of blooms
will require support when
grown as a bush.
(Handley, UK, 1972)

**'Brandt's 500 Club'**
Single  H2  Bush
*Tube* pink. *Sepals* long, pale
cerise, shading to orange.
*Corolla* cerise, pink at base
with orange flush. *Foliage*
medium green, serrated.
Growth upright and bushy.
(Brand, USA, 1955)

**'Breckland'**
Single  H2  Bush
*Tube* and *sepals* flesh pink,
flushed darker pink inside.
*Corolla* violet to mauve. Large
single bell-shaped blooms displayed prominently. Growth
strong, upright and self-branching. ('Lancelot' × 'Carlisle Bells')
(Heavens, UK, 1986)

**'Breeder's Delight'**
Single  H3  Bush
*Tube* and *sepals* neyron rose.
*Corolla* imperial purple shaded
light rose at base. *Sepals* large,
strong, held at right angles to
the *corolla*. *Foliage* light green.
Strong upright growth.
('Cloverdale Pearl' ×
'Prosperity')
(Sinton, UK, 1988)

**'Breeder's Dream'**
Double  H2  Bush
*Tube* and *sepals* white flushed
pink and tipped with light green.
*Corolla* phlox purple. Large
flowers are produced fairly
freely. *Foliage* medium green.
Growth upright and bushy.
(Jones, UK, 1961)

**'Brenda'**
Double  H2  Lax bush
*Tube* short, thick, pale pink.
*Sepals* very pale pink, tinges on
white. *Corolla* a mixture of

dark and pale pinks. *Foliage*
dark green with a definite blue
cast. Bushy and spreading
growth makes this cultivar suitable for hanging containers.
(Ryle, UK, 1980)

**'Brenda Pritchard'**
Semi-double  H2  Trailer
*Tube* long, tapering, pinkish
white with faint stripe. *Sepals*
pink, are held at the horizontal.
*Corolla* bright cerise flecked
carmine rose. *Foliage* medium
green. Fairly large blooms
freely produced. A lax grower
which will suit basket work.
(Marshall, UK, 1975)

**'Brenda White'**
Single  H2  Bush
*Tube* and *sepals* carmine.
*Corolla* bright white veined
with carmine. Smallish flowers,
of good classical shape,
produced very freely and
continuously. *Foliage* light
green. Compact and bushy
plants.
(Pacey, UK, 1986)

**F. brevilobis**
Species  H3  Bush
Red and purple flowers with
fused sepals, produced in the
leaf axils on a rather ungainly
vigorous and lax-growing bush.
(Brazil)

**'Brian C. Morrison'**
Triphylla type  H1  Bush
Terminal-flowering triphylla-
type flowers. *Tube* long, rose
red. *Sepals* trumpet-shaped,
rose red. *Corolla* bright orange.
Growth is upright and self-
branching. Best grown for exhibition work in large pots.
(Stannard, UK, 1993)

**'Brian Stannard'**
Single  H2  Trailer
*Tube* and recurving *sepals* flesh-
coloured. *Corolla* bell-shaped
with lavender hue. Heavily
multiflowered. Growth strong,
with lots of side shoots. Suitable for small baskets or hanging pots. *Foliage* medium green
with serrated edging.
(Goulding, UK, 1988)

**'Bridal Pink'**
Double  H2  Trailer
*Tube* short, pink. *Sepals*, long
light pink with light green tips.
*Corolla* fluffy pink with light
pink overlays.
(Copley Gardens, USA, 1968)

**'Bridal Veil'**
Double  H2  Trailer
*Tube* white. *Sepals* white tipped
with green. *Corolla* creamy
white. *Foliage* glossy with small
dark leaves. The large flowers
are continuously produced.
(Waltz, USA, 1963)

**'Bridesmaid'**
Double  H2  Bush
*Tube* thick, white. *Sepals*
broad, recurving, white with
light carmine blush, phlox pink
inside. *Corolla* pale lilac orchid,
deepening toward petal edges.
Medium-sized blooms pro-
duced over a long season.
*Foliage* medium green.
(Tiret, USA, 1952)

**'Brightling'**
Single  H2  Lax bush
*Tube* and *sepals* light red.
*Corolla* bright lilac rose. Flow-
ers fairly small but profuse.
*Foliage* small medium green.
Growth is lax.
(de Graaff, Holland, 1989)

**'Brighton Belle'**
Single  Triphylla type  H1
Bush
*Tube* long slender, and *sepals*
short, both rose red. *Corolla*
almost salmon pink. Growth is
spreading and self-branching.
*Foliage* retains its dark green
leaves well.
(Goulding, UK, 1985)

**'Brilliant'**
Single  H3  Bush
*Tube* long, scarlet. *Sepals* scarlet, recurving. *Corolla* violet
magenta veined with red.
Medium sized flowers freely
produced. *Foliage* medium to
dark green with serrated edging. Needs pinching back early
to form a good shape. H. and
S. 24–30in (60–75cm).
(Bull, UK, 1865)

'BOW BELLS'

'BREEDER'S DELIGHT'

'BREEDER'S DREAM'

'BRENDA WHITE'

'BRIAN C. MORRISON'

'BRIDESMAID'

**'Briony Caunt'**
Single H3 Bush
*Tube* and *sepals* waxy red.
*Corolla* purple with broad pink
stripe. Bushy growth. *Foliage*
medium green. H. and S.
24–30in (60–75cm).
(Caunt, UK, 1987)

**'British Jubilee'**
Double H2 Bush
Continuously flowering small
double. *Tube* and *Sepals* pink.
*Corolla* claret rose. *Foliage*
medium green. Named by the
British Fuchsia Society for their
Golden Jubilee.
('Igloo Maid' × *F. fulgens* var
*rubra grandiflora*)
(Bielby/Oxtoby, UK, 1988)

**'British Sterling'**
Semi-double H2 Bush
*Tube* thick, short, white. *Sepals*
white on upper side, rosy pink
on the underside, tipped with
green and reflexing to the tube.
*Corolla* lavender with faint rose
cast, delicately veined with
pink. Small flowers but profuse.
*Foliage* medium green.
(Foster, USA, 1973)

**'Brookwood Belle'**
Double H2 Bush
*Tube* and *sepals* double deep
cerise. *Corolla* white flushed
with pale pink and deep rose
veining. Very floriferous close-
jointed upright growth. *Foliage*
medium green. Excellent cultivar for the show bench. ('Ann
H Tripp' × 'Heidi Ann')
(Gilbert, UK, 1988)

**'Brookwood Joy'**
Double H2 Stiff trailer
*Tube* white. *Sepals* white tipped
with green and blush pink on the
undersurface, medium length,
broad, tips recurving. *Corolla*
hyacinth blue marbled with
phlox pink. *Foliage* medium
sized, and medium green with
lighter green underneath. Needs
frequent pinching to create good
bushy shape. ('Stanley Cash' ×
'Joan Gilbert')
(Gilbert, UK, 1983)

**'Brunette'**
Single H2 Lax bush
*Tube* long, cream. *Sepals* cream
blushed with rose on top,
recurving tips. *Corolla* opens
cardinal red with light orange-
red base and maturing to
smoky orange-red. Smallish
flowers but profuse. *Foliage*
medium green but lighter
underneath, serrated edges.
('Mephisto' ×)
(de Graaff, Holland, 1982)

**'Brutus'**
Single H3 Bush
*Tube* short, crimson cerise.
*Sepals* rich cerise. *Corolla* dark
purple, ageing to wine. *Foliage*
medium to dark green, dark
veins. A very profuse early
bloomer. Good strong upright
bushy growth. Can be used for
all types of large structures. H.
and S. 24–36in (60–75cm).
(Bull, UK, 1901)

**'Bubble Hanger'**
Single H2 trailer
*Tube* and *sepals* pale pink.
*Corolla* rose madder. Large
flowers. *Foliage* medium green.
Floriferous for the size of the
flower. Vigorous trailer. The
large fat buds give the plant its
name.
(Niederholtzer, USA, 1946)

**'Buddha'**
Semi-double H2 Bush
*Tube* and *sepals* rich wine.
*Corolla* rich wine. *Foliage*
medium green. Good upright
growth.
(Fuchsia La, USA, 1968)

**'Buenos Aries'**
Single H2 Bush
*Tube* flesh pink. *Sepals* also
flesh pink, gently upswept.
*Corolla* rose pink. *Foliage*
medium green. Large flowers
freely produced. Upright vigorous growth, short-jointed.
(Goulding, UK, 1989)

**'Bunny'**
Semi-double H2 Bush
*Tube* and *sepals* cerise. *Corolla*

lilac pink edged with slightly
darker shade of violet-rose with
a very distinct picotee edging.
*Foliage* medium green on
strong upright and bushy
plants.
(Need, UK, 1965)

**'Burning Bush'**
Single H2 Horizontal bush
*Tube* and *sepals* red. *Corolla*
reddish-purple. *Foliage* variegated reddish, yellow and
cream. Similar to 'Autumnale'
grown mainly for its superb
coloured foliage. Spreading
habit. Growth stiff, tends to
horizontal so a difficult variety
to train.
(Courcelles)

**'Buttercup'**
Single H2 Bush
*Tube* and *sepals* pale pink.
*Corolla* orange. *Foliage*
medium green. Medium-sized
flowers freely produced. The
medium upright growth makes
it ideal for bush or standard
training. Colours best in the
shade.
(Paskesen, USA, 1976)

# C

**'Caballero'**
Double H2 Lax bush or
trailer
*Tube* and *sepals* salmon pink.
*Corolla* bluish-purple to violet
with splashes of salmon pink
on outer petals. *Foliage*
medium green. Large double
blooms fairly freely produced.
(Kennett, USA, 1965)

**'Cable Car'**
Double H2 Bush
*Tube* short, heavy, white.
*Sepals* faint pink with darker
tips. *Corolla* multi-hued orchid
fading to mixed hues of rose.
*Foliage* dark green with red
veining. Upright and vigorous
growth.
(Paskesen, USA, 1968)

'BRITISH JUBILEE'

'BROOKWOOD BELLE'

'BROOKWOOD JOY'

'BRUTUS'

'BUBBLE HANGER'

'CABLE CAR'

**'Caesar'**
Double H2 Lax bush or trailer
*Tube* and *sepals* red. *Corolla*
purple fading to burgundy. The
large flowers are fairly freely
produced. Petals curl to a rose-
shaped bloom. *Foliage* medium
green. Will need supports to
make a good bush. Can be
trained as basket with weights.
(Fuchsia Forest, USA, 1967)

**'Caetar'**
Single H2 Bush
*Tube* and *sepals* salmon.
*Corolla* orange. *Foliage* mid-
green. Upright grower not
easily obtainable.
(Raiser not known, UK, 1986)

**'Caledonia'**
Single H3 Bush
*Tube* very long, cerise. *Sepals*
cerise. *Corolla* crimson, small.
Flowers medium size and very
free. *Foliage* mid- to dark
green. Good small plant, or in
garden in sheltered areas. H.
and S. 24–30in (60–75cm).
(Lemoine, France, 1899)

**'Callaly Pink'**
Single H2 Bush
*Tube* and *sepals* white flushed
pink. *Corolla* shell pink with
pink veining. *Foliage* medium
green. Medium-sized flowers
very compact and beautiful.
Growth upright and bushy.
Good bush plant if pinched
regularly.
(Ryle, UK, 1974)

**'Calverley'**
Single H2 Bush
*Tube* and *sepals* white. *Corolla*
violet, white at base. *Foliage*
medium green. Makes a good
bush or standard.
(Holmes, UK, 1993)

**'Cambridge Louie'**
Single H2 Bush
*Tube* thin, pinky-orange. *Sepals*
pinky orange, green tips,
darker underneath. *Corolla*
rosy pink with darker edges.
*Foliage* light green and rather
small. Medium-sized flowers
produced prolifically
throughout the season. Self-

branching, short-jointed.
Excellent banker for Show
work. ('Lady Isobel Barnett' ×
'Mr. A. Huggett')
(Napthen, UK, 1977)

**'Camelot'**
Single H2 Bush
*Tube* short, thick, white to
pink. *Sepals* fully reflexed,
white on top pale pink
underneath, recurving tips.
*Corolla* white to very pale pink
with pink veining. Medium-
sized flowers bell shaped and
very free. *Foliage* medium
green and rather larger than
average. Prefers shade to keep
its white colouring.
(Goulding, UK, 1983)

**'Cameron Ryle'**
Semi-double H2 Lax bush
*Tube* short, white to pale pink.
*Sepals* frosty white with pink
to red overcast. *Corolla* very
deep purple, inside palish pink.
Medium-sized blooms. *Foliage*
medium green. ('Lena Dalton'
× 'Citation')
(Ryle/Atkinson, UK, 1971)

**F. campos portoi**
Species H3 Bush
The small flowers are red and
purple. Possibly hardy in
favoured areas.
(Brazil)

**'Candlelight'**
Double H2 Bush
*Tube* white. *Sepals* upturned,
pure white on outsides and
slightly flushed pink on the
underside. *Corolla* rose with
overlapping petals of very dark
purple-lilac fading to bright
carmine. Large blooms freely
produced. *Foliage* medium
green.
(Waltz, USA, 1959)

**'Capri'**
Double H1 Lax bush
*Tube* short, thick, white. *Sepals*
are glistening white, broad.
*Corolla* deep blue-violet, heavily
petalled. Huge flowers but not
easy to grow. *Foliage* medium
green.
(Schnabel/Paskesen, USA, 1960)

**'Cara Mia'**
Semi-double H2 Trailer
*Tube* greenish-white, thin.
*Sepals* long and graceful, pale
pink. *Corolla* deepest crimson
and globular-shaped. Good-
sized flowers along entire
length of branches. *Foliage*
medium green. Good half
basket.
(Schnabel, USA, 1957)

**'Cardinal Farges'**
Semi-double H3 Bush
*Tube* and reflexed *sepals* pale
cerise. *Corolla* white, veined
with cerise. Flowers are quite
small but profuse. *Foliage*
medium green. Has a similar
fault to its parent from which
it is a sport, 'Abbe Farges', in
that the growth is very brittle.
H. and S. 24–30in (60–75cm).
(Rawlins, UK, 1958)

**'Carla Johnson'**
Single H2 Bush
*Tube* and *sepals* white tipped
with green and flushed carmine
underneath. *Corolla* sea-
lavender violet. Medium-sized
blooms of very delicate colouring. Very freely produced.
*Foliage* medium green. Good
excellent upright growth.
(Pacey, UK, 1986)

**'Carl Drude'**
Semi-double H2 Bush
*Tube* and *sepals* cardinal red.
*Corolla* white with red veins.
Medium-sized flowers very
free. *Foliage* golden bronze.
Upright and bushy.
('Strawberry Delight' ×)
(Gadsby, UK, 1975)

**'Carlisle Bells'**
Single H2 Bush
*Tube* palest pink striped with
carmine. *Sepals* white, flushed
pink underneath, tips
recurving. *Corolla* bishop's
violet shading to pale pink at
base of each petal, maturing to
spectrum violet. Medium-sized
flowers freely produced.
*Foliage* dark green, red veins,
serrated. Upright and self-
branching growth.
(Mitchinson, UK, 1983)

'CALEDONIA'

'CALVERLEY'

'CAMBRIDGE LOUIE'

'CAPRI'

'CARDINAL FARGES'

'CARLA JOHNSON'

**'Carl Wallace'**
Double H2 Bush
*Tube* and *sepals* rosy red,
short, medium thickness.
*Corolla* violet-purple. Medium
sized blooms very full and
rosette-shaped. Free-flowering.
*Foliage* medium to dark green.
(Hobson, UK, 1984)

**'Carmel Blue'**
Single H2 Bush
*Tube* long greenish-white,
narrow. *Sepals* outspread and
white, flushed palest pink on
underside. *Corolla* beautiful
blue. *Foliage* medium green.
Blooms freely produced. One
of the finest blue and white
cultivars; will make good
exhibition plant with minimum
of pinching.
(Hodges, USA, 1956)

**'Carmen Maria'**
Single H2 Lax bush or trailer
Sport of 'Leonora'. *Tube* pink.
*Sepals* long narrow stand
straight up, also pink with
green tips. *Corolla* consists of
four overlapping petals, baby
pink with deeper pink veins.
*Foliage* medium green. Growth
upright, self-branching,
vigorous. Good exhibition
plant, free-flowering.
(Breitner, USA, 1970)

**'Carmine Bell'**
Single H2 Lax bush
*Tube* long, thin, neyron rose.
*Sepals* neyron rose with
recurved tips. *Corolla* opens
rosy carmine with deep rose at
wavy petal edges, maturing to
pale carmine. *Foliage* mid-
green on top but much paler
underneath, veins green with
red mid-rib, serrated edges.
Needs early and regular
pinching. ('President Stanley
Wilson' × self)
(Caunt, UK, 1985)

**'Carnival'**
Double H2 Lax bush or
trailer
*Tube* long, white. *Sepals*
glistening white, outer sides
tinted delicate pea green.
*Corolla* brilliant spiraea red

and very long. Large blooms,
free and early. *Foliage* medium
green. Needs a great deal of
pinching to achieve shape;
makes a good half basket.
(Tiret, USA, 1956)

**'Carnoustie'**
Double H2 Bush
*Tube* and *sepals* pink. *Corolla*
frilly mixture of pale mauves
and pinks. *Foliage* lime green.
Produces large numbers of
sideshoots without pinching.
Grows well in 5in (13cm) pots.
(Goulding, UK, 1986)

**'Carol Grace'**
Double H2 Bush
*Tube* rich pink. *Sepals* recurving,
pink. *Corolla* blush pink heavily
veined with rich pink on the
extra small petals. *Foliage* dark
green, glossy. Upright and strong
growth. ('Rosemary Day' ×
'Celia Smedley')
(Day, UK, 1989)

**'Carol Hardwick'**
Double H2 Trailer
Medium-sized flowers. *Tubes*
pale pink. *Sepals* pink. *Corolla*
violet. *Foliage* medium green.
Natural trailer.
(Johnson, UK, 1990)

**'Caroline'**
Single H2 Bush
*Tube* pink. *Sepals* cream
flushed with pink, green tips,
deeper pink underneath.
*Corolla* campanula-violet
maturing to pale cyclamen
purple. *Foliage* medium green.
Flowers large, freely produced.
A near-perfect fuchsia.
('Citation' ×)
(Miller, UK, 1967)

**'Carol Roe'**
Single H2 Bush
*Tube* short, thick, creamy, white.
*Sepals* light pink on the topside
and rose pink on the lower,
tipped green and held almost at
the horizontal. *Corolla* rosy
pink. *Foliage* light green. A very
attractive plant which flowers
continuously. ('Eleanor
Leytham' × 'Pink Darling')
(Roe, UK, 1976)

**'Caron Keating'**
Single H2 Bush
Medium-sized flower. *Tube*
pink. *Sepals* light pink. *Corolla*
violet. *Foliage* medium green.
Upright growth produces a
good bush shape.
(McDonald, UK, 1989)

**'Cascade'**
Single H2 Trailer
*Tube* white flushed with carmine,
medium length, thin. *Sepals* long,
slim, white flushed carmine,
down-pointing. *Corolla* rose
bengal. *Foliage* light to medium
green, very finely serrated. The
naturally cascading growth
makes a superb basket. Most of
the flowers are produced at the
ends of the branches. ('Rolla' ×
'Amy Lye')
(Lagen, USA, 1937)

**'Casper Hauser'**
Double H2 Bush
*Tube* and *sepals* cardinal red.
*Corolla* ruby red. *Foliage*
medium to darkish-green. An
unusual and eye-catching
colouring of flower. A
delightful cultivar.
(Springer, Holland, 1987)

**'Catherine Bartlett'**
Single H2 Bush
*Tube* short, white flushed very
pale rose. *Sepals* white, flushed
pale rose and held horizontally.
*Corolla* a beautiful shade of
rose with very little veining,
but slightly lighter shade at
base of petals. *Foliage* medium
green. A very early and
continuously flowering plant
delightful in its simplicity.
Strong grower and short-
jointed, responds best when
allowed to 'break' on its own.
('Carol Peat' × 'Alison Ewart')
(Roe, UK, 1983)

**'Catherine Claire'**
Double H2 Bush
*Tube* and *sepals* carmine.
*Corolla* rose madder. Large
blooms and fairly free for a
double. *Foliage* medium green.
Strong upright growth, self-
branching.
(Clyne, UK, 1974)

'CARNIVAL'    'CARNOUSTIE'

'CAROLINE'    'CASCADE'

'CASPER HAUSER'    'CATHERINE BARTLETT'

**'Catherine Law'**
Double H3 Bush
Medium-sized flowers. *Tubes*
and *sepals* red. *Corolla*
pinkish-white. *Foliage* medium
green. H. and S. 18–24in
(45–60cm).
(Weeks, UK, 1991)

**'Cathie MacDougall'**
Double H1 Trailer
*Tube* cerise. *Sepals* upswept,
cerise. *Corolla* violet-blue,
marbled and striped various
shades of blue and pink.
Medium-sized blooms
produced in quantity. *Foliage*
medium green.
(Thorne, UK, 1960)

**'Cecile'**
Double H2 Trailer
*Tube* thick, pink. *Sepals* deep
pink, curl back from the
lavender blue *corolla*. Fairly
large flowers and plentiful for a
double. *Foliage* medium green.
(Whitfield, USA, 1981)

**'Cecil Glass'**
Single H2 Bush
*Tube* and *sepals* white flushed
pink. *Corolla* magenta-pink.
Free-flowering and very early.
*Foliage* medium green. Makes
a good bush if staked early.
(Lye, UK, 1887)

**'Celadore'**
Double H2 Trailer
*Tube* and *sepals* candy pink,
tipped eau de nil. *Corolla*
luminous candy pink. Medium-
sized flowers freely produced.
*Foliage* deep green with a
central vein of shaded pink.
Leaves heart-shaped. Growth
naturally trailing and very
vigorous. Worth trying as a
weeping standard. ('Pink
Galore' × 'Blush of Dawn')
(Hall, UK, 1981)

**'Celebration'**
Double H2 Trailer
*Tube* and *sepals* pale orange.
*Corolla*, petals variable in size
with marbled shades of orange.
*Foliage* medium green lace
edged with yellow. The colour
of the foliage brightens in the

sunshine. Very useful for full
baskets.
(Goulding, UK, 1988)

**'Celia Smedley'**
Single H2 Bush
*Tube* and *sepals* neyron rose.
*Corolla* vivid currant red.
*Foliage* largish leaves of
medium green. Growth is
extremely vigorous, with
careful pinching produces an
excellent bush or standard in
just one season. One of the
very best.
(Chance seedling from 'Pepi')
(Bellamy, UK, 1970)

**'Centenary'**
Double H2 Bush
Blush white *self* with large fully
double blooms. *Foliage* light
green with red tinge. Upright
and bushy.
(Dresman, UK, 1988)

**'Centrepiece'**
Semi-double H1 Lax bush or
trailer
*Tube* and *sepals* red. *Corolla*
starts opening with four pink
petaloids surrounding lavender
blue petals, then petaloids flare
out and the centre keeps
growing to a long corolla.
Fairly large blooms for a semi-
double. Best used in baskets as
the growth is very lax. *Foliage*
medium green.
(Fuchsia Forest, USA, 1964)

**'Ceri'**
Single H2 Bush
*Tube* and *sepals* white. *Corolla*
white faintly tinged with pink.
Medium-sized blooms freely
produced. *Foliage* medium
green.
(Holmes, E., UK, 1980)

**'Cerrig'**
Single H2 Bush
*Tube* pale pink. *Sepals* clear
rose pink held tight from
corolla. *Corolla* deep rose
slightly flared. Medium-sized
flowers. *Foliage* largish,
medium green with red mid-
rib. Strong upright grower.
(Howarth, UK, 1979)

**'Chandlerii'**
Single H2 Bush
*Tube* and *sepals* creamy white.
*Corolla* orange-scarlet.
Medium to large flowers freely
produced. Growth is upright
and bushy. *Foliage* medium
green.
(Chandler, UK, 1839)

**'Chang'**
Single H2 Bush
*Tube* orange-red. *Sepals* orange
tipped with green. *Corolla*
brilliant orange. Flowers are
small but profuse. Growth
upright and bushy and must be
stopped frequently in early
stages to keep within bounds.
*Foliage* small and medium
green. (*F. cordifolia* hybrid)
(Hazard and Hazard, USA,
1946)

**'Chantry Park'**
Single H1 Bush
Triphylla-type fuchsia fully
terminal flowering. *Tubes* long,
scarlet. *Sepals* short, horizontal
scarlet; small petals. *Corolla*
bright scarlet. Growth short-
jointed and very bushy. Makes
an excellent hanging pot or
small basket. *Foliage* medium
to olive green.
(Stannard, UK, 1993)

**'Chaos'**
Single H2 Trailer
*Tube* and *sepals* rose red.
*Corolla* cyclamen purple.
Growth self-branching and
spreading. *Foliage* medium
green. Excellent for baskets or
window-boxes.
(de Graaf, Holland, 1989)

**'Charisma'**
Single H2 Bush
*Tube* white, flushed pink.
*Sepals* white flushed pale pink
at the base with green
recurving tips. *Corolla* white,
veined pale pink. *Foliage* dark
green. Profuse flowering.
Strong upright growth.
(McDonald, UK, 1989)

'CELADORE'

'CHANG'

'CENTREPIECE'

'CHANTRY PARK'

'CHARISMA'

**'Charleston'**
Semi-double H2 Lax bush
*Tube* pinky orange. *Sepals*
orange. *Corolla* an unusual
shade of coral to smoky
orange. Large semi-double
flowers freely produced on
upright but lax bushy growth.
*Foliage* medium green. Suitable
for both bush and basket
growth with training.
(Bridgland, UK, 1986)

**'Charlie Gardiner'**
Single H2 Trailer
*Tube* short, salmon pink. *Sepals*
light orange, long, slender,
slightly reflexed. *Corolla*
apricot-coloured and flared.
Blooms prominently displayed.
Very prolific in its flowering.
*Foliage* medium green. Good
spreading growth but can be
used as a bush with supports.
(Goulding, UK, 1982)

**'Charlie Girl'**
Double H2 Bush
*Tube* short pink. *Sepals* rose
pink, opening right out and
covering tube. *Corolla* lilac
blue, paler at the base of the
petals and veined with rose.
Medium-sized blooms freely
produced. *Foliage* medium
green, outstanding veins.
Strong, upright-growing bush.
(Tanfield, UK, 1970)

**'Charlie Pridmore'**
Double H2 Bush
Medium-sized flowers. *Tube*
pink. *Sepals* white, flushed pink.
*Corolla* orange-pink shaded
white. *Foliage* medium green.
Good, strong, upright growth.
(Weeks, UK, 1989)

**'Charming'**
Single H3 Bush
Medium-sized flowers. *Tubes*
carmine. *Sepals* reddish-cerise,
well reflexed. *Corolla* rosy-
purple with cerise at the base
of the petals. *Foliage* slightly
yellowish especially light at the
tips. Growth upright and very
bushy. H. and S. 24–30in
(60–75cm). ('Arabella
Improved' × 'James Lye')
(Lye, UK, 1877)

**'Chartwell'**
Single H2/3 Bush
*Tube* white. *Sepals* long,
recurved, held well out from
the corolla, rhodamine pink
and have green tips. *Corolla*
wisteria blue lightening at the
base of the petals. *Foliage*
medium green. Medium-sized
flowers freely produced. Good
pot plant, also summer bedder.
H. and S. 18–30in (45–75cm).
('Christine Clements' ×
'Cloverdale Pearl')
(Gadsby, UK, 1977)

**'Chatsworth'**
Single H2 Bush
*Tube* crimson. *Sepals* waxy,
neyron rose on the underside
and crimson on top, green tips.
*Corolla* magenta rose. Large,
open, bell-shaped flowers. Best
colour under shady conditions.
*Foliage* medium green. Upright,
bushy, self-branching growth.
('Magenta Flash' × 'Derby
Belle')
(Gadsby, UK, 1975)

**'Checkerboard'**
Single H2 Bush
*Tube* long, red. *Sepals* recurve
slightly, start red and change
abruptly to white. *Corolla* a
deeper red than the tube, and
white at the base of the petals.
The flowers are fairly long but
are produced in profusion.
Flowers from early in the
season and is never out of
bloom. *Foliage* medium green,
finely serrated. An excellent
cultivar for the beginner and
can be trained to virtually any
shape other than basket.
(Walker and Jones, USA, 1948)

**'Checkmate'**
Single H2 Lax bush
*Tube* short, pale striped pink.
*Sepals* short, pale magenta-pink,
slightly upturned. *Corolla* Indian
magenta. Extremely floriferous
with medium-sized flowers.
*Foliage* medium to dark green,
slightly serrated. Self-branching,
lax upright and will make a
superb weeping standard. (Sport
of 'Checkerboard')
(Tolley, UK, 1980)

**'Cheers'**
Double H2 Lax bush
*Tube* light coral pink. *Sepals*
broad and sharply pointed,
streaked pale pink along the
centre, coral pink on the
outside. *Corolla* orange-red.
Very full double of medium-
sized flowers. *Foliage* dark
green with serrated edges.
Could be useful for baskets
with the assistance of
weights.
(Stubbs, USA, 1979)

**'Chessboard'**
Single H2 Bush
*Tube* pink. *Sepals* pink and
white tipped with green.
*Corolla* magenta, edged with
crimson. Medium to large
flowers freely produced.
*Foliage* medium green. Strong
upright grower.
(Colville, UK, 1975)

**'Chillerton Beauty'**
Single H3 Bush
Small flowers freely produced.
*Tube* pale rose pink. *Sepals*
pale pink, deeper underneath,
green tips. *Corolla* mauvish-
violet veined with pink, ages to
magenta. *Foliage* medium
green, smallish, leathery shiny
appearance. Strong upright
growth makes it suitable for
hedge work. H. and S. 30–36in
(75–90cm).
(Bass, UK, 1847)

**'China Doll'**
Double H2 Trailer
*Tube* cerise with darker stripes.
*Sepals* cerise red. *Corolla* white
faintly veined with red. *Foliage*
medium green. A natural
trailer. Quite floriferous.
(Walker and Jones, USA, 1950)

**'China Lantern'**
Single H2 Lax bush
*Tube* deep pink, shiny. *Sepals*
are shiny white tipped with
green, reflexed. *Corolla* rosy
pink, white at base of the
petals. Medium-sized flowers
freely produced, enhanced by
the *foliage*, deep green and
slightly serrated.
(Believed USA, 1953)

'CHARMING'

'CHESSBOARD'

'CHARLIE GARDINER'

'CHEERS'

'CHILLERTON BEAUTY'

**'Chiquita Maria'**
Double H2 Bush
*Tube* light pink. *Sepals* carmine
tipped with green. *Corolla* red.
*Foliage* dark green, lighter on
the undersurface. Best colour is
produced in bright light. The
large flowers are freely
produced.
(Stubbs, USA, 1987)

**'Chris'**
Single H2 Lax bush
*Tube* and *sepals* rose. *Corolla*
reddish-purple. *Foliage* an
attractive grey-green. Medium-
sized flowers freely produced.
The lax growth makes it
suitable for either baskets or
bushes, given the necessary
supports.
(Breemer, Holland, 1989)

**'Christ Driessen'**
Single H2 Trailer
*Tubes* long, thin. *Sepals* shorter,
rose pink; petals are a slightly
darker pink. Intermediate type
of plant. Growth is spreading
and rather unusual. Needs
continual pinching. An eye-
catching novelty. *Foliage*
yellowish-green on the upper
surface and light olive green on
the lower surface. ('Small
pipes' × 'Small Pipes')
(de Graaf, Holland, 1988)

**'Christina Becker'**
Single H2 Bush
*Tube* and partially recurving
*sepals* rosy red. *Corolla* cup
shaped rose with a porcelain
blue cast. *Foliage* medium
green. Growth is spreading and
self-branching. Excellent for
show work.
(Strumper, Holland, 1987)

**'Christine Clements'**
Single H2 Bush
*Tube* and *sepals* china rose.
*Corolla* wisteria blue maturing
to gentian blue. Medium sized
blooms very freely produced
and held well out from the
plant. Buds long and tapering.
Medium upright bush with
spreading habit. *Foliage*
medium green.
(Gadsby, UK, 1974)

**'Christine Shaffery'**
Double H2 Bush
An excellent relatively new
introduction. *Tube* short, white.
*Sepals* flyaway, white touched
with green and pink. *Corolla*
pale lavender mottled with pink.
Growth bushy and upright.
*Foliage* medium green. Worth
growing for the show bench.
(Shaffery, UK, 1993)

**'Christine Windsor'**
Single H2 Bush
*Tube* short, light red. *Sepals*
light red, fully recurved away
from the tube. *Corolla* opens
white with a single pink vein
on each petal. Maturing to
white with slight pink flush at
base. *Foliage* light green. A
self-branching medium upright
which should make a good
standard.
(Windsor, UK, 1986)

**'Christmas Candy'**
Double H2 Trailer
*Tube* short, thick, bright pink.
*Sepals* long, bright pink, paler
pink tipped with white on the
lower surface. *Corolla* white
streaked rose with wavy edges.
*Foliage* dark green on the
upper surface and lighter on
the lower. ('Ada Perry' × 'Trade
Winds')
(Stubbs, USA, 1987)

**'Christmas Holly'**
Double H2 Bush
*Tube* thin, red. *Sepals* thin,
bright red, open straight but
turn up with maturity. *Corolla*
deep purple, streaked with
crimson. Small blooms but
prolific. *Foliage* medium green
has deep serrations to the edges
giving the appearance of holly.
Self-branching, will trail if
weights used. Bush needs
staking.
(Stubbs, USA, 1977)

**'Christmas Ribbons'**
Double H2 Bush
*Tube* rhodonite red. *Sepals*
short curling back to tube, are
also rhodonite red. *Corolla*
campanula violet with
rhodonite red veining. Flowers

small, compact but very free.
Best colour in the shade.
*Foliage* medium green.
(Foster, USA, 1974)

**'Churchtown'**
Semi-double H2 Bush
*Tube* and *sepals* rhodamine
pink. *Corolla* roseine purple
edged with deep fuchsia purple.
Medium-sized blooms, very
beautiful and free-flowering.
*Foliage* medium green.
(Porter, UK, 1984)

**'Cindy Robyn'**
Double H2 Lax upright.
Large double flower. *Tube* and
*sepals* rose. *Corolla* salmon rose.
*Foliage* medium green. The
laxity of the growth lends itself
to use as a supported bush or as
a trailer in a hanging container.
(Stubbs, USA, 1982)

***F. cinerea***
Species H1 Bush
*Tube* long, narrow, funnel-
shaped, widening at base of
sepals 2in (5cm). Tube and
*sepals* dull orange. *Corolla*
orange to crimson. Flowers
rather sparsely. *Foliage* medium-
sized and light green turning to
purplish-red. In the wild grows
to approx 3m (10ft). (Colombia
and Equador).
(Berry, USA, 1978)

**'Cinnabarina'**
Single Encliandra Hybrid H3
Bush
Small bushy plant. *Flowers* tiny,
orange-scarlet. *Sepals* red,
reflexed. Ungainly when grown
under glass but very suitable as
a hardy for the outside border.
*Foliage* small medium green.
(Cultivated form of × *Bacillaris*)
(Raiser unknown, c.1829)

**'Cinnamon'**
Double H2 Trailer
*Tube* orange. *Sepals* held
horizontally, also orange.
*Corolla* reddish-orange with
orange streaks. Medium green
*foliage*. A natural trailer, and
will make excellent basket or
weeping standard.
(Storvick, USA, 1983)

'CHIQUITA MARIA'

'CINNABARINA'

**'Cinpetio'**
Single H2 Bush
Medium-sized flower. *Tube, sepals, corolla* pink. Growth upright. *Foliage* medium green. A hybrid from two species. (*F. cinerera × F. petiolaris*)
(Betje, Holland, 1991)

**'Circe'**
Semi-double H2 Bush
*Tube* and *sepals* pale pink. *Corolla* consists of four light blue petals that fade to pale lavender, pink petaloids open and spread almost flat. Large flowers freely produced. Upright growth. *Foliage* medium green.
(Kennett, USA, 1965)

**'Circus Spangles'**
Double H2 Trailer
Large flowers. *Tubes* and *sepals* white. *Corolla* red, streaked with white. *Foliage* medium green. A vigorous trailing cultivar which makes a good basket.
(Stubbs, USA, 1990)

**'Cissbury Gem'**
Single H2 Bush
*Tube* shortish red. *Sepals* recurved held half up, also red. *Corolla* phlox pink with neyron rose veining. *Foliage* mid-green, lighter underneath. Self-branching upright growth which makes an attractive bush. ('Rambling Rose' ×)
(Hobbs, UK, 1986)

**'Citation'**
Single H1 Bush
*Tube* light rose to pink. *Sepals* upturned, also light rose to pink. *Corolla* white, veined light pink at the base. Large flowers with four petals which flare to saucer shape. *Foliage* medium green. An excellent eye-catching, cultivar.
(Hodges, USA, 1953)

**'City of Adelaide'**
Double H2 Bush
*Tube* and *sepals* white. *Corolla* dark violet with white base maturing to magenta with purple edges. Large flowers.

*Foliage* large, yellow-green. A late plant to flower on rather lax, upward-growing stems. ('Pio Pico' × 'White King')
(Richardson, Australia, 1986)

**'City of Derby'**
Single H2 Bush
*Tube* crimson. *Sepals* waxy, crimson, held well up and curved over, long and narrow, a spiky effect. *Corolla* campanula violet on lighter base, opening wide giving saucer effect. Very free-flowering. *Foliage* medium green, small and narrow, self-branching medium upright. Best colour in the shade. ('Cliff's Hardy' seedling × 'Bishop's Bells')
(Gadsby, UK, 1978)

**'City of Leicester'**
Single H2 Bush
*Tube* medium length, rose bengal. *Sepals* rose bengal tipped with green. *Corolla* pale violet-purple, heavily veined with imperial purple. Medium-sized flowers, very free-flowering. *Foliage* medium green. Growth upright and bushy. A very impressive cultivar.
(Pacey, UK, 1984)

**'Clair de Lune'**
Single H2 Trailer
*Tube* and *sepals* of this delightful cultivar are salmon. *Corolla* salmon orange. *Foliage* bronze-green. A natural trailing habit will make a good basket but will also make a bush with supports.
(Rozaine-Boucharlat, France, 1880)

**'Cliantha'**
Double H2 Trailer
*Tube* greenish-pink. *Sepals* pinkish-green with green tips. *Corolla* opens magenta, matures to a lighter colouring. *Foliage* dark green on the upper surface and lighter on the lower. Medium-sized blooms produced very freely. ('Lena Dalton' ×)
(Strumper, Germany, 1989)

**'Cliff Gadsby'**
Double H2 Bush
*Tube* and *sepals* pale spiraea tipped with green, changing to a deeper shade as the flower matures. *Corolla* rose bengal. Flowers fairly large and very free for the size of bloom. *Foliage* medium green. Good compact, bushy growth.
(Gadsby, UK, 1980)

**'Cliff's Hardy'**
Single H3 Bush
*Tube* crimson, thick. *Sepals* light crimson tipped with green. *Corolla* campanula violet, paler at the base of the petals, veined scarlet. *Foliage* medium to dark green. Upright and bushy growth. Excellent for the hardy border. H. and S. 18–24in (45–60cm). ('Athela × 'Bon Accorde')
(Gadsby, UK, 1966)

**'Cliff's Own'**
Single H2 Bush
*Tube* white. *Sepals* waxy, white, pale pink on the underside, green tips. *Corolla* hyacinth blue passing to a delicate pale violet. Small to medium-sized flowers freely produced. *Foliage* light green. Excellent for show work especially in the smaller pots. Upright and bushy growth. ('Christine Clements' × 'Cloverdale Pearl')
(Gadsby, UK, 1977)

**'Cliff's Unique'**
Double H2 Bush
*Tube* short, thick, light pink. *Sepals* waxy white, flushed pink with green tips; short, broad, reflexing. *Corolla* gentian blue maturing to light violet-pink. Medium-sized blooms well formed and resemble a camelia flower. The first known double flower to be held erect. *Foliage* medium green, medium-sized, serrated leaves. Self-branching, free-flowering.
(Gadsby, UK, 1976)

'CITY OF ADELAIDE'                    'CITY OF LEICESTER'

'CLAIR DE LUNE'                              'CLIANTHA'

'CLIFF GADSBY'                              'CLIFF'S HARDY'

**'Clifton Beauty'**
Double H2 Lax bush
Large flower. *Tube* white,
thick, medium length. *Sepals*
creamy pink. *Corolla* very
full, rosy purple with
crimson pencilled edges. The
outer petals heavily streaked
with salmon. *Foliage*
medium green. The lax
growth makes it suitable for
all types of growth. Requires
full sun for best colour.
(Handley, UK, 1975)

**'Clifton Belle'**
Semi-double H2 Bush
*Tube* white, long. *Sepals*
white, tinged with the palest
pink inside, reflexed back to
stem. *Corolla* a vivid
magenta with petals of even
length. A very striking
colour combination. *Foliage*
medium green. Suitable for
bush or standard growth.
Colours develop best in the
shade.
(Handley, UK, 1974)

**'Clifton Charm'**
Single H3 Bush
*Tube* short, waxy, cerise.
*Sepals* bright cerise,
reflexed. *Corolla* deep lilac
blending to rose pink at the
base. Deep red picotee edge
and veining to the petals.
*Foliage* medium to darkish
green. H. and S. 18–30in
(45–75cm). Short-jointed
and very free-flowering.
(Handley, UK, 1981)

**'Clipper'**
Single H2 Bush
*Tube* and recurving. *Sepals*
scarlet cerise. *Corolla* rich
claret red. Early bloomer
with medium-sized flowers
and very free. Very vigorous
upright bush which could
make an excellent standard.
*Foliage* medium green.
(Lye, UK, 1897)

**'Cloth of Gold'**
Single H2 Bush
*Tube* and *sepals* red.
*Corolla* purple. Main
feature of this delightful

plant is its golden *foliage*.
The golden yellow of the
leaves fades to a bronzy
flush with maturity. Growth
is upright and bushy. Late
to flower, as is so often the
case with 'foliage' plants.
(Sport of 'Souvenir de
Chiswick')
(Stafford, UK, 1863)

**'Cloverdale'**
Single H2 Bush
*Tube* short, thin, crimson.
*Sepals* also crimson. *Corolla*
cornflower blue fading to
cyclamen purple. Flowers
small. *Foliage* small and
medium green. Growth is
upright but could be
described as dwarf. The
flowers are held horizontally
out from the plant. Suitable
for border edging or small
pot exhibition. Free-
flowering, long-lasting.
(Gadsby, UK, 1972)

**'Cloverdale Crown'**
Single H2 Bush
Medium-sized flower. *Tube*
and *sepals* pale rose. *Corolla*
white, veined with rose.
*Foliage* medium green. (Sport
from 'Cloverdale Jewel')
(Fix, UK, 1989)

**'Cloverdale Delight'**
Semi-double H2 Bush
*Tube* medium length and
width, pink. *Sepals* soft pink
held back against the tube.
*Corolla* wisteria blue fading
to violet, bell-shaped. *Foliage*
medium green. Growth
upright, self-branching. Will
make an excellent bush and
could be trained for larger
structures. ('Rosedale' ×
'Forward Look')
(Gadsby, UK, 1977)

**'Cloverdale Jewel'**
Semi-double H2 Bush
*Tube* medium length and
thickness, neyron rose.
*Sepals* held well back against
the tube, also neyron rose.
*Corolla* wisteria blue with
rose-pink veins. *Foliage*
small, medium green. Very

floriferous, strong, upright
grower which flowers over a
long period. Good in a pot
or in open garden as summer
bedder. ('Cloverdale' × 'Lady
Isobel Barnett')
(Gadsby, UK, 1974)

**'Cloverdale Joy'**
Single H2 Bush
*Tube* white. *Sepals* white
with a tinge of pink, held
well out. *Corolla* violet.
*Foliage* medium green.
Vigorous, upright bushy
growth. Very floriferous
over a long season.
('Cloverdale Pearl' ×
'Christine Clements')
(Gadsby, UK, 1979)

**'Cloverdale Pearl'**
Single H2 Bush
*Tube* medium length, white.
*Sepals* rhodamine pink
shading to white with green
tips, held well out curving
back towards tips. *Corolla*
white with pink veins.
*Foliage* small and darkish
green. A very easy to grow,
self-branching bush plant.
(Unnamed seedling × 'Grace
Darling')
(Gadsby, UK, 1973)

**'Cloverdale Pride'**
Single H2 Bush
*Tube* pale pink, medium
length and thickness. *Sepals*
rose bengal, upturned and
curving back. *Corolla*
cyclamen. *Foliage* medium
green. Upright growth, self-
branching. Makes an
excellent bush. Best colour
develops in shade. (Unnamed
seedling × 'Grace Darling')
(Gadsby, UK, 1979)

**'Cloverdale Star'**
Single H2 Bush
*Tube* white. *Sepals* white
with the underside flushed
pink and held well back.
*Corolla* wisteria blue on a
lighter base. *Foliage* medium
green. Growth self-branching
medium-sized upright, makes
an excellent bush.
(Gadsby, UK, 1976)

'CLIFTON CHARM'          'CLOTH OF GOLD'

'CLOVERDALE JEWEL'

**'Coachman'**
Single H2 Lax bush
*Tube* and *sepals* pale salmon.
*Corolla* rich orange-
vermilion. *Foliage* medium
green. Medium-sized blooms
freely produced in flushes
over a long season. The lax
growth makes it suitable for
a bush or as a basket. The
cleanness of the colouring
makes it an excellent cultivar
for all types of growth.
(Bright, UK, 1910)

**F. coccinea**
Species H3 Bush
Smallish flowers. *Tube* and
*sepals* red. *Corolla* violet
and purple. *Foliage* dark
green heart shaped leaves.
Will make a shrub in excess
of 3ft (1m).
(Kew Gardens, 1789)

**'Coconut Ice'**
Single H2 Bush
*Tube* white. *Sepals* rose on
the outside well reflexed.
*Corolla* white with rose
pink veining. Flowers
medium-sized. *Foliage*
medium green. Strong
upright growth, and is
considered to be an
improvement on its parent
'Cloverdale Pearl' which is
quite a recommendation.
Responds well to pinching.
('Iced Champagne' ×
'Cloverdale Pearl')
(Burns, UK, 1979)

**F. colensoi**
Species H3 Bush
A rather insignificant native
of New Zealand. *Tube*
green. *Sepals* greenish to
red. *Corolla* purple. Flowers
small. *Foliage* green on the
upper side, white on the
lower and very smooth.
(Hooker, New Zealand,
1867)

**F. colensoi ssp 'Bronze
Bank Peninsula'**
Native of New Zealand, this
plant is a vigorous form of
*F. colensoi* but with the
flower of *F. procumbens*.

**F. colensoi var.
'Purpurescens'**
Similar to *F. colensoi*. *Tube*
and *sepals* green. *Corolla*
purple. Growth lax upright.
(Hooker, New Zealand,
1867)

**'Collingwood'**
Double H2 Bush
*Tube* pale pink, medium
length and thickness. *Sepals*
pale pink and slightly
upturned. *Corolla* pure white
and fully double. *Foliage* is
medium green. Growth self-
branching and upright.
Could be useful in the hardy
border but will need some
protection in the winter.
(Niederholzer, USA, 1945)

**'Colne Fantasy'**
Single H2 Bush
*Tube* and *sepals* red.
*Corolla* purple. The
attractive feature of this
cultivar is the *foliage,* green
edged with yellow. Fairly
strong upright growth.
(Percival, UK, 1993)

**'Colne Greybeard'**
Single H2 Bush
Sport from 'Border Queen'.
*Tube* and *sepals* rhodamine
pink. *Corolla* amethyst violet
flushed pale pink. *Foliage*
unusual, variegated matt
silver grey with irregular
splashes of dark green.
(Percival, UK, 1989)

**'Colourful Lady'**
Semi-double H2 Trailer
*Tube* short, rose opal. *Sepals*
white, held half-way above
the horizontal. *Corolla*
mineral violet, bell shaped.
*Foliage* leek green. A natural
trailer, this cultivar will
produce a superb basket.
('La Campanella' ×
'Morning Light')
(Sharpe, New Zealand,
1987)

**'Come Dancing'**
Double H2 Trailer
*Tube* and *sepals* deep pink
tipped with yellow-green.

*Corolla* magenta rose with
salmon-rose at the base.
Flowers large. *Foliage* bright
green, rounded and
crinkled. The semi-trailing
growth makes a good
basket using weights, or a
weeping standard.
(Handley, UK, 1972)

**'Comet'**
Single H2 Bush
*Tube* and *sepals* red.
*Corolla* violet-blue. Blooms
large, produced on strong
upright growth. *Foliage*
medium green. Self-
branching, flowers early and
continues throughout
summer.
(Banks, UK, 1862)

**'Confection'**
Double H2 Lax bush
*Tube* thin, greenish-white.
*Sepals* broad white to blush
pink tipped with green.
*Corolla* white with faint
pink at base of the petals,
full and fluffy, medium-
sized. *Foliage* dark green
and is slightly serrated. The
laxity of growth makes it
suitable for both bush and
basket with the necessary
assistance.
(Stubbs, USA, 1982)

**'Congreve Road'**
Double H2 Trailer
*Tube* rose pink. *Sepals*
recurving, rose-pink.
*Corolla* dark aubergine with
rose stripes. *Foliage* medium
green. Growth spreading or
pendant. Very suitable for
hanging pots.
(Goulding, UK, 1994)

**'Connie'**
Double H3 Bush
*Tube* cerise red. *Sepals*
cerise red, broad, hang long
over corolla. *Corolla* white
flushed pale purple, deep
pink veining. Medium-sized
flowers. *Foliage* medium
green. Upright and bushy
growth. H. and S. 18–24in
(45–60cm).
(Dawson, UK, 1961)

'COACHMAN' 'COLLINGWOOD'

'COLNE FANTASY'

'COLNE GREYBEARD'

**'Conspicua'**
Single H2/3 Bush
*Tube* crimson. *Sepals* recurve back almost against the tube, crimson. *Corolla* white with cerise veins. *Foliage* dark green. Upright and vigorous-growing plant producing an abundance of flowers. Equally at home in the greenhouse as in the hardy border. H. and S. 18–24in (45–60cm). (Smith, UK, 1863)

**'Constable Country'**
Semi-double H2 Lax bush
*Tube* short, thick, orient pink. *Sepals* horizontally held, neyron rose. *Corolla* opens violet, maturing to cyclamen purple. *Foliage* dark green on top, lighter underneath with green veins, slightly serrated. The lax growth makes it suitable for bush or baskets provided it is given the necessary encouragement. (Goulding, UK, 1984)

**'Constance'**
Double H3 Bush
*Tube* pale pink. *Sepals* pale pink with green tips, deeper pink underneath. *Corolla* rosy mauve with pink tints at the base of the petals. *Foliage* medium green. A free-flowering, bushy, upright plant. Suitable for the hardy border. Trainable to any shape except basket. H. and S. 12–18in (30–45cm). (Berkley Hort. Nurseries, USA, 1935)

**'Constellation'**
Double H1 Bush
*Tube* thin, medium length, white. *Sepals* white with green tips slightly upturned. *Corolla* creamy white. *Foliage* darkish green with serrated edges. Upright growth and very free-flowering. Shaded conditions will retain the whiteness of the corolla. Subject to *botrytis*, so extreme care necessary. (Schnabel, USA, 1957)

**'Continental'**
Double H2 Bush
Double or semi-double flowers. *Tube* short, white. *Sepals* white on top, flushed pink underneath, slightly recurving. *Corolla* pink with rose picotee edges. The blooms are produced mainly towards the ends of laterals. *Foliage* medium green. Strong upright growth. Worth trying as a standard. (Goulding, UK, 1985)

**'Contramine'**
Single H2 Lax bush
*Tube* light rose. *Sepals* white flushed with rose and tipped green. *Corolla* light purple with rose at the base of the petals. *Foliage* medium green with red veins and stems. Growth rather lax, so support will be necessary. (de Graaff, Holland, 1978)

**'Copycat'**
Single H2 Bush
*Tube* rose to red in colour. *Sepals* pointed held horizontally, also red. *Corolla* almost blue. Flowers very small. *Foliage* medium to dark with slightly serrated edges. Growth upright. (Stubbs, USA, 1981)

**'Coquet Bell'**
Single H2 Bush
*Tube* medium length, deep rose madder. *Sepals* deep rose madder with green tips. *Corolla* pale mauve flushed rose mauve at the base and with distinctive red veins. The petals form the shape of a bell with slightly waved edges. *Foliage* medium green with serrated edges. Growth strong, self-branching and upright. ('Lena Dalton' × 'Citation') (Ryle-Atkinson, UK, 1973)

**'Coquet Dale'**
Double H2 Bush
*Tube* short, pinkish white. *Sepals* neyron rose and held well up. *Corolla* lilac and slightly flared. *Foliage* medium green. Upright, bushy, vigorous and self-branching. ('Joe Kusber' × 'Northumbrian Belle') (Ryle, UK, 1976)

**'Coquet Gold'**
Single H2 Lax bush
*Tube* pinkish white. *Sepals* white with pink flush on top and pink on the undersurface. *Corolla* violet purple maturing to a bell shape. *Foliage* lettuce green mostly with yellow edges. Growth is normally a self-branching bush, but as the growth is rather lax, it can be trained as a basket. Foliage at its best in shaded conditions. (Sport from 'Belsay Beauty') (Ryle, UK, 1976)

**'Coralle'**
Triphylla type Single H1 Bush
*Tube* long, thin, tapering. *Sepals* short, salmon orange. *Corolla* also salmon orange. Total length of flower approx. 2.25in (6cm). *Foliage* deep sage green with veins of a slightly paler shade, and an overall velvety sheen. Leaves fairly large 3in (7–8cm) in length. Growth upright and very vigorous. Flowers very numerous, carried at the ends of the branches. (*F. triphylla* × *F. fulgens*) (Bonstedt, Germany, 1905)

**'Corallina'**
Single H3 Bush
*Tube* carmine. *Sepals* drooping, carmine. *Corolla* purple with pink at the base of the petals. *Foliage* dark green and of medium size. Growth is a rather lax spreading bush, could be used for hedging in sheltered areas. H. and S. 18–24in (45–60cm). (*F. cordifolia* × 'Globosa') (Pince, UK, 1844)

'CONSPICUA'

'CONSTANCE'

'CONTINENTAL'

'COQUET BELL'

'COQUET DALE'

'CORALLE'

**'Coral Seas'**
Single H2 Trailer
*Tube* salmon. *Sepals* salmon
to orange. *Corolla* burnt
orange. *Foliage* medium
green. Very free-flowering
cultivar produced on lax
branches, which lend it to
being used as a basket.
(Martin, USA, 1966)

**'Coral Shells'**
Single H2 Trailing
Medium-sized flowers.
*Tubes* pale cream. *Sepals*
peach. *Corolla* red. *Foliage*
medium green. The natural
desire of the plant is to trail.
Will make a good basket.
(Riley, USA, 1991)

**F. cordifolia**
Species H1 Bush
*Tube* dark scarlet. *Sepals* are
also dark scarlet with green
tips. *Corolla* a combination
of green, yellow and white.
*Foliage* largish broad. The
flowers appear from the leaf
axils. By many no longer
considered to be a separate
species; most plants under
cultivation thought to be *F.
splendens*.
(Bontham, 1841, Guatemala)

**'Core'ngrato'**
Double H2 Bush
*Tube* long, pale coral pink.
*Sepals* coral pink on the
outside and a frosty salmon
pink on the inner. *Corolla*
opens burgundy purple,
changing to salmon
burgundy with additional
salmon-pink splashes. *Foliage*
medium green. The growth is
self-branching and upright.
(Blackwell, UK, 1964)

**'Corsage'**
Double H2 Semi-trailer
*Tube* and *sepals* ivory pink.
*Sepals* ivory pink with a pale
salmon shade on the outside
and a darker salmon on the
inside, stand straight out
until mature then straight up
against tube. *Corolla* short

but very full, thirty or more
petals, orange coral, rosette-
like. *Foliage* medium green
with red stems on the new
growth. Growth rather lax,
so will make a basket or a
bush with the necessary
supports.
(Stubbs, USA, 1979)

**F. corymbiflora**
Species H1 Bush
*Tube* scarlet, can reach up
to 2.5in (6cm) in length.
*Sepals* scarlet. *Corolla* a
deep shade of red. *Foliage*
medium green and very
large (up to 4 × 2in (10 ×
5cm)) with soft hairs on
both upper and lower
surfaces. The flowers
appear at the ends of
branches in racemes.
(Native of Ecuador and Peru)

**F. corymbiflora var. alba**
Species H1 Bush
The description for this
variety is the same as that for
*F. corymbiflora* except that
*tube* and *sepals* are white.

**'Cosmopolitan'**
Double H2 Lax bush or
trailer
*Tube* and *sepals* deep rose
pink. *Corolla* white flushed
pale pink, splashed and
veined rose pink. Large
flowers freely produced.
*Foliage* medium green. The
lax growth makes it suitable
either for a basket or as a
bush with the necessary
assistance.
(Castro, USA, 1960)

**'Costa Brava'**
Single H2 Lax bush
*Tube* long, pink with a
deeper pink stripe. *Sepals*
bright pink with reddish
overtone, long and broad,
held at the horizontal.
*Corolla* is cerise with pink at
the base of the petals. *Foliage*
yellowish, maturing to a light
green. The growth is very lax
even though the plant is self-

branching and short-jointed.
Could be useful either a bush
or a basket.
(Colville, UK, 1973)

**'Cotta Bella'**
Double H2 Trailer
*Tube* and *sepals* white.
*Corolla* rose bengal with
three neat tiers of petals.
The flowering is very free
and continuous. An
excellent basket variety.
*Foliage* is medium green.
(Bielby/Oxtoby, UK, 1989)

**'Cotta Bright Star'**
Single H2 Bush
*F. decussata/* × 'Fanfare'
cross with similar colouring
to *F. decussata* but much
bigger flowers. The strong
upright growth needs
'pinching' to stimulate
branching. *Tube* long,
Indian lake. *Sepals* small,
are similar with green tips.
*Corolla* very bright orange.
Much more floriferous than
its parents. (*F. decussata* ×
'Fanfare')
(Bielby/Oxtoby, UK, 1994)

**'Cotta Fairy'**
Semi-double H2 Stiff trailer
*Tube* white. *Sepals* white-
edged with carmine. *Corolla*
consists of pale lilac petals
and petaloids. *Foliage*
medium green. Growth
rather stiff. Will make a
good basket but will need
weights to lower the
branches.
(Bielby/Oxtoby, UK, 1989)

**'Cotta Princess'**
Double H2 Trailer
*Tube* crimson rose. *Sepals*
broad, are crimson rose.
*Corolla* rhodamine purple
with white base to the
petals and picotee edge.
*Foliage* medium to dark
green on top and lighter
beneath. A very strong-
growing plant. ('Pink
Panther' × 'Pink Panther')
(Bielby/Oxtoby, UK, 1989)

*F. CORDIFOLIA*

*F. CORYMBIFLORA* VAR. *ALBA*

'COSMOPOLITAN'

'COTTA BELLA'

**'Cotta Vino'**
Single H2 Bush
*Tube* pale pink. *Sepals* very
pale pink (rhodamine pink)
with green tips, horizontal.
*Corolla* opens very dark
purple and matures to
purple or a rich red wine. A
very unusual colour
combination and very
attractive. *Foliage* medium
to dark green. Growth
extremely vigorous.
Excellent for bush growth,
but can also be encouraged
to grow in a basket.
(Bielby/Oxtoby, UK, 1994)

**'Cotton Candy'**
Double H2 Bush
*Tube* white with pink veins.
*Sepals* white on top, pink
on the underside and with
green tip, recurving towards
the tube. *Corolla* pale pink
with cerise veining. A very
full and fluffy double,
*Foliage* dark to medium
green. The upright, bushy
growth is very vigorous.
(Tiret, USA, 1962)

**'Countess of Aberdeen'**
Single H2 Bush
A superb plant when grown
well. *Tube* short, creamy
white. *Sepals* also white and
slightly upturned. *Corolla*
small and white. *Foliage*
small, medium green.
Growth is upright and bushy.
Not the easiest of cultivars as
it is very prone to *botrytis* if
overwatered. Grown in the
shade to get the best
colouring from the flowers.
(Dobbie Forbes, UK, 1888)

**'Countess of Maritza'**
Double H2 Bush
*Tube* short, pale pink.
*Sepals* pale pink, broad and
long. *Corolla* lilac. *Foliage*
medium green. Strong
upright and bushy growth.
(Holmes, E., UK, 1977)

**'Country Girl'**
Single H2 Bush
*Tube* flesh pink. *Sepals* also
flesh pink, longish and

sometimes twist. *Corolla*
pink bengal. Blooms of
medium size. *Foliage* light
green. Growth upright and
bushy, short-jointed and
quite strong.
(Tolley, UK, 1979)

**'Court Jester'**
Double H2 Bush
*Tube* short, rose red. *Sepals*
rose red with a crêpe effect.
*Corolla* royal purple with
pink coral petals overlaying
the centre. *Foliage* medium
green. Very free-flowering on
strong, upright and bushy
growth.
(Castro, USA, 1960)

**'Cover Girl'**
Semi-double H2 Bush
*Tube* and *sepals* bright red.
*Corolla* rich blue with white
at the base of the petals.
*Foliage* medium green.
Good, strong, upright and
bushy growth.
(Haag and Son, USA, 1953)

**'Coxeen'**
Single H2 Lax bush
*Tube* dull red. *Sepals* white,
green tipped. *Corolla* rosy-
pink, white at base. Small
blooms very freely produced.
*Foliage* medium green.
Growth is rather thin but will
make a reasonable basket.
(Howlett, UK, 1936)

**'Crackerjack'**
Single H2 Trailer
*Tube* white. *Sepals* white
with a pink flush, and they
completely recurve around
the tube. *Corolla* pale
mauve-blue, white at the
base. *Foliage* light green
with a crimson vein, large
leaves. The growth is
naturally trailing and will
make a superb basket.
(Fuchsia La, USA, 1961)

**F. crassistipula**
Species H1 Bush
*Tube* approx. 1.75in
(4–5cm) scarlet pink. *Sepals*
scarlet pink tipped with dull
purple. *Corolla* deep red.

Flowers appear at the ends
of branches. *Foliage* very
large, up to 6in (15cm) long.
Leaves are dark green on the
upper surface with a purple
flush on the lower. In the
wild (Colombia), grows to
about 3m (9ft).
(Berry, Dr P., Colombia,
1979)

**'Cream Puff'**
Double H2 Trailer
*Tube* long, slender, slightly
curved, pale pink. *Sepals*
pale pink becoming white at
the tips. *Corolla* creamy
white with delicate pink
overlay on the outside
petals. Blooms large, borne
on long pedicels. *Foliage*
medium green. The plant is
a natural trailer so will
make a good basket.
(Kennett, USA, 1960)

**'Crinoline'**
Double H2 Bush
*Tube* rosy white. *Sepals* rosy
white, tipped with green.
*Corolla* a clear pale rose
pink. *Foliage* medium green.
Upright bushy growth but
tends to make very heavy
wood. A rather
temperamental grower.
(Reiter, USA, 1950)

**'Cropwell Butler'**
Single H2 Bush
*Tube* short, thick, rosy-red.
*Sepals* rosy red, held
horizontally. *Corolla*
campanula violet, slightly
flaring; medium-sized flowers
freely produced. *Foliage*
medium green on upright
and bushy growth. ('Heidi
Ann' × 'Cloverdale Jewel')
(Roe, UK, 1981)

**'Crosby Soroptomist'**
Single H2 Bush
*Tube* and *sepals* rhodamine
pink. *Corolla* pure white.
Medium-sized flowers freely
produced. *Foliage* dark
green. Good, strong bushy
growth. ('Border Queen' ×
'Joy Patmore')
(Clark, D., UK, 1989)

'COTTA VINO'

'COTTON CANDY'

'COUNTESS OF ABERDEEN'

'COVER GIRL'

'CRACKERJACK'

'CROSBY SOROPTOMIST'

## 'Cross Check'
Single H2 Lax bush
*Tube* long, neyron rose with darker rose. *Sepals* held at horizontal also neyron rose on the upper surface with white on the lower; recurving tips. *Corolla* tyrian purple with smooth edges to the petals. *Foliage* lettuce green with serrated edges. The laxity of the growth makes it suitable for either bush, standard or basket use with the necessary supports. ('Checkerboard' × 'Achievement')
(Brouwer, Holland, 1985)

## 'Crown Derby'
Double H2 Bush
*Tube* and *sepals* waxy crimson. *Corolla* centre petals white with outer petals and petaloids crimson. *Foliage* medium green. Growth upright. Very floriferous over a long season.
(Gadsby, UK, 1970)

## 'Crundale'
Single H2 Bush
*Tube* and *Sepals* rose. *Corolla* pale bishop's violet. *Foliage* medium green. Growth upright and bushy.
(Neill, UK, 1990)

## 'Crusader'
Double H2 Trailer
*Tube* and *sepals* frosty white. *Corolla* deep purple. Flowers fairly large and freely produced. *Foliage* medium green.
(Tiret, USA, 1962)

## 'Crystal Blue'
Single/semi-double H2 Bush
*Tube* greenish-white. *Sepals* white with green tips recurving right back against the tube. *Corolla* violet blue, with white at the base of each petal. *Foliage* medium green. The upright growth is self-branching but can be even better with some 'stopping'. Very free-flowering.
(Kennett, USA, 1962)

## 'Crystal Stars'
Semi-double H2 Bush
*Tube* short, thick greenish-white flushed with red. *Sepals* white, reflexed. *Corolla* white. *Foliage* medium to small, spinach green, ovoid. Upright, bushy and self-branching growth. ('Ting a Ling' × ('La Campanella' × 'Flirtation Waltz'))
(Clyne, UK, 1974)

## 'Cupcake'
Single H2 Trailer
Medium-sized flowers. *Tube* white. *Sepals* pink. *Corolla* pale magenta. *Foliage* medium green, serrated edges. The growth is naturally trailing so will make a good basket.
(Stubbs, USA, 1986)

## 'Cupid'
Single H2 Bush
*Tube* pale scarlet cerise. *Sepals* also pale scarlet cerise. *Corolla* pale bluish-magenta. *Foliage* medium to dark green. The upright bushy growth is self-branching. Flowers are small but are produced in quantity.
(Wood, UK, 1946)

## 'Curly Q'
Single H2 Lax bush/trailer
*Tube* whitish-carmine. *Sepals* pale carmine, reflex or curl back against the tube. *Corolla* violet-purple with four rolled petals. *Foliage*, small, medium green with dark purple stems. A self-branching, lax grower ideal for baskets or training as a bush with supports.
(Kennett, USA, 1961)

## 'Curtain Call'
Double H2 Trailer
*Tube* and *sepals* pale carmine shading to white. *Sepals* flushed pink on the underside, reflexing. *Corolla* rosy cerise with white at the base of each petal. *Foliage* medium green. The natural trailing of this plant makes it ideal for hanging containers, but will grow upright if staked. Very free-flowering; produces four blooms from each pair of leaf axils, not two.
(Munkner, USA, 1961)

## *F. cylindracea*
Species H1 Bush
*Tube* and *sepals* deep red. *Corolla* lighter red. The tiny flowers are borne solitarily in the leaf axils. *Foliage* partly shiny on the upper surface and hairy underneath. Belongs to the *F. encliandra* section. The strong upright shrub will attain heights of 15+ft (5+m) in its native Mexico.
(Lindley, 1938, Mexico)

## 'Cymon'
Double H2 Bush
*Tube* white. *Sepals* white flushed with carmine and with green tips. *Corolla* rich aster violet shading to carmine at base of petals. Medium-sized flowers freely produced. *Foliage* medium green. Strong, vigorous and upright bushy growth.
(Pacey, UK, 1987)

## 'Cymru'
Double H2 Bush
*Tube* short, wild silk. *Sepals* ivory, reflexed, broad. *Corolla* shell pink, very compact and full with narrow cylindrical petals. Flowers fairly large and quite prolific. *Foliage* medium green.
(Thornley, UK, 1966)

## 'Cyril Holmes'
Single H2 Bush
*Tube* thick waxy white. *Sepals* blush white with green tip and scarlet on the inside. *Corolla* rowanberry with capsicum red at base. Medium-sized flowers with four distinct petals. *Foliage* soft green. Upright, bushy plants, self-branching. ('Percy Holmes' × 'Hidcote Beauty')
(Holmes, R., UK, 1973)

'CURTAIN CALL'

'CURLY Q'          'CYMRU'

# D

**'Daisy Bell'**
Single H2 Trailer
*Tube* long, white with orange
cast, shading to green at base.
*Sepals* are pale orange shading
to apple green at the tip.
*Corolla* vermilion shading to
pale orange at the base of the
petals. Small but very
numerous flowers, the petals
forming a narrow cone. *Foliage*
small, medium green with
lighter shading beneath.
Growth naturally trailing, self-
branching and vigorous. Makes
an excellent basket or half
basket. Best colour in sun.
(Mieske, USA, 1977)

**'Dalton'**
Single H2 Bush
*Tube* and *sepals* are flesh pink,
green tipped. *Corolla* Venetian
pink, tipped with green.
medium-sized blooms freely
produced. Worth trying as a
standard; a good summer
bedder. *Foliage* medium green.
('Hawkshead' × 'Other Fellow')
(Thornley, UK, 1971)

**'Damlata'**
Single H2 Bush
*Tube* neyron rose. *Sepals*
carmine rose on the upper
surface, neyron rose on the
lower. *Corolla* tyrian purple
with turned up petal edges.
*Foliage* dark green with reddish
stems. ('Little Beauty' ×)
(Brouwer, Holland, 1987)

**'Dancing Flame'**
Double H2 Trailer
*Tube* pale orange to flesh
colour with darker stripes.
*Sepals* orange on the inside,
paler on the top side, slender,
recurving. *Corolla* orange
carmine, deeper in centre,
lighter orange on outer petals.
The medium to small flowers
are very eye catching. *Foliage*
large, medium green with
serrated edges. A good trailer
but as growth rather stiff will
require some assistance to
cover the container. With

supports will make a good
bush. ('Novella' × 'Applause')
(Stubbs, USA, 1981)

**'Danish Pastry'**
Single H2 Lax bush/trailer
*Tube* and *sepals* coral with
green tips. *Corolla* lavender to
salmon red. Large blooms on
rather lax growth. *Foliage*
medium green. Train as bush
or trailer with the necessary
supports; good as half basket.
(Fuchsia Forest, USA, 1968)

**'Danny Boy'**
Double H2 Bush
*Tube* and *sepals* pale red.
*Corolla* red, very large size.
*Foliage* medium green, largish.
Very large flowers but only
sparsely produced. Upright,
self-branching, bushy growth;
needs staking and hand
pinching to keep upright due to
weight of blooms.
(Tiret, USA, 1961)

**'Daphne Arlene'**
Single H2 Bush
This sport from 'Countess of
Aberdeen' has small but very
profuse flowers. *Tube* and
*sepals* are waxy white with a
tinge of pink. *Corolla* coral
pink. *Foliage* small and
medium green. Very similar to
'Shuna', another sport from the
same parent.
(Putley, UK, 1978)

**'Dark Eyes'**
Double H2 Bush
*Tube* short. *Sepals* short, broad,
upturned, deep red. *Corolla*
violet-blue. Petals tightly rolled
and form a solid centre.
Medium-sized blooms freely
produced. *Foliage* medium to
dark green. Growth quite
strong and upright. Try it in the
border as a temporary resident.
(Erickson, USA, 1958)

**'Dark Secret'**
Double H2 Bush
*Tube* short, greenish. *Sepals*
heavy, broad, upturned, waxy
white on the outside and pale
pink with a crêpe texture on
the inside. *Corolla* deep violet,

splashed phlox pink. Medium-
sized blooms show up well
against the very dark *foliage*.
(Hodges, USA, 1957)

**'Dark Spider'**
Single H2 Trailer
Large flowers. *Tube* short, rosy
red. *Sepals* red, long and
slender. *Corolla* purple ageing
to red with maturity, toothed
edges to the petals. *Foliage*
medium green on upper
surface, paler underneath,
serrated edges, green to reddish
veins. Being a natural trailer
will make an excellent basket.
(de Graaff, Holland, 1980)

**'Dark Treasure'**
Double H2 Bush
*Tube* and *sepals* deep pink.
*Corolla* very deep purple with
deep pink splashes at the base
of the petals. *Foliage* medium
green.The very large blooms
are quite freely produced.
Because of the weight of the
blooms some support will be
needed by the branches.
(Hobson, UK, 1985)

**'Darreen Dawn'**
Double H2 Bush
*Tube* and *sepals* creamy pink.
*Corolla* purple with pink
corners to the petals. *Foliage*
medium green. Fairly large
flowers freely produced.
(Dyos, UK, 1992)

**'Dartmoor Pixie'**
Single H2 Lax bush
*Tube* and *sepals* rhodonite red.
*Corolla* plum purple. *Foliage*
medium green. Medium-sized
flower. Growth rather lax but
the flowers are freely produced.
(Hilton, UK, 1978)

**'David'**
Single H2/3 Bush
Small single flowers freely
produced throughout the season.
*Tube* and *sepals* cerise. *Corolla*
rich purple. *Foliage* medium to
dark green. Growth rather low-
growing but bushy, will make an
excellent edging to a hardy
border. ('Pumila' × seedling)
(Wood, W.P., UK, 1949)

'DALTON'

'DANCING FLAME'

'DANISH PASTRY'

'DARK EYES'

'DARREEN DAWN'

'DAVID'

**'David Lockyer'**
Double H2 Bush
*Tube* medium length, white.
*Sepals* white on the top, white
with a pink flush underneath.
*Corolla* bright crimson red with
some of the petals splashed and
striped with white. It has a
rather unusual shape in that
there are long petals in the
centre surrounded by folds of
shorter petals. *Foliage* large,
medium green. Growth very
vigorous and upright. An
excellent bush plant.
(Holmes, E., UK, 1968)

**'David Ward'**
Double H2 Bush
*Tubes* and flyaway *sepals* flesh
pink. *Corolla*, fully ruffled,
pastel blue turning to pink.
Flowers produced at the ends
of the laterals, continuously.
*Foliage* is medium green.
Strong upright grower should
make a good show plant.
(Goulding, UK, 1989)

**'Dawn'**
Single H2 Bush
*Tube* white with pink flush,
long, rather thin. *Sepals* white,
tipped green. *Corolla* pale
violet and paler at the base of
the petals. Medium-sized
blooms freely produced.
*Foliage* medium green. Upright
and bushy growth.
(Baker, UK, 1970)

**'Dawn Carless'**
Large double H2 Bush
*Tube* white striped with green.
*Sepals* pale pink tipped with
greenish-white. *Corolla* light
pink to light mauve. Fairly
strong upright growth but will
need supports for the heavy
flowers. *Foliage* medium to
green, quite large. ('Nancy
Lou' × 'Eden Lady')
(Carless, UK, 1993)

**'Dawn Redfern'**
Double H2 Bush
*Tube* and *sepals* white, lightly
flushed with palest pink on the
inside. *Corolla* white with the
base of the petals veined with
pink. *Foliage* golden green.

Flowers perfectly formed,
produced on strong upright
growth.
(Redfern, UK, 1990)

**'Dawn Star'**
Double H2 Bush
*Tube* rose red. *Sepals* also rose
red, with a paler colouring at
the base and tipped with green.
*Corolla* aster-violet, very full.
Large blooms of good shape,
freely produced for their size.
*Foliage* medium green.
(Bellamy, UK, 1985)

**'Dawn Thunder'**
Double H2 Lax bush
*Tube* thin, flesh-coloured.
*Sepals* pink, long, broad,
slightly upturned. *Corolla*
dusky pink and purple fading
to rose and coral. Most petals
have serrated edges. Blooms
very large, freely produced for
the size. *Foliage* dark green.
(Stubbs, USA, 1975)

**'Dawning'**
Single H2 Bush
*Tube* pink. *Sepals* pink,
recurve, and have green tips as
they age. *Corolla* pink with a
faint suggestion of grey. *Foliage*
medium green. Strong growth
will produce a good specimen
very quickly.
(Shaffery, UK, 1994)

**'Debby'**
Double H2 Bush
*Tube* medium length, rose
bengal. *Sepals* rose bengal wide,
recurving. *Corolla* heliotrope
blue fading to cobalt violet,
very full. *Foliage* medium-sized,
mid-green. Growth upright,
very free-flowering. Vigilance is
necessary to form a good shape.
(Nessier, USA, 1952)

**'Deben'**
Semi-double H2 Bush
*Tube* short, ivory. *Sepals* ivory
coloured, darkening with
maturity. *Corolla* violet turning
to rose. *Foliage* medium green.
Strong, upright-growing and
self-branching plants suitable
for bushes or smaller standards.
(Goulding, UK, 1988)

**'Deben Rose'**
Single H2 Trailer
*Tube* a delicate shade of
azalea pink. *Sepals* long,
slender slightly recurved,
spinel red tipped with green.
*Corolla* mallow purple, petals
edged spinel red. Medium-sized
flowers produced early and
prolifically. *Foliage* medium
green. A natural trailer so will
make a superb basket. ('La
Campanella' × 'Shady Lady')
(Dunnett , UK, 1979)

**'Debra Hampson'**
Double H2 Bush
Sport from 'Dark Eyes'. *Tube*
short, thick, deep red. *Sepals*
red short, broad and upturned.
*Corolla* mauve. Blooms
medium-sized with curled and
rolled petals. *Foliage* dark
green with red carmine vein.
Upright, bushy and self-
branching.
(Hilton, UK, 1976)

**F. decussata**
Species H1 Bush
*Tube* and *sepals* dark red.
*Corolla* scarlet to orange-red.
Flowers usually found in the
leaf axils but occasionally
towards the ends of the
laterals. *Foliage* dark green,
spear shaped. Strong upright
grower.
(Ruiz and Pavon, Peru, 1802)

**'Dee Copley'**
Double H2 Bush
*Tube* and broad *sepals* bright
red. *Corolla* deep purple
mottled red at the base of the
petals. *Foliage* dark green.
Large blooms extremely
profuse. Upright sturdy growth.
(Copley Gardens, USA, 1964)

**'Deep Purple'**
Double H2 Trailing.
*Sepals* and *tubes* white. *Corolla*
dark violet. *Foliage* medium
green. Very strong, spreading
and versatile growth helps this
large flowered fuchsia to look
very attractive when grown in
any large hanging container.
('Blue Satin' × 'Quasar')
(Garrett, USA, 1989)

'DAVID WARD'

'DAWN STAR'

'DEEP PURPLE'

**'Delaval Lady'**
Single H2 Bush
*Tube* carmine striped with
darker shade. *Sepals* neyron
rose underneath with darker
colour shading on white, shiny
upperside. *Corolla* rhodamine
pink. Long graceful flowers
freely produced. *Foliage*
medium green.
(Ryle, UK, 1975)

**'Delicia'**
Single H2 Bush
*Tube* short white. *Sepals*
longish, slender, crimson on
top and carmine underneath.
*Corolla* small to medium,
Imperial purple maturing paler,
square shaped. Medium-sized
flowers freely produced.
*Foliage* forest green with white
veining and magenta stems,
serrated edges. The upright
growth makes it a candidate
for growing as a standard.
('Cloverdale Pearl' × 'Marin
Glow')
(Redfern, UK, 1984)

**'Delilah'**
Double H2 Bush
*Tube* rose pink. *Sepals* rose
pink, reflexing to the stem.
*Corolla* violet flecked pink and
white and matures to rosy
magenta. Short jointed growth
produced on an upright bush.
Colour best in shade.
(Handley, UK, 1974)

**'Delta's Bambi'**
Single H2 Trailing
Medium-sized flowers. *Tube*
and *sepals* deep purple. *Corolla*
robin red. *Foliage* medium
green. The natural growth of
this cultivar is trailing so will
make a good basket.
(Vreeke/van't Westeinde,
Holland, 1991)

**'Deltaschon'**
Double H2 Bush
*Tube* and *sepals* red. *Corolla*
pale pink veined red. Growth
upright and, will make a good
bush. *Foliage* medium to dark
green. (Sport from
'Tausendschon')
(Felix, Holland, 1986)

**'Delta's Delight'**
Single H2 Bush
Medium-sized flower. *Tube* and
*sepals* rose red. *Corolla* violet.
Growth fairly strong, upright.
*Foliage* medium green.
(Vreeke/van't Westeinde,
Holland, 1991)

**'Delta's Flame'**
Double H2 Bush
Medium-sized flowers. *Tube*
peach pink. *Sepals* carmine.
*Corolla* robin red. *Foliage*
medium green. Reasonably
strong. Growth upright.
(Vreeke/van't Westeinde,
Holland, 1991)

**'Delta's Glory'**
Single H2 Bush
Medium-sized flowers. *Tube*
and *sepals* reddish aubergine.
*Corolla* purple. *Foliage* mid-
green. Growth upright.
(Vreeke, Holland, 1989)

**'Delta's K.O.'**
Double H2 Bush
Very large flower. *Tube* cream.
*Sepals* cream flushed with rosy
purple. *Corolla* deep purple.
*Foliage* mid- to dark green
colouring. Growth vigorously
upright; will make an excellent
bush quite quickly.
(Vreeke/van't Westeinde,
Holland, 1991)

**'Delta's Memory'**
Single H2 Bush
Medium-sized flower. *Tube* and
*sepals* rose red to reddish-
purple. *Corolla* cream. *Foliage*
medium green. Growth
upright.
(Vreeke, Holland, 1989)

**'Delta's Paljas'**
Single H2 Bush
Medium-sized flowers. *Tubes*
dull yellow-green. *Sepals* rose.
*Corolla* dusky fuchsia purple
and dark red. *Foliage* medium
green. Growth upright.
(Vreeke/van't Westeinde,
Holland, 1991)

**'Delta's Parade'**
Double H2 Bush
Medium-sized flowers. *Tubes*

and *sepals* deep rosy red.
*Corolla* deep purple. *Foliage*
deep mid-green. Growth
upright.
(Vreeke/van't Westeinde,
Holland, 1991)

**'Delta's Rien'**
Single H2 Trailer
*Tube* white. *Sepals* white with
a touch of green. *Corolla* pale
violet. Long medium-sized
flowers are produced quite
freely. *Foliage* rather coarse
fresh green. A natural trailer
(van't Westeinde, Holland,
1989)

**'Delta's Robijn'**
Single H2 Bush
*Tube* red-purple. *Sepals* deep
red purple with darker stripes.
*Corolla* deep red purple.
*Foliage* mid-green. Very free-
flowering plant over a long
period. Strong upright growth.
(Vreeke, Holland, 1989)

**'Delta's Song'**
Single H2 Bush
*Tube* and *sepals* white. *Corolla*
Chinese rose. *Foliage* medium
green. Growth upright.
(Vreeke/van't Westeinde,
Holland, 1991)

**'Delta's Souvenir'**
Semi-double H2 Bush
*Tube* yellowish-white. *Sepals*
shell pink fading to pale green,
the underside being paler pink.
*Corolla* pale phlox violet.
*Foliage* medium green. Rather
large flowers carried on strong
upright stems.
(Vreeke, Holland, 1990)

**'Delta's Splendor'**
Single H2 Bush
*Tube* and *sepals* pink. *Corolla*
deep robin red. *Foliage* mid- to
dark green. Growth strong and
upright.
(Vreeke/van't Westeinde,
Holland, 1991)

'DELTA'S DELIGHT'

'DELTA'S K.O.'

'DELTA'S PARADE'

'DELTA'S SONG'

**'Delta's Sprinkler'**
Single H2 Trailer
*Tube* and *sepals* spiraea red.
*Corolla* robin red. *Foliage*
medium to dark green. Growth
naturally trailing.
(Vreeke/van't Westeinde,
Holland, 1991)

**'Delta's Wonder'**
Single H2 Bush
*Tube* and *sepals* of this large-
flowered single are red-purple.
*Corolla* lilac with red-purple
stripes. For the size of the
flower the plant is very free-
flowering. *Foliage* medium
green. The strong upright
growth will make a good bush.
(Vreeke, Holland, 1989)

**'Denis Bolton'**
Single H2 Bush
*Tube* dark rose. *Sepals* dark
rose, held horizontally. *Corolla*
opens purple, dark rose at base
of petals. *Foliage* medium
green on the upper surface,
paler on the lower. Growth is
strong and upright and could
make a good standard.
('Brixham Orpheus' × 'Biddy
Lester')
(Holmes, R., UK, 1989)

**F. denticulata**
Species H1 Bush
*Tube* pink. *Sepals* green, pink-
tipped. *Corolla* red. The
flowers are carried in the leaf
axils. *Foliage* very large, dark
green. Native of Peru and
Bolivia.
(Ruiz and Pavon, 1802)

**'Deori De'**
Single H2 Bush
(Deori De is the popular name
for the fuchsia in Ireland, the
Gaelic for 'God's Tears'.)
Medium-sized flowers. *Tubes*
white. *Sepals* white flushed
with pink. *Corolla* reddish-
purple splashed pink. *Foliage*
medium green. Growth upright
and bushy.
(Swinbank, UK, 1988)

**F. dependens**
Species H1 Bush
*Tubes* long, thin. *Sepals* and the

petals very short, orange to red.
Flowers are produced terminally.
*Foliage* small. Growth is self-
branching and upright. This is
one of the species that prefers to
be left alone and is happier
when kept rather dry.
(Hooker, 1837)

**'Derby Belle'**
Single H2 Bush
*Tube* and *sepals* white, flushed
with rose. *Corolla* cyclamen
purple flushed with magenta.
*Foliage* is pale green, slightly
serrated. The flowers are bell-
shaped and medium in size.
Prefers shade. ('Upward Look'
× 'Caroline')
(Gadsby, UK, 1970)

**'Derby Countess'**
Single H2 Bush
*Tube* long, white. *Sepals* waxy
white. *Corolla* violet purple
with pink at base of petals.
*Foliage* medium green. Flowers
are very large, some measuring
up to 5in (13cm) across.
Rather late in its flowering.
Needs careful pinching in early
stages. ('Sleigh Bells' × 'Pepi')
(Gadsby, UK, 1973)

**'Derby Imp'**
Single H2 Bush
*Tube* thin, crimson. *Sepals*
crimson with underside rose
red. *Corolla* violet-blue
maturing to violet purple, pink
at base of petals, cerise veining.
Flowers are small but very
dainty. *Foliage* small, wiry,
medium green colouring. Self-
branching, very free-flowering.
Will make basket, bush or
quarter standard.
(Gadsby, UK, 1974)

**'Derby Star'**
Single H2 Bush
*Tube* and *sepals* white flushed
with pink. *Corolla* wisteria blue
on a white base. Medium-sized
flowers held on horizontal
stems giving a spiking effect.
Naturally spreading and self-
branching bush plant. *Foliage*
medium green. ('Cliff's Hardy'
× 'Shy Look')
(Gadsby, UK, 1974)

**'Desire'**
Semi-double H2 Bush
*Tube* and *sepals* cream. *Corolla*
light violet-purple. Medium-
sized flowers produced on
fairly strong, upright growth.
*Foliage* medium green.
(van Aspert, Holland, 1991)

**'Desmond Davey'**
Double H2 Bush
*Tube* and *sepals* white. *Corolla*
white, veined red at the base.
*Foliage* medium green. Natural
growth upright, self-branching
and bushy.
(Holmes, R., UK, 1994)

**'Destiny'**
Double H2 Trailer
*Tube* light pink. *Sepals* light
pink on the upper surface, pink
on the lower. *Corolla* opens
reddish-purple, maturing to
violet. *Foliage* medium green
on the upper surface, light
green on the lower. Growth
rather lax, which enables it to
be used as a bush with
supports or as a basket cultivar.
(Richardson, New Zealand,
1988)

**'Devonshire Dumpling'**
Double H2 Trailer
*Tube* short, thick, white. *Sepals*
neyron rose, tipped with green.
*Corolla* white, the outer petals
flushed pink. Large flowers are
produced in great quantity and
throughout the season. The
large, white, round buds make
the name of this cultivar very
appropriate. *Foliage* medium
green. Makes an exceptional
basket and is admired by all
who see it.
(Hilton, UK, 1981)

**'Diablo'**
Double H2 Trailer
*Tube* greenish white, pink flush.
*Sepals* white, flushed carmine at
tips, crêped underneath. *Corolla*
burgundy red, outer petals
splashed red, paler at base.
*Foliage* medium green with red
veining. A natural trailer which
will make a good basket. Large
blooms if pinched early.
(Tiret, USA, 1961)

F. *DENTICULATA*

'DEVONSHIRE DUMPLING'

'DENIS BOLTON'

'DERBY IMP'

'DIABLO'

**'Diamond Wedding'**
Single H2 Bush
*Tube* short, glossy red. *Sepals*
glossy red tipped with yellow
on the upper surface, crêped
red on the lower. *Corolla*
reddish-purple veined with red.
*Foliage* medium green on the
upper surface, lighter green on
the lower. ('Hugh Morgan' ×)
(Holmes, R., UK, 1989)

**'Diana Wills'**
Double H2 Bush
*Tube* and *sepals* waxy white
heavily tipped with green.
*Corolla* spiraea red flushed
white and ruby rose fading to
ruby red. *Foliage* medium
green, serrated. Growth
naturally upright, but rather
lax. Free-flowering, self-
branching. Needs staking to
make bush. Good basket.
(Gadsby, UK, 1968)

**'Diane Brown'**
Single H2 Bush
*Tube* and *sepals* pure white.
*Corolla* a very light shade of
pink shading to white at the
base of the petals. Flowers held
horizontally. *Foliage* light to
medium green. Growth short-
jointed.
(Webb, UK, 1990)

**'Diann Goodwin'**
Single H2 Bush
*Tube* and *sepals* flesh to rose
red. *Corolla* matt red; darker.
*Foliage* medium green. Growth
strong and upright. Should
make a good exhibition plant.
(Goulding, UK, 1991)

**'Dick Swinbank'**
Double H2 Bush
*Tube* and *sepals* of this very
attractive small-flowered
cultivar are pale rose. *Corolla*
purple. *Foliage* medium green.
Growth fairly strong, upright,
self-branching and bushy.
Recommended for the show
bench.
(Swinbank, UK, 1991)

**'Didi'**
Semi-double H2 Trailer
Medium-sized flowers. *Tube*
cream, *sepals* rose. *Corolla*
violet. *Foliage* medium green.
The natural growth is to trail so
will make a good basket.
(Beije, Holland, 1989)

**'Die Fledermaus'**
Double H2 Trailer
*Tube* and *sepals* scarlet.
*Corolla* violet-blue. *Foliage*
medium green. A natural trailer
so can be used for hanging
containers.
(Blackwell, UK, 1967)

**'Die Schone Wilhelmine'**
Single H2 Bush
*Tube* and *sepals* deep shell pink
with green tips. *Corolla* shell
pink. *Foliage* medium green.
The natural growth is as an
upright bush, very suitable for
use on the patio.
(Raiser and date unknown)

**'Dilly Dilly'**
Double H2 Trailer
*Tube* white. *Sepals* pale pink on
top, deeper underneath, green
tips. *Corolla* lilac, pink at petal
base. Largish flowers are freely
produced. *Foliage* medium
green, large, slight serrations.
Although can only be described
as a semi-trailer, this plant will
make a nice basket.
(Tiret, USA, 1963)

**'Dimples'**
Double H2 Trailer
*Tube* thick, short, red. *Sepals*
red, slightly reflexing. *Corolla*
white with red veining on each
petal. Small blooms enhanced
by the medium-green *foliage*
with red stems. Best colour
obtained under shady
conditions.
(Storvick, USA, 1981)

**'Dinny Hetterscheid'**
Single H2 Trailer
Medium-sized flowers. *Tube*
and *sepals* rosy red. *Corolla*
salmon rose. *Foliage* medium
green. Growth can be described
as lax upright or trailing, so
will make a good bush or
basket with the necessary
assistance.
(de Graaff, Holland, 1989)

**'Dipton Dainty'**
Semi-double H2 Bush
*Tube* short, rhodamine pink.
*Sepals* also rhodamine pink,
curve slightly upward. *Corolla*
wisteria blue shading to a
lighter colouring. Medium-
sized flowers freely produced.
*Foliage* medium green. Good,
upright, self-branching growth.
(Ryle, UK, 1975)

**'Display'**
Single H2/3 Bush
*Tube* of this superb cultivar
pink. *Sepals* deep rose pink
arching upwards. *Corolla* deep
cerise pink and opens bell-
shaped. *Foliage* medium green
with slight serration. Growth
strong, upright and bushy.
Excellent for all exhibition
work. H. and S. 4ft (120cm)
upwards.
(Smith, UK, 1881)

**'Doc'**
Single H3 Bush
*Tube* and *sepals* red. *Corolla*
pale purple. Small flowers but
extremely free-flowering.
*Foliage* deep green. Excellent
for the front of the hardy
border as it achieves a height
of approx 9–15in (22–38cm).
(Tabraham, UK, 1974)

**'Doctor Jill'**
Double H2 Bush
*Tube* short, red-purple. *Sepals*
also red-purple, reflex
completely on the tube. *Corolla*
red purple with deeper veining.
*Foliage* medium to dark green.
(Seedling from 'Chang')
(Pugh, UK, 1978)

**'Dollar Princess'**
Double H3 Bush
*Tube* small, cerise. *Sepals* cerise,
quite broad and reflex almost to
the tube. *Corolla* purple with
cerise at the base of the petals.
*Foliage* medium to darker green
and serrated. Growth upright,
strong and self-branching. Good
for pot work or as a plant. H.
and S. 18–24in (45–60cm).
Sometimes erroneously called
'Princess Dollar'.
(Lemoine, France, 1912)

'DIAMOND WEDDING'

'DIANE BROWN'

'DICK SWINBANK'

'DISPLAY'

'DOC'

'DOLLAR PRINCESS'

**'Dolly Daydream'**
Double H2 Lax bush
*Tube* long, thin, dawn-pink.
*Sepals* neyron rose with
recurved tips and held
horizontally. *Corolla* scarlet.
Medium-sized blooms produced
in profusion. *Foliage* Paris-green
with serrated edges. Because of
the laxity of growth this cultivar
is suitable as a bush or in
hanging pots given the right
type of support and training.
('Pink Marshmallow' × *F.
fulgens*)
(Bielby, UK, 1987)

**'Domacin'**
Double H2 Trailer
*Tube* white, thin. *Sepals* pink
and partially recurving. *Corolla*
violet splashed with rose red
with red veins, fading to dark
red with paler marbling.
Growth is strong and needs
constant 'pinching' to ensure a
good basket. *Foliage* medium
green, lighter underneath, with
serrated edges and red veins.
('Pink Marshmallow' ×
'Midnight Sun')
(Richardson, Australia, 1985)

*F. dominiana*
Species H1 Bush
Flowers long, 'triphylla-type',
rosy scarlet and with rather
loose *corolla*. *Foliage* dark
greenish bronze. Growth
upright and bushy, vigorous
and free-flowering. Best grown
in a heated greenhouse (but it
will require plenty of root
room) as it is a very late
bloomer (October to January).
(*F. serratifolia* × *F. spectablis*)
(Dominy, UK, 1852)

**'Dopey'**
Double H3 Bush
*Tube* and *sepals* red. *Corolla*
purple, tinged with pink.
Flowers small but freely
produced. *Foliage* dark green.
Very dwarf and dainty. H. and
S. 9–16in (20–40cm).
(Tabraham, UK, 1974)

**'Doreen Redfern'**
Single H2 Bush
*Tube* short, white. *Sepals* white

on the upper surface, pale lilac
underneath, tipped with green.
*Corolla* methyl-violet maturing
to violet-purple. *Foliage* dark
green with serrated edges and
white veins. Dislikes bright
sunlight; and needs cool
conditions. ('Cloverdale Pearl'
× 'Marin Glow')
(Redfern, UK, 1984)

**'Doreen Stroud'**
Double H2 Lax bush or
trailer
*Tube* short, thin, rosy red. *Sepals*
light red, broad and held a little
below the horizontal. *Corolla*
fully double, lavender with frilly
petals. *Foliage* medium green.
The laxity of growth makes it
suitable for use in baskets,
especially as flowers are medium
to large and freely produced.
(Oakleigh Nurseries, UK, 1988)

**'Doris Coleman'**
Double H2 Trailer
*Tube* thin, crimson. *Sepals*
carmine striped and edged with
crimson on the upper surface.
*Corolla* methyl violet maturing
to rose purple. *Foliage* dark
green on the upper surface,
lighter on the lower. A natural,
self-branching trailer and will
make a good basket. ('Biddy
Lester' × 'Jack King')
(Holmes, R., UK, 1987)

**'Doris Hobbs'**
Single H2 Lax bush
*Tube* orchid pink. *Sepals* orchid
pink on the upper surface but
lighter on the undersurface.
*Corolla* spiraea rose in two
distinct tones. Small to medium
flowers produced very freely.
*Foliage* medium green with
dark red veining. ('Kathleen
Muncaster' × ('Harry Gray' ×
'Bicentennial'))
(Bielby/Oxtoby, UK, 1989)

**'Doris Yvonne'**
Double H2 Bush
*Tube* and *sepals* cardinal red.
*Corolla* aster violet with red
veining. *Foliage* medium green.
Medium-sized flowers carried
in profusion.
(Holmes, R., UK, 1993)

**'Dorking Delight'**
Double H2 Trailer
*Tube* and *sepals* deep rose.
*Corolla* vivid cerise. Flowers of
medium size. *Foliage* medium
green. The natural desire of the
plant is to trail.
(Meier, UK, 1994)

**'Dorothy'**
Single H3 Bush
*Tube* short, medium thick,
bright crimson. *Sepals* spread
out from the corolla, crimson.
The *corolla* violet, veined red,
red at base of petals. Medium-
sized flowers very free. *Foliage*
medium to dark green.
Considered to be hardy in the
south of England and could be
used for hedging. H. and S.
24–36in (60–90cm).
(Wood, UK, 1946)

**'Dorothy M. Goldsmith'**
Single H2 Bush
*Tube* red. *Sepals*, long, sweep
upwards almost hiding the
tube, red. *Corolla* pink with
darker pink edges. Medium-
sized, bell-shaped flowers freely
produced. *Foliage* medium
green. Growth strong and
upright.
(Goulding, UK, 1989)

**'Dorothy Shields'**
Double H2 Bush
*Tube* creamy white, moderate
length. *Sepals* held horizontally,
pink with white overtones on
top. *Corolla* opens violet,
veined pink, and matures to
light violet. *Foliage* medium
green. The upward growth is
quite strong and plants will
require early pinching to shape
successfully. ('Jackie Bull' ×
'Annabel')
(Redfern, UK, 1989)

**'Dorrian Brogdale'**
Single (Triphylla type) H1
Bush
*Tube* long. *Sepals*, outswept.
*Corolla* parrot-beaked: all pink
overlaid with orange. *Foliage*
dark green. Rather lax growth
makes it suitable for growing
in hanging containers.
(Goulding, UK, 1994)

'DOLLY DAYDREAM'

'DOROTHY'

'DOREEN REDFERN'

'DORKING DELIGHT'

'DOROTHY SHIELDS'

**'Drake 400'**
Double H2 Bush
*Tube* medium-sized, pale
carmine. *Sepals* carmine,
twisting around the tube.
*Corolla* imperial purple heavily
flushed with carmine. Medium-
sized blooms very freely
produced for a double.
Upright growth. *Foliage*
medium green.
(Hilton, UK, 1981)

**'Drama Girl'**
Double H2 Trailer
*Tube* and *sepals* pale pink.
*Corolla* blue with pink
marbling. Medium-sized, very
full blooms. *Foliage* medium
green, serrated edges. Makes a
very nice basket.
(Lockerbie, Australia,1975)

**'Drame'**
Semi-double H3 Bush
*Tube* medium length, scarlet.
*Sepals* broad, scarlet, held
horizontally, turning up at the
tips. *Corolla* purplish-red with
a definite red at the base of
each petal. Mature *foliage*
medium green, but when young
it is yellowish green. Small to
medium-sized leaves, slightly
serrated. Growth upright, self-
branching, and bushy. A good
strong plant for the hardy
border. H. and S. 18–24ins
(45–60cm).
(Lemoine, France, 1880)

**'Dr Brendan Freeman'**
Single H2 Bush
*Tube* and *sepals* rhodamine
pink shading to phlox pink.
*Corolla* white. *Foliage* medium
green. Growth of the plant is
fairly strong and upright.
(Gadsby, UK, 1977)

**'Dreamy Days'**
Single H2 Bush
*Tubes* pink. *Sepals* fully
recurving, flesh pink. *Corolla*
rose red with a hint of grey
along the margins. *Foliage*
medium green. The upright
growth makes it a good
proposition for using
as a standard.
(Goulding, UK, 1990)

**'Dr Foster'**
Single H3 Bush
*Tube* and *sepals* scarlet.
*Corolla* violet-purple, large,
full. *Foliage* medium to dark
green. Flowers quite large,
freely produced. Probably the
largest flowering 'hardy'
available today. Could be used,
especially in southern area, as a
hedge plant. H. and S. up to
3ft (90cm).
(Lemoine, France, 1899)

**'Drifter'**
Triphylla type H1 Lax bush
*Tubes* salmon, long, slightly
curved. *Sepals* smaller, similar
in colour but the short petals
are a brighter orange. *Foliage* is
mid- to dark green. Growth
spreading or pendant. Would
do well in a hanging pot.
(Stannard, UK, 1993)

**'Dr Olson'**
Double H2 Trailer
*Tube* and upturned *sepals*
bright red. *Corolla* pale orchid
pink with large central petals
surrounded by shorter,
spreading petals. Large flowers
and fairly free for the size.
*Foliage* medium green. A
natural trailer so will make a
good basket.
(Mrs D. Lyon, America, 1959)

**'Dr Robert'**
Single H2 Bush
*Tube* short, thick. *Sepals* white
the underside pale pink.
*Corolla* deep lilac shading to
pink at the base of the petals.
*Foliage* medium green. Growth
is strong, short-jointed and
upright. An excellent free-
flowering small single.
(Roe, UK, 1987)

**'Dr Topinard'**
Single H2 Bush
*Tube* and *sepals* deep rose red.
*Corolla* pure white, veined
with rose. Medium-sized
flowers very freely produced.
*Foliage* medium green. Growth
strong, self-branching and
upright. An excellent 'old'
fuchsia.
(Lemoine, France, 1890)

**'Drum Major'**
Semi-double H2 Bush
*Tube* and *sepals* white with
green tips. *Corolla* magnolia
purple with crimson flecks.
Flowers large, freely produced.
*Foliage* medium green. Growth
is upright and bushy.
(Baker, UK, 1970)

**'Du Barry'**
Double H2 Bush
*Tube* and reflexing *sepals*
softest pink. *Corolla* fuchsia
purple, the smaller outside
petals flecked and marbled
with flesh-pink. *Foliage*
medium green. Large blooms
fairly freely produced. Growth
upright and vigorous.
(Tiret, America, 1950)

**'Duchess of Albany'**
Single H2 Bush
*Tube* creamy wax. *Sepals*
recurving, white with pink
flush. *Corolla* pinkish-cerise.
Flowers medium-sized and very
free. *Foliage* bright green. The
strong upright, bushy growth
will make an excellent
standard.
(Rundle, UK, 1891)

**'Duet'**
Double H2 Trailer
*Tube* red. *Sepals* recurve to
cover the tube, bright pink.
*Corolla* pale raspberry pink.
Large flowers with some of the
petals forming a bell shape.
*Foliage* large, spring green. The
natural trailing will produce a
superb basket. Needs light
conditions for best results.
(Hall, UK, 1982)

**'Dulcie Elizabeth'**
Double H2 Bush
*Tube* rose pink, short. *Sepals*
reflexed, neyron rose, short,
broad, completely recurve over
tube. *Corolla* powder blue,
flecked with deep rose and shell
pink. *Foliage* parsley green.
Upright growth self-branching
and bushy. Free-flowering,
excellent exhibition plant, but
tends to bloom late. ('Tennessee
Waltz' × 'Winston Churchill')
(Clyne/Ames, UK, 1974)

'DRAME'

'DR ROBERT'

'DULCIE ELIZABETH'

**'Dusky Beauty'**
Single H2 Bush
*Tube* small, neyron rose. *Sepals*
horizontally held, neyron rose.
*Corolla* pale purple with pink
cast and deeper pink edges.
Small, prolific flowers. *Foliage*
medium to dark green. Growth
bushy and upright. Excellent
exhibition plant.
(Ryle, UK, 1981)

**'Dusky Rose'**
Double H2 Trailer
*Tube* deep reddish pink. *Sepals*
a clear, deep coral pink with
green tips. *Corolla* rose red,
maturing to raspberry pink,
with coral pink splashes.
*Foliage* dark green. Large
flowers, fluffy and frilled.
Growth is naturally trailing so
will make a superb basket.
(Waltz, USA, 1960)

**'Dutch Firebird'**
Single H2 Stiff trailer
*Tube* thin, rhodonite red.
*Sepals* horizontally held,
rhodonite red on top and claret
red underneath. *Corolla* tyrian
purple with smooth-edged,
overlapping petals. *Foliage*
olive green. The stiff trailing
growths will require the
assistance of weights to make a
good basket.
(de Graaff, Holland, 1985)

**'Dutch Mill'**
Single H2 Bush
*Tube* bright rose bengal. *Sepals*
also rose bengal, long, curled.
*Corolla* bell-shaped, veronica
blue. Medium-sized blooms
freely produced. *Foliage*
medium green broad, serrated.
The growth makes a good
upright bush.
(Peterson, USA, 1962)

**'Duyfken'**
Single H2 Bush
*Tube* and *sepals* light, dusky
orange-red with light green,
reflexed tips. *Corolla* pinkish-
red. *Foliage* medium green.
Growth upright and of medium
strength.
(Bromat, Australia, 1988)

# E

**'Earl of Beaconsfield'**
Single H2 Bush
*Tube* salmon pink. *Sepals* broad
and upturnèd, salmon pink with
green tips. *Corolla* vermilion.
Flowers medium-sized and
profuse. *Foliage* light to
medium green. Rather spreading
growth, vigorous, but will need
'stopping' to make a good
shape. (*F. fulgens* × 'Perfection')
(Laing, UK, 1878)

**'Earre Barre'**
Single H2 Bush
Medium-sized flower. *Tube* and
*sepals* reddish-purple. *Corolla*
white with reddish-purple base
and veins. *Foliage* medium
green. The flowers flare open
very attractively.
(de Graaff, Holland, 1989)

**'East Anglian'**
Single H2 Bush
*Tube* thick, medium length,
pale pink. *Sepals* downward-
pointing, long with turned-up
tips, and pinkish-white with
deeper stripes. *Corolla* rose
pink with an orange flush to
the base of the petals. *Foliage*
medium to dark green, with
serrated edges and red veins.
Growth is vigorous and bushy.
(Thorne, UK, 1960)

**'Easterling'**
Single H2 Bush
*Tube* and *sepals* ivory white.
*Corolla* rosy red. Flowers
medium-sized but very
floriferous. *Foliage* medium
green with serrated edges.
Growth strong, bushy and
upright. Good exhibition
cultivar.
(Goulding, UK, 1985)

**'Ebbtide'**
Double H2 Trailer
*Tube* and recurved *sepals* light
pink on the inside and white
on the outside. *Corolla* light
blue and phlox pink, changing
to lavender and phlox pink
with maturity. *Foliage* medium

green. Blooms are quite large
and can be described as
'spreading'. Very vigorous
trailing growth.
(Erickson/Lewis, USA, 1959)

**'Edale'**
Single H2 Bush
*Tube* thick, light pink. *Sepals*
rhodamine pink, slightly
upswept. *Corolla* spectrum
violet shading to imperial
purple, very compact. Large
flowers but very free. *Foliage*
medium green. Growth upright
and bushy. ('Joan Pacey' ×
'Miss Great Britain')
(Gadsby, UK, 1975)

**'Eden Beauty'**
Single H2 Trailer
*Tube* carmine. *Sepals* carmine
on the outside and crimson on
the inner, tipped green and
curve upwards gracefully.
*Corolla* fuchsia purple veined
with red, fading to magenta
rose. Large bell-shaped blooms,
very profuse. *Foliage* medium
green. Natural, self-branching,
trailer. ('Percy Holmes' ×
'Achievement')
(Holmes, R., UK, 1974)

**'Eden Dawn'**
Single H2 Bush
*Tube* pale pink. *Sepals* paler
pink, slightly reflexed.
*Corolla* pale pink. Medium-
sized flowers bell-shaped.
*Foliage* almond green and
slightly serrated. Will
produce an excellent bush or
standard.
(Mitchinson, UK, 1983)

**'Eden Lady'**
Single H2 Bush
*Tube* short, thin, pale rose.
*Sepals* Amaranth rose with a
deeper colouring underneath.
*Corolla* hyacinth blue with
slight rose colouring at base of
petals. *Foliage* medium green. Growth
upright, short-jointed, bushy. A
sister seedling to 'Border
Queen'. ('Leonora' × 'Lena
Dalton')
(Ryle, UK, 1975)

'DUYFKEN'

'EBBTIDE'

'DUSKY BEAUTY'

'DUSKY ROSE'

'EDEN BEAUTY'

**'Eden Princess'**
Single H2 Bush
*Tube* and *sepals* reddish-pink.
*Corolla* rich mallow purple.
Medium to large flowers freely
produced. *Foliage* golden
honey coloured with red
veining. Growth upright and
bushy.
(Mitchinson, UK, 1984)

**'Edie Lester'**
Single H2 Bush
*Tube* and *sepals* cherry red.
*Corolla* ruby red. *Foliage*
medium green. Growth short-
jointed and bushy, excellent for
use in small pots.
(Holmes, R., UK, 1994)

**'Edith'**
Semi-double H3 Bush
*Tube* red. *Sepals* red. *Corolla*
lavender. *Foliage* medium
green. The strong upright
growth will produce a bush
reaching a height and spread of
3ft (1m) or more. (Sport of
'Margaret')
(Brown, UK, 1980)

**'Edith Emery'**
Semi-double H2 Bush
*Tube* short, thick, waxy white.
*Sepals* white with a crêpe
reverse, reflexed. *Corolla*
amethyst violet fading to
rhodamine purple. *Foliage*
spinach green, small to medium
sized. Growth upright, strong,
self-branching and bushy.
Short-jointed, a good
exhibition plant. ('La
Campanella' × 'Flirtation
Waltz')
(Clyne, UK, 1975)

**'Edith Hall'**
*Encliandra* H1 Bush
*Tubes*, *sepals* and *corollas* red.
These are 'perfect' flowers.
*Foliage* medium green, large,
irregular. Growth strong and
bushy, but best suited to
planting in hanging pots and
hung at eye level. A bit of an
oddity.
(Breary, UK, 1987)

**'Edith Jack'**
Double H3 Bush
*Tube* and *sepals* deep pink.
*Corolla* lilac blue. The flowers
are very large and very free.
*Foliage* dark green. Growth
rather dainty, upright and
compact. H. and S. 18–24in
(45–60cm).
(Tabraham, UK, 1980)

**'Ed Lagarde'**
Double H2 Trailer
*Tube* white, short, medium
thickness. *Sepals* white, broad.
*Corolla* deep blue, very full,
frilly large bloom. *Foliage*
medium green, large, slightly
serrated. Very large-flowered
double, makes an excellent
basket.
(Pennisi, USA, 1967)

**'Edna May'**
Single H2 Bush
*Tube* brilliant scarlet. *Sepals*
and *corolla* white. *Foliage* dark
green. Very floriferous small to
medium flowers.
(Clark, UK, 1987)

**'Edna W. Smith'**
Single H2 Bush
*Tube* cerise, shortish. *Sepals*
bright cerise, tipped with green.
*Corolla* white, flushed cerise at
the base. *Foliage* medium
green. Medium-sized flowers
but very floriferous. Worth
trying as a bush or standard.
(Pacey, UK, 1985)

**'Edwin J. Goulding'**
Triphylla H1 Bush
This terminal-flowering,
triphylla-type plant has long
*tube* and *sepals* of dark red.
*Corolla* a brighter red. *Foliage*
medium to dark green.
Flowering profuse and
continuous. Excellent as a
temporary visitor to the outside
border.
(Goulding, UK, 1992)

**'Eileen Rafill'**
Single H2 Bush
*Tube* rosy cerise. *Sepals* white
with pale pink and tipped with
green. *Corolla* pale purple,

with rosy pink base to petals.
*Foliage* medium green. Growth
rather lax but will make a
good bush with supports.
(Rafill, UK, 1944)

**'Eileen Saunders'**
Single H2 Bush
*Tube* carmine, lined with
crimson. *Sepals* long, reflexing
crimson, tipped with green.
*Corolla* fuchsia purple, with
the base of the petals carmine
and veined with crimson. The
bell-shaped blooms are freely
produced. *Foliage* medium
green, paler underneath, small,
serrated. Excellent neat and
attractive bush cultivar. ('Percy
Holmes' × 'Prodigy')
(Holmes, R., UK, 1974)

**'El Camino'**
Double H2 Bush
*Tube* thin, rose red. *Sepals*
broad, rosy red. *Corolla* white,
heavily flushed and veined rose.
*Foliage* medium green. Flowers
have large central petals and
smaller spreading outer petals.
Strong, upright and bushy
growth.
(Lee, USA, 1955)

**'Elaine Ann'**
Single H2 Bush
*Tube* creamy white, slightly
veined with red. *Sepals* white
tipped with green, long and
narrow, sweeping above the
horizontal. *Corolla* also white
with a faint tinge of pink at the
base of the petals. *Foliage*
medium green. Short-jointed
cultivar which flowers
continuously and prolifically.
(('Cloverdale Pearl' × 'Sleigh
Bells') × 'Atlantic Star')
(Redfern, UK, 1989)

**'El Cid'**
Single H3 Bush
*Tube* and *sepals* deep red.
*Corolla* burgundy red. *Foliage*
medium green. Blooms
compact and well shaped, and
produced in good quantity. H.
and S. 18–24in (45–60cm).
('Empress of Prussia' ×)
(Colville, UK, 1966)

'EDITH'

'EL CAMINO'

'EDWIN J. GOULDING'

'EILEEN SAUNDERS'

'EL CID'

**'Eleanor Clark'**
Single H2 Bush
*Tube* pale is phlox pink with
deeper pink stripes. *Sepals* also
phlox pink, fully reflexed on
maturity. *Corolla* shell pink.
Medium-sized flowers freely
produced. *Foliage* light to
medium green, ovate with leaf
tip, lobed leaf base and serrate
margins. Best colour in shade.
(Sport of 'Symphony')
(Clark, UK, 1980)

**'Eleanor Leytham'**
Single H2 Bush
*Tube* and *sepals* white flushed
with pink. *Corolla* pink edged
with deeper pink on the edges of
petals. Small flowers produced
in profusion. The *foliage*
medium green, glossy, and small.
Growth bushy, free-flowering.
('Countess of Aberdeen' × 'Pink
Darling')
(Roe, UK, 1973)

**'Eleanor Rawlins'**
Single H3 Bush
*Tube* short, thick, carmine.
*Sepals* carmine, long and
upturned. *Corolla* magenta
with carmine red at the base of
the petals. *Foliage* medium
green, long and slightly
serrated. Upright, bushy plant,
self-branching, free-flowering.
H. and S. 18–24in (45–60cm).
(Wood, UK, 1954)

**'Elf'**
Single H3 Bush
*Tube* and *sepals* red. *Corolla*
cherry red. Small flowers
carried in profusion. *Foliage*
dark green. Growth is a small
bush, very compact and self-
branching. Excellent for the
edge of a hardy border. H. and
S. 6–12in (15–30cm).
(Tabraham, UK, 1976)

**'Elfrida'**
Double H3 Bush
*Tube* and *sepals* red. *Corolla*
purple. *Foliage* medium to dark
green. Very strong, bushy
grower and excellent for the
hardy border. H. and S. 24in
(60cm).
(Meillez, France, 1871)

**'Elfriede Ott'**
Triphylla type Double H1
Bush
*Tube* long. *Sepals* pointed, both
salmon pink. *Corolla* salmon
pink. *Foliage* darkish green.
Rather lax, upright growth.
('Coralle' × *F. splendens*)
(Nutzinger, Austria, 1976)

**'Elizabeth'**
Single H2 Bush
*Tube* rose opal, long, slender.
*Sepals* rose opal with green
tips, broad, tips turn up.
*Corolla* deep rich rose, with
salmon pink shading, very
compact. Long slender flowers
but very free. *Foliage* medium
green, large, finely serrated.
Difficult cultivar to train.
(Whiteman, UK, 1941)

**'Elizabeth Broughton'**
Single H2 Bush
*Tube* and *sepals* neyron rose.
*Corolla* violet purple with
white marbling. Small flowered.
*Foliage* is medium green.
Growth medium upright.
(Gadsby, UK, 1975)

**'Elizabeth Honnorine'**
Single H2 Lax bush
Medium-sized flower. *Tube*
white, flushed with green.
*Sepals* white. *Corolla* deep
purple violet. *Foliage* medium
green. Growth lax upright.
(de Cooker, Holland, 1991)

**'Elizabeth Tompkins'**
Double H2 Trailer
Medium-sized flowers. *Tubes*
short, bright red. *Sepals* broad,
recurved, also bright red.
*Corolla* very full, lilac pink
petals heavily flushed and
veined dark rose, fading to a
light purple. *Foliage* medium
green. Very strong and
vigorous, and makes a good
basket. (Sport of 'Frau Hilde
Rademacher')
(Tompkins, UK, 1993)

**'Ellen Morgan'**
Double H2 Bush
*Tube* short, thin, blush white
lined with green. *Sepals* blush
white on the outside tipped

with green and a green line
down the centre, and neyron
rose on the inside. *Corolla*
mallow purple with neyron
rose at the base of the petals.
Medium sized blooms freely
produced. *Foliage* medium
green, small to medium-sized,
broad, serrated. Upright self-
branching growth. ('Phyllis' ×)
(Holmes, R., UK, 1976)

**'Ellen van Swaay'**
Single H2 Lax bush
Medium-sized flowers. *Tubes*
and *sepals* deep carmine red.
*Corolla* light purple. *Foliage*
medium green. Growth can be
described as a lax bush.
(Stoel, Holland, 1990)

**'Elsie Downey'**
Single H2 Bush
*Tube* and *sepals* neyron rose.
*Corolla* aster violet with pink
veining. Upright-facing flowers
of medium size, produced in
good numbers. *Foliage* medium
green.
(Barnes, UK, 1991)

**'Elsie Mitchell'**
Double H2 Bush
*Tube* pink. *Sepals* pink at base,
shaded to white, green tips,
semi-reflexing. *Corolla* sea
lavender with pink blush.
*Foliage* medium green, ovate,
small to medium size. Flowers
a very nice medium size, tightly
formed. The best colour is
produced in the shade.
(Ryle, UK, 1980)

**'Elsie Vert'**
Double H2 Bush
Medium-sized flowers. *Tubes*
and *sepals* red. *Corolla* purple.
*Foliage* medium to dark green.
Good strong upright growth.
(Lemoine, France, 1898)

**'Elsine'**
Single H2 Bush
Medium-sized flowers. *Tubes*
old rose in colour. *Sepals* phlox
pink. *Corolla* petunia purple.
*Foliage* medium green. Growth
is fairly strong, upright and
bushy.
(Bogemann, Holland, 1987)

100

'ELEANOR CLARK'

'ELEANOR LEYTHAM'

'ELIZABETH'

'ELIZABETH BROUGHTON'

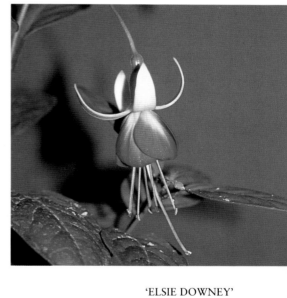

'ELIZABETH HONNORINE'

'ELSIE DOWNEY'

**'Elsstar'**
Semi-double H2 Trailer
Medium-sized flowers. *Tube*
white, striped with rose. *Sepals*
white flushed rose. *Corolla*
aubergine. *Foliage* medium
green. The trailing habit of the
plant makes it ideal for
hanging containers.
(Elsman, Holland, 1989)

**'Emile de Wildeman'**
Double H2 Bush
This fuchsia is synonymous
with 'Fascination'. *Tubes* short,
thick, carmine red. *Sepals*
carmine red, broad and
completely reflex over the tube.
*Corolla* pink flushed with
cerise veining. Flower very full.
*Foliage* medium green, slightly
serrated. Growth upright,
bushy, self-branching and very
free-flowering, especially for
the size of the flower.
(Lemoine, France, 1905)

**'Emile Zola'**
Single H2/3 Bush
*Tube* scarlet cerise. *Sepals*
reflexing, scarlet cerise. *Corolla*
bright rose magenta, compact,
medium sized. Flowers
medium-size and bell-shaped.
*Foliage* medium to darkish
green. The bushy plant carries
its flowers fairly freely.
(Lemoine, France, 1910)

**'Emily Austen'**
Single H2 Bush
*Tube* and *sepals* white to light
pink. *Corolla* rose. *Foliage*
medium green. Medium-sized
flower produced on an upright
and short-jointed bush. Very
floriferous and well worth
trying.
(Bielby/Oxtoby, UK, 1980)

**'Emma Louise'**
Double H2 Trailer
Superb small cultivar. *Tube* and
*sepals* pale rose. *Corolla* opens
blue-violet changing to mauve-
pink. *Foliage* medium green.
Trailing growth and small to
medium-sized flowers make
this an ideal plant for a
hanging pot.
(Horsham, UK, 1991)

**'Emma Massey'**
Single H2 Bush
*Tube* and *sepals* waxy red.
*Corolla* soft purple with red at
the base of the petals. *Foliage*
medium green. Fairly strong
upright and bushy growth.
(Holmes, R., UK, 1992)

**'Emma Rowell'**
Single H2 Trailer
*Tube* short, greenish white.
*Sepals* long, white tipped green
flushed pink on the underside,
and are held back against the
tube. *Corolla* white, also
flushed with pink. *Foliage*
medium green. Growth
naturally trailing.
(Rowell, UK, 1991)

**'Empress of Prussia'**
Single H3 Bush
A superb plant for permanent
planting outside. *Tube* short,
thick, scarlet. *Sepals* scarlet,
broad and held slightly above
the horizontal. *Corolla* reddish-
magenta. *Foliage* medium to
dark green, with slightly serrated
edges. Very floriferous indeed,
each leaf joint carrying up to
eight medium-sized blooms.
Very strong, self-branching and
upright in its growth. Cannot be
recommended too highly. H. and
S. up to 39in (100cm).
(Hoppe, UK, 1868)

**'Enchanted'**
Double H2 Lax bush
*Tube* short, rose red. *Sepals*
long, broad, reflexing, rosy red.
*Corolla* campanula blue, the
outer petals overlaid with pink.
The fairly large blooms are
very freely produced. *Foliage*
medium green. The growth is
rather lax so can be used for
bushes or baskets. Sister
seedling to 'Swingtime'
('Titanic' × 'Yuletide')
(Tiret, USA, 1951)

**F. encliandra ssp encliandra**
Single H2 Bush
The very small flowers and
very small foliage of this group
of fuchsias make them
extremely popular with all
types of growers. Also the

wiriness of their stems make
them the ideal subjects for use
in training around wire
supports. Axillary flowering
single. The blooms are scarlet
and are 'perfect'. The anthers,
styles and stigma are white.
The foliage is fernlike with
bright green leaves and serrated
edges.
(Steudal, 1837)

**F. encliandra ssp tetradactyla**
Single H2 Bush
Very small flowers. *Tubes* and
*sepals* rose. *Corolla* white.
*Foliage* bright green. Growth
very strong but wiry.
(Steudal, 1840)

**'Enfant Prodigue'**
Semi-double H3 Bush
*Tube* and *sepals* of this old
hardy are crimson. *Corolla*
bluish-purple, ageing to
magenta with splashes of pink
at the base of the petals.
*Foliage* mid to dark green,
small to medium size, serrated.
Growth is upright and bushy.
A very dependable cultivar. H.
and S. up to 4ft (120cm).
(Lemoine, France, 1887)

**'English Rose'**
Double H2 Bush
*Tube* and *sepals* white tipped
with green. *Corolla* imperial
purple. Flowers fairly large and
of excellent shape, freely
produced. *Foliage* medium
green. Natural growth is as a
self-branching bush.
(Pacey, UK, 1987)

**'Eppsii'**
Single H2 Bush
*Tube* light pink, long. *Sepals*
rosy cerise, tipped with green.
*Corolla* rosy magenta.
Medium-sized flowers very
freely produced. *Foliage* light
green natural growth of the
plant is as a bush. Will make a
good standard quite quickly.
(Epps, UK, 1844)

'EMPRESS OF PRUSSIA'
*F. ENCLIANDRA* SSP. *TETRADACTYLA*

'EMMA LOUISE'

'EMILY AUSTEN'

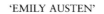

'ENFANT PRODIGUE'

**'Erica Julie'**
Double H2 Bush
*Tube* small, white, fluted. *Sepals* white, upswept, have the faintest of blushed pink near the tube. *Corolla* white with a wavy petal edge. *Foliage* lettuce green and slightly lighter underneath. Good short-jointed and self-branching plant. ('Paula Jane' × 'Flirtation Waltz')
(Tite, UK, 1986)

**'Eric Weeks'**
Semi-double H3 Bush
*Tube* pinkish-white flushed with orange. *Sepals* vermilion overlaid with pink. *Corolla* orange. *Foliage* dark green on top, medium green on the undersurface. Fairly free-flowering cultivar which can be used for the hardy border. H. and S. 24–30in (60–75cm).
(Weeks, UK, 1987)

**'Erika Koth'**
Triphylla type H1 Bush
The rather long *tube*, *sepals* and *corolla* are all rosy orange. *Foliage* olive green, leaves almost round. Strong upright grower but very frost shy. ('Coralle' × *F. boliviana*)
(Nutzinger, Austria, 1976)

**'Ernestine'**
Double H2 Trailer
*Tubes* flesh-coloured. *Sepals* slightly more orange. *Corolla* scarlet with a hint of orange. Growth very strong and spreading. *Foliage* medium green. Will make a large basket very quickly.
(Stubbs, USA, 1981)

**'Ernest Rankin'**
Single H2 Bush
Medium-sized flower. *Tube* and *sepals* deep carmine. *Corolla* blackish-purple. *Foliage* medium to dark green. Growth is lax upright and bushy.
(Wright, UK, 1991)

**'Ernie Bromley'**
Single H2 Trailer
*Tubes* and *sepals* pink. *Corolla* violet or light mauve. Flowers medium-sized. *Foliage* has a

very distinct yellow tinge to the edge of each leaf. The plant is very vigorous and self-branching. Makes an excellent basket.
(Goulding, UK, 1988)

**'Eroica'**
Single H2 Bush
*Tube* short, thick, salmon pink. *Sepals* red, sweep up at the tips. *Corolla* claret but quickly fades to red. Large flowers very freely produced. *Foliage* light green spear shaped.
(Howarth, UK, 1979)

**'Estelle Marie'**
Single H2 Bush
*Tube* greenish white, short, thick. *Sepals* white, with green tips, completely recurving. *Corolla* violet, darkening when mature, white at base of petals. Blooms small to medium-sized, held upwards and outwards. Very floriferous. *Foliage* medium to dark green. The growth is short, fairly stiff and short jointed. Perfect for summer bedding, patio tubs or on the show bench.
(Newton, USA, 1973)

**'Esther Devine'**
Single H2 Bush
*Tube* crimson. *Sepals* rich crimson, held well back from the tube. *Corolla* wisteria blue, veined with fuchsia purple at the base of the petals. Flowers very large, and freely produced. *Foliage* medium green. Growth upright and bushy. Needs regular pinching.
(Pacey, UK, 1981)

**'Eternal Flame'**
Semi-double H2 Bush
*Tube* salmon pink. *Sepals* also dark salmon-pink, tipped with green, with orange on the underside. *Corolla* smoky rose streaked with orange and salmon at the base of the petals. *Foliage* darkish green and very attractive. The many flowers are carried on strong upright growth.
(Paskesen, USA, 1941)

**'Ethel May Lester'**
Double H2 Bush
Small flowers. *Tubes* and *sepals* cardinal red. *Corolla* pansy violet. *Foliage* small, medium green. The size of the flowers and foliage make this cultivar an ideal candidate for use in 'small pots' or when attempting 'bonsai' methods.
(Holmes, R., UK, 1990)

**'Ethel Weeks'**
Semi-double H2 Lax bush
*Tube* short, thin, rose red. *Sepals* upswept with reflexing tips, rosy red on top with crepe rose-red underneath. *Corolla* whitish rose pink. *Foliage* dark green, lighter underneath. Growth is intermediate, lax for a bush and rather stiff for a trailer. Self-branching and short-jointed.
(Weeks, UK, 1986)

**'Ethel Wilson'**
Single H2 Bush
*Tube* short, pale pink. *Sepals* pale pink shading to a white tip. *Corolla* has a pink base darkening to cerise. Medium-sized flowers freely produced. *Foliage* medium green. Strong upright and bushy growth. ('Brutus' × 'Swingtime')
(Wilson, UK, 1967)

**'Eusebia'**
Double H2 Trailer
*Tube* short, white. *Sepals* long, flyway, white with rose pink flush. *Corolla* red, in strong contrast with the sepals. *Foliage* medium green. Growth strong, short-jointed and spreading. Early 'stopping' is necessary to develop bushy-type growth. Makes good baskets or weeping standards. ('Pepi' × ('Applause' × 'Bicentenial'))
(Stubbs, USA, 1982)

'ERNEST RANKIN'                    'ERNIE BROMLEY'

'ESTELLE MARIE'                    'ETERNAL FLAME'

**'Eva Boerg'**
Single/semi-double H2/3 Bush
or trailer
*Tube* greenish-white, short,
thick. *Sepals* pinkish-white on
top and green-tipped, pink crêpe
underneath, broad, reflexed.
*Corolla* pinkish-purple splashed
with pink, paler at base.
Medium-sized flowers very
freely produced. *Foliage* light
green, oval, serrated, medium-
sized. Will make a good basket,
is quite hardy as a low-growing
shrub in the border, can be
trained as a standard or as a
bush for show purposes.
H. and S. 18in (45cm).
(Yorke, UK, 1943)

**'Eva Watkins'**
Double H2 Bush
*Tube* dark red. *Sepals* dark red
on the upper surface, crêped
lighter red underneath. *Corolla*
light pink maturing to pink
with a central red vein. *Foliage*
medium green. Fairly large
blooms which are freely
produced. ('R.A.F.' × 'R.A.F.')
(Windsor, UK, 1989)

**'Eve Hollands'**
Double H2 Bush
*Tube* and *sepals* blush pink.
*Corolla* plum-coloured. *Foliage*
medium green. Growth strong,
short-jointed, self-branching
and upright.
(Goulding, UK, 1994)

**'Evening Sky'**
Double H2 Trailer
*Tube* long, thin, eau-de-nil
flushed rose bengal. *Sepals*
long, of the same colouring and
reflex. *Corolla* violet flushed
with ruby on first opening with
paler flush of ruby, pink and
orange as the flower matures.
The large full double flowers
are freely produced. *Foliage*
dark green, red veins, serrated.
The growth is of a natural
trailer so will make a superb
and eye-catching basket.
(Travis, UK, 1957)

**'Evensong'**
Single H2 Bush
This is a complete white 'self'.

*Tube* and *sepals* white. *Corolla*
white, loose, bell-shaped.
Flowers medium-sized, freely
produced. *Foliage* lightish
green, serrated. The growth is
naturally upright and compact,
self-branching.
(Colville, UK, 1967)

**'Excalibur'**
Single/semi-double H2 Bush
*Tube*, *sepals* and *corolla* of this
attractive plant are rose pink.
Petaloids are contained within
the outer ring of petals. *Foliage*
medium green. Growth stiffly
upright and self-branching.
Excellent for use on a patio or
outdoor bedding.
(Goulding, UK, 1983)

**F. excorticata**
Species H2/3 Bush
The small flowers are of
unusual appearance and
distinct in shape. Not produced
very freely on very large 'trees'
in its native New Zealand.
*Tube* and *sepals* green, turn to
purple. *Corolla* purplish-back.
The pollen on the stamens is
bright blue. The large *leaves*
are dark green and glossy on
the top surface, silvery green
underneath. Given sufficient
root room and space, will
achieve massive proportions
under glass and could be
considered hardy in some parts
of the British Isles.
(Forster, New Zealand, 1776)

**F. excorticata var purpurescens**
Species H2/3 Bush
The description of this species
is the same as that described as
*F. excorticata* with the
exception that the *corolla* is a
definite purple colour.
(Forster, New Zealand, 1776)

**'Expo '86'**
Double H2 Trailer
*Tube* pink. *Sepals* fully upswept
with green recurved tips, white
on the upper side and orange
pink underneath. *Corolla* a
very striking fluorescent red
and orange with wavy edges to
the petals. *Foliage* medium
green and much lighter on the

underside. Growth is naturally
trailing so will make a good
basket.
('Diana' × 'Corsage')
(Wood, USA, 1986)

# F

**'Fabian Franck'**
Triphylla type H1 Bush
*Tube* long, thin, flares
outwards to join the *sepals*.
Both tangerine-coloured. Short
petals of the *corolla* are a
brighter orange. Multiple
blooms carried on bushy
plants. *Foliage* medium to
darker green.
(Franck, Holland, 1991)

**'Fairy Tales'**
Semi-double H2 Trailer
*Tube* short. *Sepals* reflexing,
*corolla* all candy pink.
Medium-sized blooms very
freely produced. Plants very
short-jointed and as natural
trailer will produce a superb
basket quite quickly. *Foliage*
medium green.
(Lockerbie, Australia, 1972)

**'Falklands'**
Semi-double H2 Bush
*Tube* and *sepals* white shaded
with roseine. *Corolla* fuchsia
purple maturing to rose bengal.
The half-flared, medium-sized
blooms freely produced.
*Foliage* medium green with
distinct darker green vein and
pink stems. Growth self-
branching and short-jointed.
Will make a good bush. ('Lye's
Unique' × *F. fulgens*)
(Dunnett, UK, 1984)

**'Falling Stars'**
Single H2 Trailer
*Tube* and *sepals* pale scarlet.
*Corolla* turkey red with a slight
orange tint. Perfectly shaped
flowers produced very freely.
*Foliage* medium green, serrated.
Regular 'stopping' will be
necessary to get good bushy
and trailing effect. Worth
growing as a weeping standard.
(Reiter, USA, 1941)

'EVENING SKY'

'EVENSONG'

'EXCALIBUR'

'FABIAN FRANCK'

'FAIRY TALES'

'FALKLANDS'

**'Fancy Flute'**
Single H2 Bush
*Tube* and *sepals* white. *Corolla*
magenta, petals have red edges
and a velvety texture. *Foliage*
medium green. Medium-sized
flowers freely produced on
good, strong, upright and
bushy growth.
(Handley, UK, 1972)

**'Fancy Pants'**
Double H2 Trailer
*Tube* and *sepals* red. *Corolla*
violet maturing to a rosy red.
*Foliage* pale green, serrated.
Growth naturally spreading
and trailing, lends itself for use
in baskets.
(Reedstrom, USA, 1961)

**'Fanfare'**
Single (Triphylla type) H2
Bush
*Tube* is some 2in (5cm) long,
pink with carmine stripes.
*Sepals* light carmine tipped
with green, held halfway below
the horizontal. *Corolla* bright
vermilion. *Foliage* large, (up to
4in (10cm)) in length, dark
green. Very strong, upright and
stiff growth. Objects to
constant 'stopping'. Blooms
late in season into winter. (*F.
denticulata* × *F. leptopoda*)
(Reiter, USA, 1941)

**'Fascination'**
(Synonymous with 'Emile de
Wildeman')
Double H2 Bush
*Tube* short, thick, carmine red.
*Sepals* carmine red, broad and
completely reflex over the tube.
*Corolla* pink with cerise
veining, flushed with pink.
Flower very full. *Foliage*
medium green, slightly
serrated. Growth upright,
bushy, self-branching. Very
free-flowering for the size of
the bloom.
(Lemoine, France, 1905)

**'Fasna 1100'**
Single H2 Trailer
Medium-sized flower. *Tubes*
and *sepals* light reddish-purple.
*Corolla* aubergine. *Foliage*
medium green. The natural

trailing growth makes this
plant very useful in baskets.
(Beije, Holland, 1991)

**'Fatima'**
Single H2 Bush
Medium-sized flower *Tube* and
*sepals* salmon orange. *Corolla*
orange. *Foliage* medium green.
Growth very strong, upright.
Flowers are produced in
profusion and early in the
season.
(Giessen, Holland, 1989)

**'Feepie'**
Single H2 Bush
*Tubes* and *sepals* rose. *Corolla*
rose red, small. *Foliage* small
medium green. The plant makes
a very attractive small bush.
(Franck, Holland, 1988)

**'Fenman'**
Single H2 Bush
*Tubes* and *sepals* flesh pink.
*Corolla* pink, thickly textured.
Large blooms produced very
freely. *Foliage* medium green.
Growth strongly upright, and
will make an excellent bush or
standard.
(Goulding, UK, 1985)

**'Fergie'**
Double H2 Bush
*Tube* and *sepals* shell pink.
*Corolla* deep lavender. *Foliage*
medium green. Flowers fairly
large and are freely produced.
Makes an attractive bush.
(Bridgland, UK, 1989)

**'Fey'**
Double H2 Stiff trailer
*Tube* and *sepals* waxy white.
*Corolla* pale lavender. *Foliage*
medium green. Stiff growth
entails regular 'stopping' so
that the trailing habit can be
encouraged. Excellent in mixed
baskets and will also make a
fine semi-weeping standard.
(Lockerbie, Australia, 1970)

**'Fiery Spider'**
Single H2 Trailer
*Tube* long, thin, carmine. *Sepals*
long and narrow, pale salmon
tipped with green. *Corolla*
crimson with a pronounced

orange flush. Flowers long,
thin, produced very early in the
season. *Foliage* medium green.
An excellent basket can be
produced, but it is advised that
a number of plants are used to
get the fullness required.
(Munker, USA, 1960)

**'Filigree' ('Filigrain')**
Single H2 Bush
*Tube* and *sepals* scarlet on
topside, crimson underneath.
*Corolla* light purple with dark
veining. Flowers medium-sized,
non-flaring and bell-shaped.
*Foliage* lettuce green. Upright,
bushy growth requires early
'stopping' to achieve good
shape.
(Brouwer, Holland, 1985)

**'Finn'**
Single H2 Bush
*Tubes* ivory. *Sepals* white,
gracefully upturned. *Corolla* an
unusual shade of rusty red.
*Foliage* medium green. Flowers
produced in profusion from an
early start. Strong upright
growth and a good bushy
habit. The distinctive colouring
of the flowers is an eye catcher.
A very attractive fuchsia.
(Goulding, UK, 1988)

**'Fiona'**
Single H2 Trailer
*tube* long, white, thin. *Sepals*
flyaway, white with green tips,
long, narrow, recurve to tube
twisting slightly. *Corolla* pale
lavender gradually changing to
mauve, white at petal base.
*Foliage* medium green, finely
serrated, medium-sized. The
growth is strong and spreading.
Breaks quite naturally and its
trailing habit ensures a good
basket. Prone to *botrytis*.
(Clark, UK, 1958)

**'Fiona Jane'**
Single H2 Trailer
*Tube* and *sepals* neyron rose.
*Corolla* pale lilac with a dark
edge. *Foliage* medium green.
The natural trailing habit
makes it very suitable for
hanging containers.
(Wilkinson, UK, 1991)

'FASCINATION'

'FEY'

'FASNA 1100'

'FIERY SPIDER'

'FIONA JANE'

**'Fireflush'**
Single H2 Bush
*Tube* and *sepals* rosy red.
*Corolla* orangey-apricot.
Medium-sized flowers very
freely produced. *Foliage*
medium green. The natural
growth is upright.
(Waltz, USA, 1943)

**'Firefly'**
Single H2 Bush
Almost a self-coloured, as *tube*,
*sepals* and *corolla* are a vivid
red. *Foliage* medium green.
Medium-sized flowers freely
produced. Growth is strong
and upright. ('Pride of Exeter'
× 'Rolla')
(Niederholzer, USA, 1940)

**'Firelite'**
Double H2 Trailer
*Tube* white. *Sepals* also white
and curl on the edges. *Corolla*
a brilliant glowing carnival red.
Flowers fairly large, fluffy and
flaring, and create a superb
colour contrast. *Foliage* light
green. The growth is very lax
so can be used as a trailer or a
bush plant given the necessary
supports.
(Waltz, USA, 1965)

**'Fire Mountain'**
Double H2 Trailer
*Tube* flesh coloured. *Sepals* pale
orange slightly curving. *Corolla*
darker orange. Opens compact,
then spreads. *Foliage* medium
green, red veining on new
growth. The spreading growth
makes it a good plant to use in
baskets. Immature plants show
single and semi-double blooms.
(Stubbs, USA, 1980)

**'Firenza'**
Double H2 Bush
*Tube* short pink. *Sepals* deep
rose pink held at the
horizontal. *Corolla* deep
lavender flushed with bright
pink. *Foliage* yellowish-green,
serrated edges. The upright
growth is self-branching
and produces a good bush
shape. ('Igloo Maid' × 'Joan
Gilbert')
(Howarth, UK, 1983)

**'Firenzi'**
Single H2 Bush
*Tube* and *sepals* ruby red.
*Corolla* crimson. *Foliage*
medium green. Growth rather
lax and will need supports for
the medium-sized flowers.
('Rufus' × 'Herald')
(Roe, UK, 1981)

**'First Lady'**
Double H2 Lax bush or
trailer
*Tube* long, thick, pinkish white.
*Sepals* deep pink to coral, green
tips, slightly recurved, long
narrow. *Corolla* deep clear
pink, slightly flaring. The large
blooms are fully double.
*Foliage* dark green with red
veins, finely serrated. For a
large double this cultivar is
very free-flowering. Makes an
excellent basket or supported
bush.
(Stubbs, USA, 1973)

**'First Success'**
Species hybrid H1 Bush
*Tube* small, pink. *Sepals* very
small, light pink with recurved
tips. *Corolla* opens light pink
and matures even lighter.
Flowers very small, not
exceeding ¼in (1cm). *Foliage*
large (5 × 2½in (13 × 6cm))
medium green. Flowers very
sparse, blooms in clusters. (*F.
paniculata* × *F. splendens*)
(Weedda, Holland, 1985)

**'Flair'**
Double H2 Trailer
*Tube* and *sepals* white. *Corolla*
raspberry pink. *Foliage*
medium green. The blooms are
large and are freely produced.
The natural trailing will
produce a good basket.
(Tiret, USA, 1961)

**'Flame'**
Single H2 Bush
*Tube* and *sepals* ivory. *Corolla*
a reddish-orange. *Foliage*
medium green. The flowers are
of medium size and are freely
produced. Growth is upright,
making a good bush.
(Niederholzer, USA, 1941)

**'Flash'**
Single H3 Bush
*Tube* thin, light magenta.
*Sepals* light magenta, broad,
short. *Corolla* also a light
magenta. Might almost be
called a 'self-coloured'. *Foliage*
small, light green, finely
serrated. Although the flowers
are small they are produced in
great quantities. H. and S. up
to 30in (75cm).
(Hazard and Hazard, USA,
1930)

**'Flashlight'**
Single H3 Bush
*Tube* pale pink, very short and
thin. *Sepals* pale pink, tipped
with green. *Corolla* rose
purple. Flowers freely
produced. *Foliage* small,
medium green. H. and S. 12in
(30cm). ('Flash' × *F.
magellanica* var *alba*)
(Gadsby, UK, 1968)

**'Flat Jack O' Lancashire'**
Double H3 Bush
Large flowers. *Tube* deep red,
short. *Sepals* upswept. *Corolla*
quatrefoil light purple with red
veins. *Foliage* medium to dark
green. H. and S. 36–48in
(90–120cm).
(Jones, UK, 1991)

**'Flavia'**
Double H2 Trailer
*Tube* and *sepals* pink. *Corolla*
deep lilac. *Foliage* medium
green. Flowers large, very
freely produced. A natural
trailer so will make a good
basket.
(Tiret, USA, 1971)

**'Flim Flam'**
Single H2 Bush
*Tube* longish vermilion pink.
*Sepals* held at the horizontal,
rhodonite red on the upper side
and geranium pink on the
lower. *Sepals* tipped with
yellow-green, and reflex.
*Corolla* opens rose purple and
matures to rose red. *Foliage*
medium green with light olive
green on the undersurface.
(de Graaff, Holland, 1985)

'FIREFLY'

'FIRELITE'

'FIRE MOUNTAIN'

'FIRENZA'

'FIRST SUCCESS'

'FLASH'

**'Flirt'**
Single H2 Trailer
Flowers small. *Tubes* spinel
red. *Sepals* carmine. *Corolla*
reddish-purple. *Foliage* medium
green and the natural growth is
as a trailer.
(de Graaff, Holland, 1987)

**'Flirtation Waltz'**
Double H2 Bush
*Tube* white, short. *Sepals*
white. *Corolla* baby pink.
*Foliage* medium green. The
upright growth is strong and
self-branching. (A better shape
is produced if the growing tip
of the plant is not removed but
natural branching is allowed to
take place.) A superb cultivar
and excellent show plant but
will need care in transporting
as bruising of the petals readily
occurs.
(Waltz, USA, 1962)

**'Flocon de Neige'**
Single H2 Bush
*Tube* and *sepals* short cerise.
Medium-sized blooms. *Corolla*
creamy white, faintly flushed
with cerise. *Foliage* medium
green. The fairly strong growth
is upright, self-branching,
vigorous, free-flowering. Easy
to train.
(Lemoine, France, 1884)

**'Florence Mary Abbott'**
Single H2 Lax bush
*Tube* and *sepals* short, white.
*Corolla* white. Flowers of
medium-size and held
prominently from the plant.
*Foliage* light green. In spite of
the colouring the flowers are
slow to spoil; they are held on
spreading, self-branching
growth. Useful in hanging pots
but perhaps even better as
supported bushes in pots very
popular.
(Goulding, UK, 1983)

**'Florence Turner'**
Single H3 Bush
*Tube* pale pink, short. *Sepals*
white. *Corolla* pale pinkish-
purple. Medium-sized flowers
produced very freely early in the
season. *Foliage* medium green.

Growth upright and bushy. H.
and S. 24–30in (60–75cm).
(Turner, UK, 1955)

**'Florentina'**
Double H2 Lax bush or
trailer
*Tube* and fully recurving *sepals*
frosty white. *Corolla* burgundy
red with a slight grey cast.
*Foliage* medium green, red
veins, longish. Growth is
moderately strong and of
spreading habit. The lax
growth will require supporting
if used in pots, but is excellent
for full or half baskets.
(Tiret, America, 1960)

**'Floretta'**
Single H2 Bush
*Tube* and *sepals* white.
Medium-sized flowers. The
petals of the *corolla* are
coloured with shades of purple.
*Foliage* medium to dark green.
(Dijkstra, Holland, 1991)

**'Florrie Bambridge'**
Single H2 Bush
*Tube* long, thin, light red.
*Sepals* held half up with
recurved tips, bright light red
on top and crêped light red
underneath. *Corolla* opens
white with pink veining
maturing to plain white.
*Foliage* medium green, but is
much lighter underneath. The
flowers are large as befits a
seedling from 'Swingtime'.
(Windsor, UK, 1966)

**'Flower Dream'**
Double H2 Trailer
*Tube* rose. *Sepals* flushed rose.
*Corolla* white. A very attractive
medium-sized, but fully double
flower. *Foliage* medium green.
The growth is very willowy and
will therefore make an excellent
plant for a hanging container.
('Merry Mary' × 'Bora Bora')
(Rijff, Holland, 1983)

**'Fluffy Frills'**
Double H2 Semi-trailer
*Tube* and *sepals* claret rose.
*Corolla* amaranth pink. *Foliage*
dark green with red veining.
The large to medium-sized

flowers are freely produced.
The semi-trailing type of
growth requires frequent
'stopping' to produce best
results.
(Stubbs, USA, 1976)

**'Flyaway'**
Double H2 Bush
*Tube* short, white. *Sepals*
reflexed, white with a frosty
rose-madder reverse. *Corolla*
spectrum violet with rose-
madder flush at the base of the
petals. *Foliage* medium green,
red veins, long and pointed.
The large blooms are fairly
freely produced on an upright-
growing bush.
(Crockett, UK, 1965)

**'Fly By Night'**
Double H2 Bush
*Tube* and *sepals* cherry red.
*Corolla* fuchsia purple flushed
and edged with deep royal
purple. *Foliage* medium to dark
green. The blooms are large
and freely produced over a
long period. Growth is upright
and bushy.
(Crockett, UK, 1965)

**'Flying Cloud'**
Double H2 Lax bush
*Tube* white. *Sepals* white,
tipped with green, faint shade
of pink on the undersurface.
*Corolla* white touched with
pink at the base of the petals.
Flowers quite large and very
free. *Foliage* light to medium
green. Growth is rather lax so
supports will be needed for the
heavy blooms.
(Reiter, USA, 1949)

**'Flying Scotsman'**
Double H2 Bush
*Tubes* short, thick, white with
pale pink flush deepening with
maturity. *Sepals* dark pink on
top, lighter beneath, recurve.
The petals of the *corolla* have
rosy-red backgrounds with
white streaks. *Foliage* medium
green. Good strong upright
growth suitable for either
standards or temporary outside
bedding.
(Goulding, UK, 1985)

'FLOCON DE NEIGE'

'FLIRTATION WALTZ'

'FLUFFY FRILLS'

'FLYING CLOUD'

'FLYING SCOTSMAN'

**'Foline'**
Single H2 Bush
*Tube* purplish-red. *Sepals* dark
purplish-red. *Corolla* dark
reddish-purple. Medium-sized
flowers freely produced.
*Foliage* medium green. The
overall colour of each flower
can be described as 'aubergine'
and is considered very
attractive.
(Bogemann, Germany, 1987)

**'Foolke'**
Single H2 Bush
*Tube* and *sepals* dark magenta.
*Corolla* dark plum. *Foliage*
medium to dark green but
lighter on the undersurface.
The flowers are of medium size
and are carried on upright-
growing stems.
(Bogemann, Germany, 1987)

**'Forest King'**
Single H2 Trailer
*Tube* magenta. *Sepals* magenta,
green tips. *Corolla* magenta-
violet. The medium to large
flowers are barrel-shaped and
freely produced. *Foliage* dark
green, with red central vein,
long, oval, slightly serrated.
The natural growth is lax and
trailing so will make a good
basket.
(Tolley, UK, 1978)

**'Forget Me Not'**
Single H2 Bush
*Tube* pale pink. *Sepals* pale
flesh pink, long, narrow,
completely recurved. *Corolla*
palish-blue, matures to pale
mauve. Small flowers produced
early and in quantity. *Foliage*
medium green. Frequent
'stopping' is necessary to
encourage good bushiness.
(Banks, UK, 1866)

**'Fort Bragg'**
Double H2 Trailer
Sport of 'Enchanted'. *Tube* rose
pink. *Sepals* broad, upturned,
rose coloured. *Corolla* pale
lavender rose with bluish tinge,
petals slightly veined with rose.
*Foliage* medium green. The
flowers are large and freely
produced. The natural trailing

habit of the plant makes it an
ideal subject for hanging
containers.
(Waltx, USA, 1967)

**'Forward Look'**
Single H2 Bush
*Tube* china-rose. *Sepals* china-
rose, tipped with green.
*Corolla* wisteria blue fading to
violet. The medium-sized
flowers are held out
horizontally from the plant.
*Foliage* medium green. The
growth is upright and bushy.
(Gadsby, UK, 1972)

**'Fountains Abbey'**
Double H2 Lax bush
*Tube* white. *Sepals* pinkish-
white on the top surface, baby-
pink underneath, tipped with
green. *Corolla* lavender blue
flushed and veined pink. The
medium-sized blooms are very
free for a double. *Foliage*
medium green. Growth is lax
so will need supporting if used
as a bush. ('Coquet Bell' ×
'Blush o' Dawn')
(Akers, UK, 1981)

**'Foxgrove Wood'**
Single H2/3 Bush
The delightful flowers on this
cultivar have *tubes* and *sepals*
which are pink. *Corolla* blue.
*Foliage* medium green. Growth
upright, short-jointed, bushy.
H. and S. 24–30in (60–75cm).
(Stiff, UK, 1993)

**'Foxtrot'**
Semi-double H2 Bush
*Tube* short, pale cerise. *Sepals*
pale cerise, tipped with green
and standing well out. *Corolla*
pale lavender with a pink base.
Flowers medium-sized, freely
produced and semi-flared.
*Foliage* small and pale green,
serrated. Growth upright and
bushy. Easy to grow and train.
(Tolley, UK, 1974)

**'Francois Villon'**
Single H2 Trailer
*Tube* long, thin, carmine rose.
*Sepals* horizontal, carmine and
very narrow. *Corolla* opens
ruby red but matures to

cardinal red. Medium-sized
flowers freely produced. *Foliage*
olive green and much lighter on
the undersurface. A natural
trailer, will make a good basket.
(de Graaff, Holland, 1985)

**'Frank Sandford'**
Double H2 Trailer
Large flowers. *Tubes* peach-
coloured. *Sepals* pink. *Corolla*
delightful light pink and dark
rose. *Foliage* medium green.
The natural habit is to trail so
will make a good basket.
(Stubbs, USA, 1992)

**'Frank Saunders'**
Single H2 Bush
*Tube* and *sepals* white. Medium
to small Flowers. *Corolla* lilac
pink. Flowers, produced in
profusion, push 'up and out'.
*Foliage* dark green, small. The
upright growth makes a very
attractive pot plant.
(Dyos, UK, 1984)

**'Frank Unsworth'**
Double H2 Trailer
*Tube* of this superb, near all-
white basket cultivar pure
white. *Sepals* white, tipped
green and fly back almost to
cover the tube. *Corolla* white
with the faintest touch of pink
at base of petals. *Foliage* small
and dark green, an excellent
contrast to the flowers. Short-
jointed but lax in growth.
Responds well to pinching.
Needs shade for best colour.
(Clark, UK, 1982)

**'Franska'**
Single H2 Trailing
*Tube* and *sepals* white, striped
with rose. *Corolla* purple.
*Foliage* medium green. The
natural habit of this cultivar is
to trail, so will make a good
basket.
(Krom, Holland, 1991)

**'Franz Veerman'**
Single H2 Trailer
*Tube* and *sepals* light rose.
*Corolla* deep purple-violet.
*Foliage* medium green. A
natural trailer.
(Franck, Holland, 1989)

'FOREST KING'

'FORGET ME NOT'

'FORT BRAGG'

'FRANK UNSWORTH'

**'Frau Alice Hoffman'**
Semi-double  H3  Bush
*Tube* and *sepals* rose. *Corolla*
white, veined rose. *Foliage*
medium to dark green. Growth
upright and bushy. H. and S.
12–18in (30–45cm).
(Klese, Austria, 1911)

**'Frau Hilde Rademacher'**
Double  H2/3  Bush
*Tube* and *sepals* rich red. *Corolla*
lilac blue splashed with cerise.
Medium-sized flowers freely
produced. Petals tightly formed
within the corolla. Growth is
rather lax but makes a good
bush with supports. *Foliage*
medium green with red veins. H.
and S. 18–24in (45–60cm).
(Rademacher, Germany, 1925)

**'Frauke'**
Single  H2  Bush
Small single flowers. *Tubes* and
*sepals* crimson. *Corolla* orange.
*Foliage* medium green. The
growth is upright. (*F. speciosa*
× 'Ting a Ling')
(Bogemann, Germany, 1987)

**'Fred's First'**
Double  H2  Bush
*Tube* carmine rose. *Sepals* curl
fully, completely covering the
tube and the ovary, also
carmine rose. *Corolla* violet
tinged with pink at the base.
*Flowers* of medium size freely
produced. Growth upright and
self-branching. *Foliage* medium
green. Best colour is obtained
in shade.
(Woolley, UK, 1978)

**'Fred Standen'**
Single  H2  Bush
*Tube* and *sepals* red. Medium-
sized single. *Corolla* purple
with pink at base of petals.
*Foliage* medium green. Growth
upright and self-branching.
(Holmes, UK, 1990)

**'Fred Swales'**
Triphylla type H1  Lax bush
*Tube* long, orange. *Sepals* and
*corolla* orange. *Foliage* medium
green with red veins and stems.
The growth is lax bush or stiff
trailer. Will make a good

basket, upright or standard. An
easy and strong grower.
(Bielby/Oxtoby, UK, 1988)

**'Freeland Ballerina'**
Semi-double  H2  Bush
*Tube* and *sepals* pale pink.
*Corolla* long, soft lavender. The
medium-sized blooms are freely
produced. *Foliage* medium
green. The growth is upright,
strong and bushy.
(Stroud, UK, 1969)

**'Freestyle'**
Single  H2  Bush
*Tube* long, thick, rose bengal.
*Sepals* rose bengal, long, held
well up and out. *Corolla*
imperial purple with lighter
colouring at the base. Flowers
large, bell shaped. Very free-
flowering. *Foliage* medium to
large, deep green. Good strong
upright growth. ('Lady Isobel
Barnett' × 'Bishop's Bells')
(Gadsby, UK, 1975)

**'Friendly Fire'**
Double  H2  Bush
*Tube* small, rose madder. *Sepals*
held horizontally, recurved tips,
also rose madder. *Corolla* opens
white heavily shaded with rose
madder at least half way down
the wavy petals, paling with
maturity. *Foliage* darkish green,
paler beneath, green veins,
serrated edges. Growth is fairly
strong and upright.
(Caunt, UK, 1985)

**'Frosted Amethyst'**
Double  H2  Semi-trailer
*Tube* bright red. *Sepals* long,
broad, also bright red. *Corolla*
amethyst purple streaked with
red, pink and very pale
amethyst. Petals serrated. The
large blooms are freely
produced. *Foliage* medium
green. Excellent for use in
hanging containers.
(Stubbs, USA, 1975)

**'Frosted Flame'**
Single  H2  Trailer
*Tube* white. *Sepals* white, lightly
flushed with pink on the inside,
long and narrow, held well out
with tips curling upwards.

*Corolla* bright flame with a
deeper edge and pale pink near
base of petals. *Foliage* bright
green. Flowers long, barrel-
shaped, with overlapping petals,
produced early and in
profusion. A natural trailer
which makes a superb basket.
(Handley, UK, 1975)

**'Frosty Bell'**
Single  H2  Bush
*Tube* pink, short. *Sepals* bright
pink, long, completely reflexed
against tube. *Corolla* pure white
veined with pink. Bell-shaped
flowers, very similar to 'Ting-a-
Ling'. *Foliage* very dark green,
very large. Strong upward
growth and bushy. ('Upward
Look' × 'Ting-a-ling')
(Gadsby, UK, 1970)

**'Fruhling'**
Double  H2  Bush
*Tube* and *sepals* light red.
*Corolla* purple-blue with white
and light blue. The large
blooms are freely produced
from early in the season.
*Foliage* medium green. Growth
upright and bushy.
(Elsner, Austria, 1878)

**'Fuchsiade '88'**
Single  H2  Bush
*Tube*, *sepals* and *corolla* dark
aubergine. Flowers petite and
numerous. *Foliage* medium to
darker green. Growth upright
and fairly stiff. A very useful
fuchsia for mixed tub planting
or creating taller structures.
(de Graaff, Holland, 1988)

**'Fuchsiarama'**
Double  H2  Semi-trailer
*Tube* short, thick, red. *Sepals*
long, broad, also red reflexing
slightly at first and then
reflexing back to the tube with
maturity. *Corolla* deep blue-
purple streaked with red and
fading to magenta and pink.
The large blooms are freely
produced. *Foliage* dark green.
Habit makes it suitable for
hanging containers; some
weighting might be necessary.
(Stubbs-Barnes and Ebeling,
USA, 1975)

'FRAU HILDE RADEMACHER'      'FRED'S FIRST'

'FRED STANDEN'      'FRIENDLY FIRE'

'FROSTED AMETHYST'      'FROSTED FLAME'

**'Fuchsiarama '91'**
Single (Triphylla type) H1 Bush
Flowers long, borne at the ends
of each branch so are fully
'terminal flowering'. *Tube*,
*sepals* pink. *Corolla* short, pink.
Growth vigorous and upright.
*Foliage* medium to darker green.
Responds well to 'pinching' so
will make a good symmetrical
shape for the show bench.
(Stannard, UK, 1991)

**'Fudzi San'**
Single H2 Bush
*Tubes* funnel-shaped, dark
orange. *Sepals* horizontally
held, green. *Corolla* flared,
bright orange. Growth upright
and bushy. *Foliage* medium
green, carried in whorls. A
novelty but worth growing.
(Bogemann, Germany, 1990)

**'Fuksie Foetsie'**
Single H2 Bush
Very small flowers, *encliandra*
type. *Tubes* and *sepals* ivory
white shading to flesh pink.
*Corolla* white ageing to pink.
*Foliage* medium green, very
small. Growth upright, free-
flowering, bushy.
(van der Grijp, Holland, 1979)

*F. fulgens*
Species H1 Bush
*Tube* long, pale red. *Sepals* pale
red and yellow-green towards
the tips. *Corolla* bright red.
The very attractive flowers are
up to 5in (13cm) long. *Foliage*
very large, pale green tinged
with red. Growth very strongly
upright. One of the easiest of
the species to grow, but it does
need some extra warmth.
(Sesse and Mocino, 1888)

*F. fulgens gesneriana*
Single (species hybrid) H1
Bush
Terminal-flowering. *Tubes* long,
dull pink. *Sepals* pale red with
green tips. *Corolla* relatively
small, red. *Foliage* very large,
medium green, slightly tinged
with red. The upward growth is
very vigorous. (*F. fulgens* × *F.
splendens*)
(Hybridist and year unknown)

*F. fulgens rubra grandiflora*
Species hybrid H1 Bush
*Tubes* very long, vermilion.
*Sepals* yellowy-green. *Corolla*
vermilion. Growth strong,
upright and vigorous. Needs to
be grown in large containers or
in the greenhouse border.
*Foliage* very large, light sage
green, hairy with purple veining.
(Hybridist and year unknown)

*F. fulgens speciosa*
Full description appears under
*F. speciosa.*

**'Fuller's Pride'**
Single H2 Bush
*Tube* neyron rose. *Sepals* neyron
rose tipped with green. *Corolla*
rose purple maturing to violet-
purple. *Foliage* light to medium
green. The natural growth is as
an upright bush. Very 'showy'
plant, very floriferous.
(Lorimer, UK, 1993)

*F. furfuracea*
Species H1 Bush
Small to medium-sized flowers
sparsely borne in terminal
racemes. *Tubes* and *sepals* dark
pink to lavender or orange-red.
*Corolla* bright pink to dark
red. Foliage medium green.
(Johnston, Bolivia, 1925)

# G

**'Gala'**
Double H2 Lax bush or trailer
*Tube* and *sepals* light pink to
salmon, sepals tipped with
green. *Corolla* has a blue centre
surrounded by petals in shades
of pink, lavender and salmon.
The large flowers are fairly free
but appear later in the season.
(Martin, USA, 1966)

**'Galadriel'**
Single H2 Bush
*Tube* and *sepals* ivory white.
*Corolla* small cup shaped,
orange. The numerous blooms
are held near to the ends of the
branches. Growth is stiffly
upright. *Foliage* medium green.
(de Graaff, Holland, 1985)

**'Galahad'**
Single H2 Lax bush
*Tube* short, white. *Sepals* white
tipped with green, fully
reflexed when mature. *Corolla*
rose pink. The largish flowers
are long and slightly flared.
Very floriferous. *Foliage*
medium-sized, mid-green with
some red in the veining.
(Goulding, UK, 1983)

**'Garden Beauty'**
Double H2/3 Bush
*Tube* rose-red, thick, medium
length. *Sepals* broad, waxy,
rose red. *Corolla* violet-blue
flushed carmine and neyron
rose. Quite free-flowering for a
double. *Foliage* medium green.
The growth is upright but the
branches arch with the weight
of the blooms. H. and S.
18–24in (45–60cm).
(Gadsby, UK, 1978)

**'Garden News'**
Double H3 Bush
*Tube* pink, short, thick. *Sepals*
pink on top frosty pink
underneath, broad, short.
*Corolla* large, magenta rose.
Petals ruffled and curled.
Growth strong and upright.
*Foliage* medium green. One
definitely for the hardy border
as it is very reliable. H. and S.
30–36in (75–90cm).
(Handley, UK, 1978)

**'Garden Week'**
Double H2 Lax bush or stiff
trailer
*Tube* small, tips greenish-white
with neyron-rose flush. *Sepals*
white flushed neyron-rose on
top-side, carmine underneath,
tips twist and recurve. *Corolla*
beetroot purple splashed with
jasper red, maturing to spiraea
red with crimson carmine
splash. The flowers are very
large and flared. *Foliage* also
huge, of mid-green colouring,
serrated edges, red veins. The
growth is rather lax for an
upright but stiff for trailer.
Could be used as either bush or
in baskets with the necessary
assistance.
(Richardson, Australia, 1985)

*F. FULGENS*

*F. FULGENS RUBRA GRANDIFLORA*

'FULLER'S PRIDE'

'GALADRIEL'

'GARDEN NEWS'

'GARDEN WEEK'

**'Gartenmeister Bonstedt'**
Triphylla type H1 Bush
Self-coloured *tube*, *sepals* and
*corolla*: orange-brick red. The
flowers are very freely produced
and almost identical to 'Thalia'.
The distinguishing feature is the
distinct bulge in the tube of this
one. *Foliage* dark bronzy red-
green with a distinctive purple
sheen underneath. Growth very
upright and vigorous and
continues late into the autumn.
(*F. triphylla* ×)
(Bonstedt, Germany, 1905)

**'Gay Anne'**
Semi-double H2 Lax bush or
trailer
*Tube* claret-rose. *Sepals* also
claret rose but have crimson on
the underside. *Corolla* mallow
pink with a distinct edging of
magenta rose. Flowers long,
well shaped, produced very
freely on rather lax stems.
*Foliage* medium green,
serrated. Growth upright, self-
branching, very free-flowering,
easy to shape. Named in
honour of HRH Princess Anne.
('Leonora' × 'Joan Pacey')
(Gadsby UK, 1973)

**'Gay Fandango'**
Double H2 Trailer
*Tube* carmine pink. *Sepals*,
carmine pink on top, deeper
underneath, long, arching
upwards. Petals of *corolla* rosy,
lighter at base, tiered. Growth
is spreading and strong. *Foliage*
medium green, finely serrated.
Will grow well in a half or full
basket.
(Nelson, USA, 1951)

**'Gay Future'**
Single H2 Trailer
*Tube* short, thin, white. *Sepals*
white, slightly flushed with
neyron rose, tipped with green.
*Corolla* violet shading to white.
bell-shaped, medium-sized
flowers freely produced.
*Foliage* deep green with a very
distinct serrated edging. The
trailing and self-branching
habit makes it excellent for
hanging containers.
(Gadsby, UK, 1975)

**'Gay Parasol'**
Double H2 Bush
*Tube* ivory green, short thick.
*Sepals* white to flesh pink, not
recurving but lift above corolla
like a parasol. *Corolla*
burgundy red, rosette-
shaped.The growth is strong
and upright. *Foliage* medium
green, red veins. Excellent for
use as a show pot plant or
when grown as a standard.
(Stubbs, USA, 1979)

**'Gay Paree'**
Double H2 Lax bush or
trailer
The *tube* and *sepals* are white
tipped with green and flushed
pale carmine on the outside and
soft carmine pink on the inner.
The *corolla* is phlox pink with
purple splashes. The largish
flowers are produced early and
very freely. The *foliage* is
medium green and the growth
is as a lax bush or trailer.
(Tiret, USA, 1954)

**'Gay Senorita'**
Single H2 Bush
*Tube* short. *Sepals* rosy red.
*Corolla* dark lilac rose. Bell-
shaped flowers produced early
and freely. Good strong upright
bush. Foliage mid- to dark
green. ('Heron' × 'Pride of
Exeter')
(Schmidt, USA, 1939)

**'Gazette'**
Double H2 Lax bush
*Tube* long, rose pink. *Sepals*
are china-rose. *Corolla* methyl
violet with rose petaloids. The
flowers are large and freely
produced on a lax bush.
*Foliage* medium green.
(Baker, UK, 1970)

**'Geertien'**
Single H2 Bush
*Tube* and *sepals* deep rose.
*Corolla* reddish-purple. *Foliage*
medium green. Growth
vigorously upright.
(Veen, Holland, 1989)

**'Geesche'**
Single H2 Bush
Medium-sized flowers. *Tubes*

light rose-red. *Sepals* carmine.
*Corolla* rose, edged with
purple. *Foliage* medium green.
Growth habit is bushy.
(Bogemann, Germany, 1985)

**F. gehrigeri**
Species H1 Bush
*Tube* long, dull red. *Sepals* and
*corolla* also dull red. Blooms
carried in terminal clusters.
*Foliage* large, deep matt velvety
green with a pale green to
purplish sheen underneath.
Growth is upright and rather
unruly.
(Munz, 1943)

**'Geisha Girl'**
Double H2 Bush
*Tube* and recurving *sepals* red.
*Corolla* red-purple, very full,
no petaloids. The medium-sized
blooms are very floriferous.
*Foliage* medium green. Very
full double flowers on medium
upright bushes.
(Pugh, UK, 1974)

**'Gelre'**
Double H2 Lax bush
Medium-sized flowers. *Tubes*
cream flushed with orange.
*Sepals* carmine. *Corolla*
carmine red. Foliage medium
green. Growth rather lax.
(Beije, Holland, 1990)

**'General Charles de Gaulle'**
Single H1 Bush
Triphylla type, terminal-
flowering. The long *tube*, short
recurved *sepals* and the *corolla*
all dark salmon pink. *Foliage*
medium to dark green. Growth
is upright and can be made
bushier by frequent 'stopping'.
(Raiser and date unknown)

**'General Monk'**
Double H3 Bush
*Tube* cerise, short. *Sepals*
cerise-mauve, completely
reflexed. *Corolla* blue ageing to
mauvish-blue, veined pink,
white shading at petal base.
The medium-sized blooms are
very free. *Foliage* is medium to
dark green, serrated. H. and S.
18–24in (45–60cm).
(Raiser unknown, France)

'GAY FANDANGO'

'GAY FUTURE'

'GAY PARASOL'

*F. GEHRIGERI*

**'General Negrier'**
Semi-double H2 Bush
Medium-sized flowers. *Tubes*
and *sepals* rose. *Corolla* scarlet.
*Foliage* medium green. Growth
an upright bush.
(Meillez, France, 1848)

**'Genii'**
Single H3 Bush
This super hardy plant should
be in all collections. *Tube* and
*sepals* cerise. *Corolla* a rich
violet ageing to dark rose. The
*foliage* is its most redeeming
feature, the leaves are light
yellowish-green with red stems
when grown in full sun, tending
to green in shade. Growth is
very upright and bushy. H. and
S. 24–30in (60–75cm).
(Reiter, USA, 1951)

**'Geoff Barnet'**
Single H2 Bush
*Tube* pink. *Sepals* mid-pink,
reflexing and twisting. *Corolla*
a slightly lighter shade of pink.
Flowers small to medium.
*Foliage* dark green. Growth is
upright and self-branching.
('Miss California' ×
'Northway')
(Dyos, UK, 1987)

**'Geoffrey Smith'**
Double H3 Bush
*Tube* and *sepals* crimson.
*Corolla* pale rose veined with
crimson. *Foliage* medium
green. The upright growth will
produce a small self-branching
bush. H. and S. 18–24in
(45–60cm).
('Alice Hoffman' × 'Alice
Hoffman')
(Bielby/Oxtoby, UK, 1987)

**'Georgana'**
Double H1 Bush
*Tube* pink, medium length.
*Sepals* pink on top with green
tips, darker underneath, long.
*Corolla* consists of pastel
shades of pale blue and orchid,
veined pink. The very large
blooms are freely and
continuously produced. *Foliage*
large, bright green carried on
upright and bushy growth.
(Tiret, USA, 1965)

**'Georg Bornemann'**
Triphylla type H1 Bush
*Tube* long. *Sepals* pointed,with
green tips. *Corolla*, all salmon
pink colouring. The flowers are
produced in terminal clusters.
*Foliage* darkish olive green
with serrated edges. Growth is
strongly upright. Rather more
tolerant to frost than some
triphylla types.
(Bonstedt, Germany, 1915)

**'George Barr'**
Single H2 Bush
*Tube* white, flushed pink.
*Sepals* white with green tips.
*Corolla* violet blue, fading with
age. The flowers are small but
freely produced. *Foliage*
medium green. Growth is
upright and bushy, will make a
good standard.
(Hazard and Hazard, USA,
1930)

**'George Johnson'**
Single H2 Bush
*Tube* and *sepals* rose pink.
*Corolla* rose vermilion.
Medium-sized flowers have a
tubular formation. *Foliage*
medium green with red petiole.
Growth upright and bushy.
Worth trying as bush, shrub or
standard.
(Doyles, UK, 1977)

**'George Roe'**
Double H2 Bush
*Tube* thin, crimson. *Sepals*
thick, waxy, claret rose with
green tips, well held out.
*Corolla* white with crimson
petaloids, extra large and
solid. The blooms are exceptionally free for a large double.
*Foliage* medium green, red
veins, very finely serrated. The
growth is upright, strong and
bushy.
(Gadsby, UK, 1972)

**'George Travis'**
Double H2 Bush
*Tube* white, short, thick. *Sepals*
ivory, edged with cerise, pale
pink shading beneath, green
tips. *Corolla* a silvery blue.
The flowers are fairly large,
fully double and quite free.

*Foliage* is medium green.
Growth is a strong upright
bush. Prone to red spider mite
attack.
(Travis, UK, 1956)

**'Gerald Drewitt'**
Single H2 Bush
*Tube* deep pink. *Sepals* pink.
*Corolla* mauve-rose. Medium-
sized flowers produced from
early in the season, very free.
*Foliage* medium green. The
growth habit is upright and
this cultivar will make a good
standard. ('Mission Bells' ×
'Border Queen')
(Weeks, UK, 1984)

**'Geraldine'**
Double H2 Lax bush
Medium-sized flowers. *Tubes*
and *sepals* deep reddish-purple.
*Corolla* deep purple. *Foliage*
medium green. The habit of
growth is rather lax so will
make a bush or a basket with
the necessary supports.
(de Graaff, Holland, 1991)

**'Gerard Mathieu'**
Single H2 Bush
Flowers large. *Tube* and *sepals*
rose. *Corolla* purple with pale
pink shading at the base of the
petals. *Foliage* medium green.
The growth is vigorously
strong and upright.
(Murru, Holland, 1990)

**'Gerda Mathey'**
Single H2 Bush
*Tube* and *sepals* red. *Corolla*
purple fading to paler purple
with maturity. *Foliage* medium
green. Flowers small, erect,
best described as 'chubby'.
(Raiser and date unknown)

**'Gerharda's Aubergine'**
Single H2 Trailer
*Tube*, *sepals* and *corolla* of
this delightful cultivar are
aubergine maturing to beetroot
red. It is one of the darkest of
its kind. *Foliage* medium to
dark green. The growth habit is
spreading and very strong. Will
make a good basket or hanging
pot.
(de Graaff, Holland, 1989)

'GEOFFREY SMITH'

'GEORGANA'

'GEORGE BARR'

'GERHARDA'S AUBERGINE'

**'Gerharda's Florijn'**
Semi-double H2 Trailer
*Tube* and *sepals* flower plum
rose. *Corolla* deep purple.
Medium-sized. *Foliage* medium
green. The natural habit of this
plant is to trail, so will make a
good basket.
(de Graaff, Holland, 1991)

**'Giant Pink Enchanted'**
Double H2 Lax bush/trailer
*Tube* and *sepals* rose. *Corolla*
white suffused pink. Very large
flower. *Foliage* medium green
and quite large. The lax growth
will enable this plant to be
used as a bush, with supports
for the heavy blooms, or as a
trailing plant in baskets.
(American raiser, c.1965)

**'Gilda'**
Double H2 Bush
*Tube* short, coral. *Sepals* broad,
coral on top, salmon pink
beneath, short. *Corolla* overlaid
rose, each petal edged with
bright red. The flowers are
large and very freely produced.
*Foliage* golden green with
maroon colouring, stems and
veins darker with age. Strong
upright growth, tends to be lax.
(Handley, UK, 1971)

**'Gillian Althea'**
Double H2 Bush
Medium-sized flowers. *Tube*
white, flushed with pink. *Sepals*
deep pink. *Corolla* light blue
with orange. *Foliage* medium
green. Natural growth as a bush.
(Weeks, UK, 1991)

**'Gilt Edge'**
Single H2 Lax bush
The most interesting feature of
this cultivar is the *foliage*
medium green with a gold
edge. The *flowers* are
completely reddish-orange.
Growth is rather lax so will
need supporting.
(Endicote, UK, 1979)

**'Gipping'**
Single H2 Trailer
*Tube*, *sepals* and large bell-
shaped *corolla* all a delicate

shade of pink. *Foliage* medium
green to lemon. The natural
habit of growth is 'spreading'
and plenty of side shoots are
produced. Makes a very
attractive basket.
(Goulding, UK, 1988)

**'Girls Brigade'**
Single H2 Trailer
*Tube* and *sepals* pink. *Corolla*
rose red. *Foliage* medium
green. Easily grown, certainly
one for the beginner.
(Bielby/Oxtoby, UK, 1993)

**'Gladiator'**
Double H2 Bush
*Tube* rosy carmine, short.
*Sepals* rosy carmine, short,
broad, curling over tube.
*Corolla* white, veined and
splashed with rosy carmine.
*Foliage* dark green. The upright
growth makes this an excellent
cultivar for bushes.
(Lemoine, France, 1889)

**'Gladoor'**
Double H2 Lax bush
Medium-sized flowers. *Tube* and
*sepals* white flushed with rose.
*Corolla* deep violet. *Foliage*
medium green. Natural habit of
growth as an upright bush.
(Krom, Holland, 1990)

**'Gladys Lorimer'**
Single H2/3 Bush
*Tube* and *sepals* creamy rose.
*Corolla* purple fading to
magenta orange. *Foliage* has a
distinctive bronze tint. Natural
growth habit as a bush. Worth
trying in the hardy border. A
very attractive cultivar. H. and
S. 24–30in (60–75cm).
(Lorimer, UK, 1990)

**'Glenby'**
Double H2 Bush
*Tube* short, rose madder.
*Sepals* rose madder streaked
with pink and reflexing back to
the tube, then curling
downwards. *Corolla* amethyst
violet fading to petunia purple.
The medium-sized blooms are
very freely produced. The
*foliage* is medium green,

lanceolate with red petioles.
The upright growth is self-
branching and makes a very
good bush.
(Brazier, UK, 1972)

**'Gleneagles'**
Single H2 Bush
*Tube* short, thin, ivory. *Sepals*
short, broad, white tinged with
pink and held backwards.
*Corolla* violet to mauve. The
medium to small flowers are
carried at the ends of the
branches and are outward-
looking. *Foliage* almost yellow
when young, maturing to a
very light green. The upright
growth is very free branching.
Excellent for pots or in the
border.
(Goulding, UK, 1986)

**'Glitters'**
Single H2 Bush
*Tube* waxy white. *Sepals* have
similar colouring but are a
lovely salmon colour on the
inside; green tips. *Corolla* a
glowing orange-red. *Foliage*
medium green. The flowers are
very freely produced on strong
upright growth.
(Erickson, USA, 1963)

**'Glyn Jones'**
Semi-double H2 Bush
*Tube* and *sepals* neyron rose on
the underside with the outside
paler pink and heavily tipped
with green. *Corolla* violet-
purple with neyron rose
petaloids. Foliage light green,
helps to enhance the delightful
colour combination of the
flowers.
(Roe, UK, 1976)

**'Gloria Johnson'**
Single H2 Trailer
*Tube* long, pink. *Sepals* long,
pale pink, slightly darker on
the underside. *Corolla* a bright,
non-fading claret rose, holds its
shape well. The flower is
overall 4in (10cm) long.
*Foliage* medium green. Growth
as a natural trailer. Will make a
graceful and superb basket.
(Bielby/Oxtoby, UK, 1994)

'GILLIAN ALTHEA'

'GIRLS BRIGADE'

'GIANT PINK ENCHANTED'

'GLENBY'

'GLORIA JOHNSON'

**'Glowing Embers'**
Single H2 Lax bush/trailer
*Tube* and *sepals* watermelon-pink, thick crêpe effect. *Corolla* burnt orange to red. The large flowers are very freely produced. *Foliage* medium green. Natural growth rather lax. Will make a good bush or a basket but supports will be necessary.
(Kennett and Ross, USA, 1957)

**'Glowing Lilac'**
Double H2 Trailer
*Tube* short, white flushed pink. *Sepals* wide, white with reflexed pink tips. *Corolla* opens all lilac maturing to lilac fading to pink at the base of the petals. *Foliage* dark green on the upper surface and lighter on the lower. Veins and stems are red. A natural trailer, excellent for all hanging containers. ('Pink Marshmallow' × 'Eusebia')
(Stubbs, USA, 1987)

**'Gold Brocade'**
Single H3 Bush
*Tube* and *sepals* red. *Corolla* mauve fading to pink with maturity. Large flowers freely produced. *Foliage* deep gold-green heavily veined with purple, slowly changing to pale green with age. Upright bushy growth. H. and S. 18–24in (45–60cm).
(Tabraham, UK, 1976)

**'Gold Crest'**
Single H3 Bush
*Tube* red. *Sepals* long, also red. *Corolla* pale mauve and pink. Small flowers carried in profusion. *Foliage* golden green, the new growth being almost bright gold. Growth is upright but it does have a spreading habit. Excellent for the front of a hardy border as it only achieves H. and S. of approx 6–9in (15–20cm).
(Tabraham, UK, 1982)

**'Golden Anniversary'**
Double H2 Trailer
*Tube* sturdy greenish-white. *Sepals* white, broad, sharply pointed. *Corolla* dark violet ripening to rich ruby red.

Young *foliage* green/gold fading to light green. The natural habit is to spread, and the self-branching plants will make an excellent basket.
(Stubbs, USA, 1980)

**'Golden Arrow'**
Triphylla type H Bush.
*Tube* long, thin orange. *Sepals* green, recurving when mature, with small spurs. Petals within *corolla* tangerine. True terminal-flowering type. Growth strong and upright. *Foliage* medium to dark green.
(Goulding, UK, 1985)

**'Golden Dawn'**
Single H2 Bush
*Tube* light salmon. *Sepals* light salmon, long narrow, upturned. *Corolla* light orange shading to fuchsia pink. Medium-sized flowers freely produced. *Foliage* medium green. The natural growth is upright and bushy but it does need early 'stopping'.
(Haag, USA, 1951)

**'Golden Eden Lady'**
Single H2 Bush
*Tube* short, thin, pale rose. *Sepals* amaranth rose and deeper underneath, shading to white at the tips. *Corolla* hyacinth blue with a slight rose colouring at the base of the petals. Medium-sized flowers freely produced. *Foliage* bright yellow with green patches. Growth upright and bushy.
(Sport from 'Eden Lady')
(Cater, UK, 1982)

**'Golden Glow'**
Single H2 Lax bush
Almost a 'self' in that the *tube*, *sepals* and *corolla* are golden orange. Medium- to large-sized flowers are freely produced. *Foliage* light green. The growth is rather lax so could be used for bush or basket.
(Shutt, USA, 1968)

**'Golden Guinea Pig'**
Single H2 Bush
The *tube* and *sepals* are blush white. The *corolla* is violet purple veined with magenta.

The *foliage* is yellow. A very attractive plant. The natural growth is bushy.
(Holmes, R., UK, 1993)

**'Golden Herald'**
Single H3 Bush
*Tube* and *sepals* scarlet. *Corolla* deep purple. *Foliage* yellow. A sport from 'Herald' and it has retained the strength and vigour of its parent. Well worth growing. H. and S. 24–30in (60–75cm).
(Finder unknown)

**'Golden Jessimae'**
Single H2 Bush
Tube short, china rose. Sepals broad, also china rose. *Corolla* pale mallow purple. Medium-sized flowers freely produced. This sport from 'Jessimae' has the same upright and bushy growth as its parent. *Foliage* green and gold, very similar to 'Golden Treasure'.
(Akers, UK, 1984)

**'Golden La Campanella'**
Semi-double H2 Trailer
*Tube* white. *Sepals* white, slightly flushed with pink. *Corolla* a beautiful shade of imperial purple fading to lavender. Extremely free-flowering and very early. *Foliage* variegated, creamy yellow and green. The growth is lax and rather straggly but makes an excellent basket if more than the usual number of plants are used.
(Sport of 'La Campanella')
(Finder unknown, UK, 1980)

**'Golden Lena'**
Semi-double H2 Lax bush
*Tube* pale pink. *Sepals* pale flesh pink, half reflexed, slightly deeper in colour underneath. *Corolla* rosy magenta flushed pink and paling at the base of the petals. Medium-sized flowers very freely produced. *Foliage* has varying shades of green and gold. Growth is rather lax and could be used for baskets or supported as bush plants.
(Sport of 'Lena')
(Nottingham, UK, 1978)

'GLOWING LILAC'

'GLOWING EMBERS'

'GOLD CREST'

'GOLDEN EDEN LADY'

'GOLDEN HERALD'

**'Golden Marinka'**
Single H2 Trailer
Best known of all variegated
foliage cultivars. *Foliage* colour
combination an eye-catching
green and yellow, red veins.
*Tube* and *sepals* rich red.
Corolla a slightly darker red.
Very early and very free in its
flowering. Growth is that of a
natural trailer so will make an
excellent basket very quickly.
Best colour in maximum
sunlight. Prone to *botrytis*.
(Sport of 'Marinka')
(Weber, USA, 1955)

**'Golden Melody'**
Double H3 Bush
*Tube* and *sepals* deep pink.
*Corolla* blue fading to lavender.
Medium-sized blooms fully
double. *Foliage* a deep golden
green slowly changing to pale
green with maturity. Growth
upright, bushy and strong. H.
and S. 18–24in (45–60cm).
(Tabraham, UK, 1976)

**'Golden Peppermint Stick'**
Double H2 Bush
Sport of 'Peppermint Stick'.
*Tube* carmine. *Sepals* carmine
with a purple stripe. *Corolla*
centre petals rich royal purple,
outer petals light carmine rose
edged with purple. *Foliage* a
distinct yellowy green. Upright
and strong growth.
(Peter Dresman, UK, 1992)

**'Golden Spade'**
Double H2 Trailer
*Tube* red. *Sepals* wide,
horizontally held, also red.
*Corolla* opens pinkish-red,
matures to orange-red. *Foliage*
light olive green with red
veining. Self-branching trailing
stems will rapidly fill a basket.
(*F. magdalenae* × 'Applause')
(de Graaff, Holland, 1987)

**'Golden Swingtime'**
Double H2 Trailer
*Tube* and *sepals* waxy red.
*Corolla* white veined with red.
Large flowers freely produced,
as befits its parent 'Swingtime'.
*Foliage* a delightful golden
colour. Very strong grower.

(Sport from 'Swingtime')
(Discovered in various parts of
the UK during 1981)

**'Golden Treasure'**
Single H2 Bush
*Tube* and *sepals* scarlet.
*Corolla* purplish magenta,
compact. Flowers not
particularly attractive and
rather late coming into bloom.
However, *foliage* a delightful
variegation of green and gold.
Low-growing and could be
used as edging for a border.
(Carter, UK, 1860)

**'Golden Wedding'**
Single H2 Bush
*Tube* long, thin. *Sepals*
horizontally held, rhodamine
pink. *Corolla* cyclamen purple
with wavy petal edges.
Medium-sized flowers freely
produced. *Foliage* is pale gold
ageing to pale green, serrated
edges. Growth is upright.
(Sport from 'Pirbright')
(Muncaster, UK, 1985)

**'Gold Foil'**
Double H2 Trailer
Golden-leaved sport from
'Celebration'. *Tube* and *sepals*
orange. The petals within the
*corolla* are marbled with
shades of orange. Growth is
spreading and self-branching.
*Foliage* golden. Excellent for
hanging pots.
(Goulding, UK, 1993)

**'Gold Runner'**
Single H2 Bush
*Tube* and *sepals* pale pink.
*Corolla* rose pink. *Foliage*
variegated gold and green.
Growth upright and short-
jointed. (Sport from 'Runner')
(Tolley, UK, 1984)

**'Goldsworth Beauty'**
Single H3 Bush
Medium-sized flowers. *Tubes*
and *sepals* pale cerise. *Corolla*
reddish purple, fairly compact.
*Foliage* medium green, broad,
serrated. Growth upright and
fairly strong. H. and S.
18–24in (45–60cm).
(Slocock, UK, 1952)

**'Gordon Boy'**
Double H3 Bush
*Tube* pink. *Sepals* deep pink
with reflexed tips. *Corolla* lilac
blue and pink with smooth
petal edges. *Foliage* medium
green on the upper surface
and lighter on the lower
surface. H. and S. 18–24in
(45–60cm). ('Grace Groom' ×
'John Baker')
(Weeks, UK, 1987)

**'Gordon Thorley'**
Single H2 Bush
*Tube* pale pink. *Sepals* pale
pink rose, slightly paler on the
underside and held horizontally
to the tube. *Corolla* white,
veined with rose, each petal
slightly edged with rose. *Foliage*
medium to dark green. Growth
strongly upright, self-branching
and bushy. ('Cloverdale Pearl' ×
'Santa Barbara')
(Roe, UK, 1985)

**'Gottingem'**
Triphylla type H1 Bush
*Tube* long, tapering, orange
red. *Sepals* finely pointed,
spreading, orange-red. *Corolla*
also orange-red. *Foliage* large,
dark green, with purple mid-rib
and veining. Upright but rather
slow-growing and very frost-
shy. (*F. triphylla* ×)
(Bonstedt, Germany, 1905)

**'Gottinger Rhum'**
Single H2 Trailer
Medium-sized flowers. *Tube,
sepals, corolla* red. *Foliage*
medium to dark green.
Natural growth of the cultivar
a trailer.
(Strumper, Germany, 1984)

**'Gov. Pat Brown'**
Double H2 Trailer
*Tube* light pink. *Sepals* light
pink on top, creamy white
beneath, tipped with green and
fold back rather gracefully.
*Corolla* violet with splashes of
pink at the base of the petals.
*Foliage* pale green. Large
flowers fairly freely produced.
The habit of growth is as a
natural trailer.
(Machedo, USA, 1962)

'GOLDEN SWINGTIME'

'GOLDEN WEDDING'

'GORDON THORLEY'

'GOV. PAT BROWN'

**'Grace'**
Single H2 Lax bush
*Tube* crimson. *Sepals* crimson,
long with green tips, curl
upwards. *Corolla* cyclamen
purple and veined with
scarlet. The bell-shaped
flowers are large for a single.
*Foliage* is medium green with
red veins and stems, small,
serrated. Growth rather lax.
('Percy Holmes' × 'Jack
Acland')
(Holmes, UK, 1974)

**'Grace Darling'**
Single H2 Bush
*Tube* short, pale pink. *Sepals*
pale pink, short, broad, held
well back onto the tube.
*Corolla* white. Medium-sized
bell-shaped blooms freely
produced. *Foliage* is medium
green, small, serrated. Growth
upright, bushy, short-jointed.
('Rosedale' × 'Sleigh Bells')
(Gadsby, UK, 1972)

***F. gracillis tricolour***
Species H3 Bush
The small red and purple
flowers are carried on long
arching stems. The *foliage* is
most attractive, variegated with
light green, pink and cream. H.
and S. 36in (90cm) plus.

***F. gracillis variegata***
Species H3 Bush
*Sepals* scarlet. *Corolla* deep
purple. *Foliage* variegated with
green, red and yellow. Makes
an excellent hedging plant. H.
and S. 36in (90cm) plus.

**'Grady'**
Double H2 Bush
*Tube* and *sepals* creamy white.
*Corolla* reddish-purple.
Medium-sized fully double
blooms freely produced. The
growth is strong and upright.
*Foliage* medium green. ('Che
Belle' × 'Blush o' Dawn')
(van der Beek, Holland, 1966)

**'Graf Spee'**
Double H2 Bush
*Tube* white. *Sepals* sturdy,
upturned, white. *Corolla* large,

with irregular-shaped, rosy red
petals with pale veining.
*Foliage* medium green. The
flowers are carried at the ends
of the branches. Upright
growth, very sturdy.
(Goulding, UK, 1989)

**'Graf Witte'**
Single H3 Bush
*Tube* red, short. *Sepals* bright
red, held close to tube. *Corolla*
violet with coarse veining, bell-
shaped. *Foliage* has a
distinctive yellow tinge to the
leaves, crimson veining.
Excellent for the hardy border
or as a pot plant for show
purposes. Was responsible for
sporting 'Pixie'. H. and S.
24–36in (60–90cm).
(Lemoine, France, 1899)

**'Grand Duchess'**
Triphylla type H1 Bush
Miniature, terminal-flowering
fuchsia. *Tube* cornet-shaped,
bright orange. *Sepals* and
petals small, bright orange.
*Foliage* medium green with a
delicate purple sheen on the
reverse. The small growth is
upright and bushy. One for use
in the 'small pot' classes.
(Stannard, UK, 1993)

**'Grandma Sinton'**
Double H2 Bush
*Tube* short, white with pink
stripes. *Sepals* white with a
splash of red near the tube.
*Corolla* soft shell pink.
Medium-sized blooms fully
double; this cultivar is very
free-flowering. *Foliage* medium
green. Growth is rather lax for
a bush, so it could be
encouraged to grow in a basket
if so required. ('Pennine' ×
'Harry Gray')
(Sinton, UK, 1986)

**'Grandpa George'**
Semi-double H2 Bush
*Tube* light rose. *Sepals* light
rose striped and overlaid
magenta on upper surface,
crêped light rose with a
magenta base beneath, dark
green recurved tips. *Corolla*

white, veined with magenta.
*Foliage* medium green.
Although the growth is small
and upright the flowers are
very freely produced.
(Holmes, UK, 1988)

**'Grand Prix'**
Double H2 Bush
*Tube* and *sepals* porcelain
white with rose underneath.
*Corolla* delft rose at the base of
the petals, shading to pansy
violet with tips edged with delft
rose. Medium-sized blooms
very freely produced. *Foliage*
large, medium green. Growth is
strongly upright.
(Fuchsia La, USA, 1972)

**'Grand Slam'**
Double H2 Trailer
Very large-sized blooms. *Tube*
white. *Sepals* white with pale
crêpe pink undersides. *Corolla*
pale purple-lavender maturing
to fuchsia magenta with pink
marbling. *Foliage* large, dark
green. Natural growth as a
trailer. Needs pinching in early
stages.
(Kennett-Castro, USA, 1973)

**'Grasmere'**
Single Triphylla type H1
Trailer
*Tube* long, thin, coral red.
*Sepals* coral red with green tips,
longish, spreading. *Corolla* deep
coral pink. The flowers are held
at the ends of the branches in
bunches. *Foliage* very large,
dark green with a pink base in
younger leaves. Makes a self-
branching bush with arching
branches. Very vigorous. (*F.
cordifolia* × *F. lycioides*)
(Travis, UK, 1964)

**'Grayrigg'**
Single H3 Bush
*Tube* short, thick, white with a
green flush. *Sepals* blush pink,
have green tips and are deeper
pink on the underside. *Corolla*
soft pink. *Foliage* small and
pale green. H. and S. up to
36in (90cm). ('Silverdale' ×
'Silverdale' seedling)
(Thornley, UK, 1988)

'GRAF WITTE'

'GRANDMA SINTON'

'GRAND PRIX'

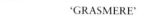

'GRASMERE'

**'Great Scott'**
Double H2 Bush
*Tube* and *sepals* carmine rose.
*Corolla* jasper red with salmon
pink petaloids. Large flowers
freely produced. *Foliage*
medium green. The growth is
strongly upright.
(Tiret, USA, 1960)

**'Green 'n Gold'**
Single H2 Bush
*Tube*, *sepals* and *corolla* a
delightful coral pink. Flowers
profuse, bell-shaped, borne in
clusters. *Foliage* small and
yellow-coloured, providing it
has full sunshine. In the shade
it will just produce green
leaves. Growth is upright and
bushy.
(Rasmussen, USA, 1954)

**'Greenpeace'**
Single H2 Bush
*Tube* and *sepals* light green,
flushed rose. *Corolla* ivory.
Medium-sized flowers
produced very freely, hang in
clusters. *Foliage* large, fuchsia
green and lighter underneath,
very serrated, light green veins.
Very rampant grower so will
need regular 'stopping' to
produce a manageable bush.
('Speciosa' × 'Ting-a-Ling')
(de Graaff, Holland,1985)

**'Greg Walker'**
Double H2 Lax bush or trailer
*Tube* white, striped with
carmine rose. *Sepals* carmine
rose flushed white on the upper
side and carmine rose
underneath; tipped with green.
*Corolla* is bishop's violet
splashed with carmine rose.
*Foliage* light lettuce green,
matures darker, serrated edging
and magenta mid-ribs. Because
of its growth habit will make a
good basket or a bush given
the necessary supports. (Sport
of 'Beryl's Choice)
(Richardson, Australia, 1982)

**'Gregor Mendel'**
Single H2 Lax bush/trailer
Medium-sized flower. *Tube* and
*sepals* carmine. *Corolla*
carmine purple. *Foliage*

medium green. Natural growth
habit very lax so will make a
good basket or bush with the
necessary supports.
(van den Bergh, Holland,
1991)

**'Gretna Chase'**
Single H2 Bush
*Tube* and *sepals* pale neyron
rose. *Corolla* a brilliant shade
of white. Medium-sized flowers
very freely produced. *Foliage*
medium green. ('Eden lady' ×
'Silver Dollar')
(Mitchinson, UK, 1988)

**'Grey Lady'**
Double H3 Bush
*Tube* and *sepals* red. *Corolla*
grey-blue fading to lavender
pink. Medium-sized blooms
very freely produced. *Foliage*
dark green. Growth is upright,
bushy and self-branching. H.
and S. 18–24in (45–60cm).
(Tabraham, UK, 1974)

**'Groene Kans Glorie'**
Single H2 Bush
*Tube* thick, rose orange. *Sepals*
salmon orange, fully reflexed to
the tube. *Corolla* is light
orange at the base of the petals
shading to deep orange on the
outer petals. The large flowers
are freely produced. *Foliage*
medium green.
(Steeves, Holland, 1978)

**'Grumpy'**
Single H3 Bush
*Tube* and *sepals* deep pink.
*Corolla* navy blue. The small
flowers are borne in profusion
throughout the season. *Foliage*
medium green. Growth stiff,
self-branching but rather
prostrate. H. and S. 9–12in
(22–30cm).
(Tabraham, UK, 1974)

**'Gruss An Graz'**
Single H2 Bush
*Tube* and *sepals* pink. Medium-
sized single flower. *Corolla* pale
violet. *Foliage* medium green.
Growth upright and self-
branching.
(Strumper, Holland, 1986)

**'Gruss aus dem Bodethal'**
Single H2, Bush
*Tube* short, thick, rich crimson.
*Sepals* crimson, short, held
horizontally. *Corolla* very dark
violet purple, almost black.
*Foliage* medium green. Growth
upright, self-branching, flowers
freely, easy to grow.
(Sattler and Belge, Germany,
1893)

**'Gustave Dore'**
Double H2 Bush
Medium flowers. *Tubes* pink.
*Sepals*, pink, long, thin.
*Corolla* white, with pinkish
veins. *Foliage* medium green.
Natural growth upright and
self-branching. Tends to be lax.
Free flowering.
(Lemoine, France, 1880)

**'Guurtje'**
Double H2 Trailer
Medium-sized flowers. *Tubes*
soft rose with light green
stripes. *Sepals* white flushed
with rose. *Corolla* light violet.
*Foliage* medium green. Natural
growth rather lax. Will make a
good basket or bush with the
right supports.
(Krom, Germany, 1989)

**'Guy Dauphine'**
Double H2 Bush
*Tube* and *sepals* carmine.
*Corolla* plum purple. Flowers
very large and free for their
size. *Foliage* medium green.
Natural growth as a bush.
(Rozaine-Boucharlet, France,
1913)

**'Gwen Dodge'**
Single H2 Bush
*Tube* is a palest waxy pink.
*Sepals* pale pink with a slight
flush of rose. *Corolla* purple
fading to white towards the
centre of the flower. The
medium-sized flowers are fully
flared and upward-looking.
Very prolific in its flowering.
*Foliage* medium green.
(Dyos, UK, 1988)

'GREG WALKER'

'GROENE KANS GLORIE'

'GRETNA CHASE'

'GREY LADY'

'GRUSS AUS DEM BODETHAL'

**'Gypsy Girl'**
Double H2 Bush
*Tube* short, cherry red. *Sepals* held well out and curving over, also cherry red. *Corolla* pale phlox purple heavily veined with rose bengal at the base of the petals. The medium-sized blooms are quite freely produced. *Foliage* medium green. Natural growth upright, self-branching and bushy.
(Pacey, UK, 1980)

# H

**'Halsall Beauty'**
Double H2 Trailer
Medium-sized flower. *Tube* and *sepals* pale pink in colour. *Corolla* light purple splashed with pink. *Foliage* medium green. The natural habit of this fuchsia is to trail so will make a good basket.
(Sinton, UK, 1990)

**'Hampshire Beauty'**
Semi-double H2 Bush
*Tube* and *sepals* white tipped with green. *Corolla* white at base shading to wisteria. Flowers medium-sized and fairly freely produced. *Foliage* variegated green and yellow. Growth is upright and bushy.
(Clark, UK, 1987)

**'Hampshire Blue'**
Single H2 Bush
*Tube* cream with pink flush. *Sepals* cream flushed pink, recurve to the tube. *Corolla* pale powder blue with white at the base of the petals. The flowers are medium-sized and extremely attractive with their pastel shades. *Foliage* medium green.
(Oakleigh Nurseries, UK, 1983)

**'Hampshire Prince'**
Double H2 Lax bush
*Tube* pink. *Sepals* rather deeper pink underneath tipped with green. *Corolla* lavender pink fading to deep pink. Blooms very large, fully double and produced freely and early in the season. *Foliage* medium green. The growth is rather lax so will make a bush or a basket with the correct supports.
(Oakleigh Nurseries, UK, 1983)

**'Hampshire Treasure'**
Double H2 Bush
*Tube* and *sepals* are a lovely shade of salmon. *Corolla* cerise and orange. *Foliage* dark green. Medium-sized blooms are extremely attractive and not dissimilar to 'Bicentennial' but smaller. ('Bicentennial' × 'Lord Lonsdale')
(Raiser unknown, UK, 1983)

**'Hanna'**
Double H2 Bush
*Tube* and *sepals* red. *Corolla* white. Flowers of medium size but freely produced; early flowering. *Foliage* medium green. Upright bushy plant.
(Elsner, Germany, date unknown)

**'Hans Van Beek'**
Single H2 Bush
Medium-sized flower. Tube pale yellow green. *Sepals* orchid rose. *Corolla* purple-mauve. *Foliage* medium green. Natural growth as an upright bush.
(Beije, Holland, 1991)

**'Happiness'**
Double H2 Bush
*Tube* rose bengal. *Sepals*, also rose bengal, curve upwards, tipped with green. *Corolla* cyclamen purple shading to rose-bengal at the base of the petals. The largish blooms are fully double. Foliage medium green. Growth upright and bushy.
(Bellamy, UK, 1984)

**'Happy'**
Single H3 Bush
*Tube* and *sepals* red. Small star-shaped flower red. *Corolla* blue. The flowers are held erect. *Foliage* pale green, the growth naturally bushy. An excellent fuchsia for the front of a border as it has H. and S. of 9–15in (22–40cm).
(Tabraham, UK, 1974)

**'Happy Anniversary'**
Double H2 Trailer
*Tube*, *sepals* and very full double *corolla* white. *Foliage* variegated greens and yellow. The growth is naturally trailing so will make an excellent basket, and will be much admired for its very large flowers.
(Raiser and date unknown)

**'Happy Fellow'**
Single H2 Bush
*Tube* light orange. *Sepals*, also light orange with green tips, upturned. Corolla orange and smoky rose. The flowers are medium-sized and extremely freely produced. *Foliage* light green. Makes a good plant for the outside border and may well prove to be hardy.
(Waltz, USA, 1966)

**'Happy Wedding Day'**
Double H2 Bush
*Tube* white. *Sepals* white with rose bengal base and margins on top, white with rhodamine purple underneath, tipped light green and recurved. *Corolla* white with wavy petal margins. The blooms are very large, round and non-flaring. *Foliage* medium green with serrated edges. The flowers are freely produced considering their size. The growth is rather lax so could be used for basketwork if required.
(Richardson, Australia, 1985)

**'Hapsburgh'**
Single H2 Bush
Medium-sized flowers. *Tube* and *sepals* white flushed with pink. *Corolla* pale parma violet. *Foliage* medium green. The upright growth is self-branching.
(Rozaine-Boucharlet, France, 1911)

**'Harbour Bridge'**
Double H2 Bush
*Tube* and *sepals* light rose. *Corolla* lavender blue flecked with rose. *Foliage* medium green. The growth is vigorously upright, the flowers large and freely produced for their size.
(Lockerbie, Australia, 1971)

'GYPSY GIRL'

'HAMPSHIRE BLUE'

'HANS VAN BEEK'

'HAPPY'

**'Harlow Carr'**
Single H2 Bush
*Tube* thin, pale pink. *Sepals* empire rose, held half way up from the horizontal. *Corolla* white. *Foliage* fairly small dark green with lighter colouring underneath. The natural growth is rather lax but upright. It is short jointed and very floriferous. ('Cloverdale Pearl' × 'Coconut Ice')
(Johns, UK, 1988)

**'Harnser's Flight'**
Single H3 Bush
*Tube* ivory white. *Sepals* white with green tips, recurving. *Corolla* pale lavender. *Foliage* medium green. Growth strongly upright. H. and S. in excess of 36in (90cm).
(Goulding, UK, 1990)

**'Harold Smith'**
Single H2 Lax bush
*Tube* and *sepals* red. *Corolla* violet purple with purple stripes. *Foliage* medium to dark green. Natural growth is rather lax upright.
(Holmes, R., UK, 1993)

**'Harriet Lye'**
Single H2 Bush
Medium-sized flower. *Tube* and *sepals* waxy white. *Corolla* mauve pink, edged with carmine. *Foliage* medium green. Growth upright and bushy. Flowers produced early and very freely.
(Lye, UK, 1887)

**'Harrow Pride'**
Double H2 Bush
*Tube* white. *Sepals* broad and upturned, white with a distinctive pink flush both inside and out. *Corolla* dark blue with some fading with maturity. Quite free-flowering for a double. *Foliage* medium green.
(Dyos, UK, 1984)

**'Harry Gray'**
Double H2 Trailer
*Tube* fairly short rose pink and lightly streaked. *Sepals* slightly recurving, white shading to rose

pink at the base and with green tips. *Corolla* fully double, white shading to rose pink at the base of the petals. *Foliage* small dark green. The short, self-branching growth and its trailing habit makes an ideal plant for hanging containers. ('La Campanella' × 'Powder Puff')
(Dunnett, UK, 1981)

**'Harry Lye'**
Single H2 Bush
*Tube, sepals* and large *corolla* are flesh pink. This cultivar is very floriferous. *Foliage* medium green. The upward growth very self-branching and short-jointed. Should make a good plant for the show bench.
(Goulding, UK, 1988)

**'Harry Taylor'**
Double H2 Trailer
*Tube* and *sepals* waxy red. *Corolla* purple, veined with red, and maturing to violet. *Foliage* medium green. Growth is very strong and bushy, but as a natural trailer will make a good basket.
(Holmes, R., UK, 1992)

**F. hartwegii**
Species H1 Bush
*Tube* long, thin, orange. *Sepals* orange. Corolla has short petals similarly coloured. The flowers, like the leaves, are held in whorls. *Foliage* dark green, and the leaves are very big. The growth is upright, but thin and rather spindly so will need supporting. Always late to come into flower.
(Colombia)

**'Harvest Glow'**
Single H2 Lax bush
*Tube* orient pink. *Sepals* held horizontally, orient pink on top and French rose underneath. *Corolla* bell-shaped, also orient pink. *Foliage* yellowish green with burnished tips and red veins and is particularly attractive in its young growth. A spreading habit and the rather lax growth, can be encouraged to make a good basket.
(Goulding, UK, 1984)

**'Hathersage'**
Double H2 Bush
*Tube* long pale pink. *Sepals* wide, carried well out from the corolla, neyron rose. *Corolla* roseine purple with red veins, shading to amaranth rose. *Foliage* medium green. The flowers are fairly freely produced. Growth is upright, self-branching and bushy. ('Joan Pacey' × 'Prosperity')
(Gadsby, UK, 1975)

**'Hathor'**
Single H2 Bush
*Tube* and *sepals* pink. *Corolla* darker pink, saucer-shaped and pointing outwards. *Foliage* medium green. The growth is very self-branching and upright.
(Springer, UK, 1985)

**F. hatsbachii**
Species H1 Bush
The small to medium-sized flowers are carried solitarily in the leaf axils. *Tube* and *sepals* red. *Corolla* violet. *Foliage* medium to dark green. The growth is rather wiry so will need supporting when pot grown.
(Berry et al, 1989)

**'Haute Cuisine'**
Double H2 Bush/trailer
A very attractive colouring on fairly large blooms. *Tube* and *sepals* very dark red. *Corolla* dark aubergine. *Foliage* medium green on the upper surfaces, but lighter on the lower. The lax growth is spreading but strong. Will make an excellent bush or a basket given the right support.
(de Graaff, Holland, 1988)

**'Hawaiian Night'**
Double H2 Trailer
*Tube* and *sepals* waxy white with light pink undersides. *Corolla* orchid mauve. *Foliage* medium green. The flowers are large and freely produced. The natural trailing habit of the plant makes it an ideal candidate for basket work.
(Fuchsia La, USA, 1968)

'HARRY GRAY'

'HARLOW CARR'

'HARRY LYE'

F. HATSBACHII

'HAUTE CUISINE'

**'Hawaiian Princess'**
Double H2 Trailer
*Tube* and *sepals* white. Flowers
fairly large double. *Corolla*
purple. *Foliage* medium green.
The growth is naturally trailing
and will make an extremely
nice basket.
(McDonald, USA, 1992)

**'Hawaiian Sunset'**
Double H2 Bush
*Tube* pale pink. *Sepals* dark
rose. *Corolla* dark red-purple
which lightens with maturity.
*Foliage* medium green. Natural
growth as a fairly strong
upright bush.
(McDonald, USA, 1990)

**'Hawkshead'**
Single H3 Bush
*Tube* short, white with a slight
greenish tinge. *Sepals* white
flushed with green, broad and
pointed. *Corolla* barrel-shaped,
also white. *Foliage* deep green,
small and with serrated edges.
The upright growth very strong
and bushy. A superb plant for
permanent use in the garden.
H. and S. in excess of 36in
(90cm). (*F magellanica* var
*molinae* × 'Venus Victrix')
(Travis, UK, 1973)

**'Hazel'**
Double H2 Lax bush
*Tube* and *sepals* neyron rose.
*Corolla* violet and neyron rose
maturing to violet, darker at
edges with neyron rose and
touches of white. *Foliage* very
large, a light lettuce green with
serrated edges and reddish
veins. The blooms are very
large, fully flared and circular.
The growth is rather lax so use
could be made of this plant in
baskets or as bushes.
(Richardson, Australia, 1985)

**'Heart Throb'**
Double H2 Bush
*Tube* pale pink, short, thick.
*Sepals* broad white with a pale
carmine blush underneath.
*Corolla* medium blue ageing to
pink, with white at the centre
and at the base of the petals.

The large wide spreading
flowers almost flat, the corolla
of larger and smaller petals
curled and folded. As flowers
mature blue and rose petals are
interspersed. *Foliage* medium
green. Growth is upright and
bushy.
(Hodges, USA, 1963)

**'Heer Hugo'**
Single H2 Bush
Medium-sized flowers. *Tube* and
*sepals* rose. *Corolla* carmine red.
*Foliage* medium green. Growth
fairly strong upright.
(van den Bergh, Holland, 1991)

**'Heidi Ann'**
Double H2 Bush
*Tube* short, thick, crimson.
*Sepals* short, broad and
reflexed, crimson cerise. *Corolla*
bright lilac-purple, veined with
cerise and lighter at the base of
the petals. There are numerous
petaloids, and the small to
medium flowers fully double.
*Foliage* small, dark green.
Upright growth self-branching
and bushy. ('Tennessee Waltz' ×
'General Monk')
(Smith, UK, 1969)

**'Heidi Weiss'**
Double H2 Bush
*Tube* short, thick, crimson.
*Sepals* short, broad, reflexing,
also crimson. *Corolla* white
with scarlet veining. Medium-
sized blooms are fully double.
*Foliage* small and darkish green.
Upright self-branching growth.
(Sport of 'Heidi Ann')
(Tacolneston, UK, 1973)

**'Heinrich Henkel'**
Triphylla type H1 Bush
*Tube* long, crimson. *Sepals* rosy
crimson flushed cinnabar.
*Corolla* bright crimson. *Foliage*
dark reddish-green flushed with
purplish-red. Growth strongly
upright. One of the most
beautiful of the triphylla
hybrids. (*F. corymbiflora* ×
'Magnifica', synonymous with
'Andenken an Heinrich
Henkel')
(Germany)

**'Heirloom'**
Double H2 Lax bush
*Tube* white with pink flush.
*Sepals* pink, green tips,
upturned. *Corolla* lavender
purple with heavy pink and
white marbling. Large flowers
fairly freely produced. *Foliage*
medium green. The growth is
rather lax for an upright so
will make a reasonable basket.
(Kennett, USA, 1968)

**'Helen Clare'**
Double H1 Bush
*Tube* a yellowish-green. *Sepals*
white with very faint pink on
the underside. *Corolla* creamy-
white with a frilly edge. *Foliage*
medium green.
(Holmes, E., UK, 1973)

**'Helene Houwen Claessen'**
Single H2 Trailer
Medium-sized cultivar. Tube
light green flushed with yellow.
*Sepals* rose, striped with white.
*Corolla* purplish-red with
purple flecks. *Foliage* medium
green. Growth is that of a
natural trailer.
(van Zoggel, Holland, 1989)

**'Hellan Devine'**
Single H2 Trailer
*Tube* pale pink. *Sepals*, also
pale pink, curl back towards
the tube. *Corolla* silver lilac.
*Foliage* medium green. Will
make a good basket as a
natural trailer.
(Pacey, UK, 1991)

*F. hemsleyana*
A purplish-mauve self. The
minute flowers are borne
solitarily in the leaf axils.
Upright-growing shrub which
would grow up to several feet
in its natural habitat.
(Costa Rica and Panama, 1937)

**'Hendrik den Besten'**
Semi-double H2 Lax bush
*Tube* pale rose. *Sepals* fuchsia
purple tipped with green.
*Corolla* dark robin red. *Foliage*
medium green. Growth rather
lax.
(Beije. Holland, 1991)

'HAWKSHEAD'

'HAZEL'

'HEIDI ANN'

'HEIDI WEISS'

'HEINRICH HENKEL'

'HELEN CLARE'

**'Hendrina Bovenschen'**
Single H2 Lax bush
*Tube* white, flushed green.
*Sepals* carmine rose. *Corolla*
purple. Large flowered cultivar.
*Foliage* medium green. The
growth is very lax so could be
used for either bush or basket
with the correct supports.
(Steevens, Holland, 1972)

**'Henk Waldenmaier'**
Double H2 Lax bush
Medium-sized flowers. *Tube*
deep shell pink. *Sepals*
cyclamen pink. *Corolla* light
rose purple. *Foliage* medium
green. The lax growth makes it
suitable for bush or basket.
(Weeda, Holland, 1990)

**'Henning Becker'**
Single H2 Bush
*Tube* red. *Sepals* red, reflex
back to the tube. *Corolla* plum
purple. The flowers are small.
*Foliage* medium green. Growth
upright and bushy.
(Strumper, Holland, 1991)

**'Henrietta Ernst'**
Single H2 Bush
*Tube* and *sepals* pale cardinal
red. *Corolla* bishop's violet
maturing to fuchsia purple
reddish veins, loose-petalled.
Flowers medium-sized and
freely produced. *Foliage*
medium green, broad, serrated.
Rather small upright growth.
(Curio, Germany, 1907)

**'Henri Poincare'**
Single H2 Bush
*Tube* medium-sized, red. *Sepals*,
also red, broad, longish and
recurve over the tube. *Corolla*
bell-shaped, violet-purple with
red veins. The bloom is fairly
long. *Foliage* darkish green
with medium-sized leaves.
Growth is rather lax and much
'stopping' required to produce
a reasonably shaped bush.
(Lemoine, France, 1905)

**'Herald'**
Single H3 Bush
*Tube* medium length, thick and
bulbous, scarlet. *Sepals*, short
and upturned, also scarlet.

*Corolla* deep bluish-purple
with cerise veining, changing to
reddish-purple on maturity.
The blooms are medium-sized.
*Foliage* light to medium green
with red veining and serrated
leaves. The growth is strongly
upright and self-branching.
(Sankey, UK, 1887)

**'Herbe de Jacques'**
Single H2 Lax bush
*Tube* scarlet, of medium length
and thickness. *Sepals* purple.
*Corolla* scarlet. The blooms are
of medium-sized. The *foliage* is
the most important feature of
this cultivar: the leaves are
variegated and mottled, with
red colouring predominant.
Could be useful for basket work
although the regular 'stopping'
required to obtain the best
colouring of the leaves will
ensure a tightly grown bush.
(Schneider, USA, 1978)

**'Heritage'**
Single H2 Bush
*Tube* crimson scarlet. *Sepals*
crimson scarlet, short, broad
and reflex. *Corolla* purple.
Flowers rather loose petalled
and of medium size. *Foliage*
medium green and serrated.
upright growth free-flowering,
although the initial growth of
the branches rather slow.
(Lemoine, France, 1902)

**'Hermiena'**
Single H2 Trailer
*Tube* and *sepals* white touched
with pink. *Corolla* dark violet
changing to rich plum. *Foliage*
medium green. The plant is self-
branching. A very floriferous
cultivar makes a superb
hanging pot or small basket.
(Lavieren, Holland, 1987)

**'Heron'**
Single H2 Bush
*Tube* short, deep cerise. *Sepals*
cerise, broad and slightly
curled at the edges. They are
held horizontally over the
corolla. *Corolla* violet magenta,
slightly veined with cerise.
*Foliage* medium green. Growth
is very strong and upright. The

plants are free-flowering and
self-branching.
(Lemoine, France, 1891)

**'Hessett Festival'**
Double H2 Bush
*Tube* white. *Sepals* long and
recurving, also white. *Corolla*
lavender blue with white
marbling. Very large. *Foliage*
medium green. A little slow
when starting its growth but a
good upright and self-branching.
(Goulding, UK, 1985)

**'Heston Blue'**
Semi-Double H2 Bush
*Tube* long, white. *Sepals* long,
narrow and upswept, white
flushed pink and with green tips.
*Corolla* smoky blue changing to
mauve as the bloom matures.
White shading at the base of the
petals. *Foliage* medium green,
and the leaves have serrated
edges. The growth is upright
and bushy. Quite free-flowering.
(Rawlins, UK, 1966)

**'Hetty Blook'**
Double H2 Lax bush
Medium-sized flowers. *Tube*
and *sepals* purple rose. *Corolla*
deep purple. *Foliage* medium
green. Very floriferous. Growth
is rather lax so the cultivar will
serve either as a bush or in a
hanging container.
(Weeda, Holland, 1990)

**'Heydon'**
Double H2 Bush
Flowers are large. *Tubes* bluish-
pink. *Sepals* off-white. *Corolla*
pale pink edged with purple
blue. *Foliage* dark green. The
growth of the plant upright
and bushy.
(Clitheroe, UK, 1981)

**'H.G. Brown'**
Single H3 Bush
*Tube* and *sepals* a deep scarlet.
*Corolla* dark lake. The small to
medium flowers freely
produced. *Foliage* dark glossy
green. The growth is low and
very bushy. Excellent for
permanent bedding. H. and S.
18–24in (45–60cm).
(Wood, UK, 1946)

'HERALD'

'HERMIENA'

'HERON'

'HESSETT FESTIVAL'

**'Hiawatha'**
Single H2 Bush
Small flowers. *Tube* white, with
rose flush, short, very thick.
*Sepals* white, with rosy flush on
top, rose pink underneath.
*Corolla* dark robin red, very
compact. *Foliage* medium
green.The upright growth is
quite bushy. ('La Campanella'
×)
(van Wijk, Holland, 1984)

**F. hidalgensis**
Species H2 Bush
Very small flowered cultivar of
the *F. encliandra* group. *Tube*,
*sepals* and *corolla* of pure
white. *Foliage* medium green
and very small. The growth is
very wiry and can be trained
into shape around wires.
(Raiser and date unknown)

**'Hidcote Beauty'**
Single H2 Lax bush
*Tube* thick, medium length,
creamy white. *Sepals* short and
broad, creamy, waxy white
with green tips. *Corolla* pale
salmon pink with a pale flush.
*Foliage* pale to medium green
with small to medium-sized
leaves. The upright growth
very strong, self-branching
and bushy. The cultivar is very
free-flowering and may be used
for either bushes or baskets.
(Webb, UK, 1949)

**'Highland Pipes'**
Single H2 Bush
Very attractive and rather
unusual flowers. *Tube* and
*sepals* beetroot purple on top,
ruby red underneath. *Corolla*
ruby red. Flowers borne in
panicles at the ends of branches.
Foliage medium to dark green.
Growth is very lax but best as a
bush plant given some support.
(*F. magdalenae* × *F. excorticata*)
(de Graaff, Holland, 1985)

**'Hilda May Salmon'**
Single H2 Bush
A plant of the 'intermediate'
type. *Tube* long, slender,
tapering, rosy red. *Sepals*
longish and narrow, held
horizontally, white terminating

rosy red at the base. *Corolla* a
deeper shade of rosy red with
orange overtones. Very
floriferous, produces six to
eight flowers at the leaf nodes.
*Foliage* mid-green with coarsely
toothed edges. Suitable for
bushes or baskets.
(Goulding, UK, 1987)

**'Hindu Belle'**
Single H2 Lax bush
*Tube* long, waxy white. *Sepals*
long, broad, upturned, white
with pink flush beneath, tipped
with green. *Corolla* rich plum
changing to red with maturity.
The flowers are large, very
long, and freely produced.
*Foliage* medium green. The
laxity of growth makes it
available for baskets or bushes.
(Monkner, USA, 1959)

**'Hinnerike'**
Single H2 Bush
*Tube*, *sepals* and *corolla* bright
orange. *Foliage* medium glossy
green, veins reddish-green,
greyish-green stems. The
growth is stiffly upright so early
'pinching' will be necessary to
achieve good bushes. Large
*encliandra*-type blooms. (*F.
cylindracea* × *F. magdalenae*)
(Bogemann, Germany, 1987)

**'Hobson's Choice'**
Double H2 Bush
*Tube* and *sepals* pink. *Corolla*
a lighter shade of pink with
delicate tints and shades.
Medium-sized blooms freely
produced. *Foliage* medium
green. Growth is upright and
bushy.
(Hobson, Britain, 1976)

**'Hokusai'**
Triphylla type H1 Bush
*Tube* long, pink. *Sepals* pink.
*Corolla* red. Flowers very long.
*Foliage* dark green with a light
purple reverse. Growth a lax
upright.
(Bogemann, Germany, 1992)

**'Holly's Beauty'**
Double H2 Trailer
*Tube* white. *Sepals* white
flushed with pale rose. *Corolla*

pale orange. *Foliage* light to
medium green. The natural
growth habit is trailing so will
make a good basket.
(Garrett, UK, 1989)

**'Honeymoon'**
Semi-double H2 Bush
*Tube* and *sepals* red. *Corolla*
veronica-blue. The flowers are
medium-sized freely produced
and open wide. *Foliage*
medium green. Growth is
upright but rather slow.
(Niederholzer, USA, 1943)

**'Horatio'**
Single H2 Trailer
*Tube* long, slender, pink. *Sepals*
pale pink, long, narrow.
*Corolla* a deeper shade of pink
(orchid pink). *Foliage* medium
green, medium-sized flowers
very freely produced. The
natural growth is as a trailer so
will make a good basket.
(Green, UK, 1975)

**'Hot Coals'**
Single H2 Bush
Medium-sized flowers. *Tube*
dark red. *Sepals* dark scarlet
red. *Corolla* dark aubergine.
*Foliage* medium to dark green.
The upright growth produced
on vigorous short-jointed and
self-branching stems.
(Carless, UK, 1993)

**'Howlett's Hardy'**
Single H3 Bush
*Tube* scarlet, thin. *Sepals*
scarlet, long, narrow, reflexed.
*Corolla* violet-purple, paler at
the base, veined with scarlet.
The flowers are large for a
hardy and fairly freely
produced. *Foliage* medium
green, long and serrated. H.
and S. 24–30in (60–75cm).
(Howlett, UK, 1952)

**'Huize Ruurlo'**
Single H2 Lax bush
Flowers are medium-sized
*Tube* and *sepals* carmine red.
*Corolla* red to purple. *Foliage*
medium to darker green.
Growth is rather lax although
it is very vigorous.
(Brouwer, Holland, 1990)

'HIAWATHA'

'HIGHLAND PIPES'

'HINNERIKE'

'HOBSON'S CHOICE'

'HONEYMOON'

'HOT COALS'

**'Hula Girl'**
Double H2 Trailer
*Tube* deep rose-pink. *Sepals* stand out flat and do not reflex, also deep rose-pink. *Corolla* white shading to pink at the base of the petals. Flowers are large. *Foliage* medium green with red veining and shaded red on the undersurface. The natural trailing habit makes this an ideal cultivar to use in baskets. (Paskesen, USA, 1972)

**'Humboldt Holiday'**
Double H2 Trailer
*Tube* thin, pinkish white. *Sepals* also pinkish-white with frosty pink on the undersurface, gradually curl upwards with a slight twist. *Corolla* violet splashed with pink, fading to white at the base of the petals. They mature to a rich violet-red. *Foliage* medium-sized with golden-green leaves veined magenta and changing to light green with maturity. The natural trailing and self-branching habit helps to make a good basket. ('Mary Ellen' × 'Cosmopolitan') (Hasset, USA, 1980)

# I

**'Ian Leedham'**
Semi-double H2 Trailer
*Tube* long, neyron rose. *Sepals* crimson and held horizontally, with recurved tips. *Corolla* tyrian purple maturing to rose bengal. The blooms are quite large with occasional cardinal red petaloids. *Foliage* mid-green, lighter on the underside. The natural habit is as a trailer, and will make a superb basket, especially from autumn-struck cuttings. (*F. magellanica* hybrid × 'Lady Kathleen Spence') (Bielby/Oxtoby, UK, 1985)

**'Iceberg'**
Single H2 Bush
*Tube* carmine, distinctly striped with red. *Sepals* reflexed, white and slightly marked red at the base. Medium-sized flowers. *Corollas* white. *Foliage* medium to dark green. Growth is fairly strongly upright and bushy. Best colour in shady conditions. ('Norman Mitchinson' × 'Baby Pink') (Mitchinson, UK, 1980)

**'Icecap'**
Single to semi-double H2 Bush
Medium-sized flowers. *Tube* and *sepals* cardinal red. *Corolla* white with slight red veining. *Foliage* medium to darker green. Very floriferous and will make a superb exhibition pot plant. ('Showcap' × 'Bon Accorde') (Gadsby, UK, 1968)

**'Ice Cream Soda'**
Semi-double H2 Lax bush
*Tube* short, light green to white. *Sepals* long and arch back, white sometimes pink. *Corolla* white to pink, sometimes completely pink; the four petals flare, giving a very frizzy look – they are surrounded by many petaloids. The large blooms are freely produced. *Foliage* a dark glossy green. Growth is rather lax and the plant can be used as bush or basket. (Castro, USA, 1972)

**'Iced Champagne'**
Single H2 Bush
*Tube* pink. *Sepals* dawn pink, reflex to show a lighter shade of pink. *Corolla* a beautiful shade of rhodamine pink. The flowers are quite long, of medium size and are very freely produced. *Foliage* light to medium green. The plant is short-jointed and self-branching; objects to constant 'pinching', preferring to be left to form a bush naturally. ('Miss California' × 'Jack Shahan') (Jennings, UK, 1968)

**'Ichiban'**
Double H2 Trailer
*Tube* short, thick, white to pink. *Sepals* also white to pink.

*Corolla* spinel pink at the base fading to cyclamen purple at the tips of the petals, maturing to china rose. Large flowers freely produced. *Foliage* large and is dark green. The growth is naturally trailing. (Fuchsia La, USA, 1973)

**'Ida Dixon'**
Double H2 Bush
Medium-sized flower. *Tube* and *sepals* red. *Corolla* purple. *Foliage* medium green. Growth habit is upright and bushy. (Dixon, UK, 1869)

**'Igloo Maid'**
Double H2 Bush
*Tube* white, long. Medium to large flowers. *Sepals* white tipped with green, short, broad. *Corolla* fully double white with the faintest touch of pink. *Foliage* yellowish-green, serrated. Natural habit of the plant is to grow upright. (Holmes, E., UK, 1972)

**'Impala'**
Double H1 Trailer
*Tube* very long, thin, ivory white. *Sepals* swept back, pale pink. *Corolla* pink. *Foliage* medium green. The growth is very slender and spreading. Excellent for hanging pots or baskets, but one that benefits from protection from adverse weather. (Moerman, Holland, 1990)

**'Imperial Crown'**
Single H2 Trailer
*Tube* and *sepals* salmon. *Corolla* a rich salmon. The flower could almost be described as a 'self-colour'; the medium-sized blooms are produced freely and early. *Foliage* medium green. Natural habit is to trail. Will make a good basket. (Haag, USA, 1953)

'HULA GIRL'                                    'HUMBOLDT HOLIDAY'

                          'ICE CREAM SODA'

'ICED CHAMPAGNE'                               'IGLOO MAID'

**'Imperial Fantasy'**
Double H2 Trailer
*Tube* greenish-white. *Sepals*
long, curved, broad, white with
reddish markings at the base.
*Corolla* imperial purple with
petaloids of pink, white and
coral variegations. *Foliage* large
and dark green with red
veining. The natural habit is to
trail so this plant makes a
superb basket.
(Stubbs, USA, 1981)

**'Impudence'**
Single H2 Bush
*Tube* light red. *Sepals* long,
slim, also light red, curling
upwards to tube. *Corolla* white
veined with rose, consists of
four round petals which open
out perfectly flat. The medium-
sized blooms are freely
produced. *Foliage* medium
green; the natural habit is to
grow as an upright bush.
(Schnabel, USA, 1957)

**'Impulse'**
Double H2 Bush
Large blooms. *Tubes* and *sepals*
white, recurving, with green
tips, flushed slightly with pink.
*Corolla* pale lilac. *Foliage*
medium green with a lighter
colouring on the lower surface.
The large blooms are quite
freely produced. Fairly strong
upright growth. ('Sweet Leilani'
× 'Sebastopol')
(Saxondale, UK, 1988)

**'Independence'**
Double H2 Bush
Large flowers. *Tube* white with
green streaks. *Sepals* white to
pink on the outside, dawn pink
on the underside. *Corolla*
currant red fading to cherry
red. *Foliage* medium-sized mid-
green with red veining. Growth
fairly strong and upright. Will
make a good bush.
(Stubbs, USA, 1976)

**'Indian Maid'**
Double H2 Trailer
*Tube* scarlet, medium length
and thickness. *Sepals* extra
long, recurved, scarlet red.
*Corolla* rich royal purple.

Large blooms very freely
produced. *Foliage* dark green.
The natural habit is trailing.
Will make a good basket. Also
makes beautiful bush if
pinched hard in early stages.
(Waltz, USA, 1962)

**'Inferno'**
Single H2 Trailer
*Tube* thick, light orange. *Sepals*
are held at the horizontal,
reflex, orange. *Corolla* reddish-
orange fading to orange at the
base of the petals. *Foliage*
medium green, lighter beneath,
red veining. A natural trailer
that will make a good basket.
(Storvick, USA, 1983)

**'Ingelore'**
Single H2 Bush
*Tubes* and *sepals* red. *Corolla*
rosy purple. *Foliage* medium
green. The natural growth is
compact, strongly erect, bushy.
(Strumper, Holland, 1991)

**'Insulinde'**
Triphylla type H1 Bush
A true terminal-flowering
triphylla type. *Tube* long,
orange. *Sepals* short, orange.
*Corolla* also orange. *Foliage*
bronze green. The growth is
bushy and self-branching. Excellent for big bedding schemes.
(de Graaff, Holland, 1991)

**'Inter City'**
Single H2 Trailer
*Tubes* white. *Sepals* white,
flushed with pink and tipped
with green. *Corolla* lilac. A
delightful flower enhanced by
the medium green *foliage*. The
natural trailing habit will
create a very good basket.
(Strumper, Holland, 1991)

**'Iolanthe'**
Triphylla type H1 Bush
*Tube* very long, thin, orange.
*Sepals* tangerine orange, rather
pendant and tipped with green.
*Corolla* orange. The long,
trumpet-shaped flowers are
borne terminally at the ends of
the branches. *Foliage* dark and
velvety in texture with some
red staining. Growth rather lax

and could be used as a basket
if so desired.
(Goulding, UK, 1987)

**'Irene L Peartree'**
Double H2 Trailer
Sport from 'Swingtime'. *Tube*
pink. *Sepals* pink, with green
tips. *Corolla* pink. *Foliage* is
medium to dark green. The
natural growth is as a
spreading bush. Will make a
good basket with the assistance
of weights.
(Peartree, UK, 1993)

**'Irene van Zoeren'**
Double H2 Bush
Medium-sized flowers. *Tube*
light orange. *Sepals* light rose-
red. *Corolla* lilac rose with a
reddish-purple border. *Foliage*
medium green. The growth is
very strong and upright.
(Beije, Holland, 1989)

**'Iris Amer'**
Double H2 Bush
*Tube* and *sepals* white, flushed
with pinkish orange. *Corolla*
bright red with shades of
carmine, the petals splashed
with orange markings. *Foliage*
deep green. This cultivar
responds to frequent 'stopping'
to develop a good bushy shape.
(Amer, UK, 1966)

**'Isis'**
Single H2 Bush
*Tube* and *sepals* red. *Corolla*
purple shading to purple red at
base of petals. Flowers medium
to large. *Foliage* dark green
with a crimson mid rib. The
growth is upright and bushy.
(de Groot, Holland, 1973)

**'Isle of Mull'**
Single H2 Bush
*Tube* light magenta with darker
veins. *Sepals* baby pink, veined
with flesh pink. *Corolla* rose
magenta splashed with pink.
The medium-sized flowers,
which have the 'coolie hat'
appearance, are freely produced.
*Foliage* is medium green, ovate,
slightly serrated. Growth is
upright, short-jointed and bushy.
(Tolley, UK, 1978)

'IMPERIAL FANTASY'

'IMPUDENCE'

'INGELORE'

'INSULINDE'

'ISLE OF MULL'

**'Isle of Purbeck'**
Single H2 Bush
Medium-sized flowers. *Tube*
white, flushed with pink. *Sepals*
pink. *Corolla* rose. *Foliage*
medium green. The natural
growth is as an upright bush.
(Swinbank, UK, 1990)

**'Isle of Wight'**
Double H2 Bush
*Tube* red. *Sepals* held half way
to the horizontal, red with
reflexed to recurved tips.
*Corolla* opens very dark
purple, matures to violet-blue.
*Foliage* dark glossy green on
the upper surface, matt dark
green on the lower. ('Royal
Velvet' × 'Lilac Lustre')
(Porter M, UK, 1989)

**'Italiano'**
Double H2 Trailer
*Tube* and *Sepals* salmon to
pink. *Corolla* deep purple
fading to burgundy. The
medium-sized flowers are very
full and freely produced.
*Foliage* medium green. The
growth is naturally trailing.
(Fuchsia Forest, USA, 1966)

**'Ivan Gadsby'**
Double H2 Bush
*Tube* greenish white, large,
thick. *Sepals* waxy white,
longish. *Corolla* magenta rose.
The very solid flowers are
freely produced. *Foliage*
medium green, long, shiny and
pointed. Growth is as an
upright bush. Does best in
shade. ('Pepi' × 'Bridesmaid')
(Gadsby, UK, 1970)

**'Ixion'**
Single H2 Trailer
*Tube* and *sepals* pink. *Corolla*
violet. Fairly large flowers.
*Foliage* medium green. The
habit of growth is naturally
trailing so will make a superb
basket.
(Raiser and date unknown)

# J

**'Jack Acland'**
Single H2 Stiff trailer
*Tube* and *sepals* pink. *Corolla*
red on opening fading to darker
pink, bell-shaped. *Foliage*
medium green. The rather stiff
arching branches grow quite
vigorously. Often confused with
'Jack Shahan' but the flowers of
the latter are lighter and the
growth is rather more lax.
(Haag and Son, USA, 1952)

**'Jack Coast'**
Single H2 Bush
*Tube* and *sepals* crimson.
*Corolla* pale violet-purple
veined with crimson. *Foliage*
medium green, slightly lighter
underneath. Growth is upright
and bushy. ('Brixham Orpheus'
× 'Beacon')
(Holmes, R., UK, 1989)

**'Jacqueline'**
Triphylla type H1 Bush
Terminal-flowering in bunches.
*Tube* long and *sepals* short, both
almost scarlet. *Corolla* orange.
*Foliage* dark green and velvety in
texture. The growth is self-
branching and upright. An
excellent cultivar. ('Gartenmeister Bonstedt', × 'Speciosa')
(Oxtoby, UK, 1987)

**'Jack Shahan'**
Single H2 Trailer
*Tube* pale rose bengal, long.
*Sepals* rose bengal, green tips,
medium length. *Corolla* also rose
bengal, very compact. The large
flowers are freely produced.
*Foliage* medium green, narrow,
serrated. The growth is lax and
will produce a fine basket which
flowers continuously over a long
period. Needs a great deal of
pinching to train to shape. Often
confused with 'Jack Acland'
whose flowers are darker and
growth somewhat stiffer.
(Tiret, USA, 1949)

**'Jack Stanway'**
Single H2 Bush
*Tube* and *sepals* rhodamine
pink with recurving tips.

*Corolla* white with pink
veining coming with maturity;
the petal edges are turned
under. The flowers are small to
medium-sized and quarter-
flared. *Foliage* sage green edged
with cream. The growth is
upright and self-branching.
With care will produce an
excellent decorative plant.
(Rowell, UK, 1985)

**'Jamboree'**
Double H2 Bush
*Tube* pinkish white. *Sepals*
salmon pink with deeper pink
underneath. *Corolla* salmon
pink and carmine. The very
large blooms have irregular
petals and the colour is
dazzling. *Foliage* large, medium
green, glossy and rather brittle.
Growth is upright and bushy.
(Reiter, USA, 1955)

**'James Travis'**
Single H2 Bush
Tiny flowers, exceedingly free-
flowering of the *breviflorae*
type. *Tube* vivid coral pink.
*Sepals* coral pink, spreading,
slightly reflexing. *Corolla*
salmon fading to dusky pink.
The flowers are followed by
decorative deep purple berries.
*Foliage* small, Lincoln green
above and lighter beneath.
Growth is shrublike. Very useful
for miniature or bonsai work.
(Travis S., UK, 1972)

**'Jam Roll'**
Double H2 Bush
*Tube* short claret red. *Sepals*
fully upswept, also claret red.
*Corolla* opens dark mauve-red
maturing to red. *Foliage*
medium green. Growth is fairly
upright and quite vigorous.
('Marinka' × )
(Brough, UK, 1986)

**'Jan Bremer'**
Single H2 Lax bush
*Tube* rather long, light red.
*Sepals* and *corolla* also light red.
Medium-sized flowers freely
produced. Foliage medium
green. The natural growth of
the plant is as a bush.
(Bremer, Holland, 1973)

148

'IXION'

'JACQUELINE'

'JACK SHAHAN'

'JAMBOREE'

### 'Jane Humber'
Double H2 Lax bush
*Tubes* venetian pink. *Sepals* also venetian pink on top, carmine rose underneath, fully reflexing with recurved tips. *Corolla* rose purple with mallow purple at the base of the petals maturing to rose purple. The large blooms are fully flared. *Foliage* medium green, lighter beneath, serrated. Growth is rather lax so is suitable for all types of training. Bushes and baskets can be grown with the necessary supporting. ('Swingtime' × 'Blush o' Dawn')
(Bielby, UK, 1983)

### 'Jane Rowell'
Double H2 Bush
*Tube* and *sepals* pale pink edged with rose. *Corolla* white, veined pink. The flowers are fairly freely produced. *Foliage* medium green.
(Raiser and date unknown)

### 'Jan Houtsman'
Single H2 Bush
*Tubes* white flushed with pink. *Sepals* dark carmine rose. *Corolla* reddish-violet. *Foliage* medium green. Growth is naturally upright.
(Giessen, Holland, 1986)

### 'Janice Ann'
Single H2 Lax bush
*Tube* and *sepals* turkey red. Medium-sized flower. *Corolla* violet blue. *Foliage* medium green. Growth is rather lax and could be used for baskets or bushes with supports.
(Holmes, R., UK, 1994)

### 'Janice Revell'
Double H2 Lax bush
*Tube* cream. *Sepals* rose on the upper surface, slightly darker on the lower. *Corolla* opens as magenta shading to white at the base of the petals. *Foliage* medium green with serrated edges. The veins and branches are red. ('Bicentennial' × 'Papa Bleuss')
(Redfern, UK, 1988)

### 'Jan Zonder Vrees'
Double H2 Bush
Medium-sized flowers. *Tubes* and *sepals* crimson. *Corolla* dark purple. *Foliage* medium green. Growth upright.
(Saintenoy, Holland, 1990)

### 'Jasper's Dondestraal'
Semi-double H2 Trailing
*Tubes* and *sepals* white. Medium-sized flower. *Corolla* violet. *Foliage* medium green. The natural trailing habit makes this a good plant for baskets. ('Dondestraal', thought to mean a scamp or naughty child.)
(Van Aspert, Holland, 1990)

### 'Jasper's Duimelot'
Single H2 Trailing
Medium-sized flower. *Tube* and *sepals* deep shell pink. *Corolla* magenta and light fuchsia purple. *Foliage* medium green. Natural trailing habit.
(van Aspert, Holland, 1991)

### 'Jasper's Groentje'
Single H2 Bush
Medium-sized flower. *Tube* and *sepals* pale green. *Corolla* light cyclamen purple. *Foliage* medium green. The natural habit is as a bush.
(van Aspert, Holland, 1991)

### 'Jasper's Likkepot'
Single H2 Bush
*Tube* and *sepals* pale rose. Flowers medium-sized. *Corolla* dark beetroot. *Foliage* medium to darker green. The growth is upright.
(van Aspert, Holland, 1991)

### 'Jasper's Ringeling'
Double H2 Trailer
*Tube* rose. *Sepals* deep rose, tipped with green. Corolla light purple; flowers are small. Foliage medium green. The natural habit is trailing.
(van Aspert, Holland, 1990)

### 'Javelin'
Single H2 Lax bush
*Tube* carmine red. Sepals cardinal red. Corolla deep purple, medium-sized flowers.

*Foliage* medium to dark green. Natural growth is rather lax. Can be used as basket or bush with the necessary supports.
(Brouwer, Holland, 1990)

### 'Jayne Lye'
Single H2 Bush
Medium-sized flower. *Tube* and *sepals* pink. Corolla mauve-pink. The upright growth is reasonably strong. Foliage medium green.
(Lye, UK, 1870)

### 'Jayne Rowell'
Double H2 Lax upright
Medium-sized flowers. *Tube* rose bengal. *Sepals* pale pink. *Corolla* white, veined with red. *Foliage* medium green. The lax growth makes this plant suitable for basket or bush.
(Rowell, UK, 1985)

### 'Jaypee'
Single H2 Bush
Small single flower. *Tube* and *sepals* red. Corolla violet-purple. *Foliage* medium green. The growth is as a small bush.
(Porter, UK, 1974)

### 'Jean Burton'
Single H2 Bush
*Tube* pale pink. *Sepals* rhodamine pink, held well back. *Corolla* pure white. The large flowers are bell-shaped and freely produced. *Foliage* medium green. The upright growth is very strong. ('Sleigh Bells' × 'Citation')
(Gadsby, UK, 1968)

### 'Jean Clark'
Single H2 Bush
*Tube* is white flushed with pink. *Sepals* white flushed pale pink on the upper surface, white flushed light pink on the lower. *Corolla* violet blue with white at the base of the petals. *Foliage* dark green on the upper surface, lighter medium green underneath. Growth is strongly upright and bushy.
('Sarah Ann' × 'Annabel')
(McDonald, UK, 1989)

'JANE HUMBER'

'JASPER'S LIKKEPOT'

**'Jean Dawes'**
Double H2 Trailer
*Tube* and *sepals* white. *Corolla*
large, a delicate shade of pink.
*Foliage* medium green. The
natural growth is to spread out
and trail so will make a super
basket. Best results are
obtained when protection is
given from strong sun and
wind.
(Goulding, UK, 1987)

**'Jean Ewart'**
Single H2 Bush
*Tube* short, china rose. *Sepals*
short pointed, curl back to
tube, also china rose. *Corolla*
amaranth rose. The medium to
small flowers are very compact
and extremely freely produced.
Foliage medium green. Growth
is upright and self-branching.
Named after a former President
of the British Fuchsia Society.
('Mipam' × 'Carol Roe')
(Roe, UK, 1981)

**'Jeanne d'Arc'**
Double H2 Bush
Medium-sized flowers. *Tube*
and *sepals* red. *Corolla* a
striking white. *Foliage* medium
green. Growth is upright and
bushy.
(Lemoine, France, 1903)

**'Je Maintiendrai'**
Single H2 Lax bush
Medium-sized flower. *Tube*
dark red. *Sepals* dark rose red
on top, light cardinal red
beneath, tips recurve. *Corollas*
opens currant red, at base of
petals, matures to claret red
with orange. *Foliage* medium
green, red veins. Natural
growth rather lax.
(de Graaff, Holland, 1979)

**'Jennette Marwood'**
Double H2 Bush
*Tube*, *sepals* and *corolla* all a
delicate shade of pastel pink.
*Foliage* yellow. The growth is
upright and bushy. The plant
was named in connection with
the BBC Children in Need
Appeal.
(Dresman, UK, 1993)

**'Jennie Rachael'**
Double H2 Bush
*Tube* thick, white. *Sepals* white,
tinged with pink, tipped with
green. *Corolla* very large, rose
red and veined with rose
bengal. The petaloids are of the
same colouring. Stamens and
pistils white. The flowers are
very large and very full. *Foliage*
dark green has leaves up to 5in
(13cm) in length.
(Cheetham, UK, 1979)

**'Jennifer Hampson'**
Double H2 Trailer
*Tube* and *sepals* are cerise.
*Corolla* rich purple. The small
flowers are perfectly shaped
and are freely produced.
*Foliage* small medium green.
The natural desire of this
fuchsia is to trail so will make
a good basket.
(Hilton, UK, 1976)

**'Jennifer Haslam'**
Single H2 Bush
*Tube* short, *sepals* flyaway both
rose red. The saucer-shaped
*corolla* is flecked with pink and
plum. *Foliage* medium green.
Growth is very firm, self-
branching and upright.
(Goulding, UK, 1994)

**'Jenny Sorensen'**
Single H2 Bush
*Tube* neyron rose. *Sepals*
neyron rose, recurved and have
green tips. *Corolla* a very pale
lilac and each petal has a
distinctive edging of dark
violet; as the plant matures so
the petals become slightly
darker with a cerise edging.
*Foliage* a glossy medium green,
and slightly paler underneath.
The growth is fairly small but
self-branching and upright.
Will make an excellent and
eye-catching small standard.
('Dusky Beauty' × 'Cloverdale
Pearl')
(Wilkinson, UK, 1987)

**'Jess'**
Single H2 Trailer
*Tube* rather long, thin, white.
*Sepals* held at the horizontal

when mature, broad crêpe
deep rose. *Corolla* large, a
vivid cerise. *Foliage* medium
green. The natural habit is to
trail, so will make an excellent
basket.
(Meier, UK, 1987)

**'Jessie Pearson'**
Double H2 Lax bush
*Tube* white, flushed with pink.
*Sepals* white, tipped with
green. *Corolla* a pale violet
blue, the outer petals streaked
with rose red fading to rosy
mauve. *Foliage* light green.
Growth is rather lax. Like
'Annabel', it will make a good
basket or a bush given the
necessary support. (Sport from
'Annabel')
(Pearson, UK, 1993)

**'Jessimae'**
Single H2 Bush
*Tube* short china rose. *Sepals*
broad china-rose. *Corolla*
mallow purple. The flowers are
small to medium-sized and
freely produced. *Foliage*
medium green. ('Countess of
Aberdeen' seedling)
(White, UK, 1980)

**'Jester'**
Semi-double H2 Bush
*Tube* cerise. *Sepals* long,
narrow, upturned, cerise.
*Corolla* a rich royal purple
turning lighter with maturity.
*Foliage* medium green. The
upright growth is fast and
sturdy.
(Holmes, E., UK, 1968)

**'Jet Fire'**
Double H2 Stiff trailer.
*Tube* long, greenish-white.
*Sepals* broad, palest pink; held
straight upright against tube,
slightly twisting and recurving.
*Corolla* reddish-cerise splashed
with pink and salmon.
*Foliage* medium green with
serrated edging. Growth is
rather lax. Could be used as a
bush or a basket but the
necessary supports will have to
be given.
(Reedstrom, USA, 1959)

'JENNY SORENSEN'

'JESS'

**'Jim Coleman'**
Single H2 Bush
*Tube* is crimson. *Sepals* crimson on the upper side and crêped crimson beneath with green tips. *Corolla* opens amethyst violet with lilac at the base of the petals and matures to lilac. *Foliage* mid-green on the upper surface and lighter on the lower. This fuchsia is a good strong upright grower which is very floriferous and holds its bell-shaped flowers semi-erect. Frequent 'stopping' will create a good bush. ('Poppet' × 'Cropwell Butler')
(Holmes, R., UK, 1987)

**'Jim Dodge'**
Double H2 Trailer
*Tube* pink. *Sepals* white. *Corolla* a delightful orchid blue. *Foliage* medium green. The growth is lax and will make an excellent basket with its freely produced medium to large flowers.
(Dyos, UK, 1993)

**F. jimenezii**
Species H1 Bush
The tiny deep red flowers are carried in terminal racemes. *Foliage* dark green flushed with purple on the underside. Leaves are fairly large, varying from 2–4in (5–10cm).
(Panama)

**'Jim Muncaster'**
Single H2 Trailer
*Tube* and *sepals* purplish-red. *Corolla* very dark purple fading to beetroot. *Foliage* medium green. The flowers are very freely produced and an extremely good basket can be obtained in a short time. The flowers appear very early in the season.
(Bielby/Oxtoby, UK, 1992)

**'Jimmy Carr'**
Double H2 Trailer
*Tube* pink. *Sepals* horizontally held, white on the upper surface and rose underneath.

*Foliage* medium green on the upper surface, light olive green underneath. The medium-sized flowers are freely produced. A natural trailing-type growth.
(Rowell, UK, 1989)

**'Joan Barnes'**
Double H2 Bush
*Tube* medium-sized white tinged with light pink. *Sepals* light pink with reflexed green tips. *Corolla* crimson, slightly darker at the base of each petal. *Foliage* medium green. Very free-flowering for a double. Upright growth is free-branching.
(Barnes, UK, 1988)

**'Joan Cooper'**
Single H3 Bush
*Tube* pale rose opal, long, thin. *Sepals* pale rose opal, reflex straight back and cover tube, tips green. *Corolla* cherry red. The smallish flowers are very freely produced. An interesting and unusual colouring of flower for a hardy. *Foliage* light green, longish, serrated. Growth upright and bushy. H. and S. 18–24in (45–60cm).
(Wood, UK, 1954)

**'Joan Gilbert'**
Double H2 Bush
*Tube* neyron rose. *Sepals* neyron rose with very distinctive green tips. *Corolla* a rich violet base splashed and mottled with salmon and pink. *Foliage* medium green. The upright growth is self-branching, close jointed and bushy. Makes an excellent bush or a standard.
(Gilbert, UK, 1977)

**'Joan Goy'**
Single H2 Bush
*Tube* and *sepals* white blushed pink with recurved tips. *Corolla* lilac pink maturing to light lilac pink. The open bell-shaped flowers are half-flared and are carried in an erect position. *Foliage* a dark shiny green with some lightening on the

undersurface. Excellent bushes can be produced from the short-jointed and self-branching growth.
(Webb, UK, 1989)

**'Joan Leach'**
Single H3 Bush
*Tube* and *sepals* are deep pink. *Corolla* light blue flushed with pink. Small flowers very freely produced on upright and bushy growth. *Foliage* medium green. The habit of growth is dwarfish, reaching a height of only 12–18in (30–45cm).
(Tabraham, UK, 1975)

**'Joan Margaret'**
Double H2 Lax bush
*Tube* white, flushed pink. *Sepals* pale rose pink tipped, green and curl back. *Corolla* a deep sugar pink, the outer petals flushed rose pink. The medium to large flowers are very freely produced. *Foliage* dark green. The natural growth is as a spreading bush.
(Hickman, UK, 1994)

**'Joan Morris'**
Single H2 Bush
*Tube* rosy-red. *Sepals* also rosy red but shading to white, green tips. *Corolla* rosy purple with white or pink streaks on each petal. Medium-sized flowers, are either single or semi-double and have many petaloids. A very eye-catching cultivar and well worth growing for its upright, vigorous and bushy growth. *Foliage* medium green.
(Dyos, UK, 1984)

**'Joanne'**
Single H2 Trailer
*Tube* short, thin, orient-pink. *Sepals* red purple tipped with green. *Sepals* quite long 1½in (3–4cm). *Corolla* red purple. The flowers are medium-sized and the colour combination is rather unusual. *Foliage* medium green. Growth is naturally trailing. (Seedling from 'Chang')
(Pugh, UK, 1982)

'JIM COLEMAN'

'JIM MUNCASTER'

'JIMMY CARR'

'JOAN BARNES'

'JOAN GOY'

'JOAN LEACH'

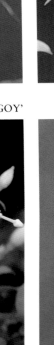

**'Joan Pacey'**
Single H2 Bush
*Tube* long, white, tinged pink.
*Sepals* pink on top, darker pink
beneath tipped with green.
*Corolla* phlox pink, veined
with rose pink. The flowers are
very prolific and of medium
size. *Foliage* medium green.
The growth is rather willowy
and will need some supporting
to make a sturdy bush. Very
vigorous. Excellent exhibition
plant. ('Rosebel' × 'Sleigh
Bells')
(Gadsby, UK, 1972)

**'Joan's Delight'**
Single H2 Bush
*Tube* short, crimson. *Sepals*
crimson. *Corolla* a rich violet-
blue. Small flowers very freely
produced. *Foliage* medium
green. The dwarf habit of the
plant makes it ideal for use in
the smaller pots. ('Wee Lass' ×
'Cloverdale')
(Gadsby, UK, 1977)

**'Joan Smith'**
Single H2 Bush
*Tube* flesh pink. reflexing.
*Sepals* flesh pink. *Corolla* soft
pink with a touch of cerise.
The medium-sized flowers are
freely produced from early in
the season. *Foliage* medium
green. The cultivar is extremely
vigorous and will achieve a
height of approx 4ft (120cm)
in a season.
(Thorne, UK, 1958)

**'Joan Young'**
Single H2 Bush
*Tube* short, red. *Sepals*
recurving, red. *Corolla* bell-
shaped is speckled pink.
*Foliage* medium green. The
upright habit of growth makes
this very useful for the border.
(Goulding, UK, 1994)

**'Joe Kusber'**
Double H2 Lax bush
*Tube* white, short. *Sepals*
white, tipped with pink, long.
*Corolla* bluish-purple with the
faintest of pink variegations.
The flowers, although full and

extremely fluffy, are very freely
produced. *Foliage* medium
green and rather large. Growth
is lax so will be useful as a
basket or as a bush if the
necessary supports are given.
(Pennisi, USA, 1968)

**'Johanna Regina'**
Semi-double H2 Bush
Medium-sized flowers. *Tube*
white flushed with rose. *Sepals*
white flushed with orange.
*Corolla* lilac. *Foliage* medium
green. Natural growth of the
plant is as an upright bush.
(Krom, Holland, 1989)

**'Johannes Novinski'**
Single H2 Bush/trailer
Medium-sized flower. *Tube*
rose striped with green. *Sepals*
plum rose. *Corolla* violet
purple. *Foliage* medium green.
The growth is very lax. Will
make a good basket or a bush
with supports.
(Baum, Holland, 1984)

**'John Baker'**
Double H2 Bush
Vigorously growing upright
cultivar with large flowers.
*Tube* and *sepals* white flushed
pink. *Corolla* white veined
with pink. *Foliage* medium
green. Quite floriferous for the
size of the bloom.
(Weeks, UK, 1987)

**'John Lockyer'**
Single H2 Bush
*Tube* pink thick, medium
length. *Sepals* a rich dark pink,
tipped with green, broad and
upturned. *Corolla* pink-purple
with red-purple edge and
inside. *Foliage* medium green.
The medium-sized flowers are
freely produced early in the
season. Upright and bushy
growth.
(Holmes, E., UK, 1969)

**'John Maynard Scales'**
Triphylla type H1 Bush
Truly terminal-flowering,
triphylla-type fuchsia. *Tube*
long, slender, orange. *Sepals*
short, an attractive orange.

*Corolla* a brighter orange.
*Foliage* medium to dark green
with a faint purple hue to the
reverse of the leaves. The
growth is strongly upright.
Very useful for large pot work.
(Goulding, UK, 1985)

**'John Yarnall'**
Double H2 Bush
*Tube* and broad *sepals* a
waxy white. *Corolla* a deep
violet-blue. *Foliage* medium
green very vigorous, bushy
plant.
(Greenwood, UK, 1991)

**'Joker'**
Double H2 Trailer
*Tube* light neyron rose, short.
*Sepals* light neyron rose, paler
towards tips which are green.
*Corolla* many shades of red
and blue. *Foliage* large, dark
green on the upper side, lighter
on the under side, red stems
and centre vein. The growth is
rather lax but the cultivar can
be used as a basket or a bush
with the right sort of support
and training. ('Lena' ×)
(de Graaff, Holland, 1976)

**'Jolanda Weeda'**
Semi-double H2 Bush
Medium-sized flowers. *Tube*
and *sepals* flame red. *Corolla*
reddish purple. *Foliage* medium
green. Growth is fairly strong
and the flowers freely
produced.
(Weeda, Holland, 1989)

**'Jomam'**
Single H2 Bush
*Tube* short, thick, rose pink.
*Sepals* recurving, slightly
twisted, also rose-pink. *Corolla*
opens pale blue-violet lightly
veined with pink maturing to
light violet-pink and slightly
flushed white at the base of the
petals. *Foliage* dark yellow-
green, paler undersides, pale
green veins, serrated. Growth is
upright and bushy. The flowers
are medium-sized, slightly
flaring, bell-shaped, profuse.
('Blue Elf' × 'Mayfield')
(Hall, UK, 1984)

'JOAN SMITH'

'JOE KUSBER'

'JOHN BAKER'

'JOHN MAYNARD SCALES'

'JOMAM'

**'Jose's Joan'**
Double H2 Trailer
*Tube* longish, white. *Sepals* white, tipped with green. *Corolla* pale violet. The blooms are large and free, and very eye-catching with this colour combination. *Foliage* medium green. The growth is lax making it suitable for both baskets or pots.
(Bellamy, UK, 1978)

**'Joy Bielby'**
Double H2 Trailer
*Tubes* short, white streaked with red. *Sepals* white with a pink overlay, recurving green tips. *Corolla* white with a rose flush. *Foliage* medium green. The growth is lax and self-branching. A delightful flower which will make a superb basket. ('Swingtime' × 'Blush o' Dawn')
(Bielby, UK, 1982)

**'Joyce Mortley'**
Double H2 Bush
Medium-sized flower. *Tube* and *sepals* waxy red. *Corolla* dark purple. *Foliage* medium to dark green. Growth is upright and bushy.
(Holmes, R., UK, 1992)

**'Joyce Sinton'**
Single H2 Bush
*Tube* is pink. *Sepals* pink on the top side, salmon pink underneath. *Corolla* orangey-red fading to orange with maturity. The long-lasting flowers are medium-sized and freely produced. *Foliage* medium green and the plants are upright in their growth and free branching. ('Orange Crush' × 'Buttercup')
(Sinton, UK, 1986)

**'Joy Patmore'**
Single H2 Bush
*Tube* white, short, thick. *Sepals* are waxy white, green tips, narrow, upturning. *Corolla* a shade of rich carmine. *Foliage* medium green. The upright growth, the ease of cultivation, and the beauty of the clear cut

colouring will make this cultivar popular for many years to come; a delightful fuchsia.
(Turner, UK, 1961)

**'Jubie-Lin'**
Double H2 Trailer
*Tube* and *sepals* red. *Corolla* deepest purple. *Foliage* medium green. A vigorously growing trailer with large flowers which, as a result of its self-branching, will make a superb basket quite quickly.
(Copley Gardens, USA, 1964)

**'Judith Alison Castle'**
Single H2 Bush
*Tube* creamy white, has a pink flush. *Sepals* reflex to tube, tipped with green, also creamy white. *Corolla* blue fading to soft pink at the base of the petals. The flowers are small but very profuse. *Foliage* medium green. Growth is upright and bushy. Will make an excellent bush. ('Dorothea Flower' × 'Hawkshead')
(Thornley, UK, 1982)

**'Judith Coupland'**
Single H2 Bush
Medium-sized flowers. *Tube* and *sepals* carmine tipped with green. *Corolla* white veined with carmine. *Foliage* medium green and the growth is strongly upright.
(Kirby, UK, 1990)

**'Jules Daloges'**
Double H2 Bush
*Tube* scarlet. *Sepals* turn right back to tube to reveal the corolla; also scarlet. *Corolla* a rich bluish violet, with pink edges to the petals. The large blooms are fully double and freely produced. *Foliage* medium to dark green. The growth is upright and bushy.
(Lemoine, France, 1907)

**'Julia'**
Double H2 Lax bush
*Tube* red. *Sepals* long, curving, red. *Corolla* blackish purple. The blooms are very large and freely produced for the size.

The growth is rather lax and can be used as a bush or a trailer. *Foliage* medium to dark green.
(Gorman, USA, 1970)

**'Julia Dietrich'**
Double H2 Bush
*Tube* cream, pink flush. *Sepals* cream, flushed pink and tipped with green. *Corolla* lavender tinged with pink. The flowers are medium-sized. *Foliage* medium green. (Sport of 'City of Pacifica')
(Casey, Australia, 1972)

**'Julie Horton'**
Semi-double H2 Trailer
*Tube* pink. *Sepals* narrow, long, pink tipped with green. *Corolla* pink with wide overlapping petals. The flowers are fairly large and freely produced. *Foliage* dark green and leathery. A natural trailer.
(Gagnon, USA, 1962)

**'Julie Marie'**
Double H2 Bush
*Tube* and *sepals* pink. *Corolla* darker pink. The flowers are fully double and 'classically' shaped. *Foliage* darkish green. The growth is fairly lax but will make an excellent bush with supports. Could also make a good basket.
(Kirby, UK, 1988)

**'June Gardner'**
Single H2 Lax bush
*Tube* short, neyron rose. *Sepals* neyron rose on the upper surface and carmine rose underneath, tipped with green; held at the horizontal. *Corolla* small, square-shaped, beetroot purple shading to rose in the centre. *Foliage* scheele's green (a golden colour), with red veining and serrated edges. A very attractive plant. The growth is rather stiff for a basket and lax for a bush so judicious training will be necessary. (('Empress of Prussia' × 'Burning Bush') × 'Mrs W. Ruddle')
(Bielby, UK, 1982)

'JOSE'S JOAN'                               'JOY BIELBY'

          'JOY PATMORE'                          'JUDITH COUPLAND'

          'JULES DALOGES'                         'JULIE MARIE'

**'Jupiter 70'**
Single H2 Bush
*Tube* slightly thick, medium length, shell pink. *Sepals* scarlet, long, upswept and green tipped. *Corolla* crimson with mandarin red at the base of the petals. Small, bell-shaped blooms. *Foliage* medium green, large, heavily serrated. The growth is strongly upright and self-branching. ('Percy Holmes' × 'San Francisco')
(Holmes, R., UK, 1970)

**'Justin's Pride'**
Single H3 Bush
*Tube* and *sepals* neyron rose. *Corolla* deep cerise pink. The medium-sized flowers are very freely produced. *Foliage* medium green. The strong upright growth and its self-branching habit requires no supporting. H. and S. 18–24in (45–60cm).
(Jones, G., UK, 1974)

# K

**'Kabibi'**
Single H2 Bush
Medium-sized flowers. *Tube* rose bengal. *Sepals* carmine. *Corolla* deep violet. *Foliage* medium green. The natural growth is as an upright bush.
(Veen, Holland, 1991)

**'Kaboutertje'**
Single H2 Trailer
Miniature flowers. *Tube* carmine, short, thin. *Sepals* carmine on the topside and crimson underneath, held half down. *Corolla* opens beetroot purple maturing to ruby red. *Foliage* small medium green, lighter beneath, serrated. The natural growth is as a stiff trailer. Self-branching with short internodes. ('Minirose' × 'Whiteknights Blush')
(de Graaff, Holland, 1985)

**'Kaleidoscope'**
Double H2 Bush
*Tube* and *sepals* red. *Corolla* various shades of purple to

pale lavender streaked with red and pink giving a multicoloured appearance which changes during the flowering season, hence the name. The very large blooms are produced fairly freely for their size. *Foliage* medium green. The natural growth is upright. Needs staking if required as a bush.
(Martin, USA, 1966)

**'Karen'**
Single H2 Bush
*Tube* and *sepals* rosy red. *Corolla* bluebird blue. *Foliage* medium green. Medium-sized blooms very freely produced, held well out from the branches. Growth is a natural upright bush. ('Upward Look' seedling ×)
(Gadsby, UK, 1968)

**'Karen Bielby'**
Single H2 Trailer
*Tube* long, thin, venetian pink. *Sepals*, are held slightly below the horizontal and twist either way, carmine rose with green tips. *Corolla* fuchsia purple. Medium-sized bell-shaped flowers extremely freely produced. *Foliage* mid-green with serrated edges to the leaves. A natural trailer which will make a superb basket. ('Arlington Hall' × 'Lustre')
(Bielby, UK, 1983)

**'Karin de Groot'**
Single H2 Trailer
*Tubes* of these medium-sized flowers. *Tube* light magenta. *Sepals* of a paler magenta. *Corolla* violet aubergine. *Foliage* medium green. The habit of the plant is as a lax bush or trailer.
(de Graaff, Holland, 1989)

**'Karin Siegers'**
Single H3 Bush
Medium-sized flowers. *Tubes* and *sepals* reddish-purple. *Corolla* carmine purple. *Foliage* medium green. The habit of growth is very stiff and

strongly upright. Excellent bush for the hardy border. H. and S. 18–24in (45–60cm).
(Stoel, Holland, 1990)

**'Kathleen Muncaster'**
Double H2 Bush
*Tube* and *sepals* dawn pink tipped with green. *Corolla* crimson. *Foliage* light green. Full double, very vigorous and fast growing. Needs 'stopping' regularly to create a manageable shape. Very floriferous.
(Bielby/Oxtoby, UK, 1987)

**'Kathleen Smith'**
Double H2 Lax bush
*Tube* venetian pink. *Sepals* fully recurved, white on the upper side, tipped green, rhodamine pink on the undersurface. *Corolla* violet, matures to bishop's violet. The medium to large blooms are bell-shaped. *Foliage* medium green. The growth is very lax for a bush but rather stiff for a trailer so judicious use of supports will be necessary to obtain either type of growth. ('Swingtime' × 'Blush o' Dawn')
(Bielby, UK, 1983)

**'Kathryn Maidment'**
Single H2 Bush
*Tube* rose. *Sepals* long, fold back to cover the tube, also rose-coloured. *Corolla* violet with deeper violet edges; petals white in the centre with red veins, gradually changing to the violet colouring. *Foliage* medium green. Growth is naturally upright.
(Creer, UK, 1982)

**'Kathy Louise'**
Double H2 Trailer
*Tube* carmine red. *Sepals* carmine, crêpe effect on underside, long, broad, curl up over tube. *Corolla* a beautiful shade of soft rose. Large blooms. *Foliage* glossy and dark green. Growth is very vigorous and trails naturally. Frequent 'stopping' is necessary to induce branching.
(Antonelli, USA, 1963)

'JUSTIN'S PRIDE'

'KAREN BIELBY'

'KARIN DE GROOT'

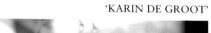

'KATHLEEN MUNCASTER'

'KATHLEEN SMITH'

**'Kathy's Prince'**
Double H2 Trailer
*Tube* and *sepals* white flushed
with pink. *Corolla* purple
quickly fading to deep red.
*Foliage* medium green. The
flowers are large and very long-
lasting, and the natural growth
is trailing. Makes a superb
basket.
(Muncaster, UK, 1992)

**'Kathy's Sparkler'**
Double H2 Lax bush/trailer
*Tube* short, thin, flesh pink
streaked with green. *Sepals* pale
to dark pink with coral pink
underneath, held horizontally
with recurving tips. *Corolla*
orchid blue variegated with pink
and maturing to cyclamen
purple; petaloids variegated
orchid pink and coral pink.
*Foliage* dark green, lighter
beneath, red veins. The growth
is rather stiff for a trailer and lax
for a bush – judicious training
will therefore be necessary.
('Hula Girl' × 'Applause')
(Stubbs, USA, 1983)

**'Katrina'**
Double H2 Bush
*Tube* and *sepals* very pale pink.
*Corolla* also very pale pink.
The blooms are medium to
large. *Foliage* medium green.
The flowers are freely
produced. Natural growth is as
an upright bush.
(Holmes, E., UK, 1968)

**'Katrina Thompsen'**
Single H2 Bush
*Tube* pink. *Sepals* palest pink,
tipped with green. *Corolla*
white. The flowers are medium-
sized. *Foliage* medium green. A
superb cultivar: extremely
floriferous, and made a great
impact when first seen on the
show circuit. Excellent for
bushes or the smaller standards.
(Wilkinson, UK, 1993)

**'Keele '92'**
Double H2 Trailer
Medium-sized flower. *Tube* and
*sepals* pink. *Corolla* pastel blue
splashed with pink. *Foliage*
medium green. The plant is

extremely floriferous. Natural
trailing habit.
(Rowell, UK, 1992)

**'Keepsake'**
Double H2 Bush
*Tube* pink, short, thick. *Sepals*
white above, flushed pink
beneath. *Corolla* dianthus
purple. Medium-sized blooms;
four central petals perfectly
cupped, surrounded by many
petals of the same colouring.
*Foliage* light green. Growth
habit is upright and bushy.
(Kennett, USA, 1961)

**'Kegworth Carnival'**
Double H2 Lax bush
*Tube* white, medium thickness
and length. *Sepals* fairly long,
and narrow white. *Corolla*
shortish, tyrian purple
changing to rose bengal. The
medium-sized blooms are freely
produced. *Foliage* medium
green. The growth is rather lax
so will make a basket or a bush
given the necessary supports.
(Smith, H., UK, 1978)

**'Kegworth Delight'**
Double H2 Bush
*Tube* white. *Sepals* broad,
short, white flushed with
carmine and tipped with green.
*Corolla* tyrian purple flushed
white at the base of the petals.
*Foliage* medium green. Very
floriferous, medium-sized
flowers. Strong upright growth.
(Smith, H., UK, 1980)

**'Kegworth Supreme'**
Single H2 Bush
*Tube* empire rose. *Sepals*
empire rose, slightly darker
underneath. *Corolla* fuchsia
purple. *Foliage* very dark
green. Growth is very strong
and upright. The flowers are of
small medium size but are very
freely produced.
(Smith, H., UK, 1978)

**'Ken Goldsmith'**
Triphylla type H1 Bush
Flowers held in bunches at the
ends of the branches. *Tube*
long and dark orange. *Sepals*
short, orange. Petals within the

*corolla* are similarly coloured.
*Foliage* medium to dark green
with a slight purple sheen on
the reverse. Strong, upright-
growing plant.
(Stannard, UK, 1991)

**'Ken Jennings'**
Single H2 Bush
*Tube* short, thick, rhodamine
pink. *Sepals* small, quite broad,
also rhodamine pink, held
horizontally. *Corolla* tyrian
purple. The flowers are medium-
sized and freely produced.
*Foliage* medium green. Growth
is naturally upright and bushy.
('Bobby Shaftoe' × 'Lustre')
(Roe, UK, 1982)

**'Kenny Dalglish'**
Double H3 Bush
*Tube* slightly fluted, scarlet.
*Sepals* a glowing scarlet.
*Corolla* purple, veined with
rose at the base. *Foliage*
darkish-green. The flowers are
produced very freely and
continuously. An excellent plant
for the hardy border. H. and S.
24–30in (60–75cm). ('Empress
of Prussia' × 'Spion Kop')
(Jones G, UK, 1988)

**'Ken Sharp'**
Single H2 Bush
*Tube* short, thickish, cream.
*Sepals* broad, pointed, white
flushed with rose, held
horizontally. *Corolla* tyrian
purple shading to pale pink at
the base of the petals. *Foliage*
medium green. Growth is fairly
strongly upright. ('Micky
Goult' × 'Lustre')
(Roe, UK, 1986)

**'Kentish Maid'**
Single H2 Bush
*Tube* narrow-waisted, jasper
red. *Sepals* carmine rose on the
outside, rose bengal on the
inner, with a distinctive green
tip; long, graceful and curve
upwards. *Corolla* beetroot
purple fading to fuchsia purple
at base of petals, Indian lake at
edges. *Foliage* medium green.
The flowers are very prolific.
Growth is naturally upright.
(Holmes, R., UK, 1976)

162

'KATHY'S SPARKLER'

'KATRINA THOMPSEN'

'KEGWORTH CARNIVAL'

'KEGWORTH DELIGHT'

**'Kernon Robson'**
Double H2 Bush
*Tube* short, pink. *Sepals* lie
back against the tube, pale red.
*Corolla* smokey red. The
flowers are fairly large and
freely produced. *Foliage*
medium green. The natural
growth is bushy.
(Tiret, USA, 1968)

**'Kerry Ann'**
Single H2 Bush
*Tube* neyron rose. *Sepals* curve
upwards, also neyron rose.
*Corolla* aster violet with slight
paling at the base of the petals.
The flowers are medium-sized
and freely produced. *Foliage*
medium green. The natural
growth is upright and self-
branching.
(Pacey, UK, 1981)

**'Khada'**
Single H2 Bush
*Tube* and *sepals* rosy red.
*Corolla* white, veined with
rose. The flowers are small but
are very prolific, held erect
through the foliage. *Foliage*
medium green. Growth is
short, compact and bushy.
('Margaret Roe' × 'Snowcap')
(Roe, UK, 1973)

**'Kiekeboe'**
Single H2 Bush
Small flowers. *Tubes* and *sepals*
light red. *Corolla* light purple
and salmon. *Foliage* medium
green. Natural growth of this
dwarf-growing plant is
spreading.
(de Graaff, Holland, 1989)

**'Kimberley'**
Semi-double H2 Trailer
*Tube* long, white. *Sepals* very
long and broad, white flushed
pink on the underside, green
tips. *Corolla* deep blue with
phlox pink marbling. The
medium to large blooms have
serrated edges to the petals and
are freely produced. *Foliage*
medium green, finely serrated.
The natural growth is as a
trailer.
(Munckner, USA, 1963)

**'Kim Broekhof'**
Single H2 Lax bush
*Tube* deep rose. *Sepals* carmine
rose. *Corolla* red flecked with
orange. *Foliage* medium green.
The natural growth is rather
lax and will need supporting to
make a good bush. Medium-
sized flower, very floriferous.
(Stoel, Holland, 1990)

**'King George'**
Single H2 Bush
Large flowers. *Tube* pink. *Sepals*
rose, long, held straight and
upturn at tips. *Corolla* light
purple with rose-pink veining.
*Foliage* medium to dark green,
serrated leaves with reddish
veins. Presented by raiser to HM
George V in 1912 with its sister
plant 'Queen Mary' ('Seedling
from 'Mrs Marshall')
(Howlett, UK, 1912)

**'King of Hearts'**
Double H2 Trailer
*Tube* and *sepals* red. *Corolla*
pale lavender with splashes of
red, pink and white on the
outer petals. The large flowers
are freely produced. *Foliage*
medium green. The growth is
naturally trailing and will make
an excellent basket. (Sport of
'Queen of Hearts')
(Fuchsia Forest, USA, 1965)

**'King's Ransom'**
Double H2 Bush
*Tube* white. *Sepals* broad,
recurved, also white. *Corolla* of
the deepest imperial purple.
The medium-sized, globular
blooms are freely produced.
*Foliage* medium green and the
natural growth is upright.
(Schnabel, USA, 1954)

**'Kiniver Joy'**
Double H2 Lax bush
*Tube* thick, bright pink. *Sepals*
bright pink, horizontally held,
long, twisted and have
recurving green tips. *Corolla*
pale pink striped with bright
pink. *Foliage* dark green.
Upright growth is rather lax,
but the arching branches carry
a heavy quantity of flowers.
(Watts, UK, 1989)

**'Kiss 'n Tell'**
Single H2 Bush
*Tube* white. *Sepals* reflexing,
waxy white with pink on the
underside. *Corolla* lavender
flushed with pink; the petals are
fluted. A very floriferous plant.
*Foliage* bright green. The natural
growth is as an upright bush.
(Hooper, UK, 1992)

**'Kit Oxtoby'**
Double H2 Trailer
*Tube* neyron rose. *Sepals*
broad, 'half up', neyron rose.
*Corolla* rose pink with darker
picotee edges. *Foliage* medium
green. Very full double,
extremely floriferous, and the
natural trailing habit makes it
superb for baskets.
(Bielby/Oxtoby, UK, 1990)

**'Kiwi'**
Double H2 Trailer
*Tube* long, greenish-white.
*Sepals* upswept, a very clear
white with green tips. *Corolla*
china rose with a touch of
purple. *Foliage* medium green,
medium size, serrated. The
blooms are very large and
freely produced.
(Tiret, USA, 1966)

**'Klein Beekestein'**
Double H2 Bush
*Tubes* pale rose. *Sepals* rose red.
*Corolla* light red to purple.
*Foliage* medium green. The
flowers are freely produced for a
large double. Growth is upright.
(van den Beek, Holland, 1986)

**'Kleine Gertnerin'**
Double H2 Lax bush
Small flowers. *Tube* and *sepals*
white, flushed rose pink.
*Corolla* pink. *Foliage* medium
green. Growth is rather lax.
(Strumper, Holland, 1985)

**'Knight Errant'**
Single H2 Bush
*Tube* and *sepals* white. *Corolla*
violet. Medium-sized flowers
freely produced. *Foliage*
variegated. Growth is upright.
(Sport from 'Tom Knights')
(Gubler, UK, 1985)

'KERNON ROBSON'

'KIMBERLEY'

'KING'S RANSOM'

'KINIVER JOY'

'KIWI'

**'Knockout'**
Double H2 Trailer
*Tubes* and *sepals* flesh pink.
*Corolla* deep purple with orange
markings on outer petals. *Foliage*
medium green, red vein. The
natural growth habit is to spread
and this can be helped by regular
'stopping' of the leading growths.
A natural trailer which will make
a good basket.
(Stubbs, USA, 1981)

**'Kolding Perle'**
Single H2 Bush
*Tube* waxy white. *Sepals* waxy
white with green tips, held low
over corolla. *Corolla* pink with
cerise and salmon shades. The
medium-sized flowers are
produced freely and early in
the season. *Foliage* pale to
medium green. A good, strong
and very dependable fuchsia.
(Raiser unknown, Denmark)

**'Kolibrie'**
Single H2 Bush
Small flower. *Tubes* and *sepals*
deep rose. *Corolla* dark red.
*Foliage* medium green. Growth
is upright and self-branching.
Not too vigorous.
(de Graaff, Holland, 1986)

**'Koningen der Fruhe'**
Single H2 Bush
*Tube* and *sepals* of this
medium-sized double are dark
red. *Corolla* violet-purple. The
growth is vigorously upright.
*Foliage* medium green.
(Hybridist and year unknown)

**'Kon Tiki'**
Double H2 Stiff trailer
*Tube* white. *Sepals* white with
pale pink flush. *Corolla* pink-
violet. The medium-sized
blooms are very freely
produced. *Foliage* medium to
dark green. The growth is
rather stiff for a trailer yet too
lax for a bush, so will need
supporting for either method.
(Tiret, USA, 1965)

**'Koralle'**
Synonymous with 'Coralle'
under which name the
description appears.

**'Kwintet'**
Single H2 Bush
*Tube* long, dark rose pink.
*Sepals* rose pink, short, held
horizontal. *Corolla* rosy red,
slightly bell-shaped. The
blooms are of medium size and
freely produced. *Foliage*
medium green. Very strong,
upright and bushy growth.
(van Wieringen, Holland,
1970)

**'Kyoto'**
Single H2 Trailer
Medium-sized flowers. *Tubes*
and *sepals* reddish-purple.
*Corolla* white, veined with
reddish-purple. *Foliage* medium
green. The natural growth is as a
trailer, will make a good basket.
(Bogemann, Germany, 1990)

# L

**'La Bergere'**
Semi-double H2 Stiff trailer
*Tube* cream blushed with red,
short, thick. *Sepals* are fully
recurved and twisted, greyish-
white. *Corolla* opens creamy
white maturing to white. The
small blooms are freely
produced. *Foliage* dark green
but lighter on the underside.
Although rather stiff in its
growth it will make an
excellent basket.
(de Graaff, Holland, 1986)

**'La Campanella'**
Semi-double H2 Trailer
*Tube* and *sepals* white slightly
flushed pink. *Corolla* a beautiful
shade of imperial purple, with
some cerise veining, maturing to
lavender. The flowers are small
but are exceptionally free and
profuse. *Foliage* small and
medium green. The growth is
trailing and self-branching. Very
rapid growth when the plants
are established. Makes an
excellent basket.
(Blackwell, UK, 1968)

**'Lace Petticoats'**
Double H2 Lax bush
*Tube* short, white. *Sepals* white

and tipped with green, short,
upturning to cover tube.
*Corolla* white with the faintest
touch of pink at the base of the
petals. *Foliage* darkish green.
The flowers are of medium size
and are freely produced.
(Tiret, USA, 1952)

**'Lady Beth'**
Double H2 Lax bush or
trailer
*Tube* pale rose. *Sepals* are the
palest rose on top, deeper pink
beneath, of thick crêpe texture,
recurving over tube. *Corolla*
bright violet blue, paler with
age. Petals splashed rose pink.
The giant blooms are fairly
freely produced considering their
size. *Foliage* medium green.
(Martin, USA, 1968)

**'Lady Boothby'**
Single H3 Bush
*Tube* crimson, short, thin.
*Sepals* crimson, short and
broad, held almost horizontal.
*Corolla* blackish-purple, pink
at base of petals, veined with
cerise. The flowers are small
but very freely produced.
*Foliage* darkish green, finely
serrated. Growth is upright and
very vigorous, very long
branches with long internodes.
H. and S. 36–48in (90–120cm).
(*F. alpestris* × 'Royal Purple')
(Rafill, UK, 1939)

**'Lady Bower'**
Double H2 Lax bush
*Tubes* and *sepals* cardinal red.
*Corolla* creamy white with outer
petaloids heavily flushed with
crimson. *Foliage* medium green.
The large blooms are freely
produced. Growth is rather lax
so will need supporting when
grown as a bush.
(Gadsby, UK, 1970)

**'Lady Heytesbury'**
Single H2 Bush
*Tube* and *sepals* waxy white.
*Corolla* deep rose to rose.
*Foliage* medium green. The
medium-sized flowers are freely
produced. Natural upright and
bushy growth.
(Wheeler, UK, 1866)

'KNOCKOUT'                                      'KON TIKI'

'KWINTET'                                        'LA CAMPANELLA'

'LACE PETTICOATS'                               'LADY BETH'

**'Lady in Grey'**
Double H2 Bush
*Tube* and *sepals* white, flushed
with pink. *Corolla* very pretty
blue overlaid with soft mauve,
darker veins. *Foliage* medium
green, serrated edges. The large
blooms are fairly freely
produced. Lax upright growth;
hard to make a basket and not
an easy variety to grow. Needs
warm situation.
(Lockerbie, Australia, 1988)

**'Lady Isobel Barnett'**
Single H2 Bush
*Tube* and *sepals* rosy red.
*Corolla* rose purple/Imperial
purple. Small to medium
flowers which are very
profusely produced. One of the
most prolific flowerers to date
carrying up to eight flowers in
each leaf node. *Foliage* medium
green. Growth is upright, self-
branching and bushy. Produces
an enormous amount of pollen
which tends to cover the leaves
making it look unsightly.
(Gadsby, UK, 1968)

**'Lady Kathleen Spence'**
Single H2 Lax bush
*Tube* whitish to pale pink.
*Sepals* whitish rose on top,
amaranth rose underneath,
long and thin. *Corolla* very
delicate lavender shade fading
to light lilac. The medium-sized
flowers are very freely
produced. *Foliage* medium
green. The lax growth enables
it to be used in baskets or pots.
(Ryle, UK, 1974)

**'Lady Ramsey'**
Single H2 Bush
*Tube* short flesh pink. *Sepals*
reflex with maturity, also flesh
pink. *Corolla* bell-shaped, violet.
The medium-sized flowers are
freely produced. *Foliage* medium
green. Very floriferous and well
worth growing for show work.
Strong growth, upright and self-
branching.
(Goulding, UK, 1981)

**'Lady's Smock'**
Single H2 Bush
*Tube* and *sepals* magenta rose.

*Corolla* lilac. The paniculata-
shaped flowers are borne
axillary. *Foliage* light olive
green with a faint flush of red
on the upper surface. Self-
branching and upright growth.
(de Graaff, Holland, 1987)

**'Lady Thumb'**
Semi-double H3 Bush
*Tube* and *sepals* light reddish-
crimson. *Corolla* white, slightly
veined with carmine. The
flowers are small but extremely
freely produced. *Foliage* small,
medium-small to green.
Growth is dwarf reaching no
more than a height and spread
of 12in (30cm). (Sport from
'Tom Thumb')
(Roe, UK, 1966)

**'La Fiesta'**
Double H2 Trailing
*Tube* short, thick, white. *Sepals*
white with green tips, broad,
tips upturn. *Corolla* light
dianthus purple; white petaloids
splashed cerise. The flowers are
fairly large and freely produced.
*Foliage* medium green. The
growth is naturally trailing and
self-branching so will therefore
make an excellent basket.
(Kennett , USA, 1962)

**'La France'**
Double H2 Bush
*Tube* scarlet, short, thick.
*Sepals* rich scarlet, short, broad,
recurving. *Corolla* rich violet-
purple with scarlet veins, pales
with maturity. The fully double
flowers are large and freely
produced. *Foliage* medium
green. The upright growth is
very strong and bushy.
(Lemoine, France, 1885)

**'Lakeland Princess'**
Single H2 Bush
*Tube* short, carmine. *Sepals*
fully recurving, white, flushed
with carmine on the outside
base. *Corolla* spectrum violet,
white at the base of each petal.
The medium-sized flowers are
very freely produced. *Foliage*
medium green. Growth upright
and fairly strong. It is self-
branching and will form a

good bush easily. ('Eden Lady'
× 'Norman Mitchinson')
(Mitchinson, UK, 1981)

**'Lakeside'**
Single H2 Lax bush
*Tube* bright pink, short, thin.
*Sepals* reddish-pink with green
tips. *Corolla* bluish-violet veined
with bright pink. *Foliage* small,
medium green. Growth is rather
lax for a bush so could be used,
with assistance, in baskets.
(Thornley, UK, 1967)

**'Lancashire Lass'**
Single H2 Bush
*Tube* short, fat, light pink with
red stripes. *Sepals* white with a
splash of red near the tube,
reflex right back to the stem.
*Corolla* hyacinth blue and
much paler at the base of each
petal. *Foliage* medium green.
The growth is tall and upright.
('Estelle Marie' × 'Pennine')
(Sinton, UK, 1986)

**'Lancelot'**
Single H2 Bush
*Tube* and *sepals* rosy red.
*Corolla* bowl-shaped, white
with pink veining. *Foliage*
medium green. The strongly
upright growth is self-
branching with many side-
shoots. Makes a splendid bush
or a standard for show work.
(Goulding, UK, 1983)

**'Land van Beveren'**
Single H2 Trailer
*Tube* and long *sepals* waxy
white. *Corolla* carmine. *Foliage*
medium green. The natural
growth of the plant is trailing.
(Saintenoy, Holland, 1988)

**'La Neige'**
Double H2 Lax bush
*Tube* white with pink flush.
*Sepals* white, tipped with
green, and have a faint touch
of pink on the underside.
*Corolla* white. The blooms are
medium-sized but freely
produced. *Foliage* medium
green, longish, serrated. The
natural growth is rather lax so
can be used for bush or basket.
(Tiret, USA, 1965)

'LADY ISOBEL BARNETT'

'LADY THUMB'

'LA FIESTA'

'LAKELAND PRINCESS'

'LANCASHIRE LASS'

'LANCELOT'

**'La Porte'**
Double H2 Bush
*Tube* and *sepals* smoky
burgundy. *Corolla* also smokey
burgundy. *Foliage* medium
green. The natural growth is as
an upright bush.
(Holmes, E., UK, 1979)

**'Larissa'**
Single H2 Bush
*Tube* and *sepals* cream. *Corolla*
neyron rose. *Foliage* medium
green. Flowers small. The
upright growth is self-
branching, short-jointed and
bushy.
(de Graaff, Holland, 1987)

**'Lark'**
Triphylla type H1 Bush
Terminal-flowering. *Tube* long
thin orange. *Sepals* short, also
orange. The petals within the
*corolla* are a darker shade of
orange. *Foliage* darker green
with distinct reddening.
Growth is rather robust. Will
make a good bush but can also
be encouraged for use in wall
baskets.
(Goulding, UK, 1988)

**'La Rosita'**
Double H2 Bush
*Tube* pink. *Sepals* recurved,
pink. *Corolla* orchid pink. The
medium-sized blooms are freely
produced. *Foliage* medium
green. The colouring of the
blooms depends upon the
amount of shade given to the
plants. The natural growth is
as an upright bush.
(Erickson-Lewis, USA, 1959)

**'Lassie'**
Double H1 Lax bush/or
trailer
*Tube* short, bright crimson.
*Sepals* very wide, also bright
crimson, glossy above and crêpe
beneath, held in a horizontal
position. *Corolla* snowy white.
The flowers are fairly large and
very full. *Foliage* dark glossy
green. The growth is rather lax
and will make a good basket
but a bush can be achieved with
supports. ('Swingtime' ×)
(Travis, S., UK, 1959)

**'Laura'**
Double H2 Trailer
*Tube* red, medium length red.
*Sepals* red, long, broad,
upturned. *Corolla* sky blue
shading to lavender, large
blooms. *Foliage* medium green.
Will make a good basket.
(Martin, USA, 1968)

**'Laura'**
Single H2 Bush
*Tube* and *sepals* light orange.
*Corolla* reddish-orange. *Foliage*
medium green. The natural
growth is strongly upright.
Very free-flowering. Excellent
for bushes or standards.
(Introduced in 1986, Raiser
unknown)

**'Laurie'**
Double H2 Trailer
*Tube* pink. *Sepals* long, slender,
pale pink, tipped with green.
*Corolla* soft rose and rhodamine
pink, four large petals in centre
and numerous outside ones.
*Foliage* lush green. The flowers
are large and heavily petalled.
(Antonelli, USA, 1963)

**'Lavender Kate'**
Double H2 Bush
*Tube* and *sepals* pink. *Corolla*
lavender blue. The flowers are
fairly large and freely produced.
The natural growth is upright.
(Holmes, E., UK, 1970)

**'Lavender Lace'**
Single H2 Trailer
*Tube* short, white. *Sepals* pink,
turn flat between the petals.
*Corolla* light lavender turning
darker with maturity. The
miniature flowers have notched
petals; unusual colouring,
*Foliage* small with serrated
edges. The growth is naturally
trailing and being self-
branching will make a good
basket.
(Francesca, USA, 1977)

**'Lavender Lady'**
Double H2 Bush
*Tube* and *sepals* pale pink.
*Corolla* pale pink and lavender.
The medium-sized blooms are
very freely produced for a

double. *Foliage* medium green
and the growth is naturally
upright and bushy.
(Senior, UK, 1972)

**'Le Berger'**
Double H2 Trailer
*Tube* white. *Sepals* long and
narrow, also white. *Corolla*
white veined with pink. The
small flowers are early, and
freely produced. *Foliage* olive
green, lighter underneath. The
natural growth is trailing so
will make a good basket.
(de Graaff, Holland, 1985)

**'Lechlade Apache'**
Triphylla type H1 Bush
Terminal-flowering triphylla.
*Tube* long, thin, red. *Sepals*
red, short and fully recurved.
*Corolla* also red. *Foliage*
darkish green, lighter on
underside, very long leaves (up
to 5in/13cm). The growth is
strong and self-branching. (*F.
simplicaulis* × *F. boliviana*)
(Wright, UK, 1984)

**'Lechlade Chinaman'**
Interspecific cross H1 Lax
bush
*Tube* stubby and non tapering,
yellow flecked with orange.
*Sepals* dark purple, small and
spiky, and are held at the
horizontal. *Corolla* very small,
the same dark purple. *Foliage*
medium green. The growth
could be described as
rampantly climbing and needs
frequent 'stopping' to achieve
any degree of control. (*F.
splendens* × *F. procumbens*)
(Wright, UK, 1983)

**'Lechlade Debutante'**
Single H1 Bush
*Tube* long and cylindrical, clear
pink and greenish-brown at the
base. *Sepals* are held at the
horizontal, reflexed tips, pale
pink, green on the upper half.
*Corolla* clear pink. The flowers
are held out horizontally from
the axils. *Foliage* medium green
with a lighter colouring
underneath. (*F. paniculata* × *F.
lampadaria*)
(Wright, UK, 1984)

'LA ROSITA'

'LAVENDER LACE'

'LAVENDER LADY'

'LECHLADE APACHE'

**'Lechlade Fireeater'**
Triphylla type H1 Bush
Terminal-flowering. *Tubes*
long, orange and red. *Sepals*
red on top, salmon underneath,
short, narrow, with green tips.
*Corolla* has petals which are
orange. *Foliage* dark green
with a purple sheen
underneath, purplish-red veins.
The growth is very strongly
upright. A greenhouse novelty.
(*F. splendens* × *F. triphylla*)
(Wright, UK, 1984)

**'Lechlade Gorgon'**
Single H1 Bush
A plant with huge leaves and
tiny flowers. *Tube* rosy purple.
*Sepals* also rosy purple, much
lighter at the tips. *Corolla* pale
mauve, petals erect and
spreading. The flowers are
produced in great quantities in
terminal-branched panicles,
very similar to sprays of lilac.
*Foliage* long, 3½–5in (9–15cm)
is deep green with paler
colouring underneath. Growth
can be very rampant and
virtually uncontrollable if the
plant is given a free root-run in
warm conditions.
(*F. arborescens* × *F. paniculata*)
(Wright, UK, 1985)

**'Lechlade Magician'**
Single H3 Bush
*Tube* and *sepals* purplish
carmine. *Corolla* dark purple
fading to brownish-red. *Foliage*
darkish green. Excellent for the
hardy border. H. and S. up to
4ft (120cm).
(Wright, UK, 1986)

**'Lechlade Martianess'**
Species hybrid H2 Bush
*Tube* long with a distinct bulge
in the middle, pale orange.
*Sepals* short, pendant, green.
*Corolla* petals also pale orange
with cream edges inside
maturing to pale orangey-pink.
*Foliage* large, light green with
slightly serrated edges. The
upright growth is very lax so
will require staking. ((*F.
splendens* × *F. fulgens*) × *F.
splendens*)
(Wright, UK, 1985)

**'Lechlade Potentate'**
Single H2 Bush
*Tube* long, red on the upper
part and brown on the lower.
*Sepals* are held slightly below
the horizontal and have reflexed
tips; red on the top and salmon
underneath. *Corolla* salmon.
The flowers are produced from
the axils. *Foliage* medium green,
paler beneath, long leaves.
Growth is tall and upright given
a good root-run. (*F. splendens* ×
*F. lampadaria*)
(Wright, UK, 1984)

**'Lechlade Rocket'**
Single H2 Bush
*Tube* long, thick, pale orange-red
browning slightly at the base.
*Sepals* fully reflexed, orange-red
on upper half and green on the
other. *Corolla* orange-red. The
flowers are held horizontally
from the axils. *Foliage* dark sage
green, paler underneath, very
long (5½in/14cm), with red
veining. The growth is lax and
needs supporting. (*F. lampadaria*
× *F. fulgens*)
(Wright, UK, 1984)

**'Lechlade Tinkerbell'**
Encliandra type H2 Bush
*Tubes*, *sepals* and *corollas* pink.
The petals recurve to hide the
sepals. The flowers are small
and held in clusters. *Foliage*
large and lightish green. With a
free root-run the growth is very
rampant and free-flowering;
flowering is reduced somewhat
when the root-run is restricted.
(*F. arborescens* × *F. thymifolia*
ssp *thymifolia*)
(Wright, UK, 1983)

**'Lechlade Violet'**
Single H2 Bush
*Tube* thin, pale purple turning
to olive green at base. *Sepals*
pale violet with green tips on
top, deeper violet underneath.
*Corolla* blackish-purple.
Flowers are produced in small
terminal or lateral
inflorescences and are held
horizontally or erect. *Foliage*
pale green darkening with age.
(*F. paniculata* × *F. colensoi*)
(Wright, UK, 1984)

**'Lee Anthony'**
Single triphylla type H1 Bush
The flowers are held in
terminal bunches. *Tube* long,
*sepals* short and even smaller
petals all rose pink. Growth is
upright and bushy. *Foliage*
medium green.
(Goulding, UK, 1994)

*F. lehmannii*
Species H1 Bush
*Tube* red. *Sepals* scarlet. *Corolla*
also scarlet, The flowers are
borne in terminal racemes.
*Foliage* medium green. The
growth is upright and shrubby
reaching over 6ft (2m) in its
natural habitat.
(Ecuador, 1943)

**'Leica'**
Double H2 Bush
Small flowers. *Tube* and *sepals*
rose pink. *Corolla* pale lilac
with purple edging. *Foliage*
medium green. The natural
growth is upright and bushy.
(Jones, UK, 1993)

**'Leicestershire Silver'**
Double H2 Bush
*Tube* and *sepals* creamy white.
*Corolla* shell pink. The
medium-sized double flowers
are carried in profusion.
*Foliage* medium green. The
growth is upright and bushy.
(Pacey, UK, 1990)

**'Lena'**
Semi-double H3 Bush/trailer
*Tube* and half-reflexed *sepals*
pale flesh-pink, slightly deeper
underneath. *Corolla* rosy
magenta flushed with pink and
paling at the base of each petal.
The medium-sized flowers are
very free and are produced in
flushes. *Foliage* medium green.
The growth is rather lax. Often
confused with 'Eva Boerg'. One
of the most versatile of all
fuchsias; can be trained into
almost any shape and equally
as useful in pots, in baskets or
in the garden.
(Bunny, UK, 1862)

'LECHLADE MAGICIAN'

'LENA'

## 'Lena Dalton'

**'Lena Dalton'**
Double H2 Bush
*Tube* and recurving *sepals* pale pink. *Corolla* lavender blue, ageing to a rosy mauve. The flowers are medium-sized and freely produced. The flowers have four cupped petals and shorter petals around the outside. *Foliage* rather small, darkish green, serrated leaves with red veining. Growth is upright and bushy.
(Reimers, USA, 1953)

**'Len Bielby'**
Triphylla type H1 Bush
A true triphylla type with the flowers produced in bunches at the ends of the branches. *Tube* long, scarlet. *Sepals* blood red. *Corolla* red. *Foliage* dark green and velvety. Upright growth is very vigorous. Excellent as a tub plant or to give added height in the border.
('Gartenmeister Bonstedt' × 'Gartenmeister Bonstedt')
(Oxtoby, UK, 1987)

**'Leo Goetelen'**
Single H2 Bush
Large flower. *Tube* cream flushed with rose. *Sepals* carmine rose. *Corolla* geranium red. *Foliage* medium green. The natural growth is upright and bushy.
(Tamarus, Holland, 1987)

**'Leonora'**
Single H2 Bush
Medium-sized bell-shaped flowers completely soft pink: *tube*, *sepals* and *corolla* all have the same delightful and restful colouring. *Foliage* medium green. The natural growth is upright and bushy. Excellent exhibition plant, very floriferous.
(Tiret, USA, 1960)

**'Lett's Delight'**
Double H2 Lax bush
Medium-sized flowers freely produced throughout the season. *Tube* and *sepals* rose pink. *Corolla* lavender pink. *Foliage* medium green. The

growth is rather lax so can be used for baskets or pots provided the necessary supports are given.
(Goulding, UK, 1986)

**'Letty Lye'**
Single H2 Bush
Medium-sized flowers. *Tubes* and *sepals* flesh pink. *Corolla* carmine crimson. *Foliage* medium green. The growth is naturally very strong and upright.
(Lye, UK, 1877)

**'Leverkusen'**
Triphylla type H1 Bush
Synonymous with 'Leverhulme'. Although classified as a triphylla type the tubes are much shorter and the flowers are carried not just in bunches at the ends of the branches but also singly in the leaf axils. *Tube*, *sepals* and *corolla* are all of the same delightful rosy cerise colouring. Very free-flowering although there can be a considerable amount of bud drop if the plant is moved from one position to another. *Foliage* medium green. Growth is upright and bushy.
(Hartnauer, Germany, 1923)

**'Lidie Bartelink'**
Single H3 Bush
Medium-sized flower. *Tube* and *sepals* deep rose red. *Corolla* spirea red. *Foliage* medium green. The natural growth is upright and bushy. Very useful for the hardy border, achieving H. and S. of 18–24in (45–60cm).
(Stoel, Holland, 1990)

**'Liebriez'**
Semi-double H3 Bush
*Tube* and *sepals* pale cerise pink. *Corolla* pinkish white veined with a deeper pink. *Foliage* smallish, medium to darker green. The flowers are fairly small but are very freely produced. Excellent for showing in smaller-sized pots.
(Kohene, Germany, 1874)

**'Liemers Lantern'**
Double H2 Trailer
*Tube* and *sepals* deep rose pink. *Corolla* magenta pink. *Foliage* medium green. The natural growth is trailing. Will make a superb basket as the large flowers are freely produced. (Sport from 'Dusky Rose')
(Giessen, Holland, 1983)

**'Lilac Dainty'**
Double H2/3 Bush
Small flowers. *Tube* and *sepals* dull red. *Corolla* lilac. *Foliage* medium green. The upright growth produces a compact bush for use in the hardy border. H. and S. 12–24in (30–60cm).
(Hobson, UK, 1982)

**'Lilac Lady'**
Semi-double H2 Bush
Medium-sized flowers. *Tube* white striped with pink. *Sepals* white, and tipped with green. *Corolla* opens violet and matures to lilac. *Foliage* medium green. The natural growth is upright and bushy.
(Redfern, UK, 1990)

**'Lilac Lustre'**
Double H2 Bush
A very attractive and beautifully formed flower. *Tubes* rose red, short. *Sepals* rose-red, broad, upturned. *Corolla* a delightful powder blue, broad pleated petals. The rich green *foliage* acts as a perfect backcloth for the freely produced flowers. Growth is upright and bushy.
(Munkner, USA, 1961)

**'Lilac Princess'**
Single H2 Bush
*Tubes* short, thick, greenish white. *Sepals* short, greenish-white on outside, flushed pale pink inside. *Corolla* a deep shade of lilac shading to pink at the base of the petals. The short-stemmed flowers are held well out; medium-sized, prolific, and are produced from early in the season. *Foliage* dark green. H. and S. 18–24in (45–60cm).
(Handley, UK, 1979)

'LENA DALTON'

'LEN BIELBY'

'LEONORA'

'LILAC LUSTRE'

### 'Lilian Clark'
Double H2 Bush
Medium-sized flowers. *Tubes* white striped with green. *Sepals* white flushed with pink, tipped green. *Corolla* violet-blue shading to pale rose at the base of each petal and veined with rose pink. *Foliage* medium green. The growth is upright and bushy.
(Taylor, UK, 1992)

### 'Lillian Windsor'
Semi-double H2 Bush
*Tube* and *sepals* light red. *Corolla* white. The flowers are medium-sized and freely produced. *Foliage* medium green. The natural growth is as an upright bush. ('R.A.F.' × 'Pacquesa')
(Windsor, UK, 1987)

### 'Lillibet'
Double H2 Trailer
*Tube* and *sepals* white, flushed with pale carmine. *Corolla* soft rose, flushed with geranium lake. *Foliage* medium green, serrated edge. The flowers are very large with long, pointed, green-tipped buds. Strong growth but as it is rather lax it is best used as a trailer.
(Hodges, USA, 1954)

### 'Lillydale'
Double H2 Lax bush/trailer
*Tube* short, white striped green. *Sepals* rhodamine pink touched white; held well up, tips reflexing. *Corolla* purple-violet flushed rhodamine pink and maturing to cyclamen purple. The flowers are very large and freely produced considering the size. *Foliage* medium green, lighter underneath, red veining. The natural growth is rather lax so is perhaps best used in a hanging container. Worth trying as a semi-weeping standard. ('Pipo Pico' × 'White King')
(Richardson, Australia, 1985)

### 'Lilo Vogt'
Triphylla type H1 Lax bush
*Tube* quite long, pink. *Sepals* pink tipped with green. *Corolla* pink. The flowers are fairly small for a triphylla type but are very freely produced. *Foliage* medium to darkish green with a faint purple sheen beneath. With training could be used for hanging containers.
(Nutzinger, Austria, 1976)

### 'Linda Goulding'
Single H2 Bush
*Tube* short, white. *Sepals* recurve, pink. *Corolla* white with pink veining, bell-shaped, very compact. The flowers are held upright towards the ends of the branches. It is a very floriferous cultivar which grows into an upright bush very easily. *Foliage* a light green.
(Goulding, UK, 1981)

### 'Lindisfarne'
Semi-double H2 Bush
*Tube* short, thick, the palest of pinks. *Sepals* held horizontally and are also pale pink, green tips, crêpe underside. *Corolla* a rich violet, deeper at the edges. Although the flowers are small they are prolific. Very short-jointed, upright growth which can develop a good bush very quickly. *Foliage* medium green with a slight reddish cast.
(Ryle/Atkinson, UK, 1974)

### 'Lindy'
Double H2 Bush
*Tube* and *sepals* flesh pink flushed with carmine. *Corolla* turkey red flushed with dianthus blue. *Foliage* medium green. The medium-sized flowers are very freely produced. Growth is upright and bushy.
(Thorne, UK, 1964)

### 'L'Ingenue'
Single H2 Bush
*Tube* short, thick, cardinal red. *Sepals* fully reflexed, long and narrow, spinel red. *Corolla* opens fuchsia purple and matures to magenta rose. Petals toothed, held horizontally. *Foliage* medium green, paler underneath. The natural growth is upright and the stems are self-branching and short jointed. ('Loeky' × 'Mazda')
(de Graaff, Holland, 1985)

### 'Linsey Brown'
Double H2 Bush
*Tube* and *sepals* pink. *Corolla* white veined with pink. *Foliage* medium green. The growth is naturally upright. Will make a good bush or a standard.
(Coupland, Britain, 1992)

### 'Lisa'
Double H2 Trailer
*Tube* bright rose pink. *Sepals* bright rose, long and broad, upturned. *Corolla* rich lavender, fading to orchid. The flowers are very large and fairly free. *Foliage* medium green.
(Antonelli, USA, 1965)

### 'Lisi'
Single H2 Trailer
Medium-sized flowers. *Tube* and *sepals* white. *Corolla* violet. *Foliage* medium green. The natural growth is trailing.
(Strumper, Austria, 1985)

### 'Little Beauty'
Single H2 Bush
*Tube* and *sepals* flesh pink. *Corolla* lavender blue. *Foliage* medium green. The growth is upright and compact. The flowers are fairly small but are produced freely over a long season.
(Raiser and year unknown)

### 'Little Jewel'
Single H2 Bush
*Tube* shiny dark carmine. *Sepals* shiny dark carmine on top, dark flat carmine underneath, star-shaped. *Corolla* light purple with carmine variegations at the base of each petal. Stamens red. The medium to large *foliage* is medium green. A strong grower.
(Soo Yun, USA, 1975)

### 'Little Ouse'
Double H2 Bush
Very large flowers. *Tubes* and *sepals* of pale pink. *Corolla* powdery blue with some pink marbling. The upright, vigorous and self-branching growth will help to make a massive plant in a season. *Foliage* is medium green.
(Goulding, UK, 1988)

'LILLIBET'

'LINDISFARNE'

'LISA'

'LITTLE BEAUTY'

'LITTLE JEWEL'

'LITTLE OUSE'

**'Little Ronnie'**
Semi-double H2 Bush
*Tube* short, light rose. *Sepals* short, broad and upturned, rosy crimson. *Corolla* dark blue ageing to mauvish-blue. The smallish flowers are produced in quantity. *Foliage* small is bright green. Growth is bushy, upright and rather stiff. (de Cola, USA, 1975)

**'Little Witch'**
Single H2 Bush
A very graceful, novelty cultivar of the semi-paniculate sort. *Tubes* and *sepals* pale lilac. *Corolla* a darker violet. The growth is upright, strong and slender. *Foliage* medium to dark green. (de Graaff, Holland, 1989)

**'Liverbird'**
Single H2 Bush
*Tube* flesh pink. *Sepals* also flesh pink. *Corolla* claret rose. The small flowers are the same colouring as 'Chang' but smaller; upward-looking. *Foliage* medium green and small. Makes good bush but requires pinching. ('Chang' ×) (Thornley, UK, 1966)

**'Liz'**
Double H2 Bush
*Tube* white. *Sepals* of the palest pink, slightly deeper underneath and tipped with green, broad and reflexed over tube. *Corolla* also of the palest pink; the petals veined and splashed with deep pink. The medium to large flowers are freely produced. Growth is upright and bushy. *Foliage* is medium green. (Holmes, R., UK, 1970)

**'Lochinvar'**
Semi-double H2 Bush
*Tube* and *sepals* pale pink, rhodamine pink underneath. *Corolla* imperial purple shading to pale pink at the base of each petal, with darker purple edges. The medium-sized flowers are rather loose and open but have an excellent

colour combination. *Foliage* dark green. The growth is medium upright, self-branching and will produce an excellent standard or bush. (Seedling × 'Valerie') (Mitchinson, UK, 1983)

**'Loeky'**
Single H2 Bush
*Tube* and *sepals* rhodonite red; the sepals have recurved tips. *Corolla* dark mallow purple and each petal has smooth edges. The medium-sized flowers open flat and saucer shaped. *Foliage* dark green. The natural growth is upright and a superb small standard can be produced. A delightful fuchsia. (de Graaff, Holland, 1985)

**'Logan Garden'**
Single H3 Bush
Very floriferous, hardy fuchsia. *Tube* pink. *Sepals* white. *Corolla* violet. *Foliage* medium green. The growth is upright and very vigorous. H. and S. in excess of 3ft (1m). (Raiser and date unknown; found in the vicinity of Logan Garden in Scotland)

**'Lonely Ballerina'**
Double H2 Lax bush/trailer
Medium-sized flowers. *Tubes* dark carmine, thin. *Sepals* short, broad, reflexing. *Corolla* white with carmine veining, carmine splashes on petals. *Foliage* medium green. The growth is rather lax and supports will be needed when training as a bush. Could make a good basket. (Blackwell, UK, 1962)

**'Long Wings'**
Single H2 Lax bush
*Tube* long, thin, rose madder. *Sepals* fully reflexed, very long and broad, curl and twist towards the tube, also rose madder. *Corolla* opens pale violet veined with rose at base and maturing to slightly lighter. The medium to large flowers are freely produced. *Foliage* medium green, lighter

underneath, serrated, green veins with red mid-rib. With supports the plant has make a reasonable upright, but is better suited for use as a basket. (Caunt, UK, 1985)

**'Lonneke'**
Single H2 Bush
Medium-sized flower. *Tube* and *sepals* red. *Corolla* rose with red veins. *Foliage* medium green. The natural growth is vigorously upright. (Beije, Holland, 1989)

**'Lorraine's Delight'**
Double H2 Trailer
*Tube* crimson. *Sepals* very long and very broad, fully reflexed neyron rose on top and crimson underneath. *Corolla* opens a mixture of fuchsia and cyclamen purple, maturing to bishop's violet with shades of crimson and carmine. The petals are veined with magenta. The large blooms are very eye-catching. *Foliage* quite large, is yellowish-green with serrated edging to the leaves. The natural growth is trailing and will make a superb basket. ('Pink Marshmallow' × 'Midnight Sun') (Richardson, Australia, 1985)

**'Lord Byron'**
Single H2 Bush
*Tube* short, thin, rich scarlet. *Sepals* broad, recurved also rich scarlet *Corolla* very dark purple but lighter at the base of each petal, red veining. The medium-sized flowers are freely produced. *Foliage* medium green. The plant is upright in its growth and very vigorous. (Lemoine, France, prior to 1877)

**'Lord Derby'**
Single H2 Bush
Medium-sized single flowers. *Tubes* and *Sepals* red. *Corolla* purple. *Foliage* medium green. The natural growth is bushy and upright. (Banks, UK, 1868)

178

'LIZ'

'LOCHINVAR'

'LOEKY'

'LONG WINGS'

'LORD BYRON'

**'Lord Lonsdale'**
Single H1 Bush
*Tube* light apricot. *Sepals* light
apricot, green tips, broad and
drooping. *Corolla* orange
peach. The very attractive
flowers are of medium size.
*Foliage* light green and has the
unfortunate habit of curling.
The growth is rather lax. Not
an easy plant to grow well.
Often confused with 'Aurora
Superba', smaller and less
vigorous.
(Raiser and date unknown,
UK)

**'Lord Roberts'**
Single H2 Bush
*Tube* short, scarlet. *Sepals*
horizontally, scarlet. *Corolla*
rich purplish-violet with scarlet
veining, pink shading at base of
petals. The flowers are largish
and freely produced. *Foliage*
medium green with red veins.
The growth is upright and
bushy.
(Lemoine, France, 1909)

**'Lorna Swinbank'**
Single H2 Bush
Very attractive small flowered
cultivar. *Tube* and *sepals* white
flushed pink. *Corolla* palest
violet blue. *Foliage* medium
green. The natural growth is
upright and self-branching  A
superb small bush can be
achieved quite quickly.
(Flemming, UK, 1990)

**'Lottie Hobby'**
*Encliandra* hybrid H2/3 Bush
Very small flowers. *Sepals* and
*tubes* light crimson. *Corolla*
light purple. *Foliage* medium
green and quite large for the
*Encliandra* type of plant.
Growth is very vigorous and
upright. Because of the wiriness
of the stems can be used to
train around any shaped
structures.
(Edwards, UK, 1839)

**'Louise Emershaw'**
Double H2 Trailer
Medium-sized flowers. *Tube*
white, long. *Sepals* white on

top with green tips, pale pink
underneath. *Corolla* jasper red
matures to cerise. The flowers
are fully double. *Foliage* dark
green, large serrated leaves.
The natural growth is trailing
so will make a superb basket.
(Tiret, USA, 1972)

**'Loulabel'**
Single H2 Bush
Medium-sized flower with open
bell shaped blooms. *Tube* pink.
*Sepals* pink and reflex back to
the tube. *Corolla* bishop's
violet. *Foliage* medium green.
The growth is upright and
bushy.
(Heavens, M., UK, 1990)

**'Love in Bloom'**
Double H2 Trailer
*Tube* flesh pink. *Sepals* white to
pale flesh, long, turn up and
reflex slightly as they mature.
*Corolla* magenta to light coral,
opening very full, some
serrated petals. *Foliage* medium
green. The cultivar has large
flowers and naturally trails so
will make a good basket.
(Stubbs, USA, 1977)

**'Love Knot'**
Double H2 Lax bush
*Tube* medium-sized, rose
madder. *Sepals* stiff and wide,
upturned are rose madder, the
edges are tinged with amethyst
violet. *Corolla* also a rosy
purple. The largish blooms are
ruffled and curled, giving an
almost square appearance when
fully open. *Foliage* bright lime
green. The growth is a rather
lax upright and can be used for
bushes or baskets as desired.
(Fuchsia La, USA, 1979)

**'Loveliness'**
Single H2 Bush
*Tube* and recurving *sepals*
waxy white. *Corolla* rosy
cerise, compact. The flowers
are medium-sized and are
produced in quantity early in
the season. *Foliage* medium
green, medium-sized, serrated.
Growth is upright and bushy.
(Lye, UK, 1869)

**'Love's Reward'**
Single H2 Bush
Small to medium-sized flowers
produced in great quantity
throughout the season. *Tube*
and *sepals* white. *Corolla*
violet-blue. *Foliage* medium
green. Growth is short and self-
branching. A superb cultivar
for the smaller pots on the
show bench. ('Estelle Marie' ×
'Carol Roe')
(Bambridge, UK, 1986)

**F. loxensis**
Species hybrid H1 Bush
*Tube* fairly long, deep orange.
*Sepals* long, narrow, pointed
and spreading, orange with
green tips. *Corolla* deep
orange. *Foliage* velvety,
medium green with serrated
edges. Growth is very upright
and rampant. Considered to be
a hybrid cross between F.
*splendens* and F. *fulgens*.
(Humboldt, 1832)

**'Loxhore Calypso'**
Single H2 Trailer
Small, long flowers. *Tube* and
*sepals* purplish-red. *Corolla* a
deeper shade of purplish-red.
*Foliage* medium green. The
growth is best described as
'slender cascading'.
(Wright, UK, 1990)

**'Loxhore Cancan'**
Single H2 Bush
*Tube* long, white flushed with
pink. *Sepals* long, pink tipped
with green. *Corolla* has long
petals which are incurved and
coloured pink-lilac. Attractive.
*Foliage* medium green. The
upright growth is rather stiff.
(Wright, UK, 1991)

**'Lucille'**
Double H2 Trailer
*Tube* long thick pink. *Sepals*
very long, curved, also pink.
*Corolla* all white. The blooms
are medium-sized, freely
produced and very 'showy'.
*Foliage* small and dark green.
The natural growth is trailing.
(Hanson, USA, 1976)

180

'LOULABEL'

'LOVELINESS'

'LOVE KNOT'

'LOVE'S REWARD'

*F. LOXENSIS*

'LUCILLE'

**'Lucinda'**
Semi-double H2 Lax bush
*Tube* whitish-pink. *Sepals*
recurving, white tipped with
pink on the outside and pale
pink on the underside. *Corolla*
pinkish-lilac. The blooms are
large and, considering their
size, are very freely produced.
*Foliage* medium green. The
growth is rather lax so the
plant excels as a half basket or
as a bush with supports. ('Baby
Pink' × 'Norman Mitchinson')
(Mitchinson, UK, 1981)

**'Lucky Strike'**
Semi-double H2 Bush
*Tube* pink. *Sepals* light ivory
pink on top with green tips,
slightly darker on the
underside. *Corolla* inside petals
are bluish-purple, the outside
petals are pink with purple
markings. The large flowers are
freely produced. *Foliage*
medium green, finely serrated
leaves. Strong upright and
bushy growth.
(Niederholzer, USA, 1943)

**'Lucy Harris'**
*Tube* and *sepals* neyron rose.
*Corolla* pure white with slight
rose veining at the base of the
petals. Each petal is sharply
pointed. The flowers are
medium-sized but are very
numerous. *Foliage* is medium
green. Growth is upright and
bushy.
(Pacey, UK, 1988)

**'Lumier'**
Single H2 Bush
*Tube* short, pink. *Sepals* pink.
*Corolla* creamy white and fully
flared. The blooms are
attractively saucer-shaped.
*Foliage* medium green. Growth
is upright and short-jointed.
Excellent for bushes or smaller
standards.
(Van der Post, Holland, 1988)

**'Lunter's Glorie'**
Single H2 Lax bush
*Tube* and *sepals* light neyron
rose. *Corolla* white. The
medium-sized flowers are quite
prolific. *Foliage* medium green.

Growth is rather lax so will
make a basket or a bush with
the right supports. ('Annabel' ×
'Iceberg')
(Appel, M., Holland, 1987)

**'Lunter's Roehm'**
Double H2 Bush
Medium-sized flowers. *Tube*
yellowish-white, faintly flushed
green. *Sepals* yellowish-white
faintly flushed pink beneath,
held well out. *Corolla* lilac
blue. *Foliage* medium green,
light green veining. Growth is
naturally upright and bushy.
('Carmel Blue' × 'Pennine')
(Appel, Holland, 1984)

**'Lunter's Trots'**
Double H2 Lax bush
*Tubes* light red. *Sepals* bright
red, on top, lighter beneath
with light yellow tips; held
horizontally. *Corolla* purple.
*Foliage* medium green. The
natural growth is rather lax so
will need support for the large,
heavy flowers. ('Trots' in Dutch
means 'Pride'.) ('White King' ×
'Dee Copley')
(Appel, Holland, 1987)

**'Lustre'**
Single H2 Bush
*Tube* and *sepals* creamy white,
short, broad. *Corolla* salmon
pink, slightly tinted with
orange. The flowers are fairly
small but are exceptionally
freely produced. *Foliage*
medium green, serrated.
Growth upright and bushy.
(Bull, UK, 1868)

**'Lutz Bogemann'**
Single H2 Lax bush
Flowers of medium-sized.
*Tubes* and *sepals* reddish-
purple. *Corolla* white. *Foliage*
medium green. The growth is
rather lax and upright so will
need some supporting.
(Haslinger, Germany, 1988)

***F. lycioides***
Species H1 Bush
Flowers are small, produced as
solitary specimens in the leaf
axils. *Tubes* and *sepals* rosy
red. *Corolla* red-purple. *Foliage*

quite small, light green.
Growth is quite lax and bushy.
(Chile)

***F. lycioides* × *magellanica***
Species hybrid H1 Bush
Medium to small flowers,
produced solitary in the leaf
axils. *Tube* thin, red. *Sepals*
reflexed, red. *Corolla* rosy
purple. *Foliage* medium to light
green. Growth is upright and
vigorous.
(Chile)

**'Lye's Excelsior'**
Single H2 Bush
*Tube* waxy white, short, thick.
*Sepals* waxy white, slightly
tinted with pink beneath, short.
*Corolla* rich scarlet cerise. The
flowers are of medium size and
freely produced. *Foliage*
medium green. Growth is
upright and bushy.
(Lye, UK, 1887)

**'Lye's Favourite'**
Single H2 Bush
*Tube* flesh pink, short. *Sepals*
flesh pink, held well out.
*Corolla* orange cerise, compact.
The medium-sized flowers are
very freely produced. Growth
is upright and bushy. Foliage
medium green, medium-sized,
serrated edges. ('Arabella
Improved' × 'James Lye')
(Lye, UK, 1886)

**'Lye's Own'**
Single H2 Bush
*Tube* and *sepals* waxy white.
*Corolla* pinkish-lilac. The
medium-sized flowers are freely
produced early in the season
and last throughout. *Foliage* is
medium green. Growth is
strong, bushy and upright.
Worth trying as a standard.
(Lye, UK, 1871)

**'Lye's Perfection'**
Single H2 Bush
*Tube* and *sepals* waxy white.
*Corolla* bright carmine. *Foliage*
medium green. The medium-
sized flowers are freely
produced. Growth is upright
and bushy.
(Lye, UK, 1884)

'LUCINDA'

'LUSTRE'

*F. LYCIOIDES*

'LYE'S EXCELSIOR'

**'Lye's Unique'**
Single H2 Bush
*Tube* and *sepals* waxy white.
*Corolla* a delightful shade of
salmon orange. The medium-
sized blooms are extremely
freely produced throughout a
long season. *Foliage* medium
green. Growth is strongly
upright and bushy. One
of Lye's most popular
introductions.
(Lye, UK, 1886)

**'Lylac Sunsa'**
Single H2 Bush
*Tube* short, rose madder. *Sepals*
are held horizontally, rose
madder on top and slightly
paler underneath, with twisting
and recurving green tips.
*Corolla* deep lavender with fine
dark rose veins. The medium-
sized flowers have an unusual
petal shape, half-flared and
bell-shaped. It is very free-
flowering. *Foliage* mid-green on
top, lighter underneath, with
serrated edges. Growth is
upright and self-branching.
('Tennessee Waltz' × 'Lye's
Unique' seedling)
(Caunt, UK, 1985)

**'Lyndhurst'**
Single H2 Lax bush
*Tube* pink. *Sepals* rosy pink,
tipped with green. *Corolla* a
lovely shade of bright cerise.
The medium-sized flowers are
very prolific. *Foliage* medium
green. The growth is vigorous
although rather lax.
('Coachman' × 'Marinka')
(Nias, A., UK, 1987)

**'Lynn Ellen'**
Double H2 Bush
*Tube* deep rose pink. *Sepals*
upturned, broad, deepest rose
pink. *Corolla* rose purple
changing to a glowing rose as
the flowers open, outer petals
with salmon pink marbling.
The blooms are large and
spreading and freely produced.
*Foliage* is medium green,
longish serrated leaves.
(Erickson, USA, 1962)

**'Lynne Marshall'**
Single H2/3 Bush
*Tube* and *sepals* pale pink.
*Corolla* lavender blue. *Foliage*
pale green. The flowers are
medium-sized and freely
produced. Growth is upright
and bushy. H. and S. 24–30 in
(60–75cm).
(Tabraham, UK, 1974)

# M

**'Mabejo'**
Double H2 trailer
Large flowers. *Tubes* cream.
*Sepals* plum red. *Corolla* has
petals which are violet blue.
*Foliage* medium green. The
growth is naturally trailing.
(van Larieren, Holland, 1991)

**'Mabel Greaves'**
Semi-double H2 Bush
*Tube* white with green stripes.
*Sepals* white tipped with green,
completely recurving. *Corolla*
white veined with pink. The
medium-sized blooms are
produced very freely, as many as
three to a leaf axil. *Foliage* pale
green. Growth is very strong and
upright. Needs heavy pinching
to achieve a good shape.
(Clark, UK, 1985)

**'Machu Picchu'**
Single H2 Bush
*Tube* empire rose. *Sepals*
empire rose on top, jasper red
underneath, green tips. *Corolla*
scarlet. The small to medium
flowers are produced very
freely. Frequent 'stopping' is
necessary to get the best shape
of plant. *Foliage* fuchsia green
with fairly large leaves. Growth
is lax for an upright but rather
stiff for a trailer.
(de Graaff, Holland, 1985)

**F. macrophylla**
Species H2 Bush
*Tubes* red. *Sepals* red tipped
with green. *Corolla* scarlet. The
flowers are medium-sized.
*Foliage* medium green. Growth
is strongly upright.
(Johnston, 1925)

**F. macrostigma**
Species H2 Bush
*Tube* pale to dark red. *Sepals*
red with dark green tips.
*Corolla* bright red. *Foliage*
medium green. The growth is
strongly upright.
(Bentham, 1844)

**'Madame Cornelissen'**
Semi-double H3 Bush
*Tube* and *sepals* rich scarlet.
*Corolla* white veined with
cerise, fairly compact. The
smallish flowers are very freely
produced throughout the
season. *Foliage* dark green,
small serrated leaves. Growth
is strong, upright and bushy.
Worth trying in favoured areas
as a hedge. H. and S. 24–30in
(60–75cm).
(Cornelissen, Belgium, 1860)

**'Madame Danjoux'**
Double H2 Bush
*Tube* short, red. *Sepals* broad,
long, carmine red. *Corolla*
pinkish-white splashed with
carmine. *Foliage* medium
green. The flowers are large
and quite full. Growth is
strongly upright and bushy.
(Salter, UK, 1843)

**'Madame Eva Boye'**
Single H2 Bush
*Tube* and *sepals* flesh pink.
*Corolla* deep wine purple
streaked with purple. The
flowers are large and very free.
*Foliage* medium green. The
growth is upright and bushy.
(Lemoine, France, 1908)

**'Madame Lanteime'**
Double H2 Bush
*Tube* and *sepals* crimson.
*Corolla* white, veined pink.
The flowers are medium-sized
and freely produced. *Foliage*
medium green. Growth is
upright and bushy, tends to
spread and become straggly.
Needs early and careful
pinching to achieve a good
plant.
(Lemoine, France, 1912)

'LYE'S UNIQUE'                           'LYNN ELLEN'

        'MABEL GREAVES'                'MADAME CORNELISSEN'

**'Madame Thibaut'**
Single H2 Bush
Large flower. *Tube* and *sepals* cerise red. *Corolla* magenta. *Foliage* medium green. The growth is vigorously upright and bushy.
(Lemoine, France, 1910)

**F. magdalenae**
Species H1 Bush
*Tube* very long, narrow, orange red. *Sepals* orange red and slightly purple at the base. *Corolla* scarlet to orange red. *Foliage* fairly large, dark green with lighter green and purple veins underneath. Very rampant upright growth.
(Munz, 1943)

**F. magellanica**
Species H3 Bush
Very hardy with small red and purple-blue flowers. *Foliage* thin and dark green. Very strong upright growth. Useful for hedges. Used in many crosses to increase the hardiness of the progeny.

**F. magellanica** var *alba*
*Tube* and *sepals* white. *Corolla* white flushed pink. Very small flowers but very free. *Foliage* medium green and small.

**F. magellanica** var *alba variegata*
Floral description as above, but *foliage* variegated with cream and green leaves.

**F. magellanica** var *aurea*
*Tube* and *sepals* red. *Corolla* purple. Long, thin flowers. *Foliage* bright golden yellow.

**F. magellanica** var *conica*
*Tube* and *sepals* red. *Corolla* purple. Flowers with a cone-shaped tube. *Foliage* medium green.

**F. magellanica** var *globosa*
*Tube* and *sepals* red. *Corolla* purple. Small but very free, round flowers. *Foliage* dark green with red stems. Will make a good hedge.

**F. magellanica** var *gracilis*
*Tube* and *sepals* scarlet red. *Corolla* purple. Smallish, thin flowers. Medium green *foliage*. Growth upright on strong wiry stems. Vigorous.

**F. magellanica** var *gracilis variegata*
*Tube* and *sepals* scarlet red. *Corolla* purple. Smallish, thin flowers. *Foliage* variegated with cream, green and pink, red veining. Strong, upright wiry stems.

**F. magellanica** var *macrostema*
Descriptions of flowers as already given for *F. magellanica* but the growth is strong and arching. Final growth is much taller than *F. magellanica*.

**F. magellanica** var *macrostema* 'Aurea'
*Tubes* and *sepals* scarlet red. *Corolla* purple. *Foliage* golden. Growth strong, upright and wiry.

**F. magellanica** var *macrostema* 'Tricolor'
*Tubes* and *sepals* scarlet red. *Corolla* purple. Leaves are variegated green and yellow with a clear contrast. Strong upright and wiry growth.

**F. magellanica** var *macrostema* 'Variegata'
*Tubes* and *sepals* scarlet red. *Corolla* purple. *Foliage* a mixture of yellow, silvery green and red. Strong upright and wiry growth.

**F. magellanica** var *molinae* 'Enstone'
*Tube* small, long and narrow, white tinged palest green. *Sepals* held out at the horizontal, white tinged palest pink. *Corolla* small, white tinged with palest lilac. *Foliage* variegated green and gold, a most beautiful combination. Growth is fairly vigorous and upright. (Sport of *F. magellanica* var *molinae*)
(Dawson, UK, 1986)

**F. magellanica** var *myrtifolia*
*Sepals* red. *Corolla* purple. Vigorous upright growth. Very small flowers; *foliage* small.

**F. magellanica** var *pumilla*
*Tube* and *sepals* scarlet. *Corolla* mauve. Very small flowers. Tiny plant suitable for a rockery. *Foliage* very small. Height no more than 12–18in (30–45cm).

**F. magellanica** *ricartonii*
*Tube* and *sepals* scarlet. *Corolla* dark purple. Thin flowers. Very free-flowering. *Foliage* medium green. Very strong upright growth. Useful for hedges.

**F. magellanica** *thompsonii*
*Tube* and *sepals* scarlet. *Corolla* palish purple. Small flowers. Not such vigorous growth. Height to approx 24in (60cm).

**F. magellanica** *versicolor*
*Tube* and *sepals* red. *Corolla* purple. Smallish flowers. *Foliage* grey-green, rose-tinted when young, and irregularly variegated creamy white. Strong upright growth, very wiry.

**'Magenta Flush'**
Double H2 Bush
*Tube* spinel-red. *Sepals* also spinel-red, tipped with green. *Corolla* magenta rose flushed with rose-red. The large flowers are freely produced for their size. *Foliage* dark green with serrated edges. Upright and bushy growth.
(Gadsby, UK, 1970)

**'Magic Flute'**
Single H2 Trailer
*Tube* very thick, waxy white. *Sepals* white, tipped with green, and held at right angles to the tube. *Corolla* clear coral rose shading to white at the base of the petals; funnel-shaped and petals overlap. The medium-sized flowers are freely produced. *Foliage* bright green. The natural growth is trailing so will make a good basket.
(Handley, UK, 1975)

F. MAGELLANICA VAR. ALBA
F. MAGELLANICA VAR. ALBA VARIEGATA

F. MAGELLANICA VAR. AUREA
F. MAGELLANICA VAR. RICARTONII

F. MAGELLANICA VAR. VERSICOLOR

**'Maharaja'**
Single H2 Trailer
*Tube* and *sepals* salmon pink.
*Corolla* very large, has petals
which are dark purple with
salmon-orange touches. *Foliage*
medium green. The natural
growth is as a trailer so will
make a superb basket.
(Castro, USA, 1971)

**'Majebo'**
Double H2 Trailer
Large flowers. *Tube* and *sepals*
white. *Corolla* is blue. *Foliage*
medium green. The natural
growth is as a trailer. Will
make a good basket.
(Raiser and date unknown)

**'Major Heaphy'**
Single H2 Bush
*Tube* reddish-orange, thin.
*Sepals* brick red and tipped
with green, short, narrow, held
well out. *Corolla* reddish-
scarlet. The flowers are small
but very freely produced.
*Foliage* medium green, serrated
leaves. Growth upright and
bushy. Dislikes a dry
atmosphere and will drop all
flowers and buds under such
conditions.
(Hybridist and year unknown,
UK)

**'Malibu Mist'**
Double H2 Lax bush
*Tube* short, white. *Sepals* held
horizontally, white on the
upper side and white tinged
pink on the lower with
recurving tips. *Corolla* opens
blue-violet streaked light pink
maturing to cyclamen purple,
with white at the base of each
petal. *Foliage* medium green
lighter underneath, red veins.
Growth is lax but will make a
basket or a bush with supports.
('Ada Perry' × 'Trade Winds')
(Stubbs, USA, 1985)

**'Mama Bleuss'**
Double H2 Trailer
*Tube* and *sepals* pink. *Corolla*
pale blue streaked with deep
blue. The large flowers are very
freely produced. *Foliage*
medium green. Growth is

rather lax for a bush and yet
stiff for a trailer.
(Tiret, USA, 1959)

**'Mancunian'**
Double H2 Trailer
*Tube* white, turning to red.
*Sepals* long, recurving with age,
white in colour. *Corolla* white
with pink veins. *Foliage*
medium green. The growth is
strong and self-branching.
Makes a superb basket.
(Goulding, UK, 1985)

**'Mantilla'**
Single H1 Trailer
Almost considered to be a
triphylla-type fuchsia as it has a
long tube with a small corolla.
*Tube*, short drooping *sepals*
and *corolla* are all bright
crimson. *Foliage* medium to
dark green. Growth is pendant
but strong; for best growth this
variety requires a warm and
well lit position. Attractive long
blooms (3½in/9cm) in clusters.
(Reiter, USA, 1948)

**'Maori Pipes'**
Triphylla type H1 Bush
Terminal-flowering. *Tube* long,
ruby red to aubergine. *Sepals*
short, same colour ruby red to
aubergine. *Corolla* slightly
brighter. *Foliage* medium to
dark green. Upright growth is
very strong. A very popular
'novelty' fuchsia. (*F. excorticata*
× *F. triphylla*)
(de Graaff, Holland, 1987)

**'Marbled Sky'**
Double H2 Bush
*Tube* and *sepals* waxy white
tipped with lime green. *Sepals*
twisted and reflexed when fully
open. *Corolla* lavender pink
flushed white at the base of
each petal. Medium-sized
flowers are of good shape and
freely produced. *Foliage*
medium green. Strong, upright
bushy growth.
(Hooper, UK, 1991)

**'Marcus Graham'**
Double H2 Bush
*Tubes* thin, white to flesh pink.
*Sepals* are salmon or pink, long

and broad. *Corolla* a delicate
shade of salmon. *Foliage*
medium green, lighter beneath.
Growth is very strong and
most suitable for large bushes
or standards. A very versatile
and attractive fuchsia.
(Stubbs, USA, 1985)

**'Marcus Hanton'**
Double H2 Bush
*Tube* rich red. *Sepals* rich red,
upturned and held well above
the horizontal. *Corolla* rich lilac
blue splashed with cerise. The
medium-sized flowers are freely
produced. *Foliage* medium
green. The upright growth is
very strong and self-branching.
(Clark, UK, 1986)

**'Margaret'**
Semi-double H3 Bush
One of the best fuchsias for a
hardy border. *Tube* carmine.
*Sepals* carmine, reflexing
completely. *Corolla* violet with
red veins, pink at petal base.
*Foliage* medium green. Upward
growth is very strong. The
flowers are produced early and
for a very long season. One for
the back of the border,
reaching a height and spread of
some 4ft (120cm).
(Wood, UK, 1939)

**'Margaret Brown'**
Single H3 Bush
A superb fuchsia for the hardy
border that will never let you
down. *Tube* and *sepals* rosy
pink. *Corolla* light rose bengal,
deeper veining. The flowers are
fairly small, but they are so
freely produced that the plant
appears positively to drip with
them throughout the season.
*Foliage* lightish green. Growth
is upright and bushy. H. and S.
24–36in (60–90cm).
(Wood, UK, 1949)

**'Margaret Ellen'**
Single H2 Bush
Medium-sized flowers. *Tube* and
*sepals* light rose, tipped with
green. *Corolla* light rose pink.
*Foliage* medium green. Growth
is upright and fairly bushy.
(Adams, UK, 1982)

'MAHARAJA'

'MAJOR HEAPHY'

'MALIBU MIST'

'MAMA BLEUSS'

'MANCUNIAN'

'MARCUS HANTON'

**'Margaret Pilkington'**
Single H2 Bush
*Tube* and *sepals* waxy white
with rose bengal veining.
*Corolla* bishop's violet
maturing to mallow purple.
Very free-flowering. *Foliage*
medium to light green. Growth
is quite strong, upright and
self-branching.
(Clark, D., UK, 1984)

**'Margaret Roe'**
Single H3 Bush
*Tube* and *sepals* rosy red.
*Corolla* pale violet-purple.
*Foliage* medium to darker
green. The medium-sized
blooms are very freely
produced. H. and S. 24–36in
(60–90cm). ('Caroline' ×
'Derby Belle')
(Gadsby, UK, 1968)

**'Margaret Rose'**
Single H2 Bush
*Tube* short, thick, neyron rose.
*Sepals* neyron rose with green
tips, open almost to the
horizontal. *Corolla* neyron rose
with spinel red picotee edging.
The medium-sized flowers are
freely produced. *Foliage*
medium green. Growth is tall,
upright and bushy.
(Hobbs, N., UK, 1976)

**'Margaret Susan'**
Single H2 Bush
*Tube* pale red. *Sepals* carmine
on top surface and lighter on
the underside, quite narrow,
reflex at right angles to the
tube and have green tips.
*Corolla* fuchsia purple with
carmine rose at the base of the
petals, veined cardinal red.
*Foliage* medium green with red
stems, serrated edges to leaves.
('Hugh Morgan' × 'Melody')
(Holmes. R., UK, 1974)

**'Margaret Swales'**
Semi-double H2 Trailer
*Tube* short, thick, ivory white
with pink at the base. *Sepals*
long and broad, waxy ivory
with green tips. *Corolla*
carmine rose shading to white
at the base of the petals. The
large petaloids are striped

carmine rose to white; the
blooms are medium-sized.
*Foliage* dark green. A natural
trailer and very free-flowering.
(Sport of 'La Campanella')
(Swales, UK, 1974)

**'Margaret Tebbit'**
Double H2 Trailer
*Tube*, *sepals* and *corolla* are all
white with a delicate hint of
pink. *Foliage* medium green.
Growth is very strong, self-
branching and short-jointed.
The natural trailing habit
makes it ideal for large
baskets.
(Dyos, UK, 1992)

**'Margaret Thatcher'**
Single H2 Bush
*Tube* short, pale pink. *Sepals*
white with greenish flush, and
recurve to the tube. *Corolla*
bluebird blue shading to
spectrum violet. *Foliage*
medium green. Growth is
vigorously upright, self-
branching and bushy.
('Christine Clements' ×
'Forward Look')
(Gadsby, UK, 1978)

**'Margaret's Pearl'**
Double H2 Trailer
Large flowered. *Tube* white.
*Sepals* also white. *Corolla* very
full, pure white. *Foliage*
medium green. The growth is
vigorous and naturally trailing.
(Australia)

**'Margarite Dawson'**
Double H2 Bush
*Tube* shortish and thick, very
pale pink striped with pale
rose. *Sepals* are held
horizontally, pale rose fading
towards the tips. *Corolla* white
with slight pale rose veining.
*Foliage* mid-green with slight
lightening underneath; the
leaves are quite large. Needs
frequent 'stopping' to make a
good bush.
(Dawson, UK, 1965)

**'Maria Landy'**
Single H2 Bush
*Tube* short, pale pink. *Sepals*
long, pale pink. Single *corolla*,

pale violet. The plant is very
floriferous. *Foliage* medium
green. Strong, upright and
bushy growth. Excellent for
show work in the smaller
pots.
(Wilkinson, UK, 1991)

**'Maria Merrills'**
Double H2 Bush
Flowers small but fully double.
*Tube* and *sepals* pink. *Corolla*
petals are pointed, white with
red veins. *Foliage* medium
green. The growth is upright
and bushy.
(Caunt, UK, 1991)

**'Marilyn Olsen'**
Single H2 Bush
*Tube* and *sepals* rosy pink.
*Corolla* white. *Foliage* medium
green. Growth is rather lax,
self-branching, short-jointed
and bushy. Can be used for
baskets or pots with supports.
A very floriferous cultivar
which made a great impact on
the show benches.
(Wilkinson, UK, 1987)

**'Marin Belle'**
Single H2 Bush
*Tube* medium length, salmon
pink. *Sepals* long, salmon pink,
and reflex over the tube.
*Corolla* bright pansy violet
with pink veins. *Foliage*
medium green. The vigorous
upright growth is self-
branching and bushy. The plant
is very free-flowering.
(Reedstrom, USA, 1959)

**'Marin Glow'**
Single H2 Bush
*Tube* short, white, medium
thickness. *Sepals* short and
broad, white with green tips.
*Corolla* bright imperial purple
tinged with pink at the base of
the petals, maturing to
magenta violet. The blooms are
of medium size and freely
produced. The vigorous growth
is upright and self-branching.
*Foliage* small to medium-sized,
serrated, medium green. An
excellent plant for the show
bench.
(Reedstrom, USA, 1954)

'MARGARET ROE'

'MARGARET TEBBIT'

'MARIA LANDY'

'MARIA MERRILLS'

'MARILYN OLSEN'

'MARIN BELLE'

**'Marinka'**
Single H2 Trailer
The yardstick against which
other basket cultivars are still
measured. *Tube* fairly long and
red. *Sepals* short, broad, red,
held over and around the petals
in the corolla when first
opening and then move to just
below the horizontal. *Corolla*
dark red and of medium size.
*Foliage* medium to dark green.
The growth is vigorous, bushy
and very free-flowering. If
exposed to cold draughts early
in the season the leaves can
become badly scorched and
marked. A superb basket can
be made very quickly.
(Rozain-Boucharlet, France,
1902)

**'Marja'**
Semi-double H2 Trailer
*Tube* short, pale rose. *Sepals*
light pink on the top and much
darker underneath. *Corolla*
carmine red. The medium-sized
flowers are freely produced on
lax growth. *Foliage* medium
green. ('Che Bella' × 'Blush o'
Dawn')
(Van der Beek, Holland, 1986)

**'Marjorie Coast'**
Single H2 Bush
*Tube* and *sepals* waxy white,
overlaid with pink. *Corolla*
amethyst blue. Medium-sized
flower. *Foliage* medium green.
The growth is vigorously
upright.
(Holmes, R., UK, 1994)

**'Mark Kirby'**
Double H2 Lax bush
*Tube* white. *Sepals* rose, have
recurved tips, and are held
horizontally. *Corolla* rose
bengal and flushed with neyron
rose. *Foliage* medium green.
The flowers are extremely large
and very freely produced
considering the size of each
bloom. Very exotic.
(Bielby/Oxtoby, UK, 1987)

**'Marlene Gilbee'**
Double H2 Lax bush
*Tube* short, light neyron rose
with a green strip. *Sepals* long

and broad, neyron rose and
white with light green recurved
tips. *Corolla* opens bishop's
purple edged with spectrum
violet maturing to imperial
purple edged with neyron rose
with touches of white. The large
bell-shaped flowers are freely
produced. *Foliage* medium
green, lighter underneath.
Longish leaves with red and
green veins. Growth is rather lax
for a bush but stiff for a basket.
('Pio Pico' × 'White King')
(Richardson, Australia, 1986)

**'Marshside'**
Semi-double H2 Bush
*Tube* thin, naples yellow
suffused with green. *Sepals*
French rose on the outside and
venetian pink underneath.
*Corolla* lilac purple veined with
turkey red and shading to
white at the base of the petals.
The medium-sized blooms are
very freely produced. *Foliage*
medium green. Growth is
upright and bushy.
(Porter, UK, 1982)

**'Martha'**
Single H2 Bush
*Tube* and *sepals* cardinal red.
*Corolla* light mauve. *Foliage*
medium green. The flowers are
medium-sized and freely
produced on strong upright
growth which is self-branching.
(Veen, Holland, 1991)

**'Martha Franck'**
Single H2 Lax bush
*Tube* long, straight, rose. *Sepals*
divergently held, bengal rose.
*Corolla* rose-coloured. *Foliage*
medium green. The growth is
rather lax so will need
supporting to make a bush.
(Franck, Holland, 1987)

**'Martin's Midnight'**
Double H2 Bush
*Tube* and *sepals* bright red.
*Corolla* deep india blue,
compact. *Foliage* medium
green. The flowers are large
and produced continuously
through the season. Growth is
upright and sturdy.
(Martin, USA, 1959)

**'Martyn Smedley'**
Single H2 Bush
*Tube* and *sepals* a waxy neyron
rose. *Corolla* blue-bird on the
inside, the outer petals wisteria
blue shaded with white. The
medium-sized blooms are held
horizontally and freely
produced. *Foliage* medium
green. The growth is strong,
upright and bushy.
(Gadsby, UK, 1968)

**'Mary'**
Triphylla type H1 Bush
*Tube* long, thin, and tapers so
that it is broad at the base of
the sepals; it is a vivid bright
crimson. *Sepals* fully reflexed,
also vivid bright crimson, as
are the fully exposed petals.
*Foliage* sage green, long and
thin, with a purple hue on the
reverse. A superb plant. (*F.
triphylla* × *F. corymbiflora*)
(Bonstedt, Germany, 1897)

**'Mary Joan'**
Double H2 Bush
*Tube* long, rose madder. *Sepals*
rose madder. *Corolla* light and
deep lavender streaked with
light and dark cerise. The
medium-sized blooms are freely
produced. *Foliage* medium green
with red veining. The growth is
upright and self-branching.
(Caunt, UK, 1983)

**'Mary Lockyer'**
Double H2 Bush
*Tube* carmine red. *Sepals* red.
The sepals have a crepe look to
the underside and green tips.
The *corolla* is pale lilac marbled
red from the top downwards.
The large blooms are fairly
freely produced. The *foliage* is
medium green and the strong
growth is upright and bushy.
(Colville, UK, 1967)

**'Mary Poppins'**
Single H2 Bush
*Tube* pale apricot. *Sepals* pale
apricot, tipped with pink.
*Corolla* orange-vermilion.
Medium-sized flower. *Foliage*
medium green. The growth is
upright and bushy.
(Need, UK, 1967)

'MARINKA'

'MARK KIRBY'

'MARLENE GILBEE'

'MARY'

'MARY LOCKYER'

'MARY POPPINS'

**'Mary Rose'**
Double H2 Bush
*Tube* fairly long, thin, rose
bengal. *Sepals* also rose bengal,
tipped with green. *Corolla*
white, flushed and veined
purple. The medium-sized
blooms are of good shape and
freely produced. *Foliage*
medium green. Growth is
strongly upright and self-
branching. Excellent for shrubs
or standards.
(Pacey, UK, 1984)

**'Mary Stilwell'**
Double H2 Trailer
*Tube* and *sepals* pinky-orange.
*Corolla* magenta, streaked with
orange. Medium-sized flowers.
*Foliage* medium green. The
rather lax but self-branching
growth makes it an ideal plant
for the hanging basket.
(Dyos, UK, 1993)

**'Masquerade'**
Double H2 Trailer
*Tube* short, greenish-white.
*Sepals* flesh colour to pink on
top, deeper pink on underside.
*Corolla* medium purple, the
outer petals pleated and
marbled pink. The very large
blooms are fairly freely
produced. *Foliage* medium
green. The natural habit of
growth is trailing so will make
a superb basket.
(Kennett, USA, 1983)

**F. matthewsii**
Species H1 Bush
*Tube* long, pink. *Sepals* pink to
red. *Corolla* darker red. The
flowers are carried terminally
in bunches. *Foliage* fairly large
and medium green.
(Peru)

**'Maureen'**
Single H2 Bush
*Tube* and *sepals* pale rose striped
with carmine. *Corolla* pale
orange-red. Medium-sized
flower. The plant is extremely
floriferous. *Foliage* medium
green. Because it has very
vigorous upright growth it is
very suitable for large structures.
(Krom, Holland, 1990)

**'Maureen Ward'**
Single H2 Trailer
*Tubes* waxy white. *Sepals*
white, tipped with rose and
flushed underneath with rose
orange. *Corolla* bright rose.
The flowers are medium-sized
and prolifically produced.
*Foliage* medium green. The
natural habit of this cultivar is
to trail so will make a superb
basket.
(Bielby/Oxtoby, UK, 1992)

**'Mauve Beauty'**
Double H2 Bush
*Tube* short, medium thickness,
cerise. *Sepals* curl and reflex
towards the tube, also cerise.
*Corolla* mauvish-lilac ageing to
pale purple with cerise veins;
loose-petalled bloom. *Foliage*
medium green. Growth is
upright and bushy. It is self-
branching and free-flowering.
(Banks, UK, 1869)

**'Mauve Wisp'**
Double H3 Bush
*Tube* and *sepals* deep pink.
*Corolla* lavender blue. The
small flowers are carried in
profusion and continuously.
*Foliage* medium green. The
growth is upright but dwarf
achieving a H. and S. only
up to approximately 12in
(30cm).
(Tabraham, UK, 1976)

**'Max Jaffa'**
Single H2 Lax bush
*Tube* small, orient pink. *Sepals*
orient pink, held slightly below
the horizontal. *Corolla*
mandarin red. The flowers are
medium-sized. *Foliage* dark
green. The growth is rather lax
so will need supporting if
grown as a bush.
(Burns, UK, 1985)

**'Mayblossom'**
Double H2 Trailer
*Tube* and *sepals* rose bengal.
*Corolla* white flushed with rose
bengal. The flowers are small
and very attractive. *Foliage*
small, round and medium
green. The natural growth is
trailing but the plant is very

short-jointed so bushes can be
achieved with staking.
(Pacey, UK, 1984)

**'Mayfield'**
Single H2 Bush
*Tube* red. *Sepals* deep rose pink
with crêpe texture on the
underside. The immature
flowers are tipped with green.
*Corolla* violet-blue and edged
slightly darker. The flowers are
bell-shaped and freely
produced. *Foliage* medium
green with fainter green
veining. Growth is upright and
self-branching.
(Pacey, UK, 1982)

**'Mazda'**
Single H2 Bush
*Tube* orangy-pink, short, very
thick. *Sepals* pale orange with
pink. *Corolla* carmine orange,
slightly paler at the base of the
petals. The bloom is longish and
bell-shaped. *Foliage* medium to
darkish green with serrated
edges to the leaves. Growth is
vigorously upright and bushy.
(Reiter, USA, 1947)

**'Meadowlark'**
Semi-double H2 Trailer
*Tube* long, thin, white. *Sepals*
white with green tips, broad
and overhang the corolla.
*Corolla* bright purple and rose
pink with white streaks; the
centre petals are longer than
the surrounding ones which are
frilled. *Foliage* medium green,
with medium to large finely
serrated leaves. The natural
growth is as a trailer so will
make a good basket.
(Kennett, USA, 1971)

**'Medallist'**
Double H2 Trailer
*Tube* short, thick, bright pink.
*Sepals* long and broad, bright
pink, deeper on undersides.
Held right up to corolla.
*Corolla* white. *Foliage* medium
green. The flowers are very
large and very full. Growth is
rather lax for a bush but will
make a good basket. ('Cyndy
Robyn' × 'Trade Winds')
(Stubbs, USA, 1984)

'MASQUERADE'

'MAYBLOSSOM'

'MAYFIELD'

'MEADOWLARK'

**'Medusa'**
Semi-double H2 Trailer
*Tube* longish, red. *Sepals* long,
curling, also red. *Corolla* white
with rose pink veining on each
petal. The blooms are very
large and have red and white
petaloids standing out from the
corolla. *Foliage* medium green.
The plant is very free-flowering
and trails quite naturally.
(de Graaff, Holland, 1976)

**'Melissa Heavens'**
Single H2 Bush
*Tube* short, claret rose. *Sepals*
fully recurved, claret rose on
top, crimson beneath. *Corolla*
fuchsia purple maturing to
tyrian purple. The medium-
sized flowers are very striking
in their colour combination.
*Foliage* medium green, small to
medium size with pale green
veins. The natural growth is
upright and self-branching.
Very floriferous, as is to be
expected with its parentage.
('Cambridge Louie' × 'Lady
Isobel Barnett')
(Heavens, UK, 1985)

**'Melody'**
Single H2 Bush
*Tube* long and thin, pale rose
pink. *Sepals* long, narrow and
reflexed, also pale rose pink.
*Corolla* pale cyclamen purple;
the blooms are very compact,
medium-sized. *Foliage* bright
green with serrated edges to
the leaves. Growth is upright
and bushy. The very easy
shaping and the quantity of
flower will always make this
cultivar popular.
(Reiter sen., USA, 1942)

**'Melody Ann'**
Double H2 Lax bush
*Tube* short, thick, white. *Sepals*
are pale pink with green tips
on top and a darker shade of
pink underneath; fairly long,
broad, curling slightly. *Corolla*
light pink. *Foliage* dark green
with crimson veins. The
growth is upright but rather
lax so will need supports to
make a good bush.
(Gagnon, USA, 1966)

**'Melting Moments'**
Double H2 Trailer
*Tube* pale pink. *Sepals* also pale
pink with dark pink veins on the
upperside and dark pink on the
lower side with green tips.
*Corolla* white with pink blotches
and pink veining. There are
many small petals. The blooms
are medium-sized but are very
full. *Foliage* medium green. The
growth is naturally trailing so
will make a good basket.
(Brough, UK, 1980)

**F. mendocini mini**
Encliandra type H1 Bush
The very small flowers have
single 'perfect' blooms. *Tube*
white, thin, short. *Sepals* white
on back, pale pink on front,
partially recurved. *Corolla* light
purple turning to dark pink,
very small. Growth is bushy
but rather lax and willowy.
The leaves are pale green. A
very versatile cultivar which
can be used for all sorts of
training shapes.
(Francesca, USA, 1975)

**'Mendocino Rose'**
Double H2 Lax bush
*Tube* thin pale pink. *Sepals* long,
broad, carmine rose and are
somewhat lighter on the outside.
*Corolla* is carmine rose to
salmon, variegated with reddish
purple lake. The extremely large
blooms are very full and flare
out when mature. *Foliage* large,
medium green. The cultivar
makes a large plant very quickly
and will need supports for the
weight of the flowers.
(Stubbs, USA, 1976)

**'Menna'**
Single H2 Bush
*Tube* medium length, bulbous,
red. *Sepals* are scarlet on the
upper surface and coral on the
lower; the tips are recurved.
*Corolla* is magenta and orange.
*Foliage* is dark green on the
upper surface and medium
green on the lower. Blooms
similar to 'Leverkusen' but
larger and more orange. Likes
full sun. ('Leverkusen' ×)
(Bogemann, Germany, 1987)

**'Meols Cop'**
Single H2 Bush
*Tube* and *sepals* blood red.
*Corolla* white with very slight
red veining. The smallish
flowers are carried in profusion.
*Foliage* medium green. The
growth is upright and bushy.
(Porter, UK, 1980)

**'Merry England'**
Double H2 Bush
*Tube* thin, medium length, rose
pink. *Sepals* broad, and reflex
over the tube, white on top and
pinkish underneath. *Corolla*
violet-purple with splashes of
rose pink at the base of the
petals. The blooms are
medium-sized. *Foliage* medium
green with finely serrated
edges. Growth is very strong,
upright and bushy.
(Gadsby, UK, 1968)

**'Merry Mary'**
Double H2 Trailer
*Tube* long, thin, pink. *Sepals*
long, broad and upturned, pink
on top and deeper pink on the
undersides. *Corolla* white with
pink veins and splashed pink
on the outer petals. The bloom
is medium-sized and fairly
compact. *Foliage* medium
green. The natural growth is as
a trailer and will make a
superb free-flowering basket.
(Fuchsia Forest, USA, 1965)

**'Mia van der Zee'**
Single H2 Trailer
*Tubes* rose pink. *Sepals* rose
pink, broad, slightly upturned.
*Corolla* rich magenta, paler at
base of petals. *Foliage* medium
green. The natural habit of this
medium-sized fuchsia is to trail
and will make a very good
basket. ('La Campanella' ×)
(de Graaff, Holland, 1978)

**'Michael Kurtz'**
Double H2 Trailer
*Tube* yellowish-white. *Sepals*
light rose. *Corolla* light purple;
flowers are large. *Foliage*
medium green. The natural
growth is as a trailer so will
make a superb basket.
(Riley, UK, 1992)

'MELTING MOMENTS'

'MERRY MARY'

**'Michelle Wallace'**
Single H2 Bush
*Tube* long, thin, creamy white
with a very slight touch of
pink. *Sepals* small, broad and
pointed, a delightful pale pink.
*Corolla* a delicate shade of
sugar pink. Very small but
delightful flowers. *Foliage*
medium green and smallish.
Growth is bushy, upright and
self-branching. (Sport of
'Countess of Aberdeen')
(Wallace, UK, 1982)

**'Micky Goult'**
Single H2 Bush
*Tube* short, white lightly flushed
pink. *Sepals* pinkish turning to a
deeper shade of pink, held at
the horizontal. *Corolla* mallow
purple. The blooms are small
and compact but extremely
floriferous. *Foliage* medium
green. Growth is vigorously
upright, self-branching and
bushy. Good exhibition plant,
also very suitable as summer
bedder. ('Bobby Shaftoe' ×
'Santa Barbara')
(Roe, UK, 1981)

**'Microchip'**
*Encliandra* type H2 Bush
Very small flowers. *Tube* and
*sepals* pink. *Corolla* pale pink.
*Foliage* small, medium green.
The growth is very thin and
wiry. Used for topiary.
(Flemming, UK, 1990)

*F. microphylla* ssp *aprica*
*Encliandra* type H2 Bush
Very small flowers. *Tube*,
*sepals* and *corolla* pink. *Foliage*
small, fern-like.
(Central America)

*F. microphylla* ssp *hemsleyana*
*Encliandra* type H2 Bush
Very small flowers. *Tube*,
*sepals* and *corolla* deep red.
*Foliage* very small.
(Central America)

*F. microphylla* ssp *hidalgensis*
*Encliandra* type H2 Bush
Very small flowers. *Tube*,
*sepals* and *corolla* pure white.
*Foliage* very small.
(Mexico)

*F. microphylla* ssp *microphylla*
*Encliandra* type H2 Bush
Very small flowers. *Tubes*,
*sepals* and *corolla* purplish-red.
*Foliage* very small.
(Mexico)

**'Midas'**
Single H2 Bush
*Tube* neyron rose. *Sepals* neyron
rose, held horizontally with tips
well recurved. *Corolla* violet
shaded rose at the base. *Foliage*
yellow to light green with red
veins. ('Grandma Sinton' ×
'Louise Faucon')
(Sinton, UK, 1988)

**'Midnight Sun'**
Double H2 Bush
*Tube* pink, long, thin. *Sepals*
broad, upturned, pink outside
and bright carmine on the
underside. *Corolla* very dark
burgundy purple, the outer
petals splashed pink and red.
The blooms are large and fairly
free. *Foliage* a rich shade of
green, finely serrated leaves.
Growth is very strongly upright.
(Waltz, USA, 1960)

**'Midwinter'**
Single H2 Bush
Small flowers. *Tube*, *sepals* and
*corolla* white. *Foliage* small
and medium green. The growth
is small and upright. Best
grown in the shade.
(Flemming, UK, year not
known)

**'Mieke Meursing'**
Single/semi-double H2 Bush
*Tube* short carmine red. *Sepals*
longish, narrow, reflexing,
carmine red. *Corolla* rose pink
with deeper veining. The
flowers are compact when first
opening, then become rather
loose; small to medium-sized.
*Foliage* medium green. Growth
is upright and bushy, self-
branching and will form into a
symmetrical bush very easily.
The leaves mark very easily
when subjected to cold
draughts. Good exhibition
plant but tends to show extra
petals and sepals.
(Hopgood, UK, 1969)

**'Miep Aalhuizen'**
Triphylla type H1 Bush
A true terminal-flowering,
triphylla-type fuchsia. *Tube*
long, thin, lavender. *Sepals*
short, *corolla* both lavender.
*Foliage* medium to dark green
with a slight purple hue on the
reverse. Growth is upright and
very strong.
(de Graaff, Holland, 1987)

**'Mikado'**
*Encliandra* type H2 Bush
The small single flowers are
perfect. *Tube*, *sepals* and
*corolla* bright orange. *Foliage*
medium green. Growth is
strong, robust and upright. Can
be used for all types of training.
(Goulding, UK, 1987)

**'Mike Oxtoby'**
Triphylla type H1 Bush
*Tube* long thin, vermilion.
*Sepals* vermilion, held down
over corolla with recurving
tips. *Corolla* small, square,
mandarin red. *Foliage* dark
green on upper surface with
dark green flushed crimson on
the lower; long, narrow leaves
with red veins, serrated edges.
The upright growth is rather
lax so will need supporting if
used as a bush. Rather stiff for
a trailer. A superb specimen of
the triphylla type of fuchsias.
(*F. triphylla* × 'Fanfare')
(Bielby, UK, 1984)

**'Millie Butler'**
Single H2 Bush
Medium-sized flowers. *Tube*
and *sepals* white. *Corolla*
orange-scarlet. *Foliage* medium
green. The natural growth is
upright and bushy.
(Clark, UK, 1990)

**'Millrace'**
Triphylla type H1 Bush
Terminal-flowering. *Tube* long,
box-shaped. *Sepals* shorter both
rose red. *Corolla* rose red.
*Foliage* medium to dark green
and has a purple sheen on the
reverse. Growth is very strong
and free-branching. Could be
useful for hanging containers.
(Stannard, UK, 1993)

198

'MICKY GOULT'  'MICROCHIP'

'MIDAS'  'MIDNIGHT SUN'

'MIEKE MEURSING'  'MIKE OXTOBY'

**'Mimi Kubischta'**
Double H2 Bush
Medium-sized flower. *Tube* and
*sepals* pale rose. *Corolla* white.
*Foliage* medium green. Growth
is fairly strong, upright and
bushy.
(Nutzinger, Austria, 1976)

**'Mina Knudde'**
Single H2 Trailer
Large flowers. *Tubes* and *sepals*
pale rose. *Corolla* pale beetroot.
*Foliage* medium green. The
natural habit is as a trailer so
will make a good basket.
(Hybridist and year unknown)

**'Ming'**
Single H2 Bush
*Tube* orange-red, short, thick.
*Sepals* orange-red flushed with
cerise, darker beneath, green
tips, short, broad. *Corolla*
cherry red paling slightly at the
base. The flowers are extremely
small, very freely produced and
are delightfully oriental in their
appearance. *Foliage* lightish
green, small, broad, serrated.
The growth is fairly strongly
upright and bushy.
(Jennings, UK, 1968)

**'Miniature Jewels'**
*Encliandra* type H1 Trailer
Very small flowers. *Tube*,
*sepals* and *corolla* whitish pink.
*Foliage* small. The growth is
thin and wiry. Can be used in
hanging containers.
(Francesca, USA, 1976)

**F. minimiflora**
*Encliandra* type H1 Bush
Very tiny flowers. *Tube* whitish
red. *Sepals* red with white
edges. *Corolla* white to red.
The flowers are borne solitary
in leaf axils. *Foliage* very small,
medium green. Thin, wiry
growth.
(Hemsley, Mexico and
Honduras, 1880)

**'Mini Rose'**
Single H2 Bush
*Tube* small, beige. *Sepals* beige
brushed with rose, small,
recurved tips. *Corolla* dark
cyclamen purple, lighter rose red

at petal base. The small flowers
are almost square shaped.
*Foliage* fuchsia green, much
lighter underneath. Growth is
upright and a small bushy plant
is produced quite easily. Very
free-flowering. It is short-jointed
and an ideal cultivar for the
smaller standards.
(de Graaf, Holland, 1985)

**'Mini Skirt'**
Double H2 Bush
*Tube* short, thin, greenish
white. *Sepals* broad, pointed,
white with green tips. *Corolla*
smoky mauve-grey rose. The
medium-sized blooms are freely
produced. *Foliage* dark green.
Best in the shade.
(Stubbs, USA, 1981)

**'Minx'**
Double H2 Bush
*Tube* flesh pink. *Sepals* very
broad, held horizontally and
have recurved tips, flame pink
on top and deep flame
underneath. *Corolla* opens
dark blue-magenta splashed
with coral pink, maturing to
blue-magenta with the same
splashing. The flowers are large
and broad. *Foliage* dark green,
much lighter underneath. The
natural growth is rather lax
and upright. Support for the
heavy blooms will be necessary.
(Brough, UK, 1986)

**'Mipam'**
Single H2 Bush
*Tube* pale carmine. *Sepals*
carmine pink, reflexing, long and
slender. *Corolla* magenta pink
flushed with carmine pink at the
base of the petals, compact. The
medium-sized flowers are very
freely produced. *Foliage* medium
green with a distinct serrated
edge to the leaves. Growth is
strong and upright.
(Gubler, UK, 1976)

**'Mirjana'**
Single H2 Lax bush
Medium-sized single flowers.
*Tube* and *sepals* crimson
flushed with rose. *Corolla* deep
purple to violet. *Foliage*
medium green. The growth is

rather lax but short-jointed,
and the flowers are prolific.
(de Graaff, Holland, 1990)

**'Mischief'**
Single H3 Bush
*Tube* and *sepals* light pink.
*Corolla* mauve, maturing
rapidly to deep pink. Very free-
flowering, giving the
impression of a pink bush.
*Foliage* dark green. Growth is
dwarf but upright. H. and S.
12–18in (30–45cm).
(Tabraham, UK, 1985)

**'Miss California'**
Semi double H2 Trailer or lax
bush
*Tube* pink, long, medium
thickness. *Sepals* medium pink,
shading to deeper pink
underneath, long, narrow.
*Corolla* white with a faintest
pink glow inside, very
compact; there is light pink
veining near the base of each
petal. The flowers are long,
medium in size and freely
produced. *Foliage* medium
green. Growth is rather lax so
needs supporting if grown as a
bush; attractive, easy to grow.
(Hodges, USA, 1950)

**'Miss Great Britain'**
Single H2 Bush
*Tube* dark pink to rose red,
medium length and thickness.
*Sepals* creamy white, tipped
with green and each has a
distinct twist. *Corolla* wisteria
blue fading to imperial purple.
The medium to large flowers
are very free but produced
rather late in the season.
*Foliage* medium green.
(Gadsby, UK, 1968)

**'Mission Bells'**
Single H2 Bush
*Tube* short, scarlet. *Sepals*
broad, reflexing, scarlet. *Corolla*
vivid purple splashed cerise at
the base of the petals. The
blooms are bell-shaped. *Foliage*
medium green, medium-sized,
serrated. The natural growth is
upright, self-branching and
bushy. Good summer bedder.
(Walker and Jones, USA, 1948)

'MIMI KUBISCHTA'

'MINA KNUDDE'

'MINI ROSE'

'MINX'

'MIPAM'

'MISCHIEF'

**'Miss Leucadia'**
Double H2 Trailer
*Tube* pink. *Sepals* pink, tipped
with green. *Corolla* soft pink.
The large blooms are flaring
and have picotee edging to the
petals. The flowers are fairly
free considering their size.
*Foliage* medium green. Growth
is naturally trailing.
(Stubbs, USA, 1971)

**'Miss Valejo'**
Double H1 Lax bush
*Tube* medium length, pale pink.
*Sepals* longish, broad, pale
pink with green tips. *Corolla*
deep pink with wide streaks of
rose pink on the petals. The
blooms are medium-sized,
compact, and freely produced.
*Foliage* medium green. The
growth is rather lax so will
require supporting.
(Tiret, USA, 1958)

**'Mistoque'**
Single H2 Bush
*Tube* and *sepals* white edged
with rose. *Corolla* lilac blue
tinged with light pink at the
base of each petal. *Foliage*
medium green. The growth
habit is upright and bushy.
Quite floriferous.
(Raiser unknown, UK, 1978)

**'Misty Blue'**
Double H2 Bush
*Tube* pink. *Sepals* pink at the
base changing to white, green
tips. *Corolla* misty lilac blue.
The flowers are very full
containing as many as fifteen
petals; very free-flowering.
*Foliage* mid-green. Growth is
upright, self-branching and
very bushy.
(Dyos, UK, 1982)

**'Misty Haze'**
Double H2 Trailer
*Tube* white, very large. *Sepals*
pure white tipped with green,
long, curve upwards to tube.
*Corolla* mineral violet slightly
flushed amethyst violet. The
large flowers are very freely
produced for their size. *Foliage*
medium green. The natural
growth is as a trailer; it will

make a very good basket.
(Bellamy, UK, 1983)

**'Misty Morn'**
Double H2 Trailer
*Tubes* flesh pink, hidden by the
frosty white, recurving *sepals*.
*Corolla* lilac blue with paler
shades of marbling. The plant is
multi-flowered. Growth trailing
and short-jointed. *Foliage*
medium green. Excellent for
hanging containers.
(Goulding, UK, 1990)

**'Misty Pink'**
Double H2 Trailer
*Tube* white streaked with
green. *Sepals* white on top,
white beneath with pink flush
near base, green tips. *Corolla*
has very pale pink and wavy
petals with pink petaloids.
*Foliage* medium green, lighter
underneath. The blooms are
quite large and very full. Will
make a superb basket.
(('Bicentennial' × 'Capri') ×
'Blush of Dawn')
(Stubbs, USA, 1983)

**'Molesworth'**
Double H2 Trailer
*Tube* medium length, cerise.
*Sepals* broad, upturned, cerise.
*Corolla* very full and fluffy
with creamy white petals which
have cerise veining. *Foliage*
medium green, small to
medium size, serrated. Growth
is very lax; better used as a
basket plant but could be used
as a bush with the necessary
supports.
(Lemoine, France, 1903)

**'Mollie Beulah'**
Double H2 Trailer
*Tube* medium length, white.
*Sepals* recurved, rose. *Corolla*
rose but opens slightly darker.
The numerous petaloids are
scarlet. *Foliage* medium green.
The natural growth is as a
trailer. Makes a superb basket.
(Bielby/Oxtoby, UK, 1988)

**'Mona Lisa'**
Single H2 Bush
*Tube* small, thin, pale pink.
*Sepals* short, narrow,

horizontally held; also pale
pink. *Corolla* pure white, short
and compact. *Foliage* medium
green. The dwarfish growth is
upright and bushy, self-
branching and very free-
flowering.
(Neiderholzer, USA, 1947)

**'Monomeith'**
Single H2 Trailer
*Tube* and *sepals* brilliant red.
*Corolla* reddish-purple. The
blooms are medium-sized but
are exceptionally freely
produced. *Foliage* medium
green. The natural trailing
makes it an ideal plant for
basketwork.
(Scrase, Australia, 1988)

**'Monsieur Joule'**
Single H2 Bush
*Tube* short, crimson. *Sepals*
short, completely recurve to
cover the tube, also crimson.
*Corolla* pale violet-purple fading
slightly at the base of the petals.
The blooms, although small, are
compact and freely produced.
*Foliage* medium green. Growth
is vigorously upright, bushy, and
self-branching.
(Lemoine, France, 1890)

**'Monsieur Thibaut'**
Single H2 Bush
*Tube* thick, cerise red. *Sepals*
broad, recurving also cerise
red. *Corolla* magenta with
cerise veining, a paler shade at
the base of the petals. The
blooms are compact and of
medium size. *Foliage* darkish
green with finely serrated edges
to the leaves. Growth is
upright, bushy and self-
branching. The flowers are
produced very freely.
(Lemoine, France, 1898)

**'Montenegro'**
Single H2 Trailer
Medium-sized flowers. *Tube*
and *sepals* light purple. *Corolla*
deep cyclamen purple. *Foliage*
medium green. The natural
growth is as a trailer. Will
make a good basket.
(Van den Bergh,
Holland, 1990)

'MISS VALEJO'

'MISTY BLUE'

'MISTY HAZE'

'MISTY PINK'

'MOLESWORTH'

'MOLLIE BEULAH'

**'Monte Rosa'**
Double H2 Bush
*Tube* medium length, pink.
*Sepals* long, narrow and
completely reflexed, also pink
with green tips. *Corolla* white
with pink veining. The blooms
are medium-sized and rather
loose. *Foliage* light to medium
green. Growth is upright, self-
branching and bushy.
(Colville, UK, 1966)

**'Montevideo'**
Double H2 Trailer
*Tube* short, flesh pink. *Sepals*
rather darker with green tips.
*Corolla* salmon and very
densely petalled. The buds on
this delightful cultivar are like
baubles. *Foliage* medium green.
The natural growth is
outwards and spreading, so
this will make a good hanging
container plant.
(Goulding, UK, 1989)

**'Montezuma'**
Double H2 Trailer
*Tube* medium length, carmine
rose. *Sepals* long and broad
with green tips, also carmine
rose. *Corolla* tyrian rose, and
the edges of the petals have a
smoky tinge; the base of each is
shaded with carmine rose.
*Foliage* medium green. The
natural growth is trailing but a
bush can be formed with the
aid of supports.
(Fuchsia La, USA, 1967)

**'Montrose Village'**
Double H2 Lax bush
*Tube* short, thickish, reddish-
purple diffused with white.
*Sepals* horizontally, white with
green tips. *Corolla* opens
spectrum violet and white,
matures to imperial purple and
white; some blooms have a
colour variation in the corolla
– this is smaller, opens violet
and white and matures to
phlox pink and white. *Foliage*
dark green. Requires early
'stopping' to make a good
bush. Very strong, upright
growth. ('Pio Pico' × 'White
King')
(Richardson, Australia, 1985)

**'Monument'**
Double H2 Bush
Medium-sized flower. *Tube* and
*sepals* carmine. *Corolla* purple.
*Foliage* medium green. The
natural growth is quite strongly
upright.
(Storey, UK, 1865)

**'Mood Indigo'**
Double H2 Lax bush
*Tube* thin, yellowish-green.
*Sepals* pale yellowish-green on
the upper surface, slightly
lighter underneath. *Corolla*
opens purple, matures to
reddish-purple with a pink
base. *Foliage* medium green on
the top, yellowish-green
underneath. Growth is rather
lax. The plant produces its
flowers very freely.
(de Graaff, Holland, 1988)

**'Moonbeam'**
Double H2 Bush
*Tube* short, yellow-green,
shaded pink. *Sepals* pale pink,
darker on the underside with a
crêpe texture, yellow-green tips;
long, narrow, upcurving. *Corolla*
white with pale pink splashes
and veining at the base. *Foliage*
large, dark green. Growth is
upright and self-branching. The
weight of the flowers will
necessitate some supporting.
(Hall, UK, 1982)

**'Moonglow'**
Double H2 Trailer
Large flowers. *Tube* white.
*Sepals* white flushed with
peach. *Corolla* white. *Foliage*
medium green, fairly large. The
natural growth is as a trailer.
(Riley, UK, 1991)

**'Moonlight Sonata'**
Single H2 Lax bush
*Tube* long, pink. *Sepals* long,
broad and upturned, also pink.
*Corolla* pale purple with pink
shading at the base, pink
veining. The blooms are
compact and of medium size.
*Foliage* medium green with
serrated edges. The lax growth
makes this cultivar suitable for
bush or basket.
(Blackwell, UK, 1963)

**'Moonraker'**
Double H2 Bush
*Tube* long, whitish. *Sepals* off-
white with pink flush on top,
green tips, underside white
shading to rose pink. *Corolla*
pale blue, fades with maturity,
serrated edging to the petals.
*Foliage* medium green. The
flowers are medium-sized and
freely produced. Growth is
upright but rather lax.
Supports may be needed.
(Clitheroe, UK, 1979)

**'Moonshot'**
Semi-double H2 Bush
*Tube* roseine purple. *Sepals*
long, broad, roseine purple
with green tips and darker
beneath. *Corolla* bishop's violet
flecked roseine purple at petal
base. *Foliage* medium green.
The upward growth is self-
branching and bushy.
(Pacey, UK, 1984)

**'Moorland Beauty'**
Semi-double H2 Bush
*Tube* red. *Sepals* neyron rose
on top, frosted neyron rose
underneath; tipped with white,
recurving. *Corolla* violet
shading to red-purple at the
base. The medium-sized flowers
are freely produced. *Foliage*
medium green. The growth is
naturally upright, self-
branching and bushy.
(Pugh, UK, 1975)

**'Morag's Baby'**
Single H2 Lax bush
Medium-sized flower. *Tube* light
pink. *Sepals* pale pink. *Corolla*
dark rose. *Foliage* medium
green. The growth is rather lax.
(Swinbank, UK, 1990)

**'More Applause'**
Double H2 Lax bush
*Tube* short, flushed ivory and
pink. *Sepals* long and very
broad, held horizontally with
recurved tips, also ivory flushed
pink. *Corolla* pink streaked with
rose. The flowers are very large
and are fully double. *Foliage*
medium green. The growth is
rather lax.
(Plows, USA, 1986)

204

'MOOD INDIGO'    'MOONBEAM'

'MOONSHOT'    'MORE APPLAUSE'

**'Morning Glow'**
Semi-double H2 Bush
*Tube* neyron rose. *Sepals*
neyron rose, held well back
from the tube. *Corolla* pale
wisteria blue shading to
gentian blue. The flowers are
medium-sized and prolific.
*Foliage* light green. Growth is
upright and bushy. ('Rosedale'
× 'Albion')
(Gadsby, UK, 1975)

**'Morning Light'**
Double H2 Lax bush
*Tube* and base of the petals
coral pink. *Sepals* white, tipped
with green, broad and
upturned, pink at the base and
edged palest pink underneath.
*Corolla* lavender splashed with
pale pink and deep pink. The
flowers are large, fully double
and eye-catching. *Foliage*
lettuce green. Growth is rather
lax, and the weight of the
flowers will need supporting. It
is prone to *botrytis*.
(Waltz, USA, 1960)

**'Morrels'**
Double H2 Bush
*Tube* crimson. *Sepals*
horizontally held, rose red
outside, neyron rose inside,
boat-shaped. *Corolla* lavender-
violet, lightly veined with
neyron rose. The medium-sized
blooms are of squarish shape.
*Foliage* darkish green with
cardinal red mid-rib. Growth is
vigorously upright but will
need regular 'stopping' as it is
not self-branching.
(Hobbs, UK, 1977)

**'Mountain Mist'**
Double H2 Bush
*Tube* greenish-white, short,
thick. *Sepals* white flushed with
rose on top, deeper pink
underneath, green tips,
upturned. *Corolla* pale silver-
grey-mauve, pink at the base of
each petal. The large flowers
are very freely produced.
*Foliage* medium green. The
natural growth is upright and
bushy.
(Crockett, UK, 1971)

**'Moth Blue'**
Double H2 Lax bush
*Tube* red, short. *Sepals* red,
long, narrow, upturning.
*Corolla* deep lilac blue. The
largish flowers are very freely
produced. *Foliage* dark green
with a distinct coppery hue.
Growth is rather lax and will
only make a bush with
supports, although a basket
can be achieved easily.
(Tiret, USA, 1949)

**'Mother's Day'**
Double H2 Trailer
*Tube* white with some green
striping. *Sepals* horizontally
held, white on the upperside
and white on the lower side
with yellowish-green recurved
tips. *Corolla* fully flared, cream
and white; the petals have a
wavy edge. *Foliage* dark green.
A natural trailer, will make a
superb basket as the large
flowers are very freely
produced.
(Richardson, Australia, 1988)

**'Moyra'**
Double H2 Trailer
Large flowers. *Tube* and *sepals*
pale pink. *Corolla* white, very
full. *Foliage* medium green.
The natural growth is as a
trailer, it is self-branching and
well worth growing in half and
full baskets.
(Johns, UK, 1990)

**'Mr A. Huggett'**
Single H3 Bush
*Tube* short, scarlet. *Sepals*
short, broad, stand out
horizontally from the tube,
recurved. *Corolla* mauvish-
pink, petals edged with purple
and pink at each base. *Foliage*
medium green. The natural
growth is upright, self-
branching and bushy. H. and S.
24–30in (60–75cm).
(Raiser unknown, UK)

**'Mr W. Rundle'**
Single H2 Lax bush
*Tube* very long, *sepals* reflexed,
both flesh pink. *Corolla* rich
orange vermillion. The flowers

are fairly large and long.
*Foliage* light green. The growth
is rather lax so this cultivar is
useful for baskets or as a
weeping standard. ('Earl of
Beaconsfield' × 'Lady
Heytesbury')
(Rundle, UK, 1883)

**'Mrs Churchill'**
Single H2 Bush
*Tube* red, thin. *Sepals* cherry
red, broad, curling upwards.
*Corolla* purplish white flecked
with deep pink and veined
cerise. The largish blooms are
bell-shaped and fairly freely
produced. *Foliage* medium
green with red veins, longish,
serrated. Growth is upright and
bushy.
(Garson, USA, 1942)

**'Mrs Florence Adams'**
Single H2 Bush
*Tube* short, creamy pink.
*Sepals* narrow, creamy pink,
slightly upturned and have
green tips. *Corolla* lilac pink
with a pink flush at the base of
the petals. The flowers are
fairly small, free-flowering, and
very compact. *Foliage* pale
green with serrated edges.
Growth is upright and bushy.
(Adams, UK, 1982)

**'Mrs Hilton'**
Semi-double H2 Bush
*Tube* thick, short, white. *Sepals*
broad and upturned, white on
the outside and flushed pink on
the inside. *Corolla* lilac with
lilac-marbled, flesh-coloured
petaloids. The medium-sized
flowers open saucer-shaped.
*Foliage* medium green. The
natural growth is as an
upright bush.
(Hilton, UK, 1976)

**'Mrs J Bright'**
Single H2 Bush
Medium-sized flower. *Tube* and
*sepals* waxy white. *Corolla*
orange. *Foliage* medium green.
The natural growth is as an
upright bush.
(Lye, UK, 1882)

'MORNING GLOW'  'MORNING LIGHT'

'MOUNTAIN MIST'  'MOTH BLUE'

'MOTHER'S DAY'  'MR A. HUGGETT'

**'Mrs Lovell Swisher'**
Single H2 Bush
*Tube* long, flesh pink. *Sepals*
tipped with green, pinkish-
white on the top and slightly
darker pink underneath, short,
narrow. *Corolla* deep old rose,
paler at the base. The flowers
are produced in great
quantities to compensate for
their smaller size. *Foliage*
medium green, medium-sized,
serrated. A very vigorous and
upright grower. Can be used
for large structures. Will benefit
from careful pinching because
otherwise makes long growths
between branches.
(Evans and Reeves, USA, 1942)

**'Mrs Marshall'**
Single H2 Bush
*Tube* thick, medium-length,
creamy white. *Sepals* held well
out from the corolla, also
creamy white. *Corolla* rosy
cerise. The flowers are compact
and of medium size, and are
produced in great quantities.
*Foliage* medium green. The
growth is upright, vigorous,
bushy and self-branching.
Needs careful watering
otherwise leaves can quickly
turn yellow and drop.
(Jones, UK, c.1862)

**'Mrs Minnie Pugh'**
Semi double H2 Bush
*Tube* short, salmon. *Sepals*
carmine rose on the outside
and frosted crimson on the
inside. *Corolla* shades from
crimson to ruby red. The
smallish flowers are freely
produced on a very compact
bushy plant. *Foliage* medium
green.
(Pugh, UK, 1969)

**'Mrs Popple'**
Single H3 Bush
*Tube* short, thin, scarlet. *Sepals*
also scarlet, short and broad.
*Corolla* violet-purple, and the
base of each petal is somewhat
paler. The petals are lightly
veined with cerise. *Foliage* dark
green, the leaves quite slender
and serrated. The natural
growth is as an upright, rather

spreading bush. H. and S.
24–30in (60–75cm).
(Elliot, UK, 1899)

**'Mrs Susan Brookfield'**
Double H2 Bush
*Tube* and *sepals* dark rose.
*Corolla* also dark rose,
streaked with purple. *Foliage*
medium to dark green with
serrated edges. The natural
growth is as an upright bush.
(Rimmer, UK, 1991)

**'Mrs Victor Reiter'**
Single H2 Lax bush
*Tube* and *sepals* creamy white.
*Corolla* pure crimson. The
largish flowers are freely
produced. *Foliage* light green
and tends to be brittle. The
growth is rather lax and will
require supports when grown
as a bush. ('Amy Lye' × 'Mrs
Rundle')
(Reiter, USA, 1940)

**'Mrs W. Castle'**
Semi-double H3 Bush
*Tube* short, rich scarlet. *Sepals*
horizontally held, also scarlet.
*Corolla* pink mauve with
veining at the base of each
petal. The fairly longish flowers
are medium-sized and freely
produced. *Foliage* dark green.
The natural growth is
vigorously upright. H. and S.
30–36in (75–90cm).
(Raiser unknown, UK, 1984)

**'Mrs W. Rundle'**
Single H2 Bush
*Tube* very long, *sepals* reflexed,
both flesh pink. *Corolla* rich
orange vermilion. The flowers
are fairly large and very long
but are very freely produced.
*Foliage* medium green. Growth
is very strong and upright.
('Earl of Beaconsfield' × 'Lady
Heytesbury')
(Rundle, UK, 1883)

**'Muirfield'**
Double H2 Trailer
Beautiful bell-shaped flower.
*Tube* and *sepals* white with red
streaks. *Corolla* lavender to
rose. *Foliage* medium green.
Growth is strong, self-

branching and very versatile.
Can be used for hanging
baskets or for bushes if
supports are provided.
(Goulding, UK, 1986)

**'Muriel'**
Semi double H2 Trailer
*Tube* long, thin, scarlet. *Sepals*
scarlet, green tips, long and
reflexed. *Corolla* light purple
veined with cerise, lighter at
base of petals. The large flowers
are freely produced. *Foliage*
medium green, serrated. The
growth is rampantly upright
and can be used as a greenhouse
climber if so desired. The
natural desire is to cascade, so
makes a good basket or
weeping standard.
(Raiser and date unknown, UK)

**'Musetta'**
Single H2 Bush
Medium-sized flower. *Tube* and
*sepals* rose red. *Corolla* pale
rose red with darker edges.
*Foliage* medium green. Growth
is bushy and upright.
(Sloots, Holland, 1988)

**'My Fair Lady'**
Double H2 Bush
*Tube* medium length, rose pink.
*Sepals* long, broad and curve
upwards, deep pink with green
tips. *Corolla* lavender maturing
to pinkish-purple. There is a
pink shading at the base of
each petal. The blooms are
rather loose-petalled. *Foliage*
medium green with serrated
edges. Growth is upright,
vigorous and extremely bushy.
This is a very free-flowering
cultivar.
(Colville, UK, 1966)

**'My Honey'**
Single H1 Trailer
*Tube* long, white. *Sepals* long,
pink on the underside and light
pink to white on the top, with
green tips. *Corolla* light
cyclamen purple with carmine
variegated base. The flowers
are fairly small. *Foliage* dark
green. The growth is naturally
trailing. A heavy bloomer.
(Palko, USA, 1976)

'MRS LOVELL SWISHER'        'MRS MARSHALL'

'MRS POPPLE'        'MRS SUSAN BROOKFIELD'

'MRS W. RUNDLE'        'MURIEL'

# N

**'Nananice'**
Single H2 Bush
*Tube* and *sepals* pure white but
splashed with carmine. *Corolla*
rose pink. The flowers are large
and freely produced. *Foliage*
very lush golden green which is
maintained throughout the
season. Growth is upright and
bushy. (Possibly a sport of
'China Lantern')
(Nice, UK, 1983)

**'Nancy Lou'**
Double H2 Bush
*Tube* pale pink. *Sepals* fully
recurving, pale pink on top,
deeper underneath, green tips;
long, broad. *Corolla* creamy
white. *Foliage* medium green,
large, serrated. The growth is
strong and upright. The
beautiful blooms are in the
classical style. Ideal as
standards or as plants in patio
tubs.
(Stubbs, USA, 1971)

**'Nanne'**
Single H2 Bush
Medium-sized flower. *Tube* and
*sepals* rose. *Corolla* is dark
purplish-violet. *Foliage* medium
green. Growth is upright and
bushy. Will take full sun.
(Breemer, Holland, 1989)

**'Napoleon'**
Single H2 Bush
Medium-sized flower. *Tube* and
*sepals* white. *Corolla* crimson.
*Foliage* medium to dark green.
Growth is fairly strongly
upright.
(Miellez, France, 1846)

**'Natalie Jones'**
Single H2 Bush
*Tube* and *sepals* white with a
hint of pink. *Corolla* pink, bell-
shaped. The flowers are
produced very freely. *Foliage*
medium green. The natural
growth is upright and self-
branching. An easy plant to
grow and the flowers display
themselves perfectly.
(Goulding, UK, 1989)

**'Natasha Sinton'**
Double H2 Trailer
*Tube* and *sepals* orchid pink.
*Corolla* orchid pink and veined
with magenta. The flowers are
medium-sized and very freely
produced. *Foliage* mid-green.
The natural growth is as a trailer.
A very eye-catching cultivar.
(Sinton, UK, 1990)

**'Nautilus'**
Double H2 Bush
*Tube* cerise, thin, medium
length. *Sepals* cerise and curve
right back to hide the tube; long,
narrow. *Corolla* white, veined
with carmine, compact. The
large blooms are quite freely
produced. *Foliage* medium to
darkish green, serrated. Growth
is upright and bushy.
(Lemoine, France, 1901)

**'Navy Blue'**
Single H3 Bush
*Tube* and *sepals* deep pink.
*Corolla* navy blue. The
medium-sized flowers are freely
produced. *Foliage* pale green.
Growth is upright and bushy
with a self-branching habit. H.
and S. 18–24in (45–60cm).
(Tabraham, UK, 1974)

**'Nel'**
Single H2 Bush
Medium-sized flower. *Tube*
light absinthe green. *Sepals*
rose. *Corolla* carmine. *Foliage*
medium green. The natural
growth is as an upright bush.
(Breemer, Holland, 1991)

**'Nell Gwynn'**
Single H2 Bush
*Tube* and *sepals* waxy orange-
salmon. *Corolla* bright orange
edged with vermilion. The
flowers are medium-sized and
produced early in the season.
*Foliage* fairly large and bright
green, a perfect foil for the
colouring of the flowers.
Growth is upright and bushy.
(Handley, UK, 1976)

**'Nellie Nuttall'**
Single H2 Bush
*Tube* very small, brilliant red.
*Sepals* small, deep crimson, held
slightly below the horizontal.
*Corolla* white with red veining;
the smallish flowers look
outward from the foliage and
are produced in great quantity
throughout the season. *Foliage*
lightish green. Growth is
upright, short-jointed and very
bushy. Compact plants are easily
formed with frequent stopping.
Always seen on the show
benches, especially in the smaller
pot classes. ('Khada' × 'Icecap')
(Roe, UK, 1977)

**'Nemerlauer'**
Semi-double H2 Trailer
*Tube* striped red rose. *Sepals*
flame red. *Corolla* reddish-
purple. *Foliage* medium green.
The flowers are large single or
semi-double and produced
quite freely. The natural
growth is rather lax so can be
used in baskets or pots with
appropriate supports.
(Weeda, Holland, 1989)

**'Neopolitan'**
*Encliandra* type H2 Bush
A novelty fuchsia which always
attracts considerable attention.
The very small flowers are
produced in white, pink or red
on the same branch and at the
same time. *Foliage* is medium
to dark green and is very fern-
like in character. The growth
very thin and wiry which
means this plant can be used to
construct all types of shapes
around wires. Very floriferous,
and as is usual with the
Encliandra type of fuchsias, the
flowers are followed by small,
shiny round black seedpods.
(Clark, UK, 1984)

**'Nettala'**
Single H2 Bush
*Tube* is dark red, short and
thick. *Sepals* short and stubby,
also dark red. *Corolla* violet
red. The blooms are of medium
size. The *foliage* is medium
green, small to medium-sized.
Growth is vigorously upright
and the plant is very free-
flowering.
(Sport of 'Chang')
(Francesca, USA, 1973)

'NANCY LOU'

'NATASHA SINTON'

'NELL GWYNN'

'NELLIE NUTTALL'

**'Neue Welt'**
Single H3 Bush
*Tube* crimson, short. *Sepals*
small, slightly upturned, rich
red. *Corolla* dark parma-violet
with carmine veins, paler at
base of petals, fading with
maturity. The flowers are very
freely produced. *Foliage*
medium green. H. and S.
24–30in (60–75cm).
(Mahnke, Germany, 1912)

**'New Fascination'**
Single H2 Bush
*Tube* medium length, bright
reddish-pink. *Sepals* reflexed,
carmine red on top and
brighter on the underside.
*Corolla* rose pink, heavily
marked with carmine splashes,
red veins. *Foliage* medium
green, serrated, medium-sized.
Growth is vigorously upright
and very free-flowering.
(Niederholzer, USA, 1940)

**'Newquay Beauty'**
Single H2 Bush
*Tube* and *sepals* white. *Corolla*
magenta pink and orange.
*Foliage* medium green. The
flowers are medium-sized and
carried in profusion. Growth is
upright and bushy.
(Weeks, UK, 1989)

**'Nice 'n Easy'**
Double H2 Bush
Medium-sized flower. *Tube* red.
*Sepals* dark rose with green
tips. *Corolla* white. *Foliage*
medium green. The natural
growth is as a bush.
(Sinton, UK, 1988)

**'Nicholas Hughes'**
Single H2 1982
*Tube* pink, medium size. *Sepals*
pink. *Corolla* cream. The
flowers are medium-sized and
produced very freely. *Foliage*
medium green, serrated edges.
The natural growth of the
plant is upright, self-branching
and bushy.
(Clark, UK, 1982)

**'Nicis Findling'**
Single H2 Bush
Small flowers. *Tube* and *sepals*

rose. *corolla* orangey-red.
*Foliage* medium green. Growth
is upright and bushy.
(Ermel, Holland, 1992)

**'Nicola Claire'**
Double H2 Trailer
*Tube* and *sepals* light pink with
deeper colouring on the
underside. *Corolla* dark red
with occasional light violet
petals dashed with bold streaks
of pink. The flowers are fairly
large and freely produced for a
double, two to each leaf axil.
*Foliage* medium green. Growth
is naturally trailing.
(Holding, UK, 1989)

**'Nicola Jane'**
Double H3 Bush
*Tubes* pinkish cerise, thick.
*Sepals* cerise pink with green
tips, broad, reflexing. *Corolla*
bluish-pink flushed with cerise.
Medium-sized loose-petalled
bloom. *Foliage* medium green.
The natural growth is upright
and bushy. H. and S. 12–18in
(30–45cm).
(Dawson, UK, 1959)

**'Nicolette'**
Single H2 Bush
*Tube* short, thick, white with a
pink flush. *Sepals* broad and
slightly recurved, pink on top
and deeper pink on the
underside, with green tips.
*Corolla* fuchsia purple, deeper
at the edges and fading to pink
at the base of the petals. The
bloom is compact and of
medium size. *Foliage* medium
green, broad, medium-sized
with serrated edges.
(Handley, UK, 1973)

**'Nicolina'**
Single H2 Lax bush
*Tube* rose-red. *Sepals* recurve to
the tube, rose bengal on top and
underneath. *Corolla* white with
an unusual picotee edging of
cyclamen purple. The open, bell-
shaped bloom is medium-sized.
*Foliage* rich green. Growth is
upright, self-branching and very
bushy. The stems are rather wiry
so will need supports when
heavily in flower. Needs early

pinching to form a reasonable
shape. ('Bishop's Bells' × 'White
Bride')
(Gadsby, UK, 1973)

**'Night and Day'**
Double H2 Trailer
Medium-sized flowers. *Tube* and
*sepals* light rose. *Corolla* violet.
*Foliage* medium green. Growth
is rather lax so will be best when
used as a basket plant.
(Brouwer, Holland, 1989)

**'Nightingale'**
Double H2 Trailer
*Tube* and *sepals* white, flushed
with pink. *Corolla* deep purple.
The flowers are large and frilly
and very freely produced for
their size. *Foliage* dark green.
The natural growth is trailing,
and an excellent basket can
soon be developed.
(Waltz, America, 1960)

**'Nightlight'**
Single H2 Bush
Small flowers. *Tube* and *sepals*
crimson pink sepals with green
tips. *Corolla* deep red. *Foliage*
medium green. Growth is very
strong and upright.
(Adams, UK, 1982)

***F. nigricans***
Species H1 Bush
*Tubes* long, thin, aubergine.
*Sepals* short also aubergine.
*Corolla* has small, dark
aubergine. The flowers appear
in the leaf axils. *Foliage* dark
green, fairly large and hairy.
Growth is weak at first,
strengthening later; a
temperamental starter.
(Venezuela)

**'Nina Wills'**
Single H2 Bush
*Tube* short, thin soft baby pink.
*Sepals* very pale flesh pink, long,
narrow and upturned. *Corolla*
soft baby pink. The medium-
sized flowers are very freely
produced and are of a neat
appearance. *Foliage* medium
green. The natural growth is as
a neat bush. (Sport of 'Forget-
me-not')
(Wills/Atkinson, UK, 1961)

'NEW FASCINATION'

'NICHOLAS HUGHES'

'NICIS FINDLING'

'NICOLA JANE'

'NIGHTINGALE'

**'Nobby Adams'**
Single H2 Bush
*Tube* short, thick, creamy.
*Sepals* very short, creamy pink
with deeper pink beneath.
*Corolla* pinky-orange with
deeper colouring at the edge of
the petals. The flowers are
small. *Foliage* medium green.
Growth is upright and bushy.
(Adams, UK, 1982)

**'Nora Henderson'**
Single H2 Trailer
*Tube* long, thin, pink. *Sepals*
slender, held horizontally, pale
pink on top, crêpe pink
underneath with green tips.
*Corolla* bell-shaped, opens
white slightly veined with pink,
maturing to a very light pink;
petals have wavy margins.
*Foliage* dark yellow-green,
paler underneath, longish with
serrated edges and green veins
shading to red near the stem.
The natural growth is as a
trailer. Will make an excellent
basket with early and regular
pinching. ('Blue Elf' ×
'Mayfield')
(Hall, UK, 1984)

**'Norman Greenhill'**
Single H2 Trailer
*Tube* and *sepals* waxy pink.
*Corolla* pinky-orange. *Foliage*
medium green. The natural
growth is as a trailer so will
make an excellent basket.
(Tite, UK, 1990)

**'Normandy Bell'**
Single H2 Lax bush
*Tube* pale pink, short. *Sepals*
pinkish white with green tips,
long, broad, slightly upturned.
*Corolla* light orchid blue with
pink veining. *Foliage* light
green quite long leaves,
serrated. The flowers are bell-
shaped and quite large. The
natural growth is as a trailer;
will make a good basket.
(Martin, USA, 1961)

**'North Cascades'**
Semi-double H2 Trailer
*Tube* thickish, white. *Sepals*
horizontally held, recurving,
white on top and pink

underneath with green tips.
*Corolla* large, broad white with
pink veining. *Foliage* yellow-
green. The natural growth is
trailing and self-branching.
('Sebastopol' × 'Pink
Marshmallow')
(Wood, USA, 1986)

**'Northern Pride'**
Double H2 Bush
*Tube* pink. *Sepals* small,
rhodamine pink on the inside
and phlox pink on the
underside. *Corolla* fuchsia
purple, the smaller outer petals
beetroot purple. Stigma white,
anthers chrysanthemum pink.
*Foliage* medium green. The
strong upward growth is self-
branching.
(Ryle, UK, 1979)

**'Northilda'**
Single H2 Bush
Medium-sized flower. *Tube*
deep pink. *Sepals* rose. *Corolla*
a delightful geranium pink.
*Foliage* medium green. The
natural growth is as an upright
bush.
(Dijkstra, Holland, 1991)

**'Northumbrian Belle'**
Single H2 Bush
*Tube* short, thick, neyron rose.
*Sepals* fairly long and narrow,
bright neyron rose. *Corolla*
aster blue, fading to petunia
purple with bengal rose veining.
The medium-sized, bell-shaped
blooms are freely produced.
*Foliage* medium green. The
upright and bushy growth is
self-branching. The best colour
develops in the shade.
(Ryle/Atkinson, UK, 1973)

**'Northway'**
Single H2 Bush
*Tube* pale pink, short, thick.
*Sepals* light pink, short, broad,
reflexing. *Corolla* cherry red,
small; compact, small bloom.
*Foliage* small, light green. The
upright growth, although
rather lax, is self-branching
and will make a superb bush.
Needs careful feeding or the
foliage becomes very pale and
the whole plant insipid; a

heavy application of nitrogen
early on will maintain quality.
('La Campanella' × 'Howlett's
Hardy')
(Golics, UK, 1976)

**'Norvell Gillespie'**
Double H2 Trailer
*Tube* white, medium length and
thickness. *Sepals* white on top,
pink underneath, long, narrow.
*Corolla* dark orchid. *Foliage*
medium green. A natural trailer,
bushy and free-flowering.
(Pennisi, USA, 1969)

**'Novato'**
Single H2 Lax bush
*Tube* long, thin, white faintly
tinged green. *Sepals* white on
top with light green tips, white
with pink tinge beneath, fairly
long. *Corolla* pale scarlet,
shading to salmon. *Foliage* very
light green. Branches are red.
The medium-sized, compact
blooms are very freely
produced. The growth is rather
lax so can be used as either
bush or basket with supports.
(Soo Yun, USA, 1972)

**'Novella'**
Semi-double H2 Lax bush
*Tube* long, thin, flesh pink.
*Sepals* long and upturning, rosy
pink. *Corolla* salmon orange,
fairly compact and of medium
size. *Foliage* medium green
with serrated edges. Growth is
rather lax so can be used as a
bush, with staking, or as a
trailer in baskets.
(Tiret, USA, 1967)

**'Noyo Star'**
Double H2 Trailer
*Tube* short, thin carmine red.
*Sepals* pink on top with
carmine streaking and tipped
green, lighter pink on the inside
shading to green. *Corolla* white
with pink streaks. The flowers
are medium-sized, and the buds
exceptionally long. *Foliage*
medium green with red veins
and red stems. The growth is a
natural trailer, the plant is self-
branching. Makes a superb
basket.
(Walker, USA, 1976)

'NORMAN GREENHILL'

'NORTHUMBRIAN BELLE'

'NORTHWAY'

'NOVELLA'

# O

**'Obergartner Koch'**
Triphylla type H1 Bush
*Tube* long, tapering, bright orange. *Tube* very thin, then bulges towards the sepals. *Sepals* are spreading and also bright orange. *Corolla* is almost hidden, the same bright orange. *Foliage* large, olive green with a purple reverse.
(Sauer, Germany, 1912)

**'Ocean Beach'**
Single H2 Bush
*Tube* light salmon. *Sepals* light salmon on the upperside and salmon underneath rather stiff and flat, tipped with green. *Corolla* salmon orange mottled with salmon rose. The small flowers are very freely produced. *Foliage* dark green with a dark red tint at the growing tip.
(Krogh, USA, 1975)

**'Oddfellow'**
Double H2 Bush
*Tube* small, pale pink. *Sepals* a delicate shade of pink with green tips. *Corolla* pure white. *Foliage* medium green. The blooms are medium-sized and freely produced. The growth is upright and self-branching.
(Dyos, UK, 1982)

**'Oldbury'**
Double H2 Trailer
*Tube* and *sepals* bright deep pink. *Corolla* pinkish-lilac marbled with bright pink and white. The medium-sized blooms are very freely produced. *Foliage* medium green. The growth is rather lax so can be used for either bush or baskets.
(Dresman, UK, 1986)

**'Oldbury Delight'**
Double H2 Trailer
*Tube* and *sepals* light pink tipped with green. *Corolla* rose pink with light pink streaks. *Foliage* medium green. The growth is lax and will make an excellent basket. ('Pink Galore' ×)
(Dresman, UK, 1990)

**'Oldbury Galore'**
Double H2 Trailer
*Tube* and *sepals* are red, tipped with green. *Corolla* a deep pink veined with red. The blooms are large and freely produced considering the size. *Foliage* medium green. The natural growth is trailing. ('Pink Galore' ×)
(Dresman, UK, 1990)

**'Oldbury Gem'**
Double H2 Trailer
*Tube* short, bright red. *Sepals* broad, also bright red. *Corolla* outer petals are bright red and splashed with purple; the inner petals are also purple. The medium-sized blooms are very compact. *Foliage* medium green. The natural growth of the plant is as a trailer, but although it is lax it can also be used as a bush or standard.
(Dresman, UK, 1986)

**'Oldbury Pearl'**
Semi-double H2 Trailer
*Tube* and *sepals* light pink. *Corolla* white with pink veining. The large flowers are very freely produced. *Foliage* medium green. The growth is naturally trailing so will make a good basket.
(Dresman, UK, 1987)

**'Old Somerset'**
Single H2 Bush
Small flowers. *Tube*, *sepals* and *corollas* red. *Foliage* a dull mid-green with pink and yellow variegations for which it is mainly grown. May be a 'sport' from 'Corralina'.
(Clapton Court, UK, 1982 (?))

**'Olive Moon'**
Semi-double H2 Bush
*Tube* and *sepals* palest pink. *Corolla* pale magenta. *Foliage* medium green. The medium-sized blooms are freely produced. Growth is upright and bushy.
(Tite, UK, 1987)

**'Olive Smith'**
Single H2 Bush
*Tube* and *sepals* carmine; the

sepals curve upwards. *Corolla* rich crimson. The flowers are quite small but are colourful and very freely produced. *Foliage* medium green. Growth is bushy and self-jointed.
(Smith, UK, 1981)

**'Olympia'**
Single H2 Bush
Medium-sized flower. *Tube* and *sepals* rose pink. *Corolla* carmine. *Foliage* medium green. The natural growth is as a short-jointed bush.
(Rozaine-Boucharlet, France, 1913)

**'Olympic Lass'**
Double H2 Trailer
*Tube* long, slender, white. *Sepals* are completely recurving, also white with rose edge, stripe and tips. *Corolla* pinkish-purple with thin purple picotee edging; long (2in/5cm), and pear shaped – rather unusual. The buds are also very long. *Foliage* medium green with heavy serration, rather lacy. Growth is rather lax, and with the heavy weight of the blooms a good basket can easily be grown.
(Sutherland, USA, 1967)

**'Omar Giant'**
Double H2 Lax bush
Very large flower. Tube and sepals light red. *Corolla* pure white. Foliage medium green. Growth is very lax so will make a good basket or a bush if the necessary supports are provided.
(Smith, UK, 1855(?))

**'Omeomy'**
Double H2 Stiff trailer
*Tube* pale pink. *Sepals* pale pink, long, narrow and upturning. *Corolla* dianthus purple overlaid with coral pink marbling. The flowers are large and tightly formed. *Foliage* medium green. Growth is rather stiff for a basket but trailing can be achieved with weights.
(Kennett, USA, 1963)

'OLD SOMERSET'

'OLIVE MOON'

'OLIVE SMITH'

'OLYMPIC LASS'

**'Onna'**
Single H2 Bush
*Tube* and *sepals* orange.
*Corolla* crimson with an
orange base to the petals.
*Foliage* medium green. The
natural growth is as an upright
and self-branching bush.
(Bogemann, Germany, 1987)

**'Oosje'**
*Encliandra* type H1 Bush
The very small single flowers
appear only in the pistillate
form. *Tube* and *sepals* red
ageing to dark red. *Corolla*
pale pink at first but reddens
with age. *Foliage* medium to
darker green. Growth is bushy
and spreading. Useful for all
types of training. (*F. parvifora*
× *F. microphylla*)
(Van der Grijp, Holland, 1973)

**'Orange Blossom'**
Single H2 Trailer
*Tube* and *sepals* pale peach.
*Corolla* vivid orange. The
flowers are fairly small with
petals folded, creating a very
attractive shape. Very free-
flowering. *Foliage* medium
green. The growth is rather lax
which assists in the making of
a good basket.
(Meier, UK, 1987)

**'Orange Cocktail'**
Single H2 Trailer
Large flowers. *Tube* pale salmon
pink, long, slender. *Sepals* pale
salmon, green tips, short, broad
and upturned. *Corolla* clear
orange in centre and at base of
petals, deeper orange at edges.
*Foliage* medium green. The
natural growth is as a trailer.
(Handley, UK, 1973)

**'Orange Crush'**
Single H2 Bush
*Tube* waxy orange salmon.
*Sepals* thick and spiky, also
orange salmon. *Corolla* bright
orange and paler at the base;
the petals overlap. The
medium-sized blooms are very
freely produced. *Foliage*
medium green. The natural
growth is as a bush.
(Handley, UK, 1972)

**'Orange Crystal'**
Single H2 Bush
*Tube* orange, medium length
and thickness. *Sepals* orange
tipped with green, long.
*Corolla* a deeper orange.
*Foliage* medium green and
quite large. The upward
growth of the bushy plant is
short-jointed. The medium-
sized flowers are freely
produced; colouring similar to
'Lord Lonsdale'.
(Handley, UK, 1980)

**'Orange Drops'**
Single H2 Lax bush
*Tube* light orange, long. *Sepals*
light orange, broad, pointed.
*Corolla* darker orange, smoky
effect on petal edges. The
flowers are medium-sized and
held out horizontally to the
plant; tend to hang in clusters.
*Foliage* fairly large and
medium green. Growth is lax
bush or stiff trailer. Ideal for
growing as a weeping standard.
(Martin, USA, 1963)

**'Orange Flare'**
Single H2 Bush
*Tubes* and *sepals* short, orange
salmon. *Corolla* light orange at
the base shading to deep orange
at the outer margins of the
petals. The flowers are medium-
sized and produced early and
very freely. *Foliage* is medium
green. Growth is upright, self-
branching and bushy. Best
colour develops in the sun.
(Handley, UK, 1972)

**'Orange Flash'**
Double H2 Trailer
*Tube* and *sepals* cerise orange.
*Corolla* bright orange on the
outer petals and purple on the
inner petals. *Foliage* medium
green. The growth is naturally
trailing.
(Dresman, UK, 1986)

**'Orange King'**
Double H2 Trailer
*Tube* white. *Sepals* pale pink on
top, rich frosty pink on
undersides, arching back.
*Corolla* opens orange and
matures to smoky pink; some

marbling of the petals. *Foliage*
medium green. The growth is
very robust and spreading.
Better when given protection
from wind and sun. Natural
trailer, will make a good basket.
(Wright, UK, 1975)

**'Orange Mirage'**
Single H2 Trailer
*Tube* pale salmon pink. *Sepals*
salmon pink with green tips,
long, broad, curling. *Corolla*
smoky orange with touches of
salmon. Medium-sized flower.
*Foliage* light green. Naturally
trailing, the plant will make a
good basket.
(Tiret, USA, 1970)

**'Orange van Os'**
Single H2 Bush
Large flowers. *Tube* and *sepals*
white with a pinkish-orange
blush. *Corolla* orange. *Foliage*
medium green. The natural
growth is as an upright, self-
branching bush.
(Raiser and date unknown)

**'Oranje Bovan'**
Single H2 Lax bush
*Tube* very long and thin, azalea
pink. *Sepals* are azalea pink
half down over corolla with
green tips recurving. *Corolla*
opens bright red-orange
maturing to brick-red with
wavy petal edges. *Foliage* large,
olive green. The lax growth
makes it suitable for baskets or
bushes given the correct
supports. Not easy to grow,
but very showy. ('Speciosa' ×)
(de Graaff, Holland, 1985)

**'Oriental Flame'**
Double H2 Stiff trailer
*Tube* pale pink. *Sepals* pale
pink on the upper surface and
pale salmon pink on the lower
surface, with recurved tips.
*Corolla* coral red streaked with
pink, maturing to bright coral
red. *Foliage* dark green on the
upper surface and lighter
underneath. The growth is
rather stiff trailing, so will
make a bush or a basket with
the correct supports.
(Stubbs, USA, 1987)

'ORANGE CRUSH'

'ORANGE CRYSTAL'

'ORANGE DROPS'

'ORANGE DROPS' SPORT

'ORANGE MIRAGE'

'ORIENTAL FLAME'

**F. orientalis**
Species H1 Bush
The small, long-tubed, orange
flowers are borne in loose
bracteate racemes.
(Ecuador)

**'Oriental Sunrise'**
Single H2 Lax bush
*Tube* short, thin, light orange.
*Sepals* light orange, tipped with
green on top, darker orange
underneath, star-shaped.
*Corolla* dark orange. The
medium-sized flowers are freely
produced. *Foliage* medium
green with red veining and
stems. The method of growth is
rather stiff for a trailer but can
be encouraged to make a
basket with weights.
(Soo Yun, USA, 1976)

**'Orient Express'**
Triphylla type H1 Bush
*Tube* long, a mixture of pink
and white. *Sepals* short,
pinkish-white and red-tipped.
*Corolla* rose pink. Very
attractive multi-coloured
blooms. *Foliage* medium green
with a slight purple reverse.
Growth is strongly upright.
Needs hard pinching to make a
good bush.
(Goulding, UK, 1985)

**'Ornamental Pearl'**
Single H2 Bush
*Tube* white. *Sepals* rhodamine
pink shading to white, tipped
with green. *Corolla* white. The
flowers are of medium size, are
well formed and extremely
floriferous. *Foliage* a very
attractive grey-green edged
with cream. There is a red hue
over the younger growth.
Growth is upright, self-
branching and very bushy.
(Sport of 'Cloverdale Pearl')
(Gubler, UK, 1984)

**'Ortenburger Festival'**
Single H2 Bush
*Tube* short, thick, red. *Sepals*
outspread, deep red. *Corolla*
violet-blue turning to reddish
with maturity; bell-shaped,
flaring. The medium-sized
blooms are very early and very

freely produced. *Foliage* is dark
green. Growth is upright, self-
branching and bushy.
(Topperwein, Germany, 1973)

**'Orwell'**
Double H2 Bush
Described as a 'novelty-type'
fuchsia by its raiser. *Tube* and
*sepals* short, pale tangerine.
*Corolla* darker orange, fully
ruffled. A very floriferous
plant. Blooms from very early
in the season. *Foliage* medium
green. Growth is upright and
bushy.
(Goulding, UK, 1988)

**'O Sole Mio'**
Single H2 Bush
*Tube* and *sepals* deep red.
*Corolla* dark purple, marbled
with reddish-pink. The
medium-sized blooms are freely
produced. *Foliage* medium
green. Growth is upright and
bushy.
(Blackwell, UK, 1960)

**'Other Fellow'**
Single H2 Bush
*Tube* white, medium length and
thickness. *Sepals* a waxy white
tipped with green, short,
narrow. *Corolla* coral pink
with white at the base of each
petal. The small flowers are
carried in profusion. Extremely
dainty and attractive fuchsia.
*Foliage* medium green, small,
finely serrated. Growth is
upright, self-branching and
bushy. A good exhibition plant,
but needs careful watering.
(Hazard and Hazard, USA, 1946)

**'Our Darling'**
Single H2 Bush
*Tube* short, narrow, deep rose
pink. *Sepals* deep rose on top,
deeper crêpe rose beneath, held
up against tube with tips
recurved. *Corolla* opens deep
violet-blue veined with rose
pink, matures to heliotrope,
flushed rose pink at base of
petals. The flowers are bell-
shaped. *Foliage* olive green,
paler beneath. The growth is
upright and self-branching.
(Hall, UK, 1984)

**'Our Gracie'**
Double H2 Bush
*Tube* and *sepals* phlox pink.
*Corolla* white, veined with rosy
red. The flower is large. *Foliage*
medium green. Growth is
upright and bushy. ('Annabel' ×
'Coquet Dale')
(Sinton, UK, 1987)

**'Our Ted'**
Triphylla type H1 Bush
Considered to be a
'breakthrough' in modern
hybridisation: the first 'White
Triphylla'. *Tube* long and
tapering white. *Sepals* white
with tips of the faintest pink.
*Corolla* also white, opens
rather more fully than most
triphylla types. *Foliage* dark
green. Not the easiest of plants
to grow, but worth persevering
with.
(Goulding, UK, 1987)

**'Ovation'**
Double H2 Trailer
*Tube* long and thin, ivory.
*Sepals* long and broad, ivory to
pink. *Corolla* deep red with
some orangey-pink in the outer
petals. The flowers are freely
produced for a medium-sized
double. *Foliage* rather large
medium green. The natural
growth is as a trailer; will
therefore make a good basket.
The best colour of flower is
achieved in filtered light.
(Stubbs, USA, 1981)

# P

**'Pacific Queen'**
Double H2 Bush
*Tube* short, thick pinkish-
white. *Sepals* short and broad,
held flat over the top of the
corolla, pink with white tips.
*Corolla* dark rose-pink fading
to bright rose very full and
'fluffy'. *Foliage* dark green
with very finely serrated
leaves. Growth is vigorously
upright, bushy and very free-
flowering.
(Waltz, USA, 1963)

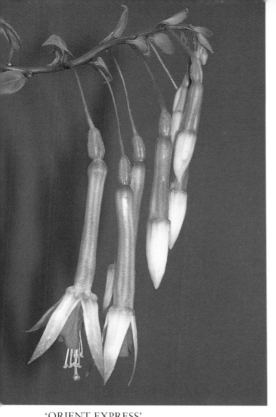

'ORIENT EXPRESS'
'ORNAMENTAL PEARL'

'ORTENBURGER FESTIVAL'
'OUR DARLING'

**'Pacquesa'**
Single H2 Bush
*Tube* short, deep red. *Sepals*
reflexing, deep red with crêpe
undersides. *Corolla* white with
red veining. *Foliage* parsley
green, almond-shaped. Growth
is upright, short-jointed and very
free-flowering. Good exhibition
plant as bush but tends to throw
semi-double flowers. ('Pacific
Queen' × 'Sheryl Ann')
(Clyne, UK, 1975)

**'Padre Pio'**
Semi-double H2 Bush
*Tube* short, thin light red
faintly streaked with darker
red. *Sepals* bright red on the
upper surface and crêped bright
red on the lower. *Corolla* dark
blue maturing to violet-red. The
petals have smooth edges.
*Foliage* light to medium green.
Growth is upright and bushy.
('Fascination' × 'Mission Bells')
(Boullemier, UK, 1987)

**'Pale Flame'**
Double H2 Trailer
*Tube* short, pale carmine. *Sepals*
long, twisting and curling, pale
carmine rose. *Corolla* opens
claret rose to carmine rose at
the base of the petals, fading to
delft rose to azalea pink; the
petals are tightly rolled but flare
with maturity. *Foliage* dark
green with red veins. Growth is
rather lax so will produce a
good basket.
(Stubbs, USA, 1978)

**F. pallescens**
Species H1 Bush
*Tube* small but longish, pale
carmine. *Sepals* white. *Corolla*
purplish. *Foliage* medium
green. The flowers are rather
small and not very free.
(Ecuador)

**'Palmengarten'**
Double H2 Lax bush
Medium-sized flower. *Tube* and
*sepals* rose. *Foliage* medium green.
The natural growth is rather
lax so supports will be needed
when training as a bush.
(Strumper, Holland, 1985)

**'Pamela Hutchinson'**
Single H2 Bush
*Tube* short, pale pink. *Sepals*
cyclamen rose with green tips.
*Corolla* light hyacinth blue.
The medium-sized flowers are
produced very freely and very
early in the season. *Foliage*
large and dark green. Growth
is upright and fairly strong.
(Gadsby, UK, 1978)

**'Pamela Knights'**
Double H2 Bush
*Tube* short, cream with pink
flush. *Sepals* flesh pink,
recurving tips. *Corolla* lavender
blue and very frilly. The flowers
are produced in profusion.
*Foliage* medium green. A fast-
growing and spreading bush.
(Goulding, UK, 1983)

**'Pan'**
Single H2 Bush
*Tube, sepals, corolla* lilac rose.
*Foliage* medium green.
Medium-sized flowers, upward-
looking in their growth. Very
attractive indeed. ('Small pipes'
× F. magdalenae)
(de Graaff, Holland, 1991)

**F. paniculata**
Species H1 Bush
The flowers are very small,
held in large, loose terminal
clusters. *Tube, sepals* and
*corolla* all small, pale lilac.
*Foliage* quite large with laurel-
like leaves. Growth is very
strong and upright, quite easy
to train. A good species for the
beginner. Sometimes referred to
as the 'Lilac Fuchsia'.
(South Mexico to Panama)

**'Pantaloons'**
Semi-double H2 Lax bush or
trailer
*Tube* longish and bulbous, pink.
*Sepals* long and broad, held out
well, light red. *Corolla* plum
purple with many petaloids
hanging down below the main
petals. *Foliage* medium green.
The natural growth is very lax
so can be used for bush or
basket. Needs pinching early to
form a basic shape.
(Fuchsia Forest, USA, 1966)

**'Papa Bleuss'**
Double H2 Lax bush
*Tube* short, greenish-white.
*Sepals* short, broad and slightly
upturned, crêpe white with
green tips on the top and white
with a pink flush underneath.
*Corolla* deep violet maturing to
reddish-purple and shaded pink
at the base of each petal.
*Foliage* medium green. Growth
is rather lax upright, bushy and
very free-flowering.
(Tiret, USA, 1956)

**'Papageno'**
Double H2 Lax bush
Medium-sized flower. *Tube* and
*sepals* dark red. *Corolla* lilac
pink. *Foliage* medium green.
Growth is rather lax for a bush
so will need supports.
(Rapp, Germany, 1982)

**'Papoose'**
Single H2 Bush
*Tube* thin, medium length,
scarlet. *Sepals* short, pointed
and held out, also scarlet.
*Corolla* very dark purple,
lighter at the base of the petals;
the blooms are small and
compact. *Foliage* medium green
with serrated edges. Growth is
self-branching, bushy but
rather lax. Staking when
training as a bush is to be
advised.
(Reedstrom, USA, 1960)

**'Paramour'**
Single H2 Bush
Medium-sized flower. *Tube* and
*sepals* cerise. *Corolla* mid blue.
*Foliage* medium green. The
natural growth is upright and
bushy.
(France, year not known)

**'Party Frock'**
Semi-double H2 Bush
*Tube* medium length, rose pink.
*Sepals* long, curling, rose pink
and have green tips. *Corolla*
pastel blue splashed with rose
and with slight rose veining.
*Foliage* medium green with red
veins. Growth is strongly
upright, self-branching and
bushy.
(Waltz, USA, 1953)

'PACQUESA'

'PALE FLAME'

F. PANICULATA

'PAPOOSE'

'PANTALOONS'

**'Pastell'**
Double H2 Bush
*Tube* neyron rose. *Sepals* curve
up tightly to the tube, neyron
rose. *Corolla* fuchsia purple
heavily flushed with azalea
pink. *Foliage* medium green.
Growth is fairly strong and
upright. ('Drake 400' ×
'Devonshire Dumpling')
(Hilton, UK, 1984)

**'Patience'**
Double H2 Bush
A double with a classical
outline. *Tube* white. *Sepals*
upturned, white. *Corolla* petals
carry a suggestion of pink on
white. *Foliage* medium green.
The upright growth is very
sturdy and strong. Excellent for
showing.
(Goulding, UK, 1987)

**'Patio Princess'**
Double H2 Bush
*Tube* and *sepals* neyron rose.
*Corolla* white veined with rose.
*Foliage* medium green. The
natural growth is upright, self-
branching and bushy. Makes a
superb plant for the patio tub.
('Cambridge Louie' × 'Estelle
Marie')
(Sinton, UK, 1988)

**'Patricia Ann'**
Double H2 Trailer
*Tube* long, striped, neyron rose
and rose pink. *Sepals* long,
white striped faint pink on top,
pale pink underneath. *Corolla*
neyron rose shading to rose
pink at the base of the petals,
veined dark pink. *Foliage*
medium to large, medium
green. The growth is naturally
trailing so will make a good
basket.
(Clements, UK, 1982)

**'Patricia Barnett'**
Single H2 Lax bush
Medium-sized flower. *Tube*
long, light rose. *Sepals* also
rose. *Corolla* dark salmon.
*Foliage* medium green. The
natural growth is upright but
rather lax. Worth using in a
basket.
(de Graaff, Holland, 1989)

**'Patricia Ewart'**
Single H2 Bush
*Tube* medium length, crimson.
*Sepals* long, narrow and
upsweeping, crimson; they keep
well clear of the corolla.
*Corolla* rhodamine pink
heavily veined with crimson.
*Foliage* medium green. Growth
is upright and naturally bushy
and self-branching. Very free-
flowering. Worth trying as bush
or smaller standard. ('Mipam'
× 'Mieke Meursing')
(Roe, UK, 1980)

**'Patty Evans'**
Double H2 Bush
*Tube* long, white with a pale
pink flush. *Sepals* long and
narrow, curve upwards, waxy
white with a rose-pink flush.
*Corolla* white with pale pink
flush and veins. The bloom is
medium-sized and very fluffy.
*Foliage* medium green with
crimson veining. Growth is
naturally upright and very
bushy. A good free-flowering
cultivar.
(Evans and Reeves, USA, 1936)

**'Paula Jane'**
Semi-double H2 Bush
*Tube* short, venetian pink.
*Sepals*, arch upwards and cover
the tube, are carmine rose. The
*Corolla* is beetroot purple
changing to ruby red as the
flower develops. There is a
pale pink flush at the base of
the *petals*. The *foliage* is
medium green. Growth is
upright and bushy. Very free-
flowering.
(Tite, UK, 1975)

**'Paula Johnson'**
Double H2 Bush
*Tube* and *sepals* white flushed
with pink; the sepals are much
darker underneath. *Corolla*
rich crimson. The two colours
contrast quite dramatically.
Flowers medium-sized, the
blooms are freely produced
for a double. *Foliage* medium
green and the upward growth
is strong and bushy.
(Pacey, UK, 1988)

**'Paul Cambon'**
Double H2 Bush
*Tube* short, thick, scarlet.
*Sepals* short and broad, slightly
reflexing, also scarlet. *Corolla*
violet-purple, very full and
fluffy. The blooms are medium-
sized. *Foliage* medium to large,
medium green with reddish
veining. Growth is upright,
bushy and free-flowering. Not
an easy one to grow, but it is
worth a try.
(Lemoine, France, 1909)

**'Paul Pini'**
Double H2 Bush
Medium-sized flower. *Tube* and
*sepals* red. *Corolla* violet
veined with pale pink; the
petals are produced in two
tiers. *Foliage* medium green.
The natural growth is upright
and bushy.
(Holmes, R., UK, 1992)

**'Paul Roe'**
Double H2 Bush
*Tube* short, medium thick,
crimson. *Sepals* narrow and
slightly upturned, also crimson.
*Corolla* violet with crimson
veining. The blooms are
medium-sized and freely
produced. *Foliage* light green.
The natural growth is upright
and bushy. ('Glyn Jones' ×
'Brutus')
(Roe, UK, 1981)

**'Pee Wee Rose'**
Single H2 Lax bush
*Tube* thin, medium length, rosy
red. *Sepals* longish, held down
over the corolla, also rosy red.
*Corolla* rosy red, small and
compact. *Foliage* medium
green. Growth is fairly lax and
will need supporting when
grown as a bush. Worth trying
as a small basket.
(Niederholzer, USA, 1939)

**'Peggy Cole'**
Single H2 Bush
Medium-sized flower. *Tube* and
*sepals* creamy white. *Corolla*
bright pink. *Foliage* medium
green. The natural growth is
rather lax upright.
(UK raiser and date unknown)

'PATIO PRINCESS'

'PEE WEE ROSE'

'PAULA JANE'

### 'Peloria'
Double H2 Bush
*Tube* long and slender, dark red. *Sepals* short and broad, dark red slightly turned up at the tips. *Corolla* central petals are purple, red petals on the outside. The medium-sized bloom is very fully double. *Foliage* medium green, the leaves very long and narrow. Growth is upright and bushy.
(Martin, USA, 1961)

### 'Pennine'
Single H2 Bush
*Tube* short, thick, carmine and striped with red. *Sepals* short, white, reddening at the base, the inside shaded pink. *Corolla* dark violet blue, paler at the base of the petals. The medium-sized flowers are very freely produced. *Foliage* medium green. The natural growth is as a self-branching bush. Colours are best in slightly shaded conditions. ('Norman Mitchinson' × 'Eden Lady')
(Mitchinson, UK, 1979)

### 'Peper Harow'
Single H2 Lax bush or trailer
*Tube* medium-sized, neyron rose. *Sepals* slightly upswept, neyron rose with green tips. *Corolla* rhodonite red with nasturtium red at the base of the petals. The blooms are small to medium-sized. *Foliage* medium green, lighter beneath, the leaves large and serrated. The growth is rather lax so can be used for bush or basket. ('Coachman' × 'Sunset')
(Holmes, R., UK, 1974)

### 'Pepi'
Double H2 Bush
*Tube* rather thick, medium length, greenish-white. *Sepals* short and broad, white and heavily flushed with rosy red. *Corolla* orange-red with marbling of a paler shade at the base of each petal; blooms very compact. *Foliage* darkish green with serrated edges. Growth is upright, free-flowering and bushy.
(Tiret, USA, 1963)

### 'Peppermint Candy'
Double H2 Trailer
*Tube* is pink. *Sepals* pink on the upper surface, dark rose on the lower surface, recurved tips. *Corolla* dark rose variegated with pink. *Foliage* yellowish-green. A natural trailer, this cultivar will make a superb basket. ('Wine and Roses' × 'Applause')
(Garrett, USA, 1989)

### 'Peppermint Stick'
Double H2 Bush
*Tube* carmine rose, short. *Sepals* upturned, carmine with a distinct white stripe running down the middle. *Corolla* centre petals are a rich royal purple, the outer petals a light carmine rose with purple edging. The medium-sized blooms are very freely produced and very solid. *Foliage* medium green. The natural growth is strong, upright and bushy. A very distinctive and well named flower.
(Walker and Jones, USA, 1950)

### 'Perky Pink'
Double H2 Bush
*Tube* medium length, pale pink. *Sepals* short, broad and upturned, pink with green tips. *Corolla* white flushed with pale pink, pink veining. The blooms are medium-sized and rather loosely formed, but are freely produced. *Foliage* medium green, the leaves are rather long and narrow with serrated edges. Growth is upright, self-branching and very bushy.
(Erickson-Lewis, USA, 1959)

### 'Perry Park'
Single H2 Bush
*Tube* short, thick, pale pink. *Sepals* pale pink on the outside, deeper pink on the inside, rather thick, reflexed. *Corolla* bright rose shading to a paler rose at the base of each petal. *Foliage* medium green. The natural growth is upright, short-jointed and self-branching. The flowers are medium-sized and very freely produced.
(Handley, UK, 1977)

### F. perscandens
Species H1 Bush
*Tube* red. *Sepals* greenish to reddish and do not reflex. *Corolla* purple. The pollen is blue, and the small flowers are followed by dark purple berries. *Foliage* greenish on the upper surface, whitish underneath, the leaves small and ovate. A naturally vigorous and climbing plant.
(New Zealand)

### 'Personality'
Double H2 Bush
*Tube* short and thick *sepals* long, both bright rosy red. *Corolla* magnolia purple changing to spiraea red, petals slightly marbled rose-pink. The large blooms are very freely produced. *Foliage* medium green. The natural growth is as an upright and strong-growing bush.
(Fuchsia La, USA, 1967)

### 'Peter Bielby'
Double H2 Bush
*Tube* long, thin, neyron rose. *Sepals* held halfway up above the horizontal, also neyron rose. *Corolla* tyrian purple with little or no fading during maturity. *Foliage* large, light green. Very strong, upright grower which requires frequent stopping in the early stages to bring out the best in the foliage and flowers. ('Swingtime' × 'Kathleen Muncaster')
(Bielby, UK, 1987)

### 'Peter Crooks'
Triphylla type H1 Lax bush
A perfect triphylla type with flowers produced in bunches at the ends of the branches. *Tubes* long, *sepals* short, both bright red. *Corolla* an intense orange-red. *Foliage* medium to dark green with a distinct purple sheen to the rear. The rather lax growth makes it suitable for use in hanging containers.
(Goulding, UK, 1985)

'PELORIA'

'PENNINE'

'PEPPERMINT STICK'

'PERKY PINK'

'PERRY PARK'

'PETER BIELBY'

**'Peter Sanderson'**
Single H2 Bush
*Tube* and *sepals* white. *Corolla*
pale lilac. Medium-sized
flowers, very floriferous.
*Foliage* medium green. The
natural growth is as an upright
bush. Very attractive.
(Heavens, UK, 1991)

**F. petiolaris**
Species H1 Bush
*Tube* very long and thin,
narrowly funnel-form, dark
pink. *Sepals* pink to pale pink,
sometimes tipped with green.
*Corolla* bright rosy pink. The
flowers are produced in the leaf
axils. *Foliage* a dull medium
green, the leaves quite large.
Best when grown under
warmer greenhouse conditions.
(Colombia and Venezuela)

**'Petite'**
Double H2 Bush
*Tube* white, flushed rose pink,
short, thick. *Sepals* upturned,
pale rose, deeper underneath,
short and broad. *Corolla* lilac
blue and bengal rose fading to
lavender blue. The small
blooms are very freely
produced from early in the
season. *Foliage* medium green.
(Waltz, USA, 1953)

**'Petit Point'**
Single H2 Bush
Small flowers. *Tube* and *sepals*
carmine; sepals deeper shade
underneath, green tips, pointed
and held well out. *Corolla*
mauve, lighter at petal base.
*Foliage* medium green. The
natural growth is as a short-
jointed upright bush. ('Alice
Hoffman' ×)
(de Graaff, Holland, 1976)

**'Petronella'**
Double H2 Bush
*Tube* and *sepals* flesh pink,
medium length. *Corolla* the
palest of lavender, full, compact.
Foliage medium green. The
natural growth is upright and
bushy. Can be made into a
good, showy standard.
('Annabel' seedling)
(Mitchinson, UK, 1986)

**'Phenomenal'**
Double H2 Bush
*Tube* scarlet, short, thin. *Sepals*
very broad, short, also scarlet.
*Corolla* rich indigo blue, paler
at the base of the petals, and
veined with carmine. The large
blooms are fairly freely
produced. *Foliage* medium
green, leaves finely serrated.
Natural growth is upright but
the weight of the blooms will
necessitate staking the
branches.
(Lemoine, France, 1869)

**'Phoebe Travis'**
Double H2 Bush
*Tube* medium length, rose pink.
*Sepals* broad and waxy, also
rose pink. *Corolla* parma violet
suffused with rose pink, the
petals short and incurved. The
medium-sized flowers are
produced freely, a very full
double. *Foliage* medium green,
The natural growth is
vigorously upright.
(Travis, UK, 1956)

**'Phoenix'**
Double H3 Bush
Medium-sized flowers. *Tube*
carmine and *sepals*. *Corolla*
purple cerise. *Foliage* medium
to dark green. Growth upright
and bushy. The plants are
excellent for the hardy border.
H. and S. 18–24in (45–60cm).
(Lemoine, France, 1969)

**'Phyllis'**
Single/semi-double H3 Bush
*Tube* short, thick, rosy red.
*Sepals* short and broad, also
rosy red, droop over corolla.
*Corolla* a slightly deeper shade
of rosy red. The flowers are
compact, and small to medium
in size. *Foliage* medium to dark
green with serrated edges.
Growth is upright and very
vigorous. Can be used for any
upright type of growth including
hedges in favoured areas. H. and
S. up to 4ft (120cm). Difficult to
train to a bushy shape, but
otherwise easy to grow; makes a
standard in one season; suitable
for beginners.
(Brown, UK, 1938)

**'Phyrne'**
Double H2 Bush
*Tube* medium length, cerise.
*Sepals* short, broad and slightly
upturned, cerise. *Corolla* white
with cerise veining in the
centre; the outer petals are
heavily marked with cerise and
much shorter. Fluffy, open
bloom, medium in size. *Foliage*
medium green, serrated, red
veins. The growth is upright
and bushy, although there is
the tendency to send out strong
horizontal branches.
(Lemoine, France, 1905)

**'Piet G. Vergeer'**
Single H2 Bush
The flowers are large. *Tube* and
*sepals* light rose. *Corolla* a
fierce red. *Foliage* medium
green. The natural growth is as
an upright bush.
(Beije, Holland, 1989)

**'Piet Hein'**
Single H2 Trailer
*Tube* neyron rose. *Sepals*
neyron rose on the upper
surface and slightly lighter on
the lower. *Corolla* opens
petunia purple maturing to
dark mallow purple. *Foliage*
dark green on the upper
surface, light olive green on the
lower. The growth is rather
stiff for a trailer but it is self-
branching. The flowers are very
freely produced.
(de Graaff, Holland, 1987)

**'Pinch Me'**
Double H2 Trailer
*Tube* thick, short, white. *Sepals*
long and narrow, white with
green tips, carried horizontally
and curl slightly. *Corolla*
bishop's purple shading to pink
at the base of the petals. The
flowers are very full, rather
loose. *Foliage* medium green, the
leaves fairly long and narrow,
slightly serrated. The plant is a
natural trailer, very bushy and
free-flowering. Makes an
excellent basket which stays in
flower over a long period. Also
summer bedder.
(Tiret, USA, 1969)

'PETRONELLA'

'PHENOMENAL'

'PHYLLIS'

'PIET G. VERGEER'

'PINCH ME'

**'Pink Aurora'**
Single H2 Bush
*Tube* and *sepals* light pink.
*Corolla* pink with a unique
orange edging to the petals.
*Foliage* medium green. The
flowers are medium-sized and
very freely produced. Growth
is naturally upright and bushy.
(Endicott, UK, 1968)

**'Pink Ballet Girl'**
Double H2 Bush
*Tube* cerise, medium length.
*Sepals* broad and upturned, also
cerise. *Corolla* pink suffused
with pale blue. The flowers are
medium to large and are fairly
compact. *Foliage* medium green
and has serrated edges. The
growth is vigorously upright,
free-flowering and bushy.
(Raiser and date unknown)

**'Pink Bon Accorde'**
Single H2 Bush
*Tube* short, medium thickness,
pink. *Sepals* slightly reflexing,
pale pink on top and rather
darker underneath, green tips.
*Corolla* pale rose pink with an
even paler shade at the base of
each petal. The flowers are small
to medium size and are held out
from the foliage, though not
quite so erect as the cultivar
'Bon Accorde'. *Foliage* medium
green and again quite small.
Growth is upright and bushy.
(Thorne, UK, 1959)

**'Pink Bouquet'**
Single/semi-double H2 Bush
*Tube* neyron rose; *sepals* also
neyron rose, tipped with green.
*Corolla* phlox pink veined with
neyron rose. The medium-sized
flowers are very freely and
continuously produced. *Foliage*
medium green. The growth is
upright and bushy.
(Pacey, UK, 1986)

**'Pink Chiffon'**
Double H2 Trailer
*Tube* is white with a pale
pinkish flush. *Sepals* recurve
slightly, are white flushed with
pale pink and have green tips.
*Corolla* pale pink and very full,
with a deeper shade of pink at

the base of each petal. *Foliage*
darkish green. The natural
growth is trailing so will make
a good basket.
(Waltz, USA, 1966)

**'Pink Cloud'**
Single H2 Bush
*Tube* short, thick, pink. *Sepals*
long, curve up towards the tube,
pale pink on top with a deeper
shade of pink underneath, green
tips. *Corolla* pale pink with
darker veining. The flowers are
rather 'fluffy' and are medium-
sized. *Foliage* medium green.
Growth is upright, bushy and
free-flowering.
(Waltz, USA, 1955)

**'Pink Crinoline'**
Double H2 Trailer
*Tube* coral pink. *Sepals* coral
pink with reflexed green tips.
*Corolla* creamy pink and lilac
with turned-under edges to the
petals. *Foliage* dark green on
the upper surface and lighter
on the lower. The growth is
naturally trailing and will make
a superb basket. ('Pink
Quartette' × 'Pink Galore')
(Weeks, UK, 1987)

**'Pink Darling'**
Single H2 Bush
*Tube* short, dark pink. *Sepals*
short and rather broad, held
horizontally, pale pink on top
and a deeper pink underneath.
*Corolla* pinkish-lilac but lighter
at the base of the petals. The
flowers are small and very
compact. *Foliage* medium
green, the leaves small with
serrated edges. Growth is
upright and bushy but careful
stopping will be necessary to
form a good symmetrical bush.
(Machada, USA, 1966)

**'Pink Dessert'**
Single H2 Bush
*Tube* short, thick, white. *Sepals*
long, narrow and reflexing,
white with a pink flush, a
deeper pink on the undersides,
green tips. *Corolla* pale pink.
The blooms are very compact,
of medium size. *Foliage*
medium green. The growth is

upright and bushy.
(Kuechler, USA, 1963)

**'Pink Fairy'**
Double H2 Bush
*Tube* pink, medium length and
thickness. *Sepals* pink, short
and broad, and turn up
towards the tube. *Corolla* pink
with darker pink veining from
the base. Small to medium-
sized blooms. *Foliage* medium
green. Growth is upright,
bushy and self-branching.
(Waltz, USA, 1954)

**'Pink Fantasia'**
Single H2 Bush
*Tube* and *sepals* of this superb
cultivar are bright pink or red.
*Corolla* fluorescent violet to
mauve. *Foliage* medium to
darker green. The flowers are
produced in great profusion
throughout the season, mainly
at the ends of the branches,
and are upward-looking. An
excellent 'show banker'.
(Webb, UK, 1989)

**'Pink Flamingo'**
Semi-double H2 Trailer
*Tube* longish, pink. *Sepals*,
broad and long, upturned to
the tube, pink with green tips.
*Corolla* pale pink with deeper
pink veining. The flowers are
very loose petalled, medium to
large in size. *Foliage* dark green
with reddish veins, the leaves
medium to large, serrated.
Growth is rather lax so will
make a superb basket. As there
is some distance between the
nodes it will be necessary to
stop the plant quite frequently
to achieve the required shape.
(Castro, USA, 1961)

**'Pink Galaxy'**
Single H2 Trailer
*Tube* white. *Sepals* white,
flushed with pink and tipped
with green. *Corolla* pale pink.
The flowers are medium-sized
and produced very freely.
*Foliage* grey/green. The growth
is vigorously trailing so frequent
stopping will be necessary to
keep it within bounds.
(Hooper, UK, 1992)

'PINK BON ACCORDE'

'PINK CHIFFON'

'PINK FAIRY'

'PINK FANTASIA'

'PINK FLAMINGO'

**'Pink Galore'**
Double H2 Trailing
*Tube* slender, medium length, pink. *Sepals* long and upturned, pink with green tips. *Corolla* very full, a soft rose pink. *Foliage* dark glossy green. The young growths on the leaves have reddish stems. Growth is naturally trailing but not the most vigorous. A beautiful cultivar when at its best.
(Fuchsia, La, USA, 1958)

**'Pink Goon'**
Double H3 Bush
*Tube* and *sepals* red. Flowers are large. *Corolla* apple blossom pink, veined with a deeper pink. *Foliage* medium green. The natural growth is as an upright bush. Upward growth is quite vigorous. H. and S. 18–24in (45–60cm).
(Hobson, UK, 1982)

**'Pink Jade'**
Single H2 Bush
*Tube* medium-sized, pink. *Sepals* reflexing, pink with green tips. *Corolla* orchid pink with a deeper picotee edging to the petals. *Foliage* medium green. Growth is rather lax but will make a good bush with supports. Very free-flowering.
(Pybon, USA, 1958)

**'Pink la Campanella'**
Single H2 Trailer
Small to medium-sized flower. *Tube* pale carmine. *Sepals* pale carmine, shade to darker at the tips on the upper surface and white on the lower surface. *Corolla* magenta maturing to carmine. *Foliage* medium green. The growth is really rather stiff for a trailer but it will make a very good basket with assistance.
(Hanson, UK, 1988)

**'Pink Lace'**
Double H3 Bush
*Tube* and *sepals* red. Flowers are large. *Corolla* pink. *Foliage* medium green. The growth is strongly upright and bushy. H. and S. 24–30in (60–75cm).
(Tabraham, UK, 1974)

**'Pink Lady'**
Single H2 Bush
*Tube* fairly long, deep crimson. *Sepals* cream, heavily flushed with pink, the tips a yellowy-green. *Corolla* pink with darker pink veins. The *flowers* are of medium size. Foliage mid-green. Growth is upright, self-branching, free-flowering and very bushy. ('Lena Dalton' × 'Citation')
(Ryle, UK, 1970)

**'Pink Marshmallow'**
Double H2 Trailer
*Tube* longish, pale pink. *Sepals* broad and reflexing, also pale pink. *Corolla* white with pink veining, with some pink shading on the petals. The flowers are very large and loose-petalled. *Foliage* light green, with medium to large serrated leaves. Growth is naturally trailing, and a superb basket can easily be grown.
(Stubbs, USA, 1977)

**'Pink Mist'**
Double H2 Lax bush
*Tube* pale pink. *Sepals* pink, tipped with green. *Corolla* white with deep pink veining. The flowers are medium-sized, very fully double, and retain good shape. *Foliage* medium green. Growth is rather lax so supports will be needed when training a bush.
(Raiser and date unknown)

**'Pinkmost'**
Double H2 Bush
*Tube* pink. *Sepals* pale green, flushed with pink. *Corolla* white veined with deep pink. *Foliage* medium green. Growth upright and bushy.
(de Graaf, Holland, 1988)

**'Pink Panther'**
Double H2 Lax bush
*Tube* medium-sized, neyron rose. *Sepals* horizontally held, recurved tips, neyron rose. *Corolla* also neyron rose and holds its colour through maturity. *Foliage* medium green. Growth is very strong and trailing. Will make a good

basket. ('Pink Marshmallow' × *F. fulgens*)
(Bielby, UK, 1985)

**'Pink Pearl'**
Double H2 Bush
*Tube* medium length, pale pink. *Sepals* recurve slightly, also pale pink. *Corolla* a deep rose pink. The flowers are very full and compact; the bloom is of medium size. *Foliage* medium green. Growth is bushy and upright, and very floriferous. Named because of its colour; subsequently renamed 'Mrs Friedlander' by Bright, after his employer who admired it.
(Bright, UK, 1919)

**'Pink Picotee'**
Single H2 Bush
*Tube* white. *Sepals* waxy white, tipped with green. *Corolla* fluorescent pink with deep rose picotee edge. *Foliage* light green. The growth is naturally upright and is short-jointed. The flowers are produced in great quantity throughout the season. Will make a superb exhibition plant.
(Hooper, UK, 1992)

**'Pink Profusion'**
Single H2 Bush
Medium-sized flower. *Tube* and *sepals* carmine rose. *Corolla* phlox pink. *Foliage* medium green. The natural growth is upright and bushy.
(Baker, UK, 1970)

**'Pink Quartette'**
Double H2 Bush
*Tube* medium length, very dark pink. *Sepals*, reddish-pink, held well away from the corolla. *Corolla* pink, consisting of four distinct tubes made by the rolled petals. *Foliage* mid-green. Growth is naturally upright and bushy.
(Walker and Jones, USA, 1949)

'PINK GALORE'

'PINK GOON'

'PINK MARSHMALLOW'

'PINK PEARL'

'PINK PICOTEE'

'PINK QUARTETTE'

**'Pink Rain'**
Single H2 Trailer
*Tube* long, thin, venetian pink.
*Sepals* are held horizontally,
neyron rose on the upper surface
and slightly darker on the lower.
*Corolla* mallow purple with a
lighter base to the petals. The
extension of the pistil and the
stamens well below the end of
the petals gives the impression of
falling pink rain. *Foliage* dark
green. Growth is naturally
trailing. A very attractive plant
when well grown.
(de Graaff, Holland, 1987)

**'Pink Surprise'**
Single H2 Bush
*Tube* and *sepals* rich red.
*Corolla* a beautiful shell pink.
The flowers are of medium size
but are fully double. *Foliage*
medium to dark green. Growth
is upright and strong. (Sport
from 'Swingtime')
(Jackson, UK, 1994)

**'Pink Temptation'**
Single H2 Bush
*Tube* longish, white flushed
with pink. *Sepals* long and
narrow, slightly upturned,
pinkish-white with green tips.
*Corolla* tyrian rose, lighter at
the base of the petals. The
blooms are of medium size and
freely produced. *Foliage*
medium green. Growth is
bushy and upright.
(Sport of 'Temptation')
(Wills, UK, 1966)

**'Pinto'**
Double H2 Trailer
*Tube* and *sepals* broad,
upturned, claret rose. *Corolla*
white, splashed with claret
rose. The very large blooms are
freely produced. *Foliage*
medium green. Growth is
naturally trailing.
(Walker and Jones, USA, 1956)

**'Pinwheel'**
Double H2 Bush
*Tube* short, flushed pink. *Sepals*
broad and pointed, turn back
slightly at the tips, pink.
*Corolla* violet. The large flat

blooms are very freely
produced. *Foliage* medium
green. The growth is upright
and bushy.
(Waltz, USA, 1958)

**'Piper's Vale'**
Triphylla type H1 Bush
A true terminal flowering
triphylla type. *Tube* long, pink.
*Sepals* shorter, a similar colour.
*Corolla* a darker shade of pink.
*Foliage* medium green. The
flowers are produced profusely.
Growth is strong but is suitable
for both upright growing or in
hanging containers.
(Stannard, UK, 1992)

**'Pirbright'**
Single H2 Bush
*Tube* long and slender,
rhodamine pink. *Sepals* long,
curl slightly upwards, also
rhodamine pink. *Corolla*
cyclamen purple. The bloom is
longish and compact. *Foliage*
medium green. Growth is
upright and self-branching.
Useful for all types of upward
growth; makes a good
exhibition plant, also summer
bedder. ('Glyn Jones' × 'Santa
Barbara')
(Roe, UK, 1981)

**'Pixie'**
Single H3 Bush
*Tube* short, carmine red. *Sepals*
short and upturned, carmine.
*Corolla* mauve purple, slightly
paler at the base of the petals,
carmine veins. Small to
medium-sized bloom, compact.
*Foliage* yellowish-green with
reddish veining. Growth is
upright, self-branching and
bushy. H. and S. 24–30in
(60–75cm).
(Russell, UK, 1960)

**'Playboy'**
Double H2 Bush
*Tube* and *sepals* red cerise.
*Corolla* a bright rosy pink,
veined with cerise. *Foliage*
medium green. The growth is
upright and bushy. ('Phyllis' ×
'Fascination')
(Homan, UK, 1969)

**'Playford'**
Single H2 Bush
*Tube* short, baby pink. *Sepals*
pink and turn upwards with
maturity. *Corolla* bluish-
mauve. The flowers are small
and rounded but are prolific.
*Foliage* mid-green with red
veining. Growth is upright,
self-branching and bushy.
(Goulding, UK, 1981)

**'Plenty'**
Single H2 Bush
*Tube* medium length, carmine.
*Sepals* held well back, neyron
rose. *Corolla* violet-purple. The
flowers are of medium size.
*Foliage* dark green. The growth
is strongly upright, short-
jointed and self-branching. The
blooms are held out from the
foliage and are produced in
great quantities. Very good
exhibition plant.
(Gadsby, UK, 1974)

**'Ploughman'**
Triphylla type H1 Bush
The flowers are produced at
the terminals. *Tube* long thin,
*sepals* shorter, and *corolla* all
red. *Foliage* medium green. The
growth is upright and of
unusual appearance. A
different and versatile fuchsia.
(Stannard, UK, 1993)

**'Plumb Bob'**
Double H2 Bush
*Tube* and *sepals* ivory with a
pink flush. *Corolla* red with
mauve undertones. Large
flowers. *Foliage* medium green.
Growth is strongly upright. An
excellent plant for the border
or as a standard.
(Goulding, UK, 1992)

**'Plymouth Sound'**
Single H2 Trailer
*Tube* rosy red. *Sepals* rosy red,
shiny on the outside but matt on
the inner side. *Corolla* magenta.
The flowers are of medium size
but freely produced. *Foliage*
medium green. The growth is
upright and bushy.
(Hilton, UK, 1978)

'PINK RAIN'

'PINTO'

'PIRBRIGHT'

'PIXIE'

'PLAYFORD'

'PLUMB BOB'

**'Poacher'**
Triphylla type  H1  Lax bush
Terminal-flowering. *Tube* long,
pink. *Sepals* almost white.
*Corolla* rosy pink. Growth is
spreading and rather elegant.
*Foliage* medium to dark green.
An excellent fuchsia, in view of
its laxity in growth, for
hanging containers.
(Stannard, UK, 1993)

**'Pole Star'**
Single  H3  Bush
*Tube* and *sepals* red. *Corolla*
brilliant white. The large flowers
are borne in great profusion.
*Foliage* rich dark green. Growth
is upright and bushy. H. and S.
18–24in (45–60cm).
(Tabraham, UK, 1974)

**'Poppet'**
Single  H2  Bush
*Tube* short and thick, waxy
carmine. *Sepals* waxy carmine
on top with a crimson base,
crêped crimson underneath;
broad with green tips. *Corolla*
roseine purple with slightly
darker edges, heavily veined
crimson. The flowers are held
semi-erect. *Foliage* medium
green, medium size, serrated,
light green veins. Growth is
upright and self-branching.
Prefers full sun.
('Beacon' seedling)
(Holmes, R., UK, 1983)

**'Popsie Girl'**
Single  H2  Bush
*Tube* and *sepals* pale orange.
*Corolla* orange. This is a
variegated form of 'Orange
Drops'. *Foliage* cream, grey-
green and pink. The flowers are
fairly large and freely produced.
Growth is rather lax.
(Dowell, UK, 1990)

**'Pop Whitlock'**
Single  H2  Bush
*Tube* very short. *Sepals* pale
pink. *Corolla* a beautiful shade
of amethyst violet. The medium-
sized flowers are very prolific.
*Foliage* variegated, light
greenish-grey with silvery sheen
and creamy white edge. Growth
is rather lax but very bushy. Will

make a very good exhibition
bush or small standard. (Sport
from 'Border Queen')
(Head, UK, 1984)

**'Postiljon'**
Single  H2  Trailer
*Tube* short and stubby, white
flushed with pink. *Sepals* short,
broad and held well out arching
over the corolla, creamy white
flushed with rose. *Corolla* rosy
purple and white at the base of
the petals. The blooms are fairly
small and very compact. *Foliage*
medium green with small
serrated leaves. Self-branching
and vigorous growth will
present a superb basket in a
season. Early flowering.
(Seedling from 'La Campanella')
(Van der Post, Holland, 1975)

**'Powder Puff'**
Double  H2  Trailer
*Tube* medium length, tyrian
rose. *Sepals* recurving, also
tyrian rose with a deeper shade
on the underside. *Corolla* apple
blossom pink. The blooms are
very compact and of medium
size. *Foliage* medium green.
The growth is naturally
trailing, self-branching and
free-flowering.
(Hodges, UK, 1953)

**'Prelude'**
Double  H2  Trailer
*Tube* white. *Sepals* broad,
upturned, also white. *Corolla*
royal purple for the four centre
petals, and splashed pink,
white and purple for the outer
petals. The medium-sized
blooms are fully double.
*Foliage* medium green with
serrated edges. Growth is
naturally trailing, vigorous and
free-flowering. Early stopping
is strongly advised.
(Kennett and Ross, USA, 1958)

**'President'**
Single  H2  Bush
*Tube* medium length, bright red.
*Sepals* long, upturned, bright
red. *Corolla* rosy purple with
slightly paler base to the petals.
The medium-sized blooms are
fairly loosely formed. *Foliage*

medium to darkish green with a
definite reddish tinge. Growth is
bushy, self-branching and quite
vigorous.
(Standish, UK, 1841)

**'President Elliot'**
Single  H2  Bush
*Tube* carmine red. *Sepals* long,
upturned, also carmine red.
*Corolla* reddish-purple, the
blooms of medium size. *Foliage*
medium green with serrated
edges to the leaves. Growth is
upright, vigorous and free-
flowering.
(Thorne, UK, 1962)

**'President Leo Boullemier'**
Single  H2  Bush
*Tube* short, fluted, white
streaked with magenta. *Sepals*
white, held well away from the
tube, fairly long and pointed.
*Corolla* bell-shaped, magenta
blue maturing to bluish pink.
The flowers are of medium-size
and freely produced. *Foliage*
dark green. ('Joy Patmore' ×
'Cloverdale Pearl')
(Burns, UK, 1983)

**'President Margaret Slater'**
Single  H2  Trailer
*Tube* long, slender, white.
*Sepals* long, slender and
curling, white with a distinct
pink flush and green tips on
top, deeper pink on the
undersides. *Corolla* mauve-
pink overlaid with salmon pink
and lighter shading at the base
of the petals. *Foliage* light to
medium green. The extremely
vigorous growth is naturally
trailing. An excellent subject
for exhibition baskets.
(Taylor, UK, 1973)

**'President Moir'**
Double  H2  Bush
*Tube* red. *Sepals* short and
wide, coral red, the tips curling
slightly. *Corolla* deep violet
flushed with coral red at the
base of the petals. The
medium-sized blooms have a
good shape. *Foliage* medium
green. The natural growth is
strongly upright.
(Moir, New Zealand, 1963)

'POP WHITLOCK'

'POSTILJON'

'PRELUDE'

'PRESIDENT LEO BOULLEMIER'

**'President Norman Hobbs'**
Single H2 Bush
*Tube* and *sepals* salmon. *Corolla*
deep orange-red and lighter at
the base of the petals. *Foliage*
medium green. The flowers are
large and very freely produced
on upright growing plants.
(Bielby/Oxtoby, UK, 1990)

**'President Roosevelt'**
Double H2 Bush
*Tube* medium length, coral red.
*Sepals* reflexing, also coral red.
*Corolla* dark violet blue. The
flowers are small but they are
freely produced. *Foliage*
medium green with serrated
edges. Growth is upright,
vigorous and bushy.
(Garson, USA, 1942)

**'President Stanley Wilson'**
Single to semi-double H2
Trailer
*Tube* long and slender, carmine.
*Sepals* carmine with green tips,
also long and slender, held
down over the corolla, turning
up slightly at the tips. *Corolla*
rosy carmine. The petals are
long and the corolla is compact
and of medium size. *Foliage*
medium green, leaves ovate,
finely serrated. Growth is
naturally trailing and vigorous.
The flowers are carried on long
stems. Frequent and early
stopping is necessary to fill a
basket completely.
(Thorne, UK, 1969)

**'President Walter Morio'**
Triphylla type H1 Bush
*Tube* and *sepals* long, pink.
*Corolla* has small orange petals.
*Foliage* medium green with a
slight purple reverse. The
upright growth is quite bushy.
(Nutzinger, Austrian, 1976)

**'President Wilf Sharp'**
Double H2 Bush
*Tube* and *sepals* pinkish red.
*Corolla* white with a tinge of
pink. The medium-sized
blooms are very freely
produced for a double. *Foliage*
medium green. The upright but
lax growth is bushy.
(Ryle, UK, 1979)

**'Preston Guild'**
Single H2 Bush
*Tube* longish and slender,
white. *Sepals* white, short,
broad and upturned; tinged
pink when grown out-of-doors.
*Corolla* violet blue-grey. The
flowers are small and compact.
*Foliage* medium green with
small finely serrated leaves.
Growth is upright and bushy.
The flowers are produced in
quantity.
(Thornley, UK, 1971)

**'Pride of the West'**
Single H2 Lax bush
*Tube* long and slender, reddish-
pink. *Sepals* reddish-pink, long,
narrow and curl upwards.
*Corolla* plum red, opens bell-
shaped. The flower is fairly
long. *Foliage* medium green.
Growth is rather lax upright so
will need stopping at an early
stage to develop a good bush
plant.
(Lye, UK, 1871)

**'Prince of Orange'**
Single H2 Bush
*Tube* a pale salmon pink.
*Sepals* short, broad and slightly
upturned, also pale salmon
pink. *Corolla* orange salmon.
The flowers are small and fairly
compact. *Foliage* light to
medium green. The growth is
upright, vigorous and bushy.
(Banks, UK, 1872)

**'Prince of Peace'**
Double H2 Lax bush
*Tube* pinkish-white. *Sepals*
large and flaring, frosty rose
pink. *Corolla* magenta fading
to rose as the bloom matures.
*Foliage* medium green with
medium to large serrated
leaves. Growth is rather lax,
semi-trailer, but vigorous and
free-flowering.
(Davis, USA, 1970)

**'Princess Dollar'**
Synonymous with 'Dollar
Princess'.

**'Princessita'**
Single H2 Trailer
*Tube* white. *Sepals* white, pink

flush underneath, long, narrow,
upturned. *Corolla* deep rose
pink. The medium-sized
flowers are freely produced.
*Foliage* medium to dark green.
Growth is naturally trailing.
Excellent exhibition baskets are
produced quite easily.
('Fandango' × 'Mrs W.
Rundle')
(Niederholzer, USA, 1940)

**'Princess Pamela'**
Double H2 Bush
*Tube* and *sepals* deep rose.
*Corolla* a vivid purple. The
large flowers are enhanced by
the fairly large, medium green,
*foliage*. Upright growth, fairly
strong and fairly free-flowering.
(Raiser unknown 1990)

**'Princess Pat'**
Semi-double H2 Trailer
*Tube* white. *Sepals* white and
slightly flushed pink. *Corolla*
imperial purple fading to
lavender blue. The small
flowers are very floriferous and
very early. *Foliage* variegated
green and creamy yellow.
Growth is self-branching and
trailing.
(Sport from 'La Campanella')
(Finder unknown, UK, 1980)

**'Princess Saranto'**
Single H2 Bush
*Tube* rose. *Sepals* white edged
with rose at the base on the
upper surface and white
flushed light pink at the base of
the lower surface, held
horizontally. *Corolla* white
veined with light pink. *Foliage*
dark green. ('Bobby Shaftoe' ×
'Sarah Ann')
(McDonald, UK, 1989)

**'Prince Syray'**
Single H2 Bush
*Tube* medium length, dawn
pink. *Sepals* short and broad,
deeper pink. *Corolla* vermilion
with neyron rose shading on
the edges. *Foliage* medium
green with serrated edges to the
leaves. The growth is upright,
bushy and free-flowering. ('Bon
Accorde' × 'Lord Lonsdale')
(White, UK, 1975)

'PRESIDENT STANLEY WILSON'                    'PRESTON GUILD'

'PRINCESSITA'                                 'PRINCESS PAMELA'

'PRINCESS PAT'                                'PRINCE SYRAY'

**F. pringsheimii**
Species H1 Bush
*Tube* fairly long, red. *Sepals*
red, slight green colouring on
the tips. *Corolla* red. The
flowers are produced in the
axils. *Foliage* small and dark
green. Requires extra warmth
to produce flowers similar to *F.
triphylla*.
(Haiti and the Dominican
Republic)

**F. procumbens**
Species H3 Trailing
A very popular and easy species
to grow, the long trailing stems
being very attractive. Very small,
upward-looking flowers. *Tube*
greenish-yellow, red at the base.
*Sepals* green, tipped with purple.
No *corolla*. The stamens carry
bright blue pollen. *Foliage* very
small and un-fuchsia-like, the
leaves being small and heart-
shaped. The seedpods should be
left on the plant after flowering,
and grow to the size and colour
of a miniature damson plum.
The seed when collected, dried
and sown will produce new
plants of the same species.
(Cunningham, New Zealand,
1834)

**'Prodigy'**
Synonymous with 'Enfant
Prodigue'.

**'Prosperity'**
Double H3 Bush
*Tube* thick and medium length,
crimson. *Sepals* long, held well
up over the tube, waxy
crimson. *Corolla* pale neyron
rose, flushed and veined rose
red. The flowers are small to
medium-sized. *Foliage* darkish
green, glossy, medium to large
serrated leaves. Growth is
upright, vigorous and free-
flowering. H. and S. 24–30in
(60–75cm). ('Bishop's Bells' ×
'Strawberry Delight')
(Gadsby, UK, 1974)

**'Pukkie'**
Single H2 Bush
*Tube* carmine rose. *Sepals*
horizontally held, carmine rose
on the upper surface and

carmine on the lower surface.
*Corolla* currant red flushed
with blue with a mandarin
orange base. The petals are
pointed. *Foliage* olive green.
(de Graaff, Holland, 1987)

**'Pumila'**
Single H3 Dwarf bush
*Tube* short and thin, crimson
red. *Sepals* short, broad and
well held out, crimson. *Corolla*
purple. The flowers are very
small and compact. *Foliage*
darkish green with small
serrated leaves. Growth is
dwarf, upright and bushy.
Good for the rockery. H. and
S. up to 12in (30cm).
(Young, UK, 1821)

**'Purbeck Medley'**
Single H2 Bush
Medium-sized flower. *Tube*
white flushed with pale green.
*Sepals* white flushed pale pink.
*Corolla* rosy purple. *Foliage*
medium green. The growth is
upright and bushy.
(Swinbank, UK, 1991)

**'Purple Heart'**
Double H2 Trailer
*Tube* long, crimson. *Sepals* long
and waxy, also crimson. *Corolla*
outer petals rose red, the inner
petals violet. *Foliage* medium to
dark green. The natural growth
is trailing and free-flowering so
will make a good basket.
(Walker and Jones, USA, 1950)

**'Purple Queen'**
Double H2 Bush
The flowers are medium-sized.
*Tube* and *sepals* cerise. *Corolla*
purple. *Foliage* medium to dark
green. The natural growth is as
an upright bush.
(Smith, UK, 1892)

**'Purple Rain'**
Single H2 Trailer
*Tube* dark reddish-purple.
*Sepals* dark reddish-purple on
the upper and lower sides,
recurving tips. *Corolla* opens
very dark purple maturing to
dark reddish-purple. *Foliage*
yellowish-green. Growth is
rather lax and can therefore be

used in hanging containers.
(de Graaff, Holland, 1988)

**'Purple Showers'**
Single H2 Bush
*Tube* and *sepals* white. *Corolla*
purple. The flowers are of
medium size and are very
prolific. *Foliage* dark green.
Growth is upright.
(Wright, UK, 1979)

**'Purple Splendour'**
Double H3 Bush
*Tube* and *sepals* crimson.
*Corolla* blue-purple. The flowers
are freely produced on strong
upright growing branches.
*Foliage* medium to dark green.
H. and S. 18–24in (45–60cm).
(Sunningdale Nurseries,
UK, 1975)

**'Purpur Klokje'**
Single H2 Bush
*Tube* and *sepals* reddish
aubergine. *Corolla* very dark
aubergine. Flowers very small
and hang in clusters. *Foliage*
medium to dark green. Growth
is small and upright. A novelty.
(de Graaff, Holland, 1989)

**'Pussy Cat'**
Single H2 Bush
*Tube* long and rather thick,
pinkish-orange. *Sepals* pinkish-
orange with green tips, pointed
and held well out. *Corolla*
pinkish-orange, rather small
and with many petaloids.
*Foliage* medium to dark green.
Growth is upright and fairly
bushy. An attractive but
novelty-type fuchsia.
('Leverkusen' × 'Checkerboard')
(Felix, Holland, 1978)

**'Put's Folly'**
Single H2 Trailer
*Tube* long and thin, pale pink.
*Sepals* creamy white on top,
flushed pale pink on the
underside, with green tips.
*Corolla* lilac rose pink, pale
pink at the base of the petals.
*Foliage* medium green, large
leaves finely serrated. Growth is
naturally trailing and very
vigorous. Makes a good basket.
(Baker, UK, 1971)

'PROSPERITY'

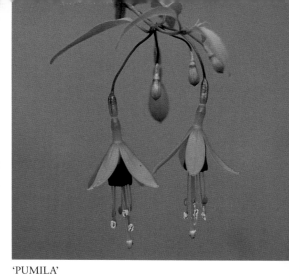

'PUMILA'

'PURPLE HEART'

'PURPLE RAIN'

'PURPLE SHOWERS'

'PURPUR KLOKJE'

*F. putumayensis*
Species H1 Bush
An orange-red self (*tube,
sepals* and *corolla* all of the
same colour). Flowers in
numerous bunches. *Foliage*
medium green, paler
underneath and hairy. Growth
is upright.
(Colombia and Ecuador)

# Q

'Quasar'
Double H2 Trailer
*Tube* medium length, white.
*Sepals* white. *Corolla* dauphin's
violet, shaded white at the base
of each petal. The flowers are
medium- to large-sized and the
blooms are very compact.
*Foliage* light green. Growth is
naturally trailing. Will make a
good basket.
(Walker, USA, 1974)

'Queen Mary'
Single H2 Bush
*Tube* thick, medium length,
pale pink. *Sepals* long, narrow
and upturned, pink with white
tips. *Corolla* rose pink
maturing to deep mauve. The
flowers are medium-sized and
compact. *Foliage* medium
green, medium-sized, serrated.
Growth is bushy and upright.
Late flowering if grown in the
garden. (See also 'King
George'.) (Seedling from 'Mrs
Marshall')
(Howlett, UK, 1911)

'Queen of Derby'
Double H2 Bush
*Tube* carmine rose. *Sepals*
broad and reflexing, also
carmine rose with green tips.
*Corolla* pale violet-purple,
flushed with pink and with
pink striping on the petals.
*Foliage* medium green.
Growth is upright and bushy.
There is the tendency for some
branches to grow horizontally.
('Rose Bower' × 'Magenta
Flush')
(Gadsby, UK, 1975)

'Query'
Single H2 Bush
*Tube* pale pink. *Sepals* pale
pink on top with green tips,
deeper pink on the undersides,
held horizontally. *Corolla*
purple with pink veins. The
flower matures to magenta.
*Foliage* medium green, rather
small and with a leathery, shiny
appearance. Growth is self-
branching and upright.
(Bass, UK, 1847)

# R

'Rachel Catherine'
Single H2 Bush
*Tube* and *sepals* deep red.
*Corolla* rich purple. The
medium-sized flowers are
flared, prolific and are held
well away from the foliage.
*Foliage* is medium green. The
growth is upright, self-
branching and bushy.
(Gadsby, UK, 1979)

'Radcliffe Beauty'
Single H2 Bush
*Tube* and *sepals* claret rose.
*Corolla* bishop's violet. The
medium-sized flowers are very
freely produced, held out
horizontally. *Foliage* medium
green. The growth is bushy and
upright.
(Gadsby, UK, 1974)

'Radcliffe Bedder'
Semi-double H2 Bush
*Tube* crimson. *Sepals* crimson,
fold right back. *Corolla*
spectrum violet. The blooms
are medium-sized. *Foliage*
medium green. Growth is
upright and bushy. ('Neil
Clyne' × 'Mipam')
(Roe, UK, 1980)

'Radings Inge'
*Encliandra* type Single H2
Bush
These are 'perfect' blooms.
*Tube, sepals* and *corollas*
salmon or pale orange. Growth
is spreading but strong. *Foliage*
small-leaved and medium green.
Very attractive as a show plant

or in mixed tubs or basket
plantings. (*F.* × *bacillaris*)
(Reiman, Holland, 1980)

'Radings Karin'
*Encliandra* type Single H2
Bush
'Perfect' flowers. *Tube* ivory at
first, turning to dull orange.
*Sepals* and the petals in the
*corolla* dull orange. The
growth is very sturdy and
bushy. *Foliage* small, medium
green. The wiry growth makes
it easy to shape as a fan,
espalier or mini-standard. (*F.* ×
*bacillaris*)
(Reiman, Holland, 1983)

'R.A.F.'
Double H2 Bush
*Tube* medium length, red. *Sepals*
short and broad, reflex to the
tube, also red. *Corolla* rose pink
veined with cerise. The flowers
are very fluffy, and medium-
sized. *Foliage* medium green.
The growth is rather lax upright,
self-branching and bushy.
(Garson, USA, 1942)

'Rahnee'
Double H2 Bush
*Tube* and *sepals* deep pink.
*Corolla* pink. *Foliage* medium
green. The flowers are of
medium size and are freely
produced. Growth is upright
and bushy.
(Colville, UK, 1966)

'Rainbow'
Double H2 Trailer
Large flowers. *Tube* carmine.
*Sepals* dark pink and recurving.
*Corolla* violet, with orange and
red on the outer petals. The
strong and spreading growth is
helped by early stopping.
*Foliage* medium green.
Excellent for full baskets.
(Nelson (American) 1958)

'Rakker'
Single H2 Bush
Medium-sized flowers. *Tube* rose-
coloured. *Sepals* rose, tipped with
green. *Corolla* rosy red. *Foliage*
medium green. The natural
growth is as an upright bush.
(Romijn, Holland, 1989)

'QUASAR'

'QUEEN OF DERBY'

'R.A.F.'

'RAINBOW'

**'Rambling Rose'**
Double H2 Trailer
*Tube* pale pink flushed with
green. *Sepals* pink with green
tips, deeper pink on the
undersides, long, broad and
curling upwards over the tube.
*Corolla* pink with deeper pink
petaloids. The blooms are
medium-sized and rather
loosely formed. *Foliage* medium
green. Growth is naturally
trailing. Constant stopping will
make a good basket.
(Tiret, USA, 1959)

**'Rambo'**
Double H2 Bush
Medium-sized flower. *Tube* and
*sepals* pale rose. *Corolla* rose
lilac with darker veins. *Foliage*
medium green. The natural
growth is as a bush. (Sport
from 'Hawaiian Night')
(Franck, Holland, 1989)

**'Ram's Royal'**
Double H2 Bush
Large flower. *Tube* red. *Sepals*
white and red at the base.
*Corolla* violet-blue splashed
with pink. *Foliage* medium
green. Growth is upright, self-
branching and bushy.
(Redfern, UK, 1988)

**'Raspberry'**
Double H2 Bush
*Tube* medium length, pinkish-
white. *Sepals* long, narrow and
upturned, also pinkish-white.
*Corolla* is raspberry rose. The
flowers are medium to large,
compact, very full doubles.
*Foliage* medium green.
(Tiret, USA, 1959)

**'Ratatouille'**
Double H2 Trailer
*Tube* and *sepals* ivory white.
*Corolla* pale aubergine. Growth
is very strong and spreading,
with plenty of sideshoots.
*Foliage* medium green. Excellent
for all hanging containers.
(de Graaff, Holland, 1988)

**'Ravenii'**
*Encliandra* H1 Bush
Larger flower than most of the
Encliandra group of fuchsias.

*Tube* and *sepals* shiny red;
*corolla* pink. *Foliage* small. The
growth is thin and wiry.
(Mexico)

**'Ravensbarrow'**
Single H2 Bush
A delightful medium-sized
flower. *Tube* and *sepals* red.
*Corolla* very dark, almost
black on opening but fading to
very dark purple with maturity.
*Foliage* dark green, the leaves
small with serrated edges.
Growth is upright and bushy.
The pollen parent is 'Gruss aus
dem Bodethal', hence the
darkness of the petal colouring.
(Thornley, UK, 1972)

**'Ray Redfern'**
Single H2 Bush
*Tube* light magenta. *Sepals* held
horizontally, also light magenta
tipped with green. *Corolla* opens
white with pink veining at the
base, maturing to pure white.
The medium-sized flowers are
freely produced. *Foliage* medium
green. The upright growth of
this cultivar makes a good bush
very easily. ('Cloverdale Pearl' ×
'Sleigh Bells')
(Redfern, UK, 1989)

**'Razzle Dazzle'**
Double H2 Lax bush
*Tube* pale pink, thin. *Sepals*
pale pink, long, broad, curled
completely to the tube. *Corolla*
dark purple with a darker edge.
The blooms are large and
produced freely for their size.
*Foliage* medium to dark green.
Natural growth is rather lax so
will be suitable for basket or
bushes with the necessary
supports.
(Martin, USA, 1965)

**'Reading Show'**
Double H3 Bush
*Tube* short, red. *Sepals* thick red.
*Corolla* a very deep blue, almost
a purple. *Foliage* medium to
dark green. The flowers are of
medium size and freely
produced throughout the season.
Useful for the hardy border. H.
and S. 18–24in (45–60cm).
(Wilson, UK, 1967)

**'Rebecca Williamson'**
Double H2 Trailer
*Tube, sepals* and *corolla* pink.
Medium-sized flowers. The
strong growth is very spreading
with plenty of sideshoots.
*Foliage* medium green. Makes
an excellent basket.
(Redfern, UK, 1986)

**'Red Imp'**
Double H3 Bush
*Tube* red. *Sepals* dark purple.
*Corolla* opens wine red and
matures to deep red. *Foliage*
dark purple green. Growth is
dwarf but upright and bushy.
H. and S. 12–18in (30–45cm).
(Tabraham, UK, 1985)

**'Red Rain'**
Single H2 Lax bush
Small flowers. *Tube, sepals* and
*corolla* red. Foliage medium
green. Growth is a lax upright.
Will need supports.
(de Graaff, Holland, 1987)

**'Red Rum'**
Double H2 Bush
*Tube* and *sepals* bright red.
*Corolla* pure white. The
medium-sized flowers are very
freely produced on strong
upright bushes. *Foliage* dark
green, red veins. A superb
fuchsia.
(Hobson, UK, 1977)

**'Red Shadows'**
Double H2 Lax bush
*Tube* and *sepals* bright
crimson. *Corolla* deep
burgundy purple maturing to
ruby red. The large flowers are
freely produced and are ruffled;
they appear to change colour
three times during maturity.
*Foliage* medium green. Growth
is rather lax so could be used
for either bush or basket.
(Waltz, USA, 1962)

'RAMBLING ROSE'

'RAM'S ROYAL'

'RATATOUILLE'

'RAVENSBARROW'

'REBECCA WILLIAMSON'

'RED SHADOWS'

**'Red Spider'**
Single H2 Trailer
*Tube* long and slender, crimson.
*Sepals* long and narrow curl
upwards, also crimson. *Corolla*
rose madder and deeper on the
edges of the petals. The bloom
is of medium size. *Foliage*
medium green. Growth is
vigorously trailing, self-
branching and free-flowering.
Needs careful pinching early on
to make a good shape.
(V. Reiter, USA, 1946)

**'Regal Robe'**
Double H2 Lax bush
*Tube* and *sepals* deep bright
red. *Corolla* deepest royal
violet-purple. The flowers are
very large with many scalloped
petals. *Foliage* medium green
with reddish veins, finely
serrated leaves. Growth is lax
upright so will need supporting
when grown as a bush.
(Erickson-Lewis, USA, 1959)

**'Reg Dickenson'**
Single H2 Bush
*Tube* short and thin, pink.
*Sepals* long and spiky, pink on
top and tipped with green,
deeper pink beneath. *Corolla*
purple with a pink base to the
petals maturing to purple. The
flowers are bell-shaped. *Foliage*
medium green, lighter
underneath. Growth is upright
and bushy.
(Redfern, UK, 1985)

**'Reg Gubler'**
Single H2 Bush
*Tube* red. *Sepals* bright mid-
red. *Corolla* violet-blue veined
with red. The medium to large
flowers are produced freely.
*Foliage* dark green. Growth is
upright and vigorous. An
excellent cultivar suitable for
all types of upright training.
('Katherine Maidment' × 'Miss
California')
(Dyos, UK, 1987)

**F. regia ssp regia**
Species H3 Bush/climber.
*Sepals* red. *Corolla* purple. The
flowers are smallish. *Foliage*
medium-sized with a

pronounced red vein. Growth is
lax but very strong so not really
suitable for training as a bush;
much happier as a climber.
(Brazil)

**F. regia ssp reitzii**
Species H3 Bush/climber
The flowers are red and purple
with spreading *sepals*. Growth
is rather shrubbier than other
*Regia*. Is hardy so could be
grown in the open garden.
(Brazil)

**F. regia ssp serrae**
Species H3 Bush/climber
The flowers are red and purple
with fused *sepals*. Hardy in the
open garden.
(Brazil)

**'Regina van Zoren'**
Semi-double H2 Bush
Medium-sized flowers. *Tube*
red. *Sepals* light red. *Corolla*
light reddish-purple. *Foliage*
medium green. The upright
growth is strong and vigorous.
(Beije, Holland, 1989)

**'Remus'**
Double H2 Bush
*Tube* pinkish. *Sepals* pale
rhodamine purple, with a
deeper colour on the underside.
*Corolla* amethyst violet with
little fading. The fairly large
blooms are freely produced.
*Foliage* medium green. Growth
is upright and bushy.
(Pacey, UK, 1984)

**'Renate'**
Double H2 Bush
*Tube* and arched *sepals* very
dark red. *Corolla* irregular in
shape and coloured dark
aubergine. *Foliage* medium
green. Growth is upright and
strong. Best seen in garden
containers when planted with
other plants.
(Raiser and date unknown)

**'Requiem'**
Single H2 Bush
Longish *tube* and *sepals* red.
*Corolla* white with red veining
towards the base of the petals.
The flowers are medium-sized

and freely produced. *Foliage*
medium green. The natural
growth is upright and bushy.
(Blackwell, UK, 1961)

**'Reverend Doctor Brown'**
Double H2 Bush
*Tube* short, thick, pale pink.
*Sepals* pale pink on top tipped
with green, deep pink inside;
completely reflexing. *Corolla*
pure white with short pink
veins at the base of the petals.
*Foliage* dark green with red
veining. Growth is upright and
self-branching. ('Sophisticated
Lady' × 'Citation')
(Taylor, UK, 1973)

**'Revival'**
Double H2 Trailer
Small *flowers. Tube* and *sepals*
light red. *Corolla* violet purple.
*Foliage* medium green. Growth
is either lax bush or a trailer.
(de Graaff, Holland, 1987)

**'Riant'**
Double H2 Lax bush
Medium-sized flower. *Tube* and
*sepals* pale primula. *Corolla*
violet and orchid pink. *Foliage*
medium green. Growth is rather
lax although an upright bush
can be trained with supports.
(Moerman, Holland, 1991)

**F. ricartonii**
**(F. magellanica var ricartonii)**
Species H3 Bush
*Tube* and *sepals* bright red.
*Corolla* dark violet. Blooms are
slender. *Foliage* medium to
dark green, the leaves longish
and thin. Growth is strong and
bushy. Excellent for the back of
a hardy border. H. and S. in
excess of 36in (90cm).
(Young, UK, 1830)

**'Ridestar'**
Double H2 Bush
*Tube* thin, scarlet. *Sepals* short
and broad, reflexing, also
scarlet. *Corolla* deep lavender
blue with cerise veining, pink
shading at base of the petals.
*Foliage* medium green with
reddish veins. Growth is upright,
self-branching and bushy.
(Blackwell, UK, 1959)

'REG GUBLER'

'RED SPIDER'
'REVEREND DOCTOR BROWN'

'RIANT'

'RIDESTAR'

**'Rieksken Boland'**
Single H2 Bush
Medium-sized flower. *Tube*
light absinthe green. *Sepals*
rose. *Corolla* carmine rose.
*Foliage* medium green. The
natural growth is as an upright
bush.
(Beije, Holland, 1991)

**'Rigoletto'**
Double H2 Bush
*Tube* short, deep red. *Sepals*
short, broad and recurved, also
deep red. *Corolla* light purple,
paler at the base of the sepals.
The medium-sized, compact
blooms have frilled edges.
*Foliage* medium green with
serrated edges to the leaves.
Growth is upright and bushy.
(Blackwell, UK, 1967)

**'Rika'**
Single H2 Bush
Small flowers. *Tube* and *sepals*
light carmine rose. *Corolla* rose
bengal. *Foliage* medium green.
The growth is naturally upright
and very vigorous.
(van der Post, Holland, 1987)

**Ri Mia**
*Encliandra* H2 Bush
Very small blooms. *Tube*,
*sepals* and *corollas* pale lilac.
*Foliage* small and medium
green. Growth is bushy but
spreading. Can be trained into
a variety of shapes like
miniature works of topiary.
(Raiser and date unknown)

**'Rina Felix'**
Triphylla type H1 Bush
Typical triphylla type, with
flowers being produced at the
terminals. *Tube* long, thin,
green shading to red. *Sepals*
short and green. *Corolla*
beetroot purple with slightly
darker shades on the petals.
Growth is upright and bushy.
*Foliage* green with pale
reverses. A most unusual
colour combination and one
worth growing. (*F. gesneriana* ×
*F. colensoi*)
(Felix, Holland, 1984)

**'Ringwood Gold'**
Double H2 Bush
*Tube* and *sepals* pink. Medium-
sized flower. *Corolla* lilac.
*Foliage* yellow. The upright
growth is bushy and self-
branching.
(Bridgland, UK, 1987)

**'Ringwood Market'**
Semi-double H2 Bush
*Tube* short, neyron rose. *Sepals*
short, broad and well held out,
also neyron rose. *Corolla*
powder blue shading at the
base of the petals to pink, fades
to lilac with maturity. The
medium-sized blooms are quite
compact. Foliage medium
green. Growth is upright,
bushy and free-flowering.
('Tristesse' × 'Susan Ford')
(Clyne, UK, 1976)

**'River Plate'**
Single H2 Trailer
Medium-sized flowers. *Tube*
white. *Sepals* white with a hint
of pink at their tips, recurving.
*Corolla* bell-shaped, also white.
The cultivar is very free-
flowering. *Foliage* medium
green. The spreading growth
makes it ideal for all types of
hanging containers.
(Goulding, UK, 1989)

**'Robbie'**
Single H2 Bush
*Tube* short, pale magenta.
*Sepals* horizontally held, pale
magenta on top fading to
white, and have green tips.
*Corolla* white, small, slightly
flaring, bell-shaped. *Foliage*
medium to light green, leaves
have red veins and serrated
edges. Growth is upright but
care must be taken with regular
stopping to develop a good
bush. ('Doctor Brendan
Freeman' × 'Ting a Ling')
(Lamb, UK, 1984)

**'Robert Bruce'**
Double H2 Lax bush or
trailer
*Tube* thinnish, white tinged with
pink. *Sepals* held horizontally,
also white tinged with pink or
red. *Corolla* bright red with

smooth petal edges. *Foliage*
dark green but much lighter
underneath. The growth is lax
upright and self-branching.
(Stubbs, USA, 1986)

**'Robert Hall'**
Single H2 Bush
*Tube* neyron rose, thick. *Sepals*
neyron rose, held clear from
the corolla. *Corolla* magenta
rose flushed with neyron rose.
The medium-sized flowers are
freely produced. *Foliage*
medium green. ('Pink Galore' ×
'Athela')
(Gadsby, UK, 1970)

**'Robert Lutters'**
Single H2 Bush
Medium-sized single flowers.
*Tubes* white flushed with rose.
*Sepals* rose. *Corolla* bengal
rose. *Foliage* medium green.
Growth is vigorously upright.
Excellent for bush training or
as standards.
(Beije, Holland, 1989)

**'Rocket Fire'**
Double H2 Bush
*Tube* magenta. *Sepals* have
reflexed tips, dark rose on the
upper surface and slightly
lighter on the lower surface.
*Corolla* has purple pleated outer
petals and dark pink inner
petals. *Foliage* dark green. The
natural growth is as an upright
bush. Good strong grower.
(Garrett, USA, 1989)

**'Rodeo'**
Triphylla type H1 Lax bush
*Tubes* long and sturdy; *sepals*
short; both dark aubergine in
colour. *Foliage* mid to dark
green. Growth is rather lax so
this very attractive, strong and
spreading fuchsia can be used in
any type of hanging container.
(Stannard, UK, 1993)

**'Roelof Sander'**
Single H2 Bush
Medium-sized flowers. *Tubes*
and *sepals* cream, flushed with
pink. *Corolla* white. *Foliage*
medium green. The natural
growth is as an upright bush.
(Veen, Holland, 1991)

'ROBBIE'

'ROBERT BRUCE'

'ROBERT LUTTERS'

'RODEO'

**'Rolla'**
Double H2 Bush
*Tube* short, pale pink. *Sepals* short and broad, also pale pink. *Corolla* pure white, tinged with pink at the base of the petals. *Foliage* light green. Growth is vigorously upright, bushy and very free-flowering. Will make an excellent large structure.
(Lemoine, France, 1913)

**'Romance'**
Double H2 Trailer
*Tube* short, thick, white with a green tinge. *Sepals* white on top with green tips, the undersides faintly flushed with pink; long and broad, and curl upwards towards the tube. *Corolla* pale violet blue in the centre, the outer petals have pink markings. The medium-sized blooms are very full and fluffy. *Foliage* long and narrow, medium green.
(Paskesen, USA, 1967)

**'Roman City'**
Double H2 Bush
*Tube* long, pale pink. *Sepals* a deeper pink, longish, held well out. *Corolla* plum purple with splashes of deep pink. The blooms are extremely large and are very full doubles. *Foliage* light green. Growth is upright with long arching branches, best in a basket or a half basket.
(Endicott, UK, 1976)

**'Ronald L. Lockerbie'**
Double H2 Trailer
*Tube* cream to pale yellow, flushed carmine. *Sepals* flushed white. *Corolla* cream to barium yellow, fading to white. *Foliage* light green. The growth is lax and long-jointed. Will make a reasonable basket. The blooms are of medium-size. When it first came to Britain, this plant was hailed as being the first 'Yellow Fuchsia'. It was a great disappointment as the colour proved to be a creamy white.
(Richardson, Australia, 1986)

**'Ron Ewart'**
Single H2 Bush
*Tube* short, thick, white. *Sepals* short and broad, turn backwards, also white. *Corolla* rose bengal, shaded to white at the base of the petals. The bloom is small and compact. *Foliage* medium green. The growth is upright, self-branching and bushy. Very good exhibition plant, bush or summer bedder. ('Bobby Shaftoe' × 'Santa Barbara')
(Roe, UK, 1981)

**'Ron Holmes'**
Single H2 Bush
*Tube* pale pink. *Sepals* pale pink on the outside, carmine rose on the inner, held at right angles to tube, tips slightly upturned. *Corolla* mandarin red overlaid with carmine. *Foliage* medium green. The growth is vigorously upright, self-branching and quite floriferous.
(Holmes, UK, 1978)

**'Ron's Pet'**
Single H2 Bush
*Tube* long and slender, pale salmon pink. *Sepals* short, narrow and well held out, pale salmon with green tips. *Corolla* salmon orange. The flowers are small and compact. *Foliage* light green, small and serrated. Growth is upright and bushy.
(Holmes, UK, 1973)

**'Roos Breytenbach'**
Triphylla type H1 Bush
Terminal flowering, true to type. *Tube* long. *Sepals* small, orange red. *Corolla* has pleated petals also orange red. The flowers are produced very prolifically throughout the season. *Foliage* medium to dark green.
(Stannard, UK, 1993)

**'Rosabell'**
Single H2 Bush
*Tube* long and slender, white. *Sepals* long and curl back towards the tube, neyron rose. *Corolla* imperial purple shading to phlox pink, paler at the base of the petals. *Foliage* medium green, medium-sized, serrated. The flowers are medium-sized and freely produced. The growth is a rather lax upright so will need

supporting when grown as a bush. ('Upward Look' ×)
(Gadsby, UK, 1971)

**'Rose Aylett'**
Double H2 Bush
*Tube* carmine red. *Sepals* reflex slightly, pale carmine. *Corolla* lilac blue, medium size, and compact. *Foliage* medium green. The natural growth is as an upright bush. Easy to grow, a nice old cultivar.
(Strutt, UK, 1897)

**'Rose Bower'**
Double H2 Bush
*Tube* crimson. *Sepals* carmine with green tips, broad and waxy, held well out. *Corolla* lilac purple shading to cyclamen purple, flushed with crimson. *Foliage* medium green serrated edges to leaves. Growth is upright, bushy and self-branching. ('La Fiesta' ×)
(Gadsby, UK, 1973)

**'Rose Bradwardine'**
Double H2 Bush
*Tube* short, dark rose pink. *Sepals* short and broad, held well over the corolla, also dark rose pink. *Corolla* lavender with splashes of orchid pink. *Foliage* mid-green, medium-sized, finely serrated. Growth is upright, bushy and self-branching.
(Colville, UK, 1958)

**'Rosebud'**
Double H2 Lax bush
*Tube* slim white. *Sepals* white and flaring. *Corolla* rosy orange with white at the base of the petals. The blooms are of medium size and very freely produced. *Foliage* small, light green. Growth is rather lax.
(Kennett, USA, 1958)

**'Rose Churchill'**
Double H2 Bush
*Tube* and *sepals* rose. *Corolla* rose pink. The medium-sized blooms are produced very freely. *Foliage* medium to dark green. The habit and growth are very similar to that of 'Winston Churchill'.
(Raiser and date unknown)

'ROLLA'

'RON EWART'

'ROSEBUD'

'ROSE CHURCHILL'

**'Rosecroft Beauty'**
Semi-double H2 Bush
*Tube* short, crimson. *Sepals*
crimson, short, broad, droop
over the corolla. *Corolla* white,
flushed and veined with cerise;
small, compact bloom. *Foliage*
pale green edged golden yellow
with shades of cream and
cerise. Growth upright and
bushy. Not a fast grower. Prone
to red spider. (Sport of
'Snowcap')
(Eden, UK, 1968)

**'Rosedale'**
Double H2 Bush
*Tube* carmine red. *Sepals*
broad, carmine on the top with
green tips, crimson on the
underside. *Corolla* magenta
rose, edged with tyrian purple.
The flowers are bell-shaped
and held horizontally. *Foliage*
medium green. Growth is
naturally upright.
(Gadsby, UK, 1973)

**'Rose Fantasia'**
Single H2 Bush
*Tube* and *sepals* deep pink.
*Corolla* pink with a hint of
mauve. *Foliage* medium green.
The growth is upright, self-
branching and very bushy. The
flowers are held at the
horizontal or higher. A very
'showy' plant. Sport from 'Pink
Fantasia', destined to supersede
its illustrious parent.
(Wilkinson, UK, 1991)

**'Rose Lace'**
Double H3 Bush
*Tube* and *sepals* deep pink.
*Corolla* rose pink. The large,
full double blooms are freely
produced and are unusual for a
'hardy'. *Foliage* dark green.
The growth is upright, arching
and fairly compact. H. and S.
24–30in (60–75cm).
(Tabraham, UK, 1982)

**'Rose Marie'**
Double H2 Lax bush
*Tube* and *sepals* pink. *Corolla*
a lighter shade of pink. Very
large blooms for a double. The
corolla is beautifully formed
with large petaloids. *Foliage*

medium green. The upward
growth is lax and arching.
(Colville, UK, 1976)

**'Rosemary Day'**
Single H2 Bush
*Tube* pale pink. Medium-sized
flower. *Sepals* pale pink on top,
deeper beneath, long and
broad. *Corolla* pale cyclamen
purple. *Foliage* is medium
green. The natural growth is as
an upright bush.
(Day, UK, 1983)

**'Rose of Castile'**
Single H2 Bush
*Tube* short, thick, white with a
greenish tinge. *Sepals* short and
pointed, held well out, white
with green tips, slight pinkish
colouring on the undersurface.
*Corolla* reddish purple shading
to white at the base of the
petals; there is a white streak in
the centre of each one. The
bloom is small and compact.
*Foliage* medium green with
serrated edges. Growth is
upright and bushy, very
vigorous and free-flowering.
(Banks, UK, 1855)

**'Rose of Castile Improved'**
Single H2 Bush
*Tube* short, pale pink. *Sepals*,
broad and held well out over the
corolla, pink on top with green
tips, and a deeper shade of pink
underneath. *Corolla* opens
reddish-violet with deep pink
veins, ageing to reddish-purple.
The blooms are medium-sized
and fairly compact. *Foliage* light
to medium green. Growth is
upright, bushy, strong and free-
flowering.
(Lane, UK, 1871)

**'Rose of Denmark'**
Single H2 Lax bush/trailer
*Tube* slender, white. *Sepals* white
on top, faintly flushed pink, with
green tips on top, the undersides
a deeper pink. *Sepals* short,
broad and upturned. *Corolla*
rosy purple with rose-pink veins,
shaded pink at the base of each
petal. Medium-sized, rather
loose bloom. *Foliage* is medium
green, rather long leaves, slightly

serrated. Growth is upright and
bushy though rather lax.
(Banks, UK, 1864)

**'Rose Reverie'**
Double H2 Bush
*Tube* cream. *Sepals* neyron rose
on topwith green tips, deeper
neyron rose underneath.
*Corolla* solferino purple flushed
and veined with slightly darker
shades of solferino purple and
rose madder. The blooms are
fairly large and compact.
*Foliage* dark green, long and
pointed, medium-sized.
(Crockett, USA, 1969)

**'Rose Winston'**
Double H2 Bush
Fairly large flower. *Tube* and
*sepals* red. *Corolla* pink rose
with red veins. Foliage medium
green. Growth is upright and
bushy.
(Raiser and date unknown)

**'Roslyn Lowe'**
Double H2 Trailer
*Tube* pinkish white with a dull
green strip. *Sepals* horizontally
held, neyron rose on the upper
surface and carmine rose on the
lower; tips recurved, green.
*Corolla* deep violet and neyron
rose maturing to violet purple
and neyron rose. The blooms
are very wide and flared and
carry many violet and neyron-
rose petaloids. *Foliage* is matt
green on top, lettuce green
underneath, the leaves large with
red and green veins, serrated
edges. ('Pink Marshmallow' ×
'Midnight Sun')
(Richardson, Australia, 1985)

**'Rosy Frills'**
Double H2 Trailer
*Tube* greenish white. *Sepals*
short and broad, pale pink
inside and very pale pink outside
with pale green tips. *Corolla*
deep rose edged with red; the
outer petals are streaked with
salmon. The blooms are very
full and compact. *Foliage* dark
green with red veins and stems.
A good basket cultivar as it is
very free-flowering.
(Handley, UK, 1979)

'ROSECROFT BEAUTY'

'ROSE FANTASIA'

'ROSE OF CASTILE'

'ROSE OF CASTILE IMPROVED'

'ROSE OF DENMARK'

'ROSE REVERIE'

**'Rosy Ruffles'**
Double H2 Trailer
*Tube* pale pink. *Sepals* white
fading to pink on the upper
surface and salmon pink on the
lower. *Corolla* rose with wavy
petal edges. *Foliage* dark green
on the upper surface and
lighter on the lower. Growth is
naturally trailing. ('Hula Girl'
× 'Applause')
(Stubbs, USA, 1987)

**'Rough Silk'**
Single H2 Trailer
*Tube* long, pale pink. *Sepals*
long, slender and upward
curling, pale pink with green
tips. *Corolla* deep wine red
shading to pink at the base of
the petals. The bloom is fairly
long and compact. *Foliage* light
to medium green, medium-
sized, serrated edges to leaves.
The natural growth is as a
trailer and is self-branching.
Quite vigorous in its growth
and so difficult to keep in
check. Basket or half basket.
(Baker, UK, 1970)

**'Royal and Ancient'**
Single H2 Bush
*Tube*, *sepals* and *corolla* pink.
The flowers are large, bell-
shaped and have wavy edges to
their petals. *Foliage* dark and
glossy. Growth is upright and
free. Excellent for bushes or
standards.
(Goulding, UK, 1986)

**'Royal Purple'**
Single to semi-double H2
Bush
*Tube* short and thick, deep
cerise. *Sepals* cerise, broad,
held slightly above the
horizontal. *Corolla* purple,
slightly paler at petal base,
veined with red. Foliage
medium green. Growth is
upright and very strong.
(Lemoine, France, 1896)

**'Royal Sovereign'**
Semi-double H2 Bush
*Tube* short, crimson. *Sepals*
crimson top, spiraea red
underneath, held well out.
*Corolla* creamy white. The

medium-sized flowers are freely
produced. *Foliage* medium
green, medium-sized, leaves
serrated. Growth is upright and
bushy.
(Gadsby, UK, 1970)

**'Royal Touch'**
Double H2 Bush
*Tube* rose pink. *Sepals* rosy
pink, broad and recurve slightly.
*Corolla* royal purple. *Foliage*
medium green. The blooms are
large and freely produced for
their size. The natural growth is
upright and bushy.
(Tiret, USA, 1964)

**'Royal Velvet'**
Double H2 Bush
*Tube* medium length, crimson.
*Sepals* short and broad, held
well out over the corolla, also
crimson. *Corolla* deep purple,
the outer petals splashed with
crimson. The blooms are very
full, fluffy and of medium to
large size. *Foliage* medium
green, finely serrated edges to
leaves. Growth is upright and
very vigorous. The plant is
bushy and self-branching. A
really first class cultivar which
makes an excellent exhibition
plant.
(Waltz, USA, 1962)

**'Royal Wedding'**
Single H2 Bush
*Tube* white, striped with pink.
*Sepals* white tinged pink,
pagoda-shaped. *Corolla* ivory
white, and produces its best
colour in shade. The medium-
sized flowers are bell-shaped.
*Foliage* medium green. Growth
is upright, self-branching and
bushy.
(Dunnett, UK, 1982)

**'Roy Walker'**
Double H2 Bush
*Tube* white with pale pink
flushing. *Sepals* white to pink
and are reflexed. *Corolla* white,
round and flaring. The flowers
are of medium size. *Foliage*
medium green, medium size.
Growth is upright and bushy.
A very free-flowering bush.
(Fuchsia La, USA, 1975)

**'Rozientje'**
Single H2 Lax bush
Medium-sized flowers. *Tube*
and *sepals* pale orange, striped
with red. *Corolla* light rosy
purple. *Foliage* medium green.
The natural growth is as an
upright, although rather lax,
bush.
(Weeda, Holland, 1990)

**'Ruby'**
Semi-double H2 Bush
*Tube* orange. *Sepals* orange,
tipped with green. *Corolla*
dusky orange-cerise. The
medium-sized blooms are quite
freely produced. The colour
combination is extremely
attractive. *Foliage* medium
green. Growth is upright and
bushy; will produce a good
standard.
(Dresman, UK, 1986)

**'Ruby Wedding'**
Double H2 Trailer
*Tube* and *sepals* ruby. *Corolla*
orangy red. The large flowers
are produced quite freely.
*Foliage* medium green. The
natural growth is as a trailer;
this cultivar will make a very
good basket.
(Forward, UK, 1990)

**'Ruddigore'**
Single H2 Bush
*Tube* long and robust, orange.
*Sepals* short, narrow and
slightly recurved, a slightly
paler colour of orange, the tips
prominently green. *Corolla* a
brighter orange. *Foliage*
medium green. The natural
growth is upright and bushy.
(Goulding, UK, 1987)

**'Ruffles'**
Double H2 Trailer
*Tube* short and waxy, pink.
*Sepals* broad and upturned, deep
pink with green tips. *Corolla*
deep violet in centre, small outer
petals marbled with pink. The
blooms are large, petals ruffled,
and are freely produced. *Foliage*
medium green. The natural
growth is as a trailer; will make
a good basket.
(Erickson, USA, 1960)

254

'ROYAL PURPLE'

'ROYAL VELVET'

'RUDDIGORE'

'ROY WALKER'

'RUFFLES'

**'Rufus'**
Single H3 Bush
*Tube*, *sepals* and *corolla* are all
bright turkey red. The flowers
are medium-sized and are
produced very freely
throughout the season. *Foliage*
medium green, medium to
large, leaves slightly serrated.
The natural growth of the
plant is as an upright bush. H.
and S. 24–30in (60–75cm).
Excellent for the hardy border
and will never let you down.
Often incorrectly called 'Rufus
the Red'.
(Nelson, USA, 1952)

**'Ruth King'**
Double H2 Trailer
*Tube* pink, medium length and
thickness. *Sepals* pink,
recurving. *Corolla* lilac and
white, compact. The large
blooms are freely produced.
*Foliage* medium green. The
natural growth is as a trailer.
An excellent plant for hanging
containers.
(Tiret, USA, 1967)

# S

**'Sailor'**
Single H2 Bush
*Tube* cream, veined with red.
*Sepals* long, white tipped green.
*Corolla* violet fading to
lavender purple. The buds are
long and pear-shaped. *Foliage*
medium green. Growth is
upright and spreading. The
flowers are medium to large.
(Redfern, UK, 1994)

**'Sally Ann'**
Double H2 Trailer
*Tubes* white. *Sepals* white on top
with green tips, pale pink
underneath. *Corolla* consists of
different shades of rose. The
flowers are largish and freely
produced. *Foliage* medium green.
Growth is naturally trailing.
(Pennisi, USA, 1971)

**'Salmon Cascade'**
Single H2 Trailer
*Tube* dark salmon. *Sepals* pale

pink shading to white, tipped
with green. *Corolla* deep
orange red. *Foliage* fairly large,
medium green. The growth is
naturally trailing, and a superb
basket can be produced quite
easily.
(Bielby/Oxtoby, UK, 1991)

**'Salmon Glow'**
Single H2 Trailer
*Tube* fairly long, salmon.
*Sepals* salmon, tipped with
green. *Corolla* orange salmon,
of very clean appearance.
*Foliage* small to medium, light
green. The long and slender
flowers are produced very
freely. The growth is rather lax.
Good as a spreading bush or
perhaps better in a basket.
(Handley, UK, 1978)

**'Sam's Song'**
Double H2 Trailer
*Tube* pale pink. *Sepals* broad,
white flushed with pink, coral
pink underneath. *Corolla* wine
rose, short and square-shaped.
Very free-flowering, with
medium-sized flowers. *Foliage*
medium green. The natural
growth is spreading so will
make a good basket.
(Hooper, UK, 1993)

*F. sanctae rosae*
Species H1 Bush
The single flowers are
produced in dense whorls at
the ends of the branches. *Tube*
long, thin, orange. *Sepals*
small, orange. *Corolla* orange.
*Foliage* green with a slight
metallic sheen. Growth is
spreading and is quite easy.
(Bolivia)

**'Sandboy'**
Single H2 Bush
*Tube* short, thin, pink. *Sepals*
very deep pink, small, narrow
and curl well back to the tube.
*Corolla* very dark mauve,
flushed with light mauve at the
base of the petals. The smallish
flowers are bell-shaped and
very prolifically produced.
*Foliage* medium green. The
natural growth is upright and
bushy. Makes a very good

exhibition bush. One of the
few fuchsias which will keep its
buds indoors, and which can
withstand central heating. It
will continue to bloom inside
all through the winter if given
enough light. Easy to
propagate, although cuttings
will start budding as soon as
they have rooted; the buds
must be removed until flowers
are wanted. (('Ballet Girl' ×
'Fascination') × (seedling × ?))
(Hall/Atkinson, UK, 1967)

**'San Diego'**
Double H2 Trailer
*Tube* and *sepals* pinkish white.
*Corolla* rosy red. The large
blooms are freely produced.
*Foliage* medium green. The
natural growth of the plant is
as a trailer. Will make a good
basket.
(Tiret, USA, 1964)

**'Sangria'**
Double H2 Bush
*Tube* white. *Sepals* white on
the top side but pale pink
underneath. *Corolla* vivid
currant red flashed with white
at the base of the petals. The
fully double blooms are of
medium size. *Foliage* medium
green. The natural growth is as
an upright bush. ('The Speed
Bird' × 'Candlelight')
(Bridgland, UK, 1986)

**'San Mateo'**
Double H2 Trailer
*Tube* and *sepals* deep pink.
*Corolla* very dark violet with
pink splashes. The extremely
large blooms are freely
produced for their size. *Foliage*
medium green. The natural
growth is trailing. Will make a
lovely weeping standard.
(Niederholzer, USA, 1946)

**'Sanrina'**
Single H2 Bush
Medium-sized flowers. *Tube*
and *sepals* aubergine. *Corolla*
also aubergine. *Foliage* medium
to dark green. Growth is
naturally upright and bushy.
('First Kiss' × 'Foolke')
(Kempink, Holland, 1988)

'RUFUS'

'SALMON CASCADE'

'SAN DIEGO'

'SALMON GLOW'

'SAN MATEO'

**'Santa Claus'**
Double H3 Bush
*Tube* and *sepals* bright red.
*Corolla* white with red veins.
The small blooms are very
freely produced. *Foliage*
medium green. Growth is
naturally upright and bushy. H.
and S. 18–24in (45–60cm).
(Hazard, USA, date unknown)

**'Santa Cruz'**
Double H3 Bush
*Tube* crimson, thick. *Sepals*
dark crimson, short and broad,
upturned to tube. *Corolla*
rather darker crimson. *Foliage*
large and bronzed, ovate,
serrated. The natural growth is
strongly upright. The plant is
very sturdy and self-branching.
H. and S. 18–30in (45–75cm).
(Tiret, USA, 1947)

**'Sapphire'**
Double H2 Bush
*Tube* short, creamy white.
*Sepals* flushed pink on the
outside, clear pink inside.
*Corolla* deep purplish-blue.
The blooms are medium-sized
and very freely produced,
though unfortunately they
arrive rather late in the season.
*Foliage* small, dark green.
Growth is upright and bushy.
(Waltz, USA, 1954)

**'Sarah Ann'**
Single H2 Bush
Medium-sized flower. *Tube*
white. *Sepals* white flushed
pink. *Corolla* silvery lavender
maturing to pale lilac. *Foliage*
medium green. The growth is
naturally upright and bushy.
(McDonald, UK, 1987)

**'Sara Helen'**
Double H2 Bush
*Tube* and *sepals* white, turning
pink. *Corolla* tyrian purple,
lighter at base of petals, fades
with maturity. The large
blooms are very full and fairly
freely produced. *Foliage*
medium green. Growth is
strong and upright.
(Colville, UK, 1969)

**'Sarah Eliza'**
Double H2 Trailer
*Tube* and *sepals* white, flushed
with the palest pink. *Corolla*
white, the outer petals flushed
with pink. *Foliage* light green.
The growth is naturally trailing
and will make a superb basket.
The flowers are very large and
fully double. As with all
'whites', the best colour is
achieved when grown in partial
shade.
(Clements, UK, 1992)

**'Sarah Greensmith'**
Single H2 Trailer
*Tube* rose. *Sepals* rose, tipped
with green. *Corolla* lavender.
*Foliage* medium green. The
natural growth is trailing. A
superb basket can be achieved
very easily.
(Caunt, UK, 1989)

**'Sarah Jane'**
Double H2 Bush
*Tube* short, rose-pink. *Sepals*
short and broad, also rose-
pink. *Corolla* lilac, darker
shaded at the base of the
petals. The blooms are small
and compact. *Foliage* medium
green. The growth is upright
and bushy. A very free-
flowering fuchsia.
(Putley, UK, 1974)

**'Sarah Louise'**
Single H2 Bush
*Tube* short, red. *Sepals* held
half-way above the horizontal,
rose with slightly paler
colouring underneath, tips
recurving slightly. *Corolla*
opens violet shading to rose,
maturing to reddish-violet. The
petal edges are smooth. *Foliage*
medium green. The natural
growth is upright and bushy.
('Loeky' × 'Eden Lady')
(Crawshaw, UK, 1988)

**'Sarong'**
Double H2 Lax bush
*Tube* short, white, thin. *Sepals*
long, twisting, white flushed
with pink. *Corolla* violet
purple. The blooms are large,

very ragged and untidy, and
fairly freely produced for a
double. *Foliage* large, medium
green. The natural growth is
rather lax. When grown as a
bush the branches will require
assistance to support the
weight of the blooms.
(Kennett, USA, 1963)

**'Saskia'**
Single H2 Bush
Small flowers. *Tube* white
striped with green. *Sepals*
crimson flushed with pink.
*Corolla* pale rose purple.
*Foliage* medium green. The
natural growth is as an upright
bush.
(Strumper, Holland, 1988)

**'Satchmo'**
Single H2 Bush
Medium-sized flower. *Tube* and
*sepals* robin red. *Corolla* deep
aubergine. *Foliage* medium
green. The natural growth is as
an upright bush.
(de Graaff, Holland, 1988)

**'Satellite'**
Single H2 Bush
*Tube* short, rather thick,
greenish white. *Sepals* broad
and slightly reflexing, white
with green tips. *Corolla* dark
red fading to bright red with
streaks of white down the
centre of each petal. *Foliage*
medium green. The growth is
upright and bushy. A very
distinctive-looking cultivar and
one well worth growing.
Beware of *botrytis*.
(Kennett, USA, 1965)

**'Saturnus'**
Single H2 Bush
*Tube* short, red. *Sepals* very
long, well held out from the
corolla, also red. *Corolla* light
purple veined with red, a paler
shade at the base of each petal.
The flowers stand well out
from the foliage. *Foliage*
medium green. Growth is
upright and bushy. (*F. regia
typica* × 'Henrietta Ernst')
(de Groot, Holland, 1970)

'SARAH ELIZA'

'SARAH GREENSMITH'

'SARAH LOUISE'

'SARONG'

'SASKIA'

'SATELLITE'

**'Saxondale'**
Semi-double H2 Bush
*Tube* crimson. *Sepals* also
crimson, small and broad.
*Corolla* amaranth rose and
veined rose red. The blooms
are small. *Foliage* medium
green, the leaves are small.
Growth is dwarf but upright
and bushy. Excellent plant for
the rockery. ('Trase' × 'Lady
Thumb')
(Gadsby, UK, 1973)

**'Saxondale Sue'**
Double H2 Bush
*Tube* short, thick, white striped
with green. *Sepals* white with
yellowish-green recurved tips.
*Corolla* white with wavy petal
edges. *Foliage* medium green.
Growth is upright and bushy
but needs frequent stopping to
get the best shape.
(Richardson, Australia, 1988)

**F. scabriuscula**
Species H1 Bush
The fairly small flowers are
borne solitarily in the upper
leaf axils. *Tube* and *sepals*
bright red. *Corolla* red. *Foliage*
medium to dark green. The
natural growth is as a low
spreading shrub.
(Ecuador)

**'Scarborough Jamboree'**
Semi-double H2 Bush
Medium-sized flower. *Tube* and
*sepals* scarlet. *Corolla* white
veined with scarlet. *Foliage*
medium green. The natural
growth, although lax, is as an
upright bush.
(Clarke, UK, 1989)

**'Scarborough Rock'**
Single H2 Bush
Medium-sized flower. *Tube* and
*sepals* pink. *Corolla* white.
*Foliage* medium green. The
upright growth makes this a
good plant for the patio tub.
(Raiser and date unknown)

**'Scarborough Rosette'**
Double H2 Bush
*Tube* and *sepals* flesh pink.
*Corolla* rosette-shaped, violet
maturing to dark red. Growth

is bushy and upright. *Foliage*
medium green. A good plant
for the show bench.
(Raiser and date unknown)

**'Scarborough Seasprite'**
Semi-double H2 Lax bush
Medium-sized flower. *Tube* and
*sepals* scarlet. *Corolla* purple
veined with scarlet. *Foliage*
medium to dark green. The
natural growth is rather lax
although it can be encouraged
to form a good bush.
(Clarke, UK, 1989)

**'Scarborough Starshine'**
Single H2 Lax bush
Medium-sized flower. *Tube* and
*sepals* pale pink. *Corolla*
magenta. *Foliage* medium
green. The rather lax growth
will necessitate the use of
stakes to form a good upright
bush.
(Clarke, UK, 1989)

**'Scarcity'**
Single H3 Bush
*Tube* short, thick, deep scarlet.
*Sepals* short and upturned, also
deep scarlet. *Corolla* deep
purple shading to scarlet at the
base of the petals. *Foliage*
medium green with serrated
edges to the leaves. Growth is
upright and bushy. H. and S.
18–30in (45–75cm).
(Lye, UK, 1869)

**'Scarlet Ribbons'**
Triphylla type H1 Bush
*Tube* very long and narrow,
red. *Sepals* short and scarlet
red with green tips, recurving.
*Corolla* small, scarlet. *Foliage*
long and thin, yellowish-green.
The flowers are borne in
largish terminal clusters, and
are very similar to those of *F.
boliviana*.
(Schneider, USA, 1984)

**'Schneeball'**
Semi-double H2 Bush
*Tube* reddish pink. *Sepals* long
and curl back over the tube,
also reddish pink. *Corolla*
white with pinkish veining. The
flowers are medium-sized and
loose-petalled. *Foliage* pale

green. Growth is upright, self-
branching and bushy. The
flowers are very freely
produced throughout the
season.
(Twrdy, Germany, 1874)

**'Schneewitchen'**
Single H2 Bush
*Tube* short, thick, dark pink.
*Sepals* short, broad and slightly
upturned at the tips, also dark
pink. *Corolla* pinkish-purple.
The flowers are small and
compact. *Foliage* medium
green, small and slightly
serrated. Growth is vigorously
upright and bushy.
(Klein, Germany, 1878)

**'Schneewitcher'**
Single H2 Bush
*Tube* short, medium thickness,
red. *Sepals* short, broad and
slightly upturned, also red.
*Corolla* violet purple with red
veins. The flowers are open
and bell-shaped. *Foliage*
medium green with red veins.
The growth is upright and
bushy. The plants are self-
branching, vigorous and free-
flowering.
(Hoeck, Germany, 1884)

**'Schonbrunner Schuljubilaum'**
Triphylla type H1 Bush
*Tube* large and long, tapering
with a distinct twist in the
middle, rosy-red. *Sepals*
narrow, pointed and spreading,
also deep rosy-red; held half-
way below the horizontal and
partially hide the corolla.
*Corolla* orange-red. *Foliage*
darkish green with a prominent
crimson mid-rib. Upright, stiff
and 'lanky'-type growth.
('Coralle' × *F. fulgens*)
(Nutzinger, Austria, 1976)

**'Schone Wilhelmine'**
Single H2 Bush
Medium-sized flowers. *Tube*
and *sepals* deep shell pink; the
sepals have green tips. *Corolla*
shell pink. *Foliage* medium
green. The natural growth is
bushy so will make a superb
plant for the patio.
(Raiser and date unknown)

'SCARBOROUGH ROCK'

'SCARCITY'

'SCHNEEBALL'

'SCHONBRUNNER SCHULJUBILAUM'
'SCHONE WILHELMINE'

**'Scotch Heather'**
Double H2 Bush
*Tube* white, streaked with pink.
*Sepals* white on the top side
and flushed pink underneath,
tipped green, short, wide and
flaring. *Corolla* hyacinth blue
to mallow purple, slightly
flared. The medium-sized
blooms are freely produced.
*Foliage* light green. Growth is
upright and bushy.
(Foster, USA, 1974)

**'Sealand Prince'**
Single H3 Bush
*Tube* light red, quite thick.
*Sepals* long, narrow and
upturned, light red. *Corolla*
violet-purple fading to reddish-
purple. The medium-sized
flowers are numerous. *Foliage*
medium green. The natural
growth is as an upright bush.
(Walker Bees Nurseries, UK,
1967)

**'Sea Shell'**
Double H2 Bush
*Tube* pink, rather thick. *Sepals*
fully reflexed, whitish pink.
*Corolla* pink, veined with a
deeper pink. The flowers are
quite large and free. *Foliage*
dark green. Growth is upright
and bushy.
(Evans, USA, 1954)

**'Sebastopol'**
Double H2 Trailer
*Tube* short white. *Sepals* long,
broad and recurving, white and
pink. *Corolla* white, variegated
in pale pink. The blooms are
largish and very free for their
size. *Foliage* medium green.
The growth is naturally
trailing.
(Pennisi, USA, 1968)

**F. serratifolia**
Species H1 Bush
(Synonymous with
*F. denticulata*)
*Tube* red, longish and hairy.
*Sepals* red with green tips.
*Corolla* scarlet to crimson.
*Foliage* dark green, reddish on
the underside. Growth is
upright and shrubby.
(Peru, Bolivia)

**F. sessilifolia**
Species H1 Bush
*Tube* scarlet. *Sepals* greenish-
red. *Corolla* scarlet. The
flowers are produced quite
freely in clusters at the ends of
the laterals, and are each
approx 1in (3cm) long. *Foliage*
darkish green, quite large.
(Colombia)

**'Seventh Heaven'**
Double H2 Trailer
*Tube* short, thick, greenish-
white with green streaks. *Sepals*
long, broad and curving, white
shading to pink as the flower
matures. *Corolla* orange-red
shading to orange and white at
the base of the petals. The
flowers are large and free for
their size. *Foliage* medium
green. The natural desire of the
plant is to trail. Weights will
probably be required to achieve
a superb basket.
(Stubbs, USA, 1981)

**'Severn Queen'**
Single H2 Bush
*Tube* thin, very pale pink,
medium length. *Sepals* also
very pale pink, medium size.
*Corolla* is rose bengal and
semi-flared. *Foliage* scheoles
green. The growth is upright,
free-flowering, self-branching
and short-jointed.
(Tolley, UK, 1978)

**'Shady Blue'**
Single H2 Bush
*Tube* short and bulbous,
pinkish carmine. *Sepals* long,
broad, held well out from the
corolla, also pinkish carmine.
*Corolla* pale violet-blue, shaded
pink at the base of each petal.
The flowers are medium-sized
and compact. *Foliage* medium
green, leaves medium to large,
serrated. Growth is vigorously
upright. Needs early pinching
to make a good bush. Does
well indoors or out. ('Upward
Look' × 'Caroline')
(Gadsby, UK, 1970)

**'Shady Lady'**
Double H2 Bush
*Tube* pink. *Sepals* broad,

crêped on the underside, also
pink. *Corolla* white. The
blooms are very large and
fairly freely produced. The
edges of the numerous petals
are slightly serrated. *Foliage*
medium green. The natural
growth of this cultivar is as an
upright bush.
(Stubbs, USA, 1970)

**'Shangri La'**
Double H2 Lax bush
*Tube* medium length, dark
pink. *Sepals* broad and
upturned, dark pink to red.
*Corolla* pale pinkish-white with
pink veining. The flowers are
very large and very full. *Foliage*
mid-green, medium-sized.
Growth is rather lax so can be
used as a trailer or a bush as
required.
(Martin, USA, 1963)

**'Shanley'**
Single H2 Bush
*Tube* long, pale salmon orange.
*Sepals* also pale salmon orange
with green tips, short, broad
and well held out. *Corolla* pale
orange. *Foliage* medium green,
rather large, with serrated
edges. The growth is vigorously
upright and bushy. A very free-
flowering cultivar.
(Shutt, USA, 1968)

**'Sharon Alsopp'**
Double H2 Bush
*Tube* and *sepals* carmine.
*Corolla* white. The medium-sized
blooms are well shaped and
freely produced for a double.
*Foliage* medium green. Growth
is short-jointed and bushy.
(Pacey, UK, 1983)

**'Sharon Caunt'**
Double H2 Bush
*Tube* medium-length, rose
madder. *Sepals* rose madder on
the upper surface, pale rose
madder on the lower; the tips
are slightly reflexed. *Corolla*
white lightly veined with rose
madder. *Foliage* mid-green with
paler areas on the upper
surface. The growth is strongly
upright and bushy.
(Caunt, UK, 1987)

'SEA SHELL'

F. SESSILIFOLIA

'SHADY LADY'

'SHANLEY'

**'Sharpitor'**
*Tube* small and thin, pale
pinkish-white. *Sepals* pale
pinkish-white, short, fairly
broad, well held out. *Corolla*
very slightly darker than the
sepals. The flowers are small
and compact. *Foliage* the most
redeeming feature of this plant,
variegated pale cream and
green, small and has a serrated
edging. Growth is upright and
bushy. It is self-branching but is
late coming into flower. A slow
grower but one that always
creates an impression, when
well grown, on the show
bench. Difficult to propagate.
Thought to be a sport of *F.
magellanica* var *molinae*; plants
revert quite easily.
(National Trust, Sharpitor, UK,
c.1974)

**'Shaun Rushton'**
Double H2 Bush
Medium-sized flower. *Tube* and
*sepals* pale pink. *Corolla*
amethyst violet maturing to
lilac. *Foliage* medium green.
Growth is upright and bushy.
(Horton, UK, 1991)

**'Shawna Ree'**
*Encliandra* type H2 Bush
*Tube* very small, thin, deep red.
*Sepals* tiny, deep red,
horizontal, tips recurve.
*Corolla* very small, deep red.
*Foliage* very small, medium to
dark green on top, lighter
underneath. The growth is
upright but very thin and wiry.
('Mendocino Mini' ×)
(Pike, UK, 1985)

**'Sheila Crooks'**
Double H2 Bush
*Tube* and *sepals* brilliant red.
*Corolla* bluish-purple. *Foliage*
medium green. The growth is
upright and very bushy.
(Crooks, UK, 1985)

**'Sheila Kirby'**
Single H2 Bush
*Tube* short, rosy red. *Sepals* white
flushed with rose at the base,
tipped with green. *Corolla* deep
violet, whitish at the base of each
petal. *Foliage* medium green.

Growth is upright, short-jointed
and bushy. The small to medium-
sized flowers are freely produced.
(Kirby, UK, 1993)

**'Shelford'**
Single H2 Bush
*Tube* short, thick, fluted, baby
pink. *Sepals* long and narrow,
also baby pink shading to
white at the tips, tipped with
green; held horizontally.
*Corolla* white with slight pink
veining at the base of the
petals. The medium-sized
flowers are rather tubular in
shape. *Foliage* dark green. The
natural growth is as an upright
bush. An extremely successful
exhibitors' banker.
(Roe, UK, 1986)

**'Shelley Lynn'**
Double H2 Trailer
*Tube* and *sepals* clear white.
*Corolla* clear deep lilac. The
largish blooms are very freely
produced. *Foliage* medium green.
The growth is as a natural trailer.
Makes a superb basket.
(Tiret, USA, 1968)

**'Sherwood'**
Single H3 Dwarf bush
*Tube* short, carmine. *Sepals*
short and pointed, also
carmine. *Corolla* neyron rose
veined with carmine. The
flowers are small and compact.
*Foliage* medium green. Growth
is upright and bushy, but very
small and dwarf-like. Good for
the front of a hardy border.
Early to flower. H. and S. up to
12in (30cm). ('Trase' × 'Lady
Thumb')
(Gadsby UK, 1973)

**'Shining Knight'**
Single H2 Bush
*Tube* short, pale pink. *Sepals*
pale pink edged with carmine
rose on the upper surface,
crêped pale pink on the lower.
*Corolla* aster violet when first
open, maturing to lavender
blue with slightly turned-under
petal edges. *Foliage* deep green.
Growth is strong, upright and
short-jointed.
(Hall, UK, 1987)

**'Shooting Star'**
Semi-double H2 Lax bush
*Tube* short, salmon red. *Sepals*
long, narrow and well held out,
also salmon red. *Corolla* purple
in the centre with the outer
petals and the petaloids
splashed salmon red and pink;
the centre opens bell-shaped.
*Foliage* medium green. The
growth is rather lax although
vigorous. Needs 'stopping'
frequently in the early stages of
training.
(Martin, USA, 1965)

**'Showtime'**
Double H2 Bush
*Tube* short, white. *Sepals* also
white, flushed with carmine
rose with much deeper shade
underneath. *Corolla* rich ruby
red but much paler at the base
of the petals. The compact
blooms are freely produced for
a double. The plant is upright
and bushy.
(Pacey, UK, 1987)

**'Shuna'**
Single H3 Bush
*Tube* medium-sized, warm
pink. *Sepals* short and broad,
mid-pink. *Corolla* a warm mid-
pink. The flowers are very
compact on opening, but
spreading slightly with
maturity. *Foliage* mid- to
darkish green, small and with
serrated edges. Growth is
upright and self-branching. The
smallish flowers are produced
in great profusion. Makes very
good exhibition plant, but not
easy to grow. (Sport of
'Countess of Aberdeen')
(Travis, UK, 1973)

**'Shy Look'**
Single H2 Bush
*Tube* short and thick, rose
pink. *Sepals* crimson, short,
broad and well held out.
*Corolla* roseine purple. The
flowers are of medium size, the
blooms produced very freely
and held erect. *Foliage* is
medium green, small to
medium size. Growth is upright
and bushy. ('Upward Look' ×)
(Gadsby, UK, 1972)

'SHEILA CROOKS'

'SHEILA KIRBY'

'SHELFORD'

'SHELLEY LYNN'

## 'Sid Drapkin'

**'Sid Drapkin'**
Single H2 Trailer
Medium-sized flower. *Tube*
pink. *Sepals* light pink. *Corolla*
red. *Foliage* medium green. The
natural habit of the plant is to
trail.
(Drapkin, USA, 1991)

**'Sierra Blue'**
Double H2 Trailer
*Tube* short and thick, white.
*Sepals* short, broad and slightly
upturned, white with green
tips. *Corolla* silvery blue with
pinkish veining, shaded white
at the base of the petals.
*Foliage* mid-green. The natural
growth habit is trailing so will
make a good basket.
(Waltz, USA, 1957)

**'Silver Anniversary'**
Double H2 Lax bush
*Tube* white. *Sepals* fully
reflexed, white on the upper
surface, white tinged with
orchid on the lower. *Corolla*
opens a lovely silvery blue
maturing to silvery orchid blue.
Medium-sized, flaring bloom.
*Foliage* medium green on top,
lighter beneath. ('Sugar Blues'
× 'Pink Marshmallow')
(Stubbs, USA, 1985)

**'Silverdale'**
Single H3 Bush
*Tube* short, ivory. *Sepals* quite
long for a small flower, *eau-de-
nil* flushed with very soft pink
and tipped with green. *Corolla*
pastel lavender, compact,
barrel-shaped. The small
flowers are very freely
produced. *Foliage* small and
pale green. The upright growth
makes it very useful for the
hardy border. H. and S. 36in +
(90cm +). (*F. magellanica* var
*molinae* × 'Venus Victrix')
(Travis, UK, 1962)

**'Silver Dawn'**
Double H2 Bush
*Tube* long, white. *Sepals* long,
white, broad, heavily tipped
with green. *Corolla* a beautiful
shade of aster violet shading to
rhodanite red at the base of the
petals; the whole changes to

imperial purple with maturity.
Long, fairly compact bloom.
*Foliage* medium green. The
upright growth is very bushy.
(Bellamy, UK, 1983)

**'Silver Dollar'**
Single H2 Bush
*Tube, sepals* and *corolla* are all
white. Considered by many to
be the most perfect white ever
produced. The medium-sized
flowers have rolled petals
which hold their shape. They
need shade to assist in the
retention of the white colour.
*Foliage* medium to light green.
The natural growth is upright
and bushy.
(Mitchinson, UK, 1985)

**'Silver Pink'**
Single H3 Bush
*Tube* and *sepals* deep pink.
*Corolla* silvery pink. The
medium-sized flowers are very
freely produced. *Foliage*
medium green. Growth is
upright and bushy. H. and S.
18–24in (45–60cm).
(Tabraham, UK, 1978)

**'Simon J. Rowell'**
Single H2 Bush
Medium-sized flowers. *Tubes*
short, a dull red colour. *Sepals*
pink with red streaks. *Corolla*
a rosy purple. *Foliage* medium
green. The upward growth is
quite bushy.
(Rowell, UK, 1991)

**F. simplicaulis**
Species H1 Bush
*Tubes* long; *sepals* short; petals
small; all crimson. The flowers
are held in terminal corymbs.
Growth is upright and quite
vigorous. *Foliage* darkish green
with a satin texture, quite
large. Does not respond to
frequent stopping.
(Central Peru)

**'Sincerity'**
Double H2 Bush
*Tube* long and slender, white
flushed with pale pink. *Sepals*
long, broad, slightly reflexed
white on top and flushed pink

with a deeper pink on the
undersides. *Corolla* fairly full,
white. The blooms are of
medium size. *Foliage* medium
green. The natural growth
of the plant is upright and
bushy.
(Holmes, UK, 1968)

**'Siobhan'**
Semi-double H2 Bush
*Tubes* rose pink. *Sepals* held
well out, white flushed pink at
the base, slightly deeper pink
on the underside. *Corolla*
white, faintly tinged with pink
at the base of the petals.
*Foliage* mid-green. Growth is
upright and bushy. ('Joe
Kusber' × 'Northumbrian
Belle')
(Ryle, UK, 1976)

**'Sir Alfred Ramsey'**
Single H2 Bush
*Tube* empire rose, short, thick.
*Sepals* neyron rose, medium
length and held well up to the
tube with recurved tips.
*Corolla* opens violet-purple
maturing to tyrian red, small,
flaring, bell-shaped. The large
flowers are freely produced.
*Foliage* pale green, leaves
longish with green veins and
serrated edges. Growth is very
strong and upright.
(Goulding, UK, 1984)

**'Siren'**
Double H2 Bush
*Tube* and *sepals* deep red.
*Corolla* violet with red veins.
*Foliage* medium to dark green.
The flowers are very full and
large. The upright growth is
very sturdy and bushy.
(Baker, UK, 1970)

**'Sister Ann Haley'**
Single H2 Bush
*Tube* rose. *Sepals* rose on top,
crêped light rose underneath,
green tips, recurved. *Corolla*
white veined with rose, maturing
to white with very slight
pinking. *Foliage* medium green.
Growth is rather small but
upright and self-branching. The
plant is very free-flowering.
(Crawshaw, UK, 1988)

266

'SIERRA BLUE'

'SILVER DAWN'

'SILVER DOLLAR'

*F. SIMPLICAULIS*

'SIREN'

'SISTER ANN HALEY'

**'Skyway'**
Single H2 Bush
*Tube* pale pink. *Sepals*
rhodamine pink, pale on top,
deeper underneath, green tips;
long, broad, held well out.
*Corolla* hyacinth blue, edged
with blue-bird blue; the inside
of the petals wisteria blue. The
flowers are medium-sized and
very freely produced. *Foliage*
medium green, leaves long with
serration. Growth is upright
and bushy. ('Jean Burton ×
'Rosabell')
(Gadsby, UK, 1970)

**'Sleepy'**
Single H3 Bush
*Tube* and *sepals* pale pink.
*Corolla* lavender blue, fading
to pink. The small flowers are
produced continuously. *Foliage*
pale green. Growth is upright
and bushy although of a dwarf
habit. H. and S. 12–18in
(30–45cm).
(Tabraham, UK, 1954)

**'Sleigh Bells'**
Single H2 Bush
*Tube* short, white. *Sepals* long,
narrow and recurving, white
with pale green tips. *Corolla*
bell-shaped, of medium size and
also white. *Foliage* medium
green with serrated edges.
Growth is upright and bushy.
(Schnabel, USA, 1954)

**'Slender Lady'**
Single H2 Bush
*Tube* medium length, white.
*Sepals* long, slender and pointed,
waxy white, flushed pink.
*Corolla* violet fading to fuchsia
purple. The blooms are long and
compact. *Foliage* bright green,
serrated. Growth is upright and
bushy. ('Pepi' × 'Sleigh Bells')
(Gadsby, UK, 1970)

**'Small Pipes'**
Triphylla type H1 Bush
A true terminal-flowering
fuchsia. The long *tubes*, *sepals*
and *corolla* are all pale lilac.
The growth is upright, free-
branching and symmetrical.
The colour of the flowers
intensifies when the plants are

grown out of doors. *Foliage*
medium to dark green.
(*F. paniculata* × *F. triphylla*)
(de Graaff, Holland, 1987)

**'Smoky'**
Semi-double H2 Trailer
*Tube* pale orange. *Sepals* rosy
red. *Corolla* smoky magenta
rose. *Foliage* medium green.
The growth is strong and
spreading, but if helped by
early stopping this plant will
make a good trailing basket.
(de Graaff, Holland, 1987)

**'Smoky Mountain'**
Double H2 Trailer
*Tube* reddish-pink. *Sepals*
whitish-pink on the upper
surface and pink on the lower,
with green tips, recurved.
*Corolla* opens smoky purple
maturing to smoky maroon
with smooth edges to the petals.
*Foliage* dark green on the upper
surface and lighter on the lower.
(Wood, USA, 1987)

**'Sneezy'**
Single H3 Bush
*Tube* and *sepals* red. *Corolla* a
deep blue purple. The small
flowers are very freely
produced. *Foliage* light green.
Growth is upright and bushy
but dwarf in habit. H. and S.
12–18in (30–45cm).
(Tabraham, UK, 1974)

**'Snowcap'**
Semi-double H3 Bush
*Tube* short, scarlet. *Sepals* short,
broad and held well out, also
scarlet. *Corolla* white with
reddish veins. The flowers are
small to medium-sized and
rather loose-petalled. *Foliage*
medium to darkish green, leaves
small, serrated. Growth is
upright, self-branching and very
floriferous. H. and S. 24–30in
(60–75cm). Needs a great deal
of pinching in the early stages to
make a good shape.
(Henderson, UK)

**'Snowdrift'**
Double H2 Trailer
*Tube* dark rose pink with light
green streaks. *Sepals* rose red

with green tips, short, broad
and held right over the top of
the corolla. *Corolla* pure white
but with some reddish veining.
The flowers are very full
double and fluffy. *Foliage* dark
green. Growth is rather lax so
can be used as a trailer for
baskets or in pots with
supports.
(Colville, UK, 1966)

**'Snowfire'**
Double H2 Bush
*Tube* medium length, pink.
*Sepals* white, wide and tapering,
recurve on maturity. *Corolla*
bright pink to coral with some
white variegation. The bud
shows rose-pink streaks before
opening. *Foliage* dark green.
Growth is upright and bushy.
(Stubbs, USA, 1978)

**'Snow Goose'**
Double H2 Lax bush
*Tube* short. *Sepals* upswept,
ivory white tinged with pink.
*Corolla* petals white with pink
veins. *Foliage* medium green.
This self-branching fuchsia is
ideal for use in hanging
containers.
(Shaffery, UK, 1994)

**'Snowstorm'**
Single H2 Bush
*Tube* thin, greenish-white.
*Sepals* completely reflex, white
with green tips. The *corolla* is
white, of medium size and with
compact blooms. *Foliage* mid-
green, medium-sized. Growth is
upright, bushy and free-
flowering.
(Handley, UK, 1976)

**'Snow White'**
Double H2 Trailer
*Tube* white with very faint pink
streaks, long and thin. *Sepals*
white, held straight back to the
tube, tipped with green. *Corolla*
white with petaloids of the
same colour. *Foliage* is mid-
green, leaves medium-sized with
serrated edges. The natural
growth is as a trailer. Best
colour in the shade. ('Shelley
Lyn' × seedling)
(Dunnett, UK, 1982)

'SLEEPY'

'SLEIGH BELLS'

'SMOKY MOUNTAIN'

'SNOWCAP'

'SNOWFIRE'

**'Snowy Summit'**
Double H2 Trailer
*Tube* white, medium length and thickness. *Sepals* long and broad, also white. *Corolla* white. The blooms are of medium size and freely produced for a double. *Foliage* medium green with red veins. The natural growth is trailing.
(Stubbs, USA, 1975)

**'So Big'**
Double H2 Trailer
*Tube* long and slender, pale pink. *Sepals* pale pink with green tips, slightly darker on the underside, long and recurving. *Corolla* creamy white with slight pink veining. The flowers are large and rather loose petalled. *Foliage* large, light green with serrated edging. Growth is naturally trailing. Excellent for baskets,
(Waltz, USA, 1955)

**'Sofie'**
Single H2 Bush
Medium-sized flower. *Tube* and *sepals* white. *Corolla* deep purple. *Foliage* medium green. The natural growth is as an upright bush.
(de Graaff, Holland, 1991)

**'Software'**
Double H2 Trailer
Medium-sized flowers. *Tubes* white. *Sepals* pink, faintly tipped with green. *Corolla* orchid pink. *Foliage* dark green. The natural growth is as a trailer.
('Fuchsia Fan' × 'Applause')
(Klein, USA, 1987)

**'Sonata'**
Double H2 Bush
*Tube* short, white with a greenish tinge. *Sepals* short, broad and reflexing, with green tips. *Corolla* white with pink veining; very fluffy with numerous small outer petals. *Foliage* mid-green with longish serrated leaves.
(Tiret, USA, 1960)

**'Son of Thumb'**
Single H3 Bush
*Tube* and *sepals* cerise. The *corolla* is lilac, fairly compact.

The small flowers are very prolific throughout the season. The *foliage* is medium to darker green. A delightful, dwarf-growing fuchsia, the short, bushy growth making it an ideal plant for the front of a hardy border. H. and S. 12–18in (30–45cm).
(Sport of 'Tom Thumb')
(Gubler, UK, 1978)

**'Sophie Claire'**
Triphylla type H1 Bush
A true terminal-flowering type of fuchsia. *Tube*, *sepals* and *corolla* bright orange. *Foliage* medium green. The blooms point upwards and outwards. Growth is short, upright and bushy.
(Stannard, UK, 1991)

**'Sophie's Surprise'**
Triphylla type H1 Bush
A true terminal-flowering type of fuchsia. *Tube*, *sepals* and *corolla* bright orange. The blooms are held upright and point outwards. The growth is short, upright and bushy. *Foliage* medium green with irregular variegation.
(Stannard, UK, 1992)

**'Sophisticated Lady'**
Double H2 Trailer
*Tube* short, pale pink. *Sepals* very long and broad, held slightly below the horizontal and out from the corolla, are also pale pink. *Corolla* white, very full and compact. Corolla is short, but the bloom is medium- to large-sized. *Foliage* medium green with reddish veins, small to medium-sized, serrated. The natural growth is trailing.
(Martin, USA, 1964)

**'Southgate'**
Double H2 Lax bush
*Tube* medium length, pale pink. *Sepals* short and upturned, pale pink on the outside and slightly deeper on the undersides. *Corolla* soft pink with deeper pink veining. The flower is medium-sized, and the bloom is very full and fluffy. *Foliage* medium green, leaves long and

serrated. Growth is rather lax and upright. Suitable for bushes or baskets.
(Walker and Jones, USA, 1952)

**'South Seas'**
Semi-double H2 Lax bush
*Tube* medium length, white, flushed with pale pink. *Sepals* white, flushed pink and are long, broad and recurving. *Corolla* pink and compact. *Foliage* mid-green with serrated edges to the leaves. Growth is rather lax, but vigorous.
(Castro, USA, 1963)

**'South Today'**
Double H2 Bush
*Tube* and *sepals* pale pink. *Corolla* very full, coral pink streaked with pale pink. *Foliage* medium green. The large blooms are freely produced on upward-growing stems.
(Porter, M., UK, 1991)

**'Southwell Minster'**
Single H2 Bush
*Tube* and *sepals* rhodonite red. The sepals held well back from the tube. *Corolla* bishop's violet. The small flowers are very dainty and extremely freely produced. *Foliage* medium green. Growth is strongly upright and is useful for the outside border.
('Glyn Jones' × 'Neil Clyne')
(Roe, UK, 1979)

**'Space Shuttle'**
Single H2 Bush
*Tube* longish, red. *Sepals* rhodonite red on the upper surface and crimson underneath, with yellow-green recurved tips. *Corolla* opens light yellow with an orange base, maturing to light orange. The long-tubed small flowers are very unusual and the plant flowers the whole year round. *Foliage* light fuchsia green on top, olive green underneath, medium size with green veins and serrated edges. Growth is lax upright or trailer. Needs heavy pinching to make any good shape. (*F. speciosa* × *F. splendens*)
(de Graaff, Holland, 1985)

'SO BIG'

'SONATA'

'SON OF THUMB'

'SOPHIE CLAIRE'

'SOUTH TODAY'

'SOUTHWELL MINSTER'

**F. speciosa**
Species hybrid H1 Bush
*Tube* long, and together with
the *sepals*, a dull red. *Corolla*
vermilion. *Foliage* very large,
olive green in colour and
typical of its parents. (*F.
splendens* × *F. fulgens*)

**'Spion Kop'**
Double H2 Bush
*Tube* short, rose red. *Sepals*
reflex, also rose red. *Corolla*
white with rose-red veins. The
blooms flare slightly, are
medium-sized and compact.
There are also petaloids which
are white and veined red.
*Foliage* dull green, medium-
sized, serrated. Growth is
upright and bushy. The plant is
very free-branching and
produces its medium-sized
flowers in quantity.
(Jones, UK, 1973)

**F. splendens**
Species H1 Bush
*Tube* rose to bright red,
compressed in the middle.
*Sepals* green, sometimes reddish
at the base. *Corolla* green and
ovate. *Foliage* medium green,
paler on the underside. The
stems and the branches are
greenish to red. Growth is
upright and very bushy.
(Mexico, Guatemala,
Costa Rica)

**'Spring Classic'**
Semi-double H2 Bush
*Tube* pink. *Sepals* pink with
light green recurved tips.
*Corolla* opens violet maturing
to pinkish-violet; smooth edges
to the petals. The petaloids are
violet, lighter at the base and
with rose streaks. *Foliage* light
green. The veins, stems and
branches are red. Natural
growth is upright and bushy.
(Laburnum, UK, 1987)

**'Squadron Leader'**
Double H2 Trailer
*Tube* and *sepals* white. *Corolla*
a very pale shade of pink. The
flowers are medium-sized and
frilly, produced very freely,
mainly at the branch ends from

early in the season. *Foliage*
medium green. The growth is
short-jointed and very bushy.
(Goulding, UK, 1986)

**'Stad Elburg'**
Double H2 Trailer
Medium sized flowers. *Tube*
medium length, glossy carmine
red. *Sepals* crimson red, long
and broad, reflexing slightly.
*Corolla* violet blue streaked with
red and pink, fades to rosy
purple. *Foliage* medium green,
green veins, slightly serrated.
The natural growth is as a
trailer. Will make a good basket.
(Beek, Holland, 1982)

**'Stadt Bredevoort'**
Single H2 Bush
Medium-sized flower. *Tube* and
*sepals* spirea red. *Corolla* deep
robin red. *Foliage* medium
green. The natural growth is as
a rather lax upright. Could be
good for weeping standards.
(Kempinck, Holland, 1988)

**'Stadt Leonberg'**
Double H2 Lax bush
Medium sized flower. *Tube* and
*sepals* light rose. *Corolla*
cyclamen purple. *Foliage*
medium green. The growth is
upright but rather lax.
(Baum, Holland, 1983)

**'St Andrews'**
Single H2 Bush
*Tube* and recurving *sepals*
sparkling white. *Corolla* a clear
baby pink. The medium-sized
flowers are irregularly formed,
and several flowers are usually
formed from each leaf axil; the
petals are particularly clear
baby pink. *Foliage* medium
green. The growth is upright
and bushy.
(Goulding, UK, 1986)

**'Stanley Cash'**
Double H2 Trailer
*Tube* short and thick, white.
*Sepals* white with green tips,
short and broad. *Corolla* deep
royal purple, box-shaped. The
medium-sized blooms are very
compact and hold their shape
well over a long period. *Foliage*

medium green. Growth is
trailing, fairly vigorous and free-
flowering. Can be used as a bush
if stopping occurs at an early
stage. A very attractive cultivar,
but tends to fade badly as it ages.
(Pennisi, USA, 1970)

**'Stan's Choice'**
Single H2 Bush
Medium sized flower. *Tube*
rose. *Sepals* claret rose, with
crêped claret rose on the under
surface. *Corolla* white veined
with neyron rose. *Foliage* apple
green, slightly lighter
underneath. The growth is
short-jointed and very bushy.
(Hall, UK, 1987)

**'Star Ros'**
Single H2 Trailer
*Tube* short, white. *Sepals* long,
elegant and upswept, white
tipped with light rose. *Corolla*
clear rose. *Foliage* darkish
green. The natural growth is as
a trailer. Will make a very
attractive basket.
(Caunt, UK, 1985)

**'Stathern Surprise'**
Single H2 Bush
*Tube* crimson. *Sepals* carmine
rose. *Corolla* phlox purple,
heavily veined with crimson.
The medium-sized flowers are
very freely produced. The
growth is upright, short-jointed
and bushy.
(Pacey, UK, 1988)

**'Steeley'**
Double H2 Lax bush
*Tube* white, striped with
magenta. *Sepals* long and
broad, held horizontally, white
with very light purple shading
on the underside, green tips
recurving. *Corolla* opens deep
violet with neyron rose at the
base of the petals and matures
to cyclamen purple with rose at
the base. The blooms are very
large and fairly free. *Foliage*
medium green, lighter underneath. The growth is somewhat
lax for a bush yet rather stiff
for a trailer. ('Pio Pico' ×
'White King')
(Richardson, Australia, 1985)

F. SPECIOSA

'SPION KOP'

'STANLEY CASH'

'STEELEY'

**'Steeretje'**
Single H2 Bush
*Tube* of medium length, pink with a hint of aubergine. *Sepals* slightly pendant, also pink with aubergine. *Corolla* light aubergine. *Foliage* medium green. The growth is stiffly upright. Best grown under protection.
(Weeda, Holland, 1987)

**'Stella Ann'**
Triphylla type H1 Bush
*Tube* rather thick, tapering, poppy red. *Sepals* short, rather broad, chinese coral tipped with green; they point downwards and are held half-way below the horizontal. *Corolla* short, petals indian orange. The flowers are carried in large clusters at the ends of laterals. *Foliage* dark olive green with dark purple mid-ribs and strawberry-red undersides, the leaves large with heavy serrated edging. The growth is very vigorous and upright.
(Dunnett, UK, 1974)

**'Stevie Doige'**
Double H2 Lax bush
*Tube* white, veined with pink. *Sepals* whitish-pink and tipped yellowish-green. *Corolla* white veined with pink, with long streaks of pink on each outer petal. The blooms are large with long, whitish-pink buds. *Foliage* yellowish-green. The growth is rather lax so will make either a basket or a bush.
('Annabel' × 'Margaret')
(Weeks, UK, 1986)

**'Storm Petrel'**
Double H2 Bush
*Tube* and *sepals* brilliant white. *Corolla* deep blue. The medium-sized blooms have very clean-cut colouring. *Foliage* medium green. The growth is upright and bushy.
(Holland, 1980s)

**'Stormy Sunset'**
Double H2 Trailer
*Tubes* white with a pink flush. *Sepals* pink and partially recurving. *Corolla* violet and pink. *Foliage* dark green. The growth is naturally trailing, but assistance can be given by early and frequent stopping. Good for all types of hanging containers.
(Stubbs, USA, 1976)

**'Strawberry Delight'**
Double H2 Trailer
*Tube* medium length and thickness, crimson. *Sepals* crimson, short, broad, reflexed. *Corolla* white with pink veining, numerous petaloids white flushed pink. Ragged, loose-petalled, medium bloom. *Foliage* green and bronze with yellow overtones. Growth is spreading and very strong. Excellent for all types of hanging containers. ('Trase' × 'Golden Marinka')
(Gadsby, UK, 1970)

**'Strawberry Sundae'**
Double H2 Trailer
*Tube* short, white. *Sepals* broad, white tipped with green. *Corolla* pink with a slight touch of lilac. The large blooms are freely produced for their size. *Foliage* large, medium green. Growth is naturally trailing.
(Kennett, USA, 1958)

**'Strawberry Supreme'**
Double H2 Bush
*Tube* and *sepals* waxy crimson. *Corolla* white flushed carmine rose well down into outer petaloids. The large blooms are produced early and very freely. *Foliage* medium green, medium-sized, serrated leaves. The growth is upright and bushy. ('Trase' × 'Golden Marinka')
(Gadsby, UK, 1970)

**'String of Pearls'**
Semi-double H2 Bush
*Tube* pale rose, short and thick. *Sepals* pale china rose with green tips, held well back. Corolla pale rose purple with lavender veins. The flowers are medium-sized and are carried right down the stems like 'strings of pearls'. *Foliage* light to medium green, small, serrated leaves. The upright growth is quite strong. An excellent bush for all purposes. Not easy to train into any recognized shape. (*F. lycioides* seedling)
(Pacey, UK, 1976)

**'Subliem'**
Single H2 Lax bush
Medium-sized single or semi-double flower. *Tube* shell pink. *Sepals* strawberry. *Corolla* violet. *Foliage* medium green. The natural growth is as a rather lax upright bush.
(Moerman, Holland, 1990)

**'Sugar Almond'**
Double H2 Bush
*Tube* and *sepals* creamy white flushed with pink; the sepals are pink underneath. *Corolla* pale pink flushed rose pink. The medium-sized blooms are freely produced. *Foliage* medium green. Growth is upright and bushy. (('Angela Leslie' × 'Blush of Dawn') ×)
(Hobson, UK, 1978)

**'Sugar Blues'**
Double H2 Trailer
*Tube* white, tinged pink. *Sepals* white on the top side and have touches of pink underneath, long. *Corolla* dark blue fading to violet blue, extremely long and beautiful with pink blending from the centre into the blue. The large flowers are fairly freely produced. *Foliage* is medium green. The natural growth is as a trailer so an excellent basket can be produced.
(Martin, USA, 1964)

**'Sugar Plum'**
Single H2 Lax bush
*Tube* short thick, cherry red. *Sepals* bright cherry red with a crêpe texture underneath, held horizontally and curling at tips. *Corolla* pale lavender and veined bright pink. The good-sized flowers are bell-shaped. *Foliage* yellowish-green. Growth is rather lax upright. It is possible to use in baskets if assisted by weights.
(Hall, UK, 1982)

274

'STORMY SUNSET'    'STRAWBERRY DELIGHT'

'STRAWBERRY SUNDAE'    'STRAWBERRY SUPREME'

'STRING OF PEARLS'    'SUGAR BLUES'

**'Suikerbossie' ('Sugarbush')**
Single H2 Bush
*Tube* small, light lime green
with a pink flush. *Sepals*
empire rose on top, carmine on
the undersides, green tips
recurving slightly. *Corolla*
purple and fades with age.
*Foliage* dark olive green on
top, lighter underneath. The
small flowers are very freely
produced. The natural growth
is upright and self-branching.
(*F. magellanica* var.
*longipedunculata* ×)
(Brouwer, Holland, 1985)

**'Sultan'**
Double H2 Lax bush
Medium-sized flower. *Tubes*
and *sepals* are pink. *Corolla*
burgundy red. *Foliage* medium
green. The natural growth is
rather lax and upright.
(Strumper, Holland, 1984)

**'Summer Night'**
Double H2 Stiff trailer
Medium-sized flower. *Tube*
rose-coloured. *Sepals* reddish-
purple, and the *corolla*
aubergine. *Foliage* medium
green. The growth is rather
stiff for a trailer but very lax
for a bush. Supports will need
to be given.
(Kempinck, Hoilland, 1989)

**'Sunkissed'**
Double H2 Trailer
Medium-sized flowers. *Tubes*
white, short, thick. *Sepals*
azalea pink beneath, green tips;
short, broad, reflexed. *Corolla*
jasper red with pink marbling,
fairly compact. *Foliage* medium
green. The growth is rather lax
so can be used for either
hanging containers or as bush
plants if the necessary supports
are provided.
(Tiret, USA, 1957)

**'Sunningdale'**
Triphylla type H1 Bush
A true terminal-flowering
fuchsia. *Tube* long, thin,
coloured orange. *Sepals* short,
pendant, orange. *Corolla* also
orange. *Foliage* light green and
bronzy. Growth is upright and

self-branching. As it retains its
lower leaves very well it is
justifiably popular with
exhibitors.
(Goulding, UK, 1986)

**'Sunny'**
Single H2 Lax bush
*Tube* and *sepals* pale coral.
*Corolla* red with burnt edges.
The small flowers are very
freely produced. *Foliage*
medium green. The growth is
lax so can be used for either
hanging containers or as
bushes.
(Fuchsia Forest, USA, 1968)

**'Sunny Smiles'**
Single H2 Trailer
*Tube* long, pale pink. *Sepals*
long, narrow, held well out,
carmine rose tipped with green
on top, undersides empire rose.
*Corolla* crimson flushed with
claret rose. The flowers are
bell-shaped and large for a
single. *Foliage* medium green.
The natural growth is as a
trailer. Pinch early to train to
shape. ('Pink Galore' ×
'Athela')
(Gadsby, UK, 1968)

**'Sunray'**
Single H2 Bush
*Tubes* red, short. *Sepals* red on
top, deeper shade on underside,
reflexed. *Corolla* mauve, small,
compact. The beauty of this
fuchsia lies in its *foliage* which
is a mixture of light green,
cream, edges and flushed red.
Growth is upright and bushy.
The plant is very versatile but
is best used in patio tubs.
*Foliage* varies considerably
according to the conditions
under which it grows.
(Rudd, UK, 1872)

**'Sunset'**
Single H2 Bush
*Tube* pink, short. *Sepals* pale
pink on top, deeper pink
underneath, tipped with green.
*Corolla* glowing coral.
Medium-sized flowers are
freely produced. The blooms
open bell-shaped and appear
early in the season. *Foliage*

light green with reddish veins,
serrated. The upward growth is
very strong and bushy.
('Rolla' × 'Aurora Superba')
(Niederholzer, USA, 1938)

**'Supernova'**
Single H2 Bush
*Tube* very short, glossy deep
pink. *Sepals* glossy deep pink
on top and matt mid-pink
underneath. *Corolla* white,
veined mid-pink at base. The
flowers are medium-sized and
flare like hooped petticoats,
upward-looking and very
freely produced. *Foliage*
medium green. Short-jointed,
strong upright and bushy
grower.
(Clitheroe, UK, 1984)

**'Superstar'**
Single H2 Bush
*Tube* and *sepals* phlox pink
tipped with green. *Corolla* rose
purple edged with deeper
purple. The medium-sized
blooms are produced in great
numbers. The natural growth is
strongly upright and bushy.
('Cambridge Louie' × 'Estelle
Marie')
(Sinton, UK, 1988)

**'Susan Allen'**
Single H2 Bush
*Tube* short, crimson. *Sepals*
short, broad, crimson. *Corolla*
cyclamen purple. The blooms
are of medium size and freely
produced. *Foliage* dark green
with reddish stems. Growth is
upright, bushy and self-
branching. ('Albion' ×
'Rosedale')
(Allen, UK, 1974)

**'Susan Daley'**
Single H2 Bush
*Tube* small, white. *Sepals* also
white, tipped with green and
fold back towards the tube.
*Corolla* tyrian purple at the edge
of the petals, fading through
magenta to almost white at the
base. The fairly small flowers
are freely produced. *Foliage*
medium green. Growth is
upright and bushy.
(Porter, UK, 1985)

276

'SUIKERBOSSIE'

'SUNRAY'

'SUNNY SMILES'

'SUPERNOVA'

**'Susan Ford'**
Double H2 Bush
*Tube* short and thin, neyron rose. *Sepals* neyron rose with a crêpe effect on the underside, short, broad, reflexing. *Corolla* imperial purple fading to cyclamen purple. The flowers are rosette-shaped. *Foliage* dark green with serrated edges. Growth is upright, self-branching, bushy. ('La Campanella' × 'Winston Churchill) (Clyne, UK, 1974)

**'Susan Green'**
Single H2 Trailer
*Tube* and *sepals* pale pink; sepals have green tips. *Corolla* bell-shaped, coral pink. *Foliage* medium green. Growth is fairly strong and even with good self-branching stems. Superb baskets can be made with comparative ease. Worth trying as weeping standard. (Caunt, UK, 1981)

**'Susan Jill'**
Double H2 Bush
Medium-sized flower. *Tube* white flushed with pale pink. *Sepals* pale pink. *Corolla* spectrum violet. *Foliage* medium green. The growth is strongly upright and bushy. ('Paula Jane' × 'Blush o' Dawn') (Tite, UK, 1987)

**'Susan Skeen'**
Single H2 Bush
Medium-sized flower. *Tube* and *sepals* apple-blossom pink. *Corolla* apple-blossom white. *Foliage* medium green. The natural growth is as an upright bush. Its habit is short-jointed, self-branching and bushy. (Webb, UK, 1993)

**'Susan Travis'**
Single H3 Bush
*Tube* and slightly recurving *sepals* deepish pink. *Corolla* rose pink and paling towards the base of the petals. *Foliage* medium green. The medium-sized flowers are freely produced on strong branches. H. and S. 24–30in (60–75cm). (Travis, UK, 1958)

**'Susie Olces'**
Double H2 Trailer
*Tube* white. *Sepals* large and broad, also white. *Corolla* pale blue. The largish blooms are freely produced. *Foliage* medium green. The growth is rather lax. Can be used in baskets or as bushes with the necessary supports. (Martin, USA, 1960)

**'Swanley Gem'**
Single H2 Bush
*Tube* medium length, scarlet. *Sepals* short, broad and reflexing, also scarlet. *Corolla* violet with reddish veins and a paler shade of scarlet at the base of the petals. The flower opens saucer-shaped and becomes paler as the bloom ages. *Foliage* mid-green, the leaves fairly small. Growth is upright, self-branching and bushy. (Cannell, UK, 1901)

**'Swanley Yellow'**
Single H2 Bush
*Tube* long, orange-pink. *Sepals* narrow and upturned, also orange-pink. *Corolla* rich orange-vermilion, small and compact, blooms long and slender. *Foliage* bronzy green with medium to large serrated leaves. Growth is upright, vigorous and bushy. The flowers are freely produced. Needs early pinching to make a decent shape. (Cannell, UK, 1900)

**'Sweetheart'**
Single H2 Bush
*Tube* long, white. *Sepals* short reflexing, white with a pink flush on the undersides, with green tips. *Corolla* pinkish-cerise shaded white at the base of the petals. The flowers are medium-sized and bell-shaped. *Foliage* medium green with small serrated leaves. The upright growth is vigorous and self-branching. Good exhibition variety, but watch out for *botrytis*. (Van Weiringen, Holland, 1970)

**'Sweet Lavender'**
Semi-double H2 Bush
*Tube* and *sepals* a delicate pale pink. *Corolla* lavender. *Foliage* medium green. The natural growth is as an upright and self-branching bush. (Meier, UK, 1994)

**'Sweet Leilani'**
Double H2 Bush
*Tube* short, thick, pale pink. *Sepals* short, broad and curl up over the tube, pale pink. *Corolla* pale lavender blue, very full and ruffled; pink markings on the outer petals. *Foliage* light to medium green. (Tiret, USA, 1957)

**'Sweet Revenge'**
Double H2 Bush
The medium length *tube* is neyron rose. The broad *sepals* are also neyron rose. The *corolla* is hyacinth blue shading to wisteria blue. The *petaloids* are neyron rose. The *foliage* is medium green and the *leaves* are long and narrow. ('Rose Bower' × 'Magenta Flash') (Gadsby, UK, 1975)

**'Swingtime'**
Double H2 Trailer
*Tube* medium length and thickness, scarlet. *Sepals* broad and reflexing, also scarlet. *Corolla* pure white with scarlet veining. The flowers are very full and fluffy. *Foliage* medium to darkish green with red veins. Growth is lax upright but very vigorous. If the branches are allowed to grow to a reasonable length and weights are placed at the ends, an excellent basket can be developed. (Tiret, USA, 1950)

*F. sylvatica*
Species H1 Bush
*Tube* pink. *Sepals* small, pink on pale red. *Corolla* crimson to purplish-red. The smallish flowers are carried in terminal racemes. *Foliage* medium green. Growth is as a low shrub. Synonymous with *F. atroruba* and *F. nigricans*. (Bentham, Colombia, 1845)

278

'SUSAN FORD'

'SUSAN JILL'

'SWANLEY GEM'

'SWINGTIME'

'SWEETHEART'

**'Sylvia Barker'**
Single H2 Bush
*Tube* long, waxy white. *Sepals* held well out, also waxy white and have green tips. *Corolla* scarlet with a slight smoky cast. The blooms are fairly small but are freely produced. *Foliage* dark green with veins that stand out. Growth is rather lax. (Barker, UK, 1973)

**x'Sylvia Dyos'**
Double H2 Trailer
*Tube* white. *Sepals* recurving, white flushed with coral. *Corolla* pink marbled orange. The medium-sized flowers are very freely produced. *Foliage* medium green. Growth is rather lax so will make an ideal plant for hanging containers. (Dyos, UK, 1993)

**'Sylvia Foster'**
Double H2 Lax bush
*Tube* pale pink. *Sepals* pink on the upper surface and crêped pink on the lower. *Corolla* opens as pink and matures to light pink; the edges of the petals are very wavy. *Foliage* medium green. Growth is rather lax but will make a bush or basket if required. (Foster, UK, 1988)

**'Sylvy'**
Single H2 Bush
*Tube* short, barrel-shaped, bright pink. *Sepals* also bright pink. *Corolla* deep rose. The small flowers are produced in great quantity. *Foliage* strong, medium to dark green. Growth is upright, self-branching and bushy. ('Jack Acland' × 'Liebreiz') (Dyos, UK, 1978)

# T

**'Taddle'**
Single H2 Bush
*Tube* short, thick, deep rose pink. *Sepals* short and broad, reflex completely, rose pink. *Corolla* white with pinkish veins. The blooms are compact and of medium size. The *flowers* are very freely produced. *Foliage* light to medium green. The natural growth is upright, strong and bushy. (Gubler, UK, 1974)

**'Taffeta Bow'**
Double H2 Trailer
*Tube* short, pink. *Sepals* carmine rose, long and with a crêpe effect on the undersides. *Corolla* purple-violet with serrated edges to the petals; it opens compact and flares as it ages. The flowers are very attractive, medium- to large-sized. *Foliage* dark green with crimson veins. The natural growth is as a rather stiff trailer. Very free-flowering for the size of the blooms. (Stubbs, USA, 1974)

**'Taffy'**
Single H2 Trailer
*Tube* long, white flushed with pink. *Sepals* long and narrow, pink on the top with a stripe running down the centre, a deeper shade of pink underneath, with green tips. *Corolla* salmon pink. The petals are long and serrated. *Foliage* light green with heavily serrated leaves. Growth is very vigorous and naturally trailing; can be rampant, and difficult to train to any recognized shape. (Martin, USA, 1961)

**'Tamar Isobel'**
Single H2 Bush
*Tube* pale pink. *Sepals* palish pink, fully recurved. *Corolla* reddish-purple. The flowers are medium-sized but very prolific. *Foliage* medium green. The natural growth is as a strong upright bush. ('Joy Patmore' × 'Border Queen') (Mitchinson, UK, 1988)

**'Tam o' Shanter'**
Double H2 Bush
*Tube* and *sepals* flesh pink. *Corolla* dark purple verging on hyacinth blue, streaked with varying shades of pink. The medium to largish blooms are freely produced. *Foliage* medium green. The growth is strong and upright. (Mitchinson, UK, 1984)

**'Tamworth'**
Single H2 Bush
*Tube* medium length, pure white. *Sepals* have green tips and reflex slightly, also pure white. *Corolla* white at the base, then a band of salmon pink turning to rich purple at the edge of the petals. The blooms are medium-sized and fairly compact. The flowers are very freely produced. *Foliage* light green. Growth is upright, vigorous and bushy. (Handley, UK, 1976)

**'Tangerine'**
Single H2 Bush
*Tube* long, medium thickness, dark flesh pink. *Sepals* greenish flushed carmine with green tips, short, medium width; held well out from the corolla. *Corolla* brilliant salmon orange. The flowers are fairly small, very freely produced, rather compact in form. *Foliage* fairly large, dark green. Growth is vigorously upright and will require early stopping to obtain any sort of shape. (*F. cordifolia* ×) (Tiret, USA, 1949)

**'Tania Leanne'**
Single H2 Bush
*Tube* light neyron rose. *Sepals* light neyron rose with yellow-green recurved tips. *Corolla* opens spectrum violet veined magenta, maturing to imperial purple veined neyron rose. A number of petaloids, imperial purple heavily splashed with neyron rose. *Foliage* scheele's green with red veins. Upward growth is quite strong but early 'stopping' is recommended. ('Pink Marshmallow' × 'Midnight Sun') (Richardson, Australia, 1987)

'SYLVIA FOSTER'

'TADDLE'

'TAFFETA BOW'

'TAMAR ISOBEL'

'TANGERINE'

**'Tanya Bridger'**
Double H2 Bush
*Tube* long and thin, white.
*Sepals*, broad and reflexed, also
white. *Corolla* pale lavender
with pink tinge on the outer
petals. The flowers are of
medium size, compact and very
free-flowering. *Foliage* pale
green with finely serrated edges,
ovate. Growth is upright, self-
branching and bushy.
(Bridger, UK, 1958)

**'Tarra Valley'**
Single H2 Bush
'Species hybrid'. *Tube* olive
green. *Sepals* light green with
reflexed tips. *Corolla* dark plum.
*Foliage* mid-green on the upper
surface, olive green on the lower.
(*F. colensoi* × *F. splendens*)
(Felix, Holland, 1987)

**'Task Force'**
Single H2 Bush
*Tube* long, white. *Sepals* held
well above the horizontal,
white on top, flushed pale lilac
underneath. *Corolla* square-
shaped, opens cyclamen purple
and matures to magenta. The
flowers are quite large and
freely produced. *Foliage* very
large, forest green, a slight
distraction from the flowers.
Growth is vigorously upright
and bushy. Will need frequent
stopping to acquire the desired
shapes. ('Cloverdale Pearl' ×
'Celia Smedley')
(Redfern, UK, 1984)

**'Tausendschön'**
Double H2 Bush
*Tube* and *sepals* lacquer red.
*Corolla* soft pink. The large
blooms are produced early and
freely. *Foliage* medium green.
The natural growth is upright
and bushy.
(Nagel, Germany, 1919)

**'Ted Heath'**
Double H2 Bush
*Tube* and *sepals* cream with
suffused tints of delicate pink.
*Corolla* soft cream with faint
pink shading at the base of the
petals. The blooms are large
and fully double. *Foliage*

medium green. Growth is
strong and upright.
(Clark, UK, 1977)

**'Ted Perry'**
Double H2 Lax bush
*Tube* white. *Sepals* reflexing,
white flushed with pink.
*Corolla* white flushed pink at
the base of the petals. *Foliage*
medium green. The growth is
lax upright, self-branching and
bushy.
(Pacey, UK, 1988)

**'Television'**
Double H2 Lax bush
*Tube* medium length, white.
*Sepals* white on top, pale pink
on the underside. *Corolla* deep
orchid, splashed with fuchsia
pink. The flowers are of
medium size and fairly compact.
*Foliage* medium green. Growth
is rather lax so could be used
for bushes or baskets.
(Walker and Jones, USA, 1950)

**'Tempo Doeloe'**
Single H2 Trailer
*Tube* medium-sized, light
neyron rose. *Sepals* light
neyron rose on the upper
surface, neyron rose on the
lower. *Corolla* magenta with a
rose base, and smooth to wavy
petal edges. *Foliage* light to
medium green. The growth is
rather lax for a bush yet rather
stiff for a basket; either could
be used but the necessary
supports will need to be given.
(de Graaff, Holland, 1987)

**'Temptation'**
Single H2 Bush
*Tube* long, thickish, white
flushed with pink. *Sepals* long,
broad, held well out from the
corolla, also white with a pink
flush. *Corolla* bright reddish-
orange shading to white at the
base of the petals. *Foliage*
darkish green, leaves longish
and serrated. Growth is upright
and bushy.
(Peterson, USA, 1959)

**'Tennessee Waltz'**
Semi-double H2 Bush
*Tube* medium length, rose

madder. *Sepals* long, broad and
upward curving, also rose
madder. *Corolla* lilac lavender
with splashes of rose to the
petals. The bloom is of medium
size but the flowers are rather
loose and the petal length is
uneven. *Foliage* medium green,
medium-sized, leaves serrated.
Growth is vigorously upright,
self-branching and very
free-flowering.
(Walker and Jones, USA, 1950)

**'Terrysue'**
Single H2 Lax bush
*Tube* long and thin, light
salmon pink. *Sepals* long and
slender, held horizontally and
well out, salmon pink on top
and a little deeper underneath,
recurving green tips. *Corolla*
opens deep salmon and
matures to a slightly paler
colour; square and slightly
flared. *Foliage* medium green,
medium-sized, green veins,
serrated. The growth is rather
lax for a bush yet rather stiff
for a trailer. ('Coachman' ×
'Lye's Unique')
(Caunt, UK, 1984)

**'Teupel's Erfolg'**
Double H2 Bush
Medium sized flower. *Tube* pale
red. *Sepals* pale red striped
with red. *Corolla* light old rose.
*Foliage* medium green. The
natural growth is as an upright
bush.
(Teupel, Germany, 1935)

**'Texas Longhorn'**
Double H2 Trailer
*Tube* long and fairly slender,
scarlet. *Sepals* very long,
narrow scarlet and droop
downwards. *Corolla* white
with cerise veins. The flowers
are very large and long. *Foliage*
mid-green with reddish veins.
The natural growth is very lax
and can be used as a trailer.
Flowers are produced
intermittently during the
season. The size of the bloom
does not really compensate for
the dearth of flowers that it
exhibits.
(Fuchsia La, USA, 1961)

'TASK FORCE'

'TAUSENDSCHÖN'

'TENNESSEE WALTZ'

'TEUPEL'S ERFOLG'

'TEXAS LONGHORN'

**'Thalia'**
Triphylla type H1 Bush
*Tube* long and very slender,
deep flame red. *Sepals* small
and pointed, also flame red.
The petals in the corolla are
very small and are orange-
scarlet. The flowers are
produced in great quantity
throughout the season in
terminal racemes. *Foliage* dark
olive green with magenta veins
and ribs; the reverse of the
leaves is a delightful light
purple. Growth is vigorously
upright. Early stopping is
advised to encourage the
plant into the best bushy
shape.
(Bonstedt, Germany, 1905)

**'Thamar'**
Single H2 Bush
Small pansy-eyed bloom held
outwards and upwards. *Tube*
and *sepals* white. *Corolla*
petals are pale blue with white
insertions. *Foliage* medium
green. The growth is naturally
upright and bushy. One that
catches the eye when exhibited.
(Springer, UK, 1987)

**'Thames Valley'**
Semi-double H2 Trailer
*Tube* and *sepals* pale pink.
*Corolla* mauve. *Foliage*
medium green. Growth is
naturally spreading, short-
jointed and free-flowering. The
natural growth is as a trailer;
will make a good plant for a
hanging container.
(Clyne, UK, 1976)

**'That's It'**
Semi-double H2 Lax bush
*Tube* thick, middle length
smoky orange-red. *Sepals* long
and broad curl upwards,
orange red, deeper on the
underside. *Corolla* orchid
purple shaded pink at the base
of the petals, veined reddish.
*Foliage* medium green,
medium-sized, finely serrated.
Growth is upright and bushy
but rather lax. Will need
support for the large heavy
blooms.
(Fuchsia La, USA, 1968)

**'The Aristocrat'**
Double H2 Bush
*Tube* long, creamy white. *Sepals*
pale rose pink and have white
tips. *Corolla* flaring, central
petals creamy white and veined
with rose, outer petals pale rose
pink; the edges of the petals are
serrated. *Foliage* medium green.
Growth is upright, self-
branching and vigorous.
(Waltz, USA, 1953)

**'The Doctor'**
Single H2 Trailer
*Tube* long and broad, pale flesh
pink. *Sepals* flesh pink on top
and slightly darker on the
undersides, held well out from
the corolla. *Corolla* rosy salmon,
compact and medium-sized.
*Foliage* mid-green. Growth is
rather lax for a bush but tends
to be rather stiff for a trailer.
(Castle Nurseries, UK, date
unknown)

**'The Girl's Brigade'**
Single H2 Stiff trailer
*Tube* and *sepals*. *Corolla* red.
The flowers are produced very
freely over a long season. *Foliage*
medium green. The natural
growth is rather stiff for a trailer
and yet rather lax for a bush. A
strong-growing plant that needs
to be stopped just twice to get
the number of branches to make
an acceptable plant.
(Bielby/Oxtoby, UK, 1993)

**'The Madame'**
Double H2 Bush
*Tube* medium length, pale red.
*Sepals* short, broad and
reflexed, also pale red. *Corolla*
burgundy red, full and
compact. The blooms are of
medium size. *Foliage* medium
green with serrated edges.
Growth is strong and upright.
(Tiret, USA, 1963)

**'The Patriot'**
Double H2 Trailer
*Tube* medium length, pink.
*Sepals* white flushed pink with
green tips, fairly broad and
reflexing. *Corolla* white, blooms
very loose and with many
petaloids. *Foliage* large, medium

green and has serrated edges.
The natural growth is vigorously
trailing and free-flowering.
(Tiret, USA, 1971)

**'Therese Dupuis'**
Single H3 Bush
*Tubes* and *sepals* crimson.
*Corolla* reddish-purple; flowers
large. *Foliage* medium to dark
green. The upward growth of
the plant is very strong and
vigorous. H. and S. 36–48in
(90–120cm).
(Lemoine, France, Year
unknown)

**'The Rival'**
Double H2 Lax bush
*Tube* long and fairly thick,
white. *Sepals* white with a pink
flush on top, the lower sides a
deeper shade of pink; long and
broad, curl upwards and out.
*Corolla* lavender, pink, and
deeper pink shades. The petals
are long, and the bloom is
fairly large and compact.
*Foliage* medium green. The
growth is rather lax.
(Walker, USA, 1970)

**'The Tarns'**
Single H3 Bush
*Tube* short, pale pink. *Sepals*
very long, pale pink with a rose
reverse long, narrow, reflexing.
*Corolla* violet-blue paling to
rose at the base of the petals.
The medium-sized flowers are
very freely produced. *Foliage*
dark green, small, narrow,
heavily serrated. Growth is very
strong, upright and hardy. H.
and S. 36–48in (90–120cm).
(Travis, UK, 1962)

**'Theroigne de Mericourt'**
Double H1 Bush
*Tube* pale cerise, short. *Sepals*
broad, short, scarlet-crimson.
*Corolla* creamy white veined
cerise at the base. *Foliage*
medium green with cerise veins.
Although the blooms are very
large they are freely produced.
Growth is upright and bushy
although early stopping will be
necessary to promote the
bushiness.
(Lemoine, France, 1903)

'THAT'S IT'

'THE DOCTOR'

'THE MADAME'

'THE PATRIOT'

'THEROIGNE DE MERICOURT'

**'Think Pink'**
*Encliandra* type H2 Bush
Very small flowers. *Tube* and
*sepals* dark rose. *Corolla* rose.
*Foliage* medium green. The
natural growth is strongly
upright and bushy.
(Plows, USA, 1989)

**'This England'**
Double H2 Lax bush/trailer
*Tube* longish, white faintly
tinged with orchid pink. *Sepals*
broad, white with the base and
tips tinged with orchid pink,
recurving up to the tube. *Corolla*
white faintly tinged with orchid
pink. The large frilly blooms are
fully double. *Foliage* large,
golden-green maturing to mid-
green. Growth is semi-trailing,
the lax habit being suitable for
baskets or weeping standards.
(Sport of 'La France')
(Brackenbury, UK, 1982)

**'Thompsonii'**
Single H3 Bush
*Tube* and *sepals* scarlet. *Corolla*
purple. The smallish but long
flowers are very freely produced.
*Foliage* medium green, fairly
long and thin. The upward
growth is very vigorous. H. and
S. 36–48in (90–120cm).
(*F. magellanica* ×)
(Thompson, UK, 1840)

**'Thornley's Hardy'**
Single H3 Lax bush
*Tube* white, slender and of
medium length. *Sepals* narrow
and upturned, white with green
tips. *Corolla* cerise shading to
white at the base of the petals.
The flowers are fairly small and
compact. *Foliage* mid-green
with finely serrated edges to the
leaves. Growth is rather lax so
will need supporting as a bush.
(Thornley, UK, 1970)

**'Three Cheers'**
Single H2 Bush
*Tube* long and slender, bright
red. *Sepals* long, narrow and
reflexing, are bright red. *Corolla*
dark-blue veined red, with a
white mark at the base of each
petal. The medium-sized flowers
open flat. *Foliage* medium

green. Growth is upright, bushy
and very free-flowering.
('Swanley Gem' seedling)
(Greer, UK, 1969)

**'Three Counties'**
Single H2 Bush
*Tube* scarlet cerise. *Sepals*
cerise, short, broad, reflexing.
*Corolla* bluish-violet. The large
to medium-sized flowers are
very freely produced. *Foliage*
medium green. The natural
growth is as an upright bush.
(Raiser and date unknown)

**'Thunderbird'**
Double H2 Trailer
*Tube* neyron rose, long and
slender. *Sepals* neyron rose, long
and narrow, held well back from
the corolla. *Corolla* vermilion
with a paler rose shading at the
base of each petal. The blooms
are rather long but very
compact. *Foliage* medium green.
Makes a superb basket.
(Tiret, USA, 1957)

**F. thymifolia**
Species H1 Bush
*Tube* white, reddening with age.
*Sepals* white, and spread.
*Corolla* white becoming reddish-
purple as it matures. The very
small flowers are carried in
profusion. *Foliage* small,
medium green on top and paler
underneath. The natural growth
is upright and bushy with very
wiry, slender branches.
(Mexico and Guatamala)

**F. thymifolia** ssp **minimiflora**
Species H1 Bush
*Tube* whitish to reddish. *Sepals*
whitish to reddish, reflexed and
spreading. *Corolla* white to
reddish. *Foliage* medium green
on top but paler underneath;
slightly larger than *F.
thymifolia*. The small flowers
are produced on long, wiry and
slender branches.
(Mexico)

**F. thymifolia** ssp **thymifolia**
Species H1 Bush
As given above, except that the
flower is pink maturing to
purple.

**F. tilletiana**
Species H1 Bush
*Tube* long, tapering pink.
*Sepals* neatly turned up and
curl well back. The long pink
stamens are tipped with yellow
anthers and are devoid of any
corolla. The flowers are carried
at the ends of the branches.
*Foliage* medium green, leaves
rather sparse, but judicious
stopping will encourage as
many as three branches from a
single node; a reasonably thick,
bush-type plant can therefore
be produced.
(Venezuela)

**'Timlin Brened'**
Triphylla type H1 Bush
*Tube* long, flamingo pink.
*Sepals* short, shell pink with
green tips. *Corolla* petals are
short, oval and coral pink.
*Foliage* deep olive green with
red veins and satin sheen; the
leaves are large. Growth is
vigorously upright, bushy and
free-flowering.
(Baker/Dunnett, UK, 1974)

**'Tineke'**
Single H2 Bush
Medium-sized flower. *Tube* and
*sepals* pale rose, tipped with
green. *Corolla* rosy purple.
*Foliage* medium green. The
natural growth is upright and
bushy.
(Breemer, Holland, 1990)

**'Ting a Ling'**
Single H2 Bush
*Tube* thick, medium length,
white. *Sepals* white, long and
narrow, curl upwards. *Corolla*
bell-shaped, medium sized and
also white. *Foliage* medium
green, medium-sized, serrated.
Growth is vigorously upright
and free-flowering. It has two
faults: it is prone to *botrytis*; it
tends to mark easily.
(Schnabel-Paskesen, USA,
1959)

'THIS ENGLAND'

'THORNLEY'S HARDY'

'THREE COUNTIES'

'TING A LING'

**'Tinkerbell'**
Single H3 Bush
*Tube* and *sepals* red. *Corolla*
white. The small flowers are
bell-shaped and carried in
profusion. *Foliage* dark green.
The growth is upright yet
dainty and arching. Very
suitable for rockeries or the
front of a hardy border. H. and
S. 6–12in (15–30cm).
(Tabraham, UK, 1976)

**'Tintern Abbey'**
Single H2 Bush
*Tube* and *sepals* light cerise.
*Corolla* is rosy lilac. The small
flowers are carried in
profusion. Growth is upright
and bushy. *Foliage* medium
green. Will make a very good
bush or a standard.
(Gunter, UK, 1970)

**'Toby Bridger'**
Double H2 Bush
*Tube* white, short, thickish.
*Sepals* bright pink with green
tips; short, broad, held over
corolla. *Corolla* pink, veined
with a deeper pink. The largish
flowers are very freely
produced. *Foliage* darkish
green. The natural growth is as
an upright bush.
(Bridger, UK, 1958)

**'Tolling Bell'**
Single H2 Bush
*Tube* short, thick, scarlet.
*Sepals* also scarlet, broad,
recurving. *Corolla* pure white
veined with cerise. The largish
flowers are very freely
produced. The name is rather
appropriate as the flowers are
in the shape of a perfect bell.
*Foliage* mid-green, medium-
sized, serrated. The growth is
upright and bushy.
(Turner, UK, 1964)

**'Tom Hobson'**
Double H2 Bush
Flowers medium-sized. *Tube*
and *sepals* are pale pink.
*Corolla* multicoloured rose and
purple. *Foliage* medium green.
The natural growth is upright,
self-branching and bushy.
(Hobson, UK, 1980)

**'Tom Knights'**
Single H2 Bush
*Tube* short, flesh-coloured.
*Sepals* small, flesh-coloured,
held well up with recurving
tips. *Corolla* small lavender
blue to muted violet. The
cultivar is very floriferous and
outward pointing. *Foliage* light
to medium green. Growth is
upright, self-branching and
bushy. Makes a superb show
plant in larger pots.
(Goulding, UK, 1983)

**'Tom Redfern'**
Double H2 Bush
*Tube* medium sized, almost pure
white. *Sepals* horizontally held,
white on top and white faintly
touched with pink underneath;
recurved green tips. *Corolla*
violet-blue with white markings
at the base of the petals,
maturing to violet. *Foliage* dark
sage green. The growth is
naturally upright and bushy.
(Redfern, UK, 1987)

**'Tom Silcock'**
Semi-double H2 Bush
*Tube* medium sized, white.
*Sepals* fully up, white flushed
with pink on the upper surface,
white flushed rose on the lower.
*Corolla* dark violet with pink at
the base of the petals. *Foliage*
dark green.
(McDonald, UK, 1989)

**'Tom Thorne'**
Semi-double H2 Bush
*Tube* medium length, white.
*Sepals* white on top with green
tips, the undersides flushed
with pink. *Corolla* white with
pale pink veining. The flowers
are medium sized and rather
loose-petalled. *Foliage* medium
green. Growth is upright, self-
branching and free-flowering.
(Bridger, UK, 1959)

**'Tom Thumb'**
Single H3 Bush
*Tube* short and thin, carmine.
*Sepals* short, held down from
the horizontal, also carmine.
*Corolla* mauve-purple. The
flowers are small and very
compact. *Foliage* small,

medium green with finely
serrated edging. Growth is
upright and bushy, self-
branching and free-flowering.
H. and S. 12–18in (30–45cm).
(Baudinat, France, 1850)

**'Tom West'**
Single H2 Bush
*Tube* small, red. *Sepals* short,
broad, also red, held well out.
*Corolla* purple, small and
compact. *Foliage* (for which
this plant is usually grown)
variegated pale greyish-green
and cream, the leaves medium-
sized. Growth is rather lax
upright, but self-branching
and fairly vigorous. The best
foliage colour comes with the
fresh young shoots; regular
stopping provides a colourful
plant.
(Meillez, France, 1853)

**'Tom Woods'**
Single H2 Lax bush
*Tube* short, waxy white. *Sepals*
also waxy white. *Corolla*
purple fading to magenta with
maturity. The small flowers are
very prolific. *Foliage* pale
green. The growth is lax
upright and short-jointed.
(Golics, UK, 1980)

**'Topaz'**
Double H2 Trailer
*Tube* medium length and
thickness, light coral to white.
*Sepals* white flushed light coral
on top, deeper underneath.
*Corolla* centre petals violet
purple with topaz marbling,
outer petals coral pink and
topaz marbled violet-purple.
Petals ruffled. Medium-sized
blooms. *Foliage* dark green
with roundish leaves.
(Kennett, USA, 1961)

**'Topper'**
Semi-double H2 Bush
*Tube* and *sepals* red. *Corolla*
dark blue with a white cloud
over the centre of each petal.
The medium-sized, flowers are
freely produced. *Foliage* dark
green, slim. The growth is
upright and bushy.
(Brown and Soules, USA, 1952)

'TINTERN ABBEY'

'TOBY BRIDGER'

'TOLLING BELL'

'TOM THUMB'

'TOM KNIGHTS'

**'Torch'**
Double H2 Bush
*Tube* waxy, shiny pink. *Sepals* shiny pink on the outside with green tips, heavily flushed with salmon on the inside; broad and reflexing. *Corolla* has two distinct colours, purplish-red in the centre and orange salmon on the outer petals. The medium-sized, fairly compact flowers are freely produced. The colouring is very distinctive and very showy. *Foliage* light to medium green, medium-sized, ovate, serrated.
(Munkner, USA, 1963)

**'Torchlight'**
Single H2 Bush
*Tube* and *sepals* brilliant crimson. *Corolla* pure white with crimson veining at the base of the petals. The large flowers are very freely produced. *Foliage* medium green. The natural growth is as an upright and free-branching bush.
(Pacey, UK, 1987)

**'Torvill and Dean'**
Double H2 Bush
*Tube* pale cerise. *Sepals* also pale cerise tipped with green, medium length and width, held well out. *Corolla* almost pure white, slightly veined and flushed with cerise. The large double blooms are very freely produced. *Foliage* a very attractive dark green, nicely enhancing the colour of the flowers. The upright growth is very strong and bushy. A fitting tribute for the world-famous ice dancers.
(Pacey, UK, 1985)

**'Tour Eiffel'**
Single H2 Lax bush
*Tube* bulbous, salmon pink. *Sepals* short and broad, also salmon pink. *Corolla* rosy purple shading to salmon pink at the base of the petals. The flowers are of medium size and freely produced. *Foliage* bronze green with red stems and central vein. The natural growth is rather lax.
(de Graaff, Holland, 1976)

**'Tower of London'**
Double H2 Bush
Medium-sized flowers. *Tube* and *sepals* cerise. *Corolla* petals purplish violet. *Foliage* medium green. The natural upright growth is quite strong and bushy.
(Bundy, UK, 1870)

**'Towi'**
Semi-double H2 Stiff trailer
*Tube* red. *Sepals* upswept, rosy red. *Corolla* petals violet with red streaks and marbling, ragged and ruffled. Growth is rather lax but sturdy and self-branching. *Foliage* medium green. A rather unusual flower but looks well in hanging containers.
(Bosman, Holland, 1989)

**'Tracie Ann'**
Double H2 Trailer
*Tube* medium-sized, neyron rose. *Sepals* upswept, venetian pink and carmine rose at the base of the tube. *Corolla* campanula violet maturing to mallow purple. The fully flared blooms are of medium size and fully double. *Foliage* upper surface dark green, the lower surface medium green. The growth is rather lax for a bush, and although rather stiff for a basket, will do well when grown in containers. ('Harry Gray' × 'Elsie Mitchell')
(Johns, UK, 1988)

**'Trade Winds'**
Double H2 Lax bush
*Tube* white. *Sepals* white and pink. *Corolla* white with pink at the base of the petals. The small blooms are very freely produced. *Foliage* medium green. The growth is rather lax so is useful for hanging containers.
(Fuchsia La, USA, 1968)

**'Trail Blazer'**
Double H2 Trailer
*Tube* long and slender, crimson. *Sepals* which are long, narrow and reflexed, also crimson. *Corolla* rosy mauve, paler at the base of the petals. The flowers are medium-sized and fairly compact. *Foliage* is mid-green with serrated edges. Growth is naturally trailing.
(Reiter, USA, 1951)

**'Trailing King'**
Single H2 Trailer
Small flowers. *Tube* coral pink. *Sepals* strawberry red. *Corolla* petals deep carmine red. *Foliage* medium green. The natural desire of the plant is to trail.
(Brown, UK, 1936)

**'Trailing Queen'**
Single H2 Trailer
*Tube* fairly thin, medium length, red. *Sepals* red, narrow, held well out. *Corolla* dull red, compact. The medium-sized flowers are freely produced. *Foliage* bronzy red, long, branching. Growth is naturally trailing and vigorous. Needs a great deal of pinching, but will make an excellent half basket.
(Kohene, Germany, 1896)

**'Trase'**
Double H3 Bush
*Tube* medium length, carmine. *Sepals* short, broad and upturned, also carmine. *Corolla* white veined with carmine, with a carmine flush at the base of the petals. The small to medium blooms are fairly full and compact. *Foliage* medium green with small and finely serrated edges. Growth is upright and bushy, self-branching and free-flowering. H. and S. 24–30in (60–75cm).
(Dawson, UK, 1956)

**'Traudchen Bonstedt'**
Triphylla type H1 Bush
*Tube* long, light rose. *Sepals* light rose pink. *Corolla* light salmon pink, the petals short and compact. *Foliage* light sage green with paler veins and ribs; reddish tinge on the reverse of the leaves. Growth is upright, and the flowers are carried in bunches at the ends of the branches.
(Bonstedt, Germany, 1905)

'TORVILL AND DEAN'

'TOW!'

'TRAIL BLAZER'

'TRAILING QUEEN'

'TRASE'

**'Trewince Twilight'**
Single H2 Bush
*Tube* short and fairly thick,
white. *Sepals* short, broad and
reflexing, also white. *Corolla*
pale mauve pink. The flowers
are very compact. *Foliage*
medium to dark green. Growth
is upright and bushy, self-
branching and free-flowering.
Good exhibition plant,
although the colour is not as
outstanding as its parent.
(Sport of 'Marin Glow')
(Jackson, UK, 1972)

**'Tricia'**
Double H2 Bush
*Tube* and *sepals* white with a
hint of pink. *Corolla* magenta
but paler at the base of the
petals. *Foliage* medium green.
Growth is upright, and the
plant is very floriferous
considering the large size of the
blooms.
(Raiser and date unknown)

**F. triphylla**
Species H1 Bush
*Tube* red, and hairy on the
outside length 1¼in (3cm).
*Sepals* red. *Corolla* red at the
tips but slightly lighter at the
base. *Foliage* dark greeny-
bronze with reddish veins, the
leaves long and narrow, 3in
(8cm), appearing in groups of
three or four. The natural
growth is low and shrubby.
The young stems are reddish.
(Haiti)

**F. triphylla dominica**
The long flowers with flared
tubes are bright orange, and
carried in terminal racemes.
The foliage is a dull green
colour with a flushed purple
reverse.
(Haiti)

**'Tristesse'**
Double H2 Bush
*Tube* medium length, pale rose
pink. *Sepals* rose pink, short,
broad and reflexed, have green
tips. *Corolla* lilac blue. The
flowers are small to medium in
size. *Foliage* medium green,
small to medium-sized, leaves

serrated. Growth is upright,
self-branching, and the plant
very free-flowering.
(Blackwell, UK, 1965)

**'Troika'**
Semi-double H2 Bush
*Tube* medium length, rose red;
paler in colour when grown in
warm conditions. *Sepals* white,
broad and well held out.
*Corolla* light blue shading to
lilac rose. The flowers are of
medium size and are very
compact. Stamens pink. *Foliage*
medium green. Growth is
bushy but rather lax, upright,
vigorous and very free-
flowering. Needs early stopping
to ensure a good bush.
(de Graaff, Holland, 1976)

**'Tropicana'**
Double H2 Trailer
*Tubes* long, thin, greenish-
white and tinged with pink.
*Sepals* rosy pink with green
tips, slightly darker pink on the
underside. *Corolla* orange, fully
double and fairly compact with
numerous petaloids. *Foliage*
light green, the leaves quite
long and with serrated edges.
The natural growing habit is to
trail so a good basket can be
developed.
(Tiret, USA, 1964)

**'Tropic Sunset'**
Double H2 Trailer
*Tube* short, carmine. *Sepals*
carmine, short, broad and
point downwards. *Corolla* dark
purple, paler at the base of the
petals, splashed with pink. The
flowers are small to medium-
sized, but the bloom is very
compact. *Foliage* reddish-
bronze tipped with green. The
stems are red and the leaves
small, ovate, the edges serrated.
The natural growth is as a
trailer. It is self-branching, very
vigorous and free-flowering.
('Autumnale' ×)
(Tiret, USA, 1964)

**'Trubell'**
Single H2 Bush
*Tube* short and thick, reddish
pink. *Sepals* reddish pink, long,

narrow and reflex back to the
tube. *Corolla* bell-shaped,
purple with cerise veins; the
colour becomes paler at the
base of the petals. *Foliage*
medium green, medium to
large, long and serrated.
Growth is bushy and upright.
The plant is vigorous and free-
flowering. ('Bishop's Bells' ×)
(Gadsby, UK, 1970)

**'Trudy'**
Single H2 Bush
*Tube* medium length, pale
pink. *Sepals*, short, recurve to
the tube, pink on top and a
slightly darker shade of pink
underneath. *Corolla* bell-
shaped, cyclamen pink and is
very compact. *Foliage* medium
green, medium-sized, ovate,
serrated. Growth is upright,
fairly vigorous, bushy and
free-flowering. ('Chillerton
Beauty' ×)
(Gadsby, UK, 1970)

**'Trumpeter'**
Triphylla type H1 Trailer
*Tube* long and thick, pale
geranium lake. *Sepals* short
and pointed, the same
colouring. *Corolla* also pale
geranium lake, the petals short
and fairly compact. The long
blooms darken as the flower
matures. *Foliage* bluish-green.
The flowers are carried on long
wiry stems. Growth is naturally
trailing so a good basket can
be developed.
(Reiter, USA, 1946)

**'Tsjiep'**
Single H2 Bush
*Tube* longish, cream. *Sepals*
held horizontally, cream
blushed with rose. *Corolla*
small and dainty, opens blood
red maturing to claret rose; the
petals appear rather waxy.
*Foliage* fuchsia green on top,
lighter underneath. The natural
growth is as an upright bush.
Excellent for the smaller
standards. ('Mephisto' ×
'Countess of Aberdeen')
(de Graaff, Holland, 1985)

'TREWINCE TWILIGHT'

'TROIKA'

'TROPICANA'

'TROPIC SUNSET'

'TSJIEP'

**'Tuonella'**
Double H2 Bush
*Tube* medium length, reddish-pink. *Sepals* long, broad and reflexing, also reddish-pink. *Corolla* pale lavender blue with reddish veins and reddish shading at the base of the petals. The medium-sized blooms are very compact. *Foliage* medium green. Growth is upright and bushy. A very free-flowering double.
(Blackwell, UK 1969)

**'Tutone'**
Double H2 Lax bush
*Tube* short, pink. *Sepals* broad and reflexing, also pink. *Corolla* greyish-blue and pink, fully double and compact. *Foliage* dark green. Growth is rather lax so it can be used as either a bush or a basket with the necessary supports. Early stopping is advised.
(Machado, USA, 1963)

**'Tutu'**
Double H2 Bush
*Tube* short, greenish-white. *Sepals* long and spreading, greenish-white on top, flushed pale pink on the undersurface. *Corolla* pale rhodamine purple flecked with aster violet. The flowers are medium to large and open, the bloom rather flat. *Foliage* medium green. Growth is upright, bushy and free-flowering.
(Reiter, USA, 1952)

**'Twiggy'**
Single H2 Trailer
Small flower. *Tube* neyron rose. *Sepals* rhodonite red with green tips, held fully up to tube. *Corolla* lilac mauve with red veins, maturing to rose purple. *Foliage* medium green. The natural growth is as a trailer. ((*F. lycoides* × *F. magellanica*) ×)
(de Graaff, Holland, 1985)

**'Twink'**
Triphylla type H1 Bush
*Tube* short and stubby, *sepals* small, both bright crimson. *Corolla* also bright crimson.

The flowers are produced at first in the axils but gradually become terminally presented. *Foliage* medium to dark green with a faint purple sheen to the reverse. Growth is strong, upright and bushy. A very versatile plant which will be of value in the garden.
(Stannard, UK, 1993)

**'Twinkling Stars'**
Single H2 Bush
*Tube* short and thick, pale rosy pink. *Sepals* pale pink on top, slightly deeper shade of pink underneath; short, narrow and pointed. *Corolla* fuchsia pink, short, the petals well held out. *Foliage* medium green. Growth is upright and bushy. A beautifully named plant as the flowers usually have five sepals as opposed to the expected four, and the 'star' shape is shown to perfection. Plants with multiple sepals *can* now be shown in fuchsia shows without penalty.
(Handley, UK, 1976)

**'Two Tiers'**
Double H2 Lax bush
*Tube* long, thin, azalea pink. *Sepals* long, broad, fly well back to the tube, azalea pink on the upper surface but deeper pink underneath. *Corolla* pale beetroot purple. The largish blooms are unusual, with four petaloids at a lower level than the main corolla when the flower is four or five days old, forming a two tier bloom. *Foliage* medium green. The growth is rather lax but vigorous. Excellent for bushes or baskets, but the necessary supports must be given.
(Porter, UK, 1985)

# U

**'U.F.O.'**
Single H2 Bush
*Tube* short and thick, white, flushed pale pink. *Sepals* white, long and narrow, and reflex

right back to the tube. *Corolla* lilac lavender, white at the centre of the petals which open almost completely flat, saucer-shaped. *Foliage* medium green, small to medium-sized, serrated leaves. The growth is upright, vigorous, self-branching and very free-flowering.
(Handley, UK, 1972)

**'Uillean Pipes'**
Single H2 Lax bush
*Tube* magenta, but has a darker base. *Sepals* magenta on the upper surface, pale magenta on the lower; the tips reflex and are dark magenta. *Corolla* light rose with wavy petal edges. *Foliage* dark green on the upper surface, lighter with a red tinge on the reverse. The growth is lax but vigorous and self-branching. Will make a good basket or an upright with supports. (*F. paniculata* × *F. sanctae-rosae*)
(de Graaff, Holland, 1987)

**'Ullswater'**
Double H2 Bush
*Tube* long, pale pink. *Sepals* pale pink, long, broad and upswept. *Corolla* orchid blue fading to orchid purple, paler at the base of the petals. The flowers are fairly large and compact. *Foliage* medium green, ovate and has serrated edges to the leaves. Growth is upright and bushy.
(Travis, UK, 1958)

**'Ultramar'**
Double H2 Bush
*Tube* short and thick, white. *Sepals* also white, long and broad, recurve slightly. *Corolla* pale lavender blue with numerous petaloids of a pinkish-white shade. The flowers are fully double and medium to large in size. *Foliage* medium green with reddish veins. Growth is vigorously upright and bushy. The plant is very free-flowering.
(Reiter, USA, 1956)

'TUTONE'

'TUTU'

'TWINKLING STARS'

'TWO TIERS'

**'Uncle Charley'**
Semi-double H2 Bush
*Tube* thin, rose red. *Sepals* long
and narrow, curl up towards
the tube, also rose red. *Corolla*
lilac lavender. The flower is an
open bell shape and of medium
size. *Foliage* medium green,
serrated leaves. The growth is
vigorously upright and bushy.
A very free-flowering bush is
easily developed.
(Tiret, USA, 1949)

**'Uncle Jinks'**
Single H2 Trailer
*Tube* and *sepals* pink. *Corolla*
purple with a little white
shading. The small or medium-
sized blooms are produced in
profusion. *Foliage* small, mid-
green, pointed leaves. Growth
is pendulous so will make a
superb basket quite easily. The
flowers are similar to but larger
than its parent 'Auntie Jinks'.
(Wilson, UK, 1985)

**'Uncle Steve'**
Double H2 Trailer
*Tube* pale pink, medium length
and thickness. *Sepals* pale pink,
long, broad and outswept. The
*corolla* is plum purple. *Foliage*
medium green. The large
blooms are produced quite
freely. The natural growth is as
a trailer and will make a good
basket.
(Tiret, USA, 1962)

**'Upward Look'**
Single H2 Bush
*Tube* short, carmine. *Sepals*
short and broad, also carmine
and have green tips. *Corolla*
pale roseine purple. The short
flowers are very full and held
erect, similar to one of its
parents 'Bon Accorde', but has
much deeper colouring. *Foliage*
dull medium green, medium-
sized, serrated. Growth is
strong upright and bushy.
('Athela' × 'Bon Accorde')
(Gadsby, UK, 1968)

# V

**'Vale of Belvoir'**
Single H2 Lax bush
*Tube* thick, neyron rose. *Sepals*
also neyron rose, tipped with
green, curl back. *Corolla*
spectrum violet flushed with
rose, fading to pale imperial
purple. The flowers are medium-
sized and very freely produced.
*Foliage* medium green. The
natural growth, being rather lax,
can be used for growing bushes
or baskets. ('Rosedale' × 'Lady
Isobel Barnett')
(Gadsby, UK, 1973)

**'Valerie'**
Single H2 Bush
*Tube* short, empire rose and
striped with red. *Sepals* fully
reflexed, white and tipped with
green. *Corolla* violet flushed
pink at the base of each petal.
*Foliage* medium green. The
medium-sized flowers are
produced in great profusion.
Growth is upright and strong.
('Norman Mitchinson' ×
('Simonside' × 'Lindisfarne'))
(Mitchinson, UK, 1981)

**'Valerie Ann'**
Double H2 Trailer
*Tube* and *sepals* creamy white,
flushed with pink. *Corolla* white
flushed pink. The medium-sized
blooms are very freely produced
and very compact. The natural
habit of growth is trailing, so
this plant will make a good
basket quite quickly.
(Hall, UK, 1963)

**'Valerie Cottrell'**
Single H2 Bush
*Tube* and *sepals* scarlet.
*Corolla* white, veined red. The
medium-sized flowers are very
freely produced. *Foliage* an
unusual citrus green colouring.
Growth is upright, bushy and
short-jointed.
(Porter, UK, 1985)

**'Valiant'**
Single H2 Bush
Large flower. *Tube* and *sepals*
cerise. *Corolla* rose red. *Foliage*

medium green. The natural
growth is as an upright bush.
(Jennings, UK, 1850)

**'Vanessa Jackson'**
Single H2 Trailer
*Tube* medium thick, salmon red.
*Sepals* long, held well out from
the corolla, salmon orange.
*Corolla* salmon orange shading
to orange red, then to cardinal
red at the edges. The edges of
the petals flare out sharply and
then overlap. *Foliage* medium
green tinged with bronze. The
growth is naturally trailing, and
the cultivar will make a good
free-flowering basket.
(Handley, UK, 1980)

**'Vanity Fair'**
Double H2 Bush
*Tube* long, of medium thickness,
white tinged with pale green.
*Sepals* white with green tips
flushed pink on the underside,
short, broad and reflexing.
*Corolla* pale pink. The flowers
are of medium size and are very
full and fluffy. *Foliage* medium
green with large serrated leaves.
Growth upright and bushy.
(Schnabel-Paskesen, USA,
1962)

*F. vargasiana*
Species H1 Bush
The long *tube*, *sepals* and
*corolla* are all the same shade
of red. There are green tips on
the ends of the sepals. *Foliage*
very large, dark green with
crimson mid-ribs. Growth is
very strongly upright and
spreading. In order to flower it
needs a certain amount of root
restriction. Rampant growth
can be obtained given the right
moist and humid conditions.
(Peru)

**'Variegated Brenda White'**
Single H2 Bush
*Tube* and *sepals* carmine.
*Corolla* bright white. The small
flowers are very freely
produced. *Foliage* cream and
green. Growth is upright and
bushy. A delightful small single.
(Sport from 'Brenda White')
(1986)

'UNCLE CHARLEY' 'UNCLE STEVE'

'UPWARD LOOK' 'VANESSA JACKSON'

**'Variegated Swingtime'**
Double  H2  Lax bush
*Tube* and *sepals* rich red.
*Corolla* milky white and faintly
veined pink. The largish
blooms are very freely
produced. *Foliage* variegated
with green and golden leaves.
The growth is rather lax for a
bush and rather stiff for a
basket. (Sport of 'Swingtime')
(Baker, UK, 1987)

**'Variegated White Joy'**
Single  H2  Bush
*Tube* short, white. *Sepals*
broadish, held horizontally,
white with a slight pink flush.
*Corolla* white and a perfect bell
shape. The flowers are small to
medium in size but are
produced prolifically. *Foliage*
an attractive green and gold
variegation. The growth is
upward and bushy.
(Dyos, UK, 1984)

**'Velma'**
Single  H2  Bush
*Tube* short, off-white. *Sepals*
reflex right back over the tube,
also off-white maturing to deep
pink. *Corolla* a deep pink
maturing to purple with short
and round petals. The flowers
are of medium size. *Foliage*
large, light green. Growth is
upright and bushy. ('Serena
Blue' × 'Fancy Flute')
(Adams, UK, 1979)

**F. venusta**
Species  H1  Bush
*Tube* long and thin trumpet-
shaped, orange. *Sepals* short,
also orange. *Corolla* petals are
orange and spreading. Growth
is rather lax but upright and
produces many sideshoots.
*Foliage* is very robust. Although
slow to flower the blooms are
really very beautiful.
(Colombia and Venezuela)

**'Venus Victrix'**
Single  H2  Bush
*Tube* white, very small and
thin. *Sepals* very small, white
with green tips, narrow and
well held out. *Corolla* violet-
purple shading to white at the
base of the petals. The bloom
is very small and compact.
*Foliage* medium green, small
and longish, serrated edges to
the leaves. Growth is upright,
but this cultivar is very slow
and difficult to grow. The first
white-sepalled fuchsia known.
(Gulliver, UK, 1840)

**'Vera Wilding'**
Single  H2  Bush
*Tube* and *sepals* white. *Corolla*
violet. *Foliage* medium green.
The natural growth is as an
upright bush. It is self-
branching, and the small,
delightful flowers are produced
in quantity.
(Heavens, UK, 1990)

**'Victorian'**
Double  H2  Bush
*Tube* short, pink. *Sepals* broad
and upturned, pink. *Corolla*
pink. The bloom is fully double,
medium-sized and compact.
*Foliage* medium green. Growth
is upright and bushy.
(Paskesen, USA, 1971)

**'Vienna Waltz'**
Double  H2  Trailer
*Tube* medium length, darkish
pink. *Sepals* broad and
reflexing, dark pink. *Corolla*
rich lavender splashed with
pink and red. The flowers are
medium to large and flare.
*Foliage* dark green. Growth is
naturally trailing, short-jointed
and free-flowering. (Sport of
'Dusky Rose')
(Nix Nursery, USA, 1971)

**'Vincent d'Indy'**
Double  H2  Bush
*Tube* and *sepals* carmine-cerise.
*Corolla* rich violet-purple
suffused with carmine. The
blooms are very large, though
unfortunately not very freely
produced. *Foliage* medium
green. The growth is upright
and bushy.
(Lemoine, France, 1901)

**'Vincent van Gogh'**
Single  H2  Bush
*Tube*, *sepals* and *corolla* of this
medium-sized single flower are
all the same delightful pink.
*Foliage* medium green. The
natural growth is as an upright
bush.
(Van der Post, Holland, 1984)

**'Violet Bassett-Burr'**
Double  H2  Bush
*Tube* short, greenish-white and
pink. *Sepals* very long and
upswept and completely hide
the tube; white tipped with
green, pink at the base. *Corolla*
pale lilac, paler at the base.
The blooms are very full and
are freely produced. *Foliage*
dark green. Growth is upright
and bushy.
(Holmes, E., UK, 1972)

**'Violet Lace'**
Double  H3  Bush
*Tube* and *sepals* red. *Corolla*
violet splashed with pink. The
large blooms are freely
produced, and are rather
unusual in a 'hardy' fuchsia.
*Foliage* dark green. A very
compact, upright bush is easily
produced. H. and S. 24–30in
(60–75cm).
(Tabraham, UK, 1982)

**'Violet Rosette'**
Double  H2  Bush
*Tube* long, bright carmine.
*Sepals* long and broad, also
bright carmine, reflexed
straight back to the tube.
*Corolla* deep violet-purple,
shading to red at the base of
the petals. The blooms are very
full and fluffy, medium-sized.
*Foliage* bright green with finely
serrated edges to the leaves.
(Kuechler, USA, 1963)

**'Viva Ireland'**
Single  H2  Lax bush
*Tube* thin, pale pink. *Sepals*
long, narrow and recurving, also
pale pink. *Corolla* lilac-blue,
lighter at the base of the petals.
*Foliage* medium green, the leaves
long, narrow and have serrated
edges. The growth is rather lax
but is self-branching and free-
flowering. Excellent for bedding
or when grown in hanging
containers.
(Nessier, USA, 1956)

'VENUS VICTRIX'

'VERA WILDING'

'VIENNA WALTZ'

'VIOLET LACE'

'VIOLET ROSETTE'

**'Vivian Miller'**
Single H2 Bush
*Tube* neyron rose. *Sepals*
neyron rose, held well back
against the tube. *Corolla* aster
violet. Medium-sized blooms
on a strong, upright-growing
plant. *Foliage* pale green. Very
free-flowering and will make
an excellent plant for the show
bench.
(Roe, UK, 1980)

**'Vivienne Davis'**
Triphylla type H1 Bush
Most of the flowers are carried
at the terminals. *Tube* pink,
medium length and quite broad.
*Sepals* short, pink. *Corolla*
petals also pink. *Foliage*
medium green with a slight
purple reverse. Growth is
upright and strong. An excellent
plant for the garden display.
(Stannard, UK, 1993)

**'Vivienne Thompson'**
Semi-double H2 Bush
*Tube* medium-sized, rhodamine
pink. *Sepals* also rhodamine
pink edged with neyron rose,
and with green tips. *Corolla*
white with neyron rose veins at
the base. The blooms are of
medium size. *Foliage* medium
green. The self-branching,
upright growth will produce a
very acceptable bush. ('Tolling
Bell' × 'Border Queen')
(Reynolds, UK, 1983)

**'Vi Whitehouse'**
Single H2 Bush
Medium-sized flower. *Tube*
white. *Sepals* greenish-white
slightly flushed pink on the
underside, curve up to touch
the tube. *Corolla* neyron rose
veined with carmine. *Foliage*
medium green. The growth is
upright and bushy, and the
plants are very free-flowering.
(Pacey, UK, 1987)

**'Vobeglo'**
Single H2 Dwarf bush
*Tube* short and thick, pink.
*Sepals* held well out from the
corolla, rose red. *Corolla* lilac
purple, the petals slightly
darker at the edges. *Foliage*

medium green, the leaves very
small. Growth is upright but
rather dwarf; the flowers stand
out in an erect position.
Excellent for the front of a
border or as a rockery plant.
('Pallas' (*F. regia typica* × 'Bon
Accorde') × 'Henriette Ernst')
(de Groot, Holland, date
unknown)

**'Voltaire'**
Single H2 Bush
*Tube* thick and medium length,
scarlet. *Sepals* short, broad and
slightly reflexed, also scarlet.
*Corolla* magenta purple with
reddish veins. The bloom is of
medium size and freely
produced. *Foliage* medium
green with serrated edges to the
ovate leaves. Growth is upright
and bushy.
(Lemoine, France, 1897)

**'Voodoo'**
Double H2 Bush
*Tube* short, dark red. *Sepals*
long, broad and upturned, also
dark red. *Corolla* dark
purplish-violet, very full
double. The flowers, although
very large, are very freely
produced. *Foliage* medium to
darkish green, medium-sized
leaves. Growth is upright and
bushy.
(Tiret, USA, 1953)

**'Vulcan'**
Semi-double H2 Bush
*Tube* medium length, china
rose. *Sepals* neyron rose on the
underside, china rose on top;
green tips. *Corolla* neyron rose
at the base shading to ruby red
at the tips. *Foliage* lettuce green
with red veins. Growth is
upright, vigorous, self-branching
and bushy. The flowers are
produced in quantity.
(Pugh, UK, 1975)

**F. vulcanica**
Species H1 Bush
*Tube* long, thin, dark orange.
*Sepals* short, also dark orange.
*Corolla* petals almost red. The
blooms appear in the leaf axils
in whorls of three or four.
*Foliage* matt green and of

medium size. Growth is very
strong, shrubby and spreading.
A large container is necessary
to prevent too much restriction
of the root system.
(Columbia and Ecuador)

---

**'Waldfee'**
*Encliandra* type H2 Bush
Very small flowers. *Tubes* soft
lilac pink. *Sepals* fold back
completely over the tube, also
soft lilac pink. *Corolla* very
small, the same colouring.
*Foliage* large for this type of
plant, matt forest green in
colour. The natural growth is
as a very lax upright grower.
As with all the *Encliandra*
types of plant the stems are
very thin and wiry. Another
ideal candidate for using when
manufacturing all types of
topiary. (*F. michoacanensis* ×)
(Travis, UK, 1973)

**'Walsingham'**
Semi-double H2 Lax
bush/trailer
*Tube* palest pink and off-white.
*Sepals* have a similar colouring
on top, but are rose pink
underneath; held horizontally.
*Corolla* a lovely pale lavender
lilac. The flowers are of
medium size and very freely
produced. The edges of the
petals have a very attractive
crimpled appearance. *Foliage*
emerald green. The natural
growth is rather lax, and
excellent baskets and half
baskets have been produced for
show purposes. ('Northumbrian
Belle' × 'Blush o' Dawn')
(Clitheroe, UK, 1979)

**'Waltraud Strumper'**
Single H2 Bush
Medium-sized flowers. *Tube*
and *sepals* white striped with
reddish-purple. *Corolla*
reddish-purple. *Foliage* fairly
large, medium green in colour.
The upright growth is strong
and vigorous.
(Strumper, Holland, 1985)

'VOBEGLO'

'VOODOO'

'WALSINGHAM'

'WALDFEE'

'WALTRAUD STRUMPER'

**'Waltzing Matilda'**
Double H2 Bush
*Tube* medium-sized, pale pink.
*Sepals* light pink on the upper
surface, pink on the lower
surface, with recurved tips.
*Corolla* opens pale pink,
matures to pale pink veined
with rose; the outer petals are
streaked with rose. The bloom
is quite large and very full and
fluffy. *Foliage* light green with
red veins. Growth is rather lax
upright.
(Bromat, Australia, 1989)

**'Walz Bella'**
Single H2 Bush
Medium-sized flower. *Tube*
orange carmine. *Sepals* mandarin
orange on top, lighter orange
underneath, held horizontally.
*Corolla* scarlet. *Foliage* medium
green. The natural growth is as
an upright bush.
(Waldenmaier, Holland, 1987)

**'Walz Blauwkous'**
Double H2 Bush
Medium-sized flowers. *Tube* and
*sepals* light rose. *Corolla* dark
purple. *Foliage* medium green.
The growth is strongly upright.
(Waldenmaier, Holland, 1989)

**'Walz Brandaris'**
Single H2 Bush
*Tube* long and thick, crimson.
*Sepals* held half down, short
and broad, crimson on the
upper surface and scarlet
underneath. *Corolla* signal red,
small and square. The small to
medium-sized flowers are very
freely produced. *Foliage* dark
green on top, medium green
beneath. The natural growth is
upright and bushy. Needs
careful pinching. ('Chang' ×)
(Waldenamier, Holland, 1985)

**'Walz Bugel'**
Single H2 Lax bush/trailer
Large flowers. *Tube* reddish-
purple. *Sepals* reddish-purple.
*Corolla* has the same
colouring. *Foliage* medium
green. Growth is rather lax so
this plant can be used for bush
or basket work.
(Waldenmaier, Holland, 1989)

**'Walz Citer'**
Single H2 Lax bush
Medium-sized flower. *Tube* and
*sepals* white flushed with rose.
*Corolla* salmon pink. *Foliage*
medium green. The natural
growth is as a rather lax bush.
(Waldenmaier, Holland, 1989)

**'Walz Doedelzak'**
Single H2 Bush
Medium-sized flowers. *Tube*
and *sepals* rose red. *Corolla*
rose pink. *Foliage* medium
green. The natural growth is
upright and bushy.
(Waldenmaier, Holland, 1987)

**'Walz Drum'**
Single H2 Bush
Very floriferous. *Tube* peach
pink. *Sepals* cyclamen pink.
*Corolla* mauve pink. *Foliage*
light to medium green. The
natural growth is as an upright
bush.
(Waldenmaier, Holland, 1990)

**'Walz Freule'**
Single H2 Trailer
*Tube* short, medium width,
carmine rose. *Sepals* neyron
rose with slightly darker colour
on the underside. *Corolla* lilac,
fades with age. *Foliage* medium
green on top, spring green
beneath, leaves medium-sized,
serrated edges. The natural
growth is as a trailer. Best used
as a basket. ('Amelie Aubin' ×)
(Waldenmaier, Holland, 1985)

**'Walz Gamelan'**
Single H2 Lax bush
Medium-sized flowers. *Tube*
and *sepals* white striped with
rose, tipped with green. *Corolla*
robin red maturing to purple.
*Foliage* medium to dark green.
The growth is naturally upright
and bushy.
(Waldenmaier, Holland, 1991)

**'Walz Gitaar'**
Single H2 Bush
Small flowers. *Tube* and *sepals*
orange. *Corolla* lilac rose.
*Foliage* medium green. The
natural growth is as an upright
bush.
(Waldenmaier, Holland, 1989)

**'Walz Harp'**
Single H2 Trailer
*Tube* salmon rose in colour.
*Sepals* orange. *Corolla* dark red
shading to orange at the base
of the petals; large flowers.
*Foliage* medium to dark green.
The natural growth is trailing.
(Waldenmaier, Holland, 1988)

**'Walz Jubelteen'**
Single H2 Bush
*Tube* and *sepals* pale pink.
*Corolla* pinkish-orange. The
flowers are small and profuse,
and are upward facing. *Foliage*
medium green. The growth is
rather stiff and makes a good
bush plant. Good show
potential, a very attractive plant.
(Waldenmaier, Holland, 1990)

**'Walz Kalebas'**
Single H2 Bush
Medium-sized flowers. *Tube*
and *sepals* light rose red.
*Corolla* middle red. *Foliage*
mid-green. The natural growth
is upright and bushy.
(Waldenmaier, Holland, 1989)

**'Walz Kattesnoor'**
Single H2 Bush
Medium-sized flowers. *Tube*
white. *Sepals* white on top with
rose on the undersurface.
*Corolla* blue. Foliage medium
green. Growth is naturally
upright.
(Waldenmaier, Holland, 1989)

**'Walz Klavier'**
Single H2 Trailer
Flowers medium-sized. *Tube*
pink. *Sepals* pink, striped with
green. *Corolla* scarlet. *Foliage*
medium green. The natural
growth is rather lax so can be
used as either a bush or a basket
with the necessary supports.
(Waldenmaier, Holland, 1987)

**'Walz Knipperbol'**
Single H2 Bush
Flowers of medium size. *Tube*
azalea pink. *Sepals* scarlet.
*Corolla* spinel red. *Foliage*
medium to dark green. The
natural growth is as an upright
bush.
(Waldenmaier, Holland, 1986)

'WALTZING MATILDA'

'WALZ BELLA'

'WALZ BRANDARIS'

'WALZ CITER

'WALZ GITAAR'

'WALZ KNIPPERBOL'

**'Walz Lucifer'**
Single H2 Bush
*Tube* moderately long and thin, pink. *Sepals* recurving, pink. *Corolla* bright orange. The flowers are of medium size. *Foliage* medium green. Growth is upright and self-branching.
(Waldenmaier, Holland, 1991)

**'Walz Luit'**
Single H2 Bush
Triphylla type of flower. *Tube*, *sepals* and *corolla* petals of orange. *Foliage* medium green with a slight glaze on the leaves. Growth is upright and strong. Excellent for all types of pot work.
(Waldenmaier, Holland, 1989)

**'Walz Mandoline'**
Double H2 Trailer
*Tube* orange, of medium length. *Sepals* short, also orange. *Corolla* is very tightly pleated, very bright orange. *Foliage* medium green. The natural growth is as a spreading bush and will therefore trail over the edge of a hanging container.
(Waldenmaier, Holland, 1984)

**'Walz Meermin'**
Single H2 Lax bush
Small flower. *Tubes* short and thick, venetian pink. *Sepals* short, chartreuse green, lighter beneath ageing to claret rose. *Corolla* pink. *Foliage* medium green. The natural growth is rather lax. The plant can be developed for use as a bush or in a hanging container.
('Speciosa' × 'Walz Bruintje')
(Waldenmaier, Holland, 1985)

**'Walz Parasol'**
Single H2 Trailer
*Tubes* and *sepals* dark peach. *Corolla* cup-shaped, is also dark peach. *Foliage* medium green. The growth is strong but spreading. Will make a good plant for a hanging container.
(Waldenmaier, Holland, 1981)

**'Walz Piano'**
Single H2 Lax bush
Medium-sized flowers. *Tube* red.

*Sepals* rose to white. *Corolla* lilac rose. *Foliage* medium green. The natural growth, being rather lax, is suitable for growing as a bush or a basket.
(Waldenmaier, Holland, 1989)

**'Walz Sprietje'**
Single H2 Bush
Medium-sized flowers. *Tubes* cream. *Sepals* cream flushed with rose and with green tips. *Corolla* red. *Foliage* medium green. The natural growth of the plant is as an upright bush.
(Waldenmaier, Holland, 1989)

**'Walz Tam Tam'**
Double H2 Bush
Medium-sized flowers. *Tube* and *sepals* dark red. *Corolla* dark lilac to aubergine. *Foliage* mid-green. The upright growth is very vigorous and bushy.
(Waldenmaier, Holland, 1988)

**'Walz Telescoop'**
Single H2 Lax bush
Medium-sized flowers. *Tubes* and *sepals* blood red. *Corolla* geranium rose. *Foliage* medium to dark green. The upward growth is very vigorous and bushy.
(Waldenmaier, Holland, 1987)

**'Walz Toeter'**
Single H2 Bush
Medium-sized flowers. *Tubes* and *sepals* red. Corolla orange red. Foliage light to medium green. The upward growth is upright and bushy.
(Waldenmaier, Holland, 1987)

**'Walz Triangel'**
Double H2 Trailer
*Tube* white. *Sepals* white and orange on the upper surface, reddish-orange on the lower, with light apple-green recurved tips. *Corolla* dark orange on the outer petals, and reddish-orange with red shading to lilac on the inner petals. The flowers are three-quarter flared and bell-shaped. *Foliage* light green. The natural growth is trailing so will make a good basket.
(Waldenmaier, Holland, 1988)

**'Walz Trommel'**
Single H2 Lax bush
Medium-sized flower. *Tube* rose. *Sepals* cyclamen rose. *Corolla* deep mauve-purple. *Foliage* medium to dark green. The natural growth is as an upright lax bush. Although the stems are a little stiff for a trailer it might be worth experimenting.
(Waldenmaier, Holland, 1989)

**'Walz Tuba'**
Triphylla type H1 Bush
*Tube* long, red. *Sepals* red. *Corolla* deep magenta. *Foliage* dark to olive green. The natural growth is as an upright bush.
(Waldenmaier, Holland, 1985)

**'Walz Vuurpijl'**
Single H2 Trailer
Medium-sized flowers. *Tubes* long, yellowish-green. *Sepals* pale yellow-green, peachy-orange underneath. *Corolla* strawberry red with orange flush. *Foliage* medium green. The natural desire of the plant is to trail. A good basket can be developed quite easily.
(*F. speciosa* × 'Mrs W. Rundle')
(Waldenmaier, Holland, 1985)

**'Walz Waterfall'**
Single H2 Trailer
Medium-sized flowers. *Tubes* pale yellow. Sepals cream on top, orient pink beneath. *Corolla* opens fuchsia purple, matures redder. *Foliage* medium to dark green, medium size, serrated. The natural desire of a plant with this name is to cascade. ('Normandy Bell' × 'Mrs W. Rundle')
(Waldenmaier, Holland, 1985)

**'Wapenfeld's Bloei'**
Single H2 Bush
Paniculate type, a hybrid with 'perfect' flowers. *Tube* rose pink. *Sepals* recurving, rose pink. *Corolla* are orange. Growth is very strong and there are many sideshoots. *Foliage* medium green. The strength of the growth would make it a suitable plant to use as a pillar.
(Kamphuis, Holland, 1991)

'WALZ LUCIFER'

'WALZ LUIT'

'WALZ MANDOLINE'

'WALZ PARASOL'

'WALZ TRIANGEL'

**'War Paint'**
Double H2 Bush
*Tube* short white. *Sepals* broad,
flaring, white. *Corolla* dianthus
purple with coral-pink
marbling, fading to reddish-
purple. The blooms are large
and freely produced. *Foliage*
also very large, medium green
in colour. Growth is upright
and bushy. Supports are needed
for the foliage and the flowers.
(Kennett, USA, 1960)

**'Warton Crag'**
Single H2 Bush
*Tube* short, striped greenish-
white and flesh pink. *Sepals*
long and tapering, white, pink
at the base, held horizontally;
spiky but curl over with
recurved green tips on
maturity. *Corolla* light magenta
pink and pale pink. There are
also a number of thick crêpe
petaloids. The flowers are
medium-sized. *Foliage* dark
green with serrated edges.
Growth is bushy and upright.
(Thornley, UK, 1973)

**'Wassernymph'**
Single H2 Bush
*Tube* and *sepals* the palest of
pale pinks. *Corolla* salmon
orange. The flowers are of
medium size and very freely
produced. *Foliage* light to
medium green. Growth is
strongly upright and the
flowers are produced
continually from early in the
season.
(Believed from Holland, 1985)

**'Waveney Gem'**
Single H2 Trailer
*Tube* and *sepals* white. *Corolla*
pink with a mauve flush. The
medium-sized flowers are very
freely and continuously
produced from early in the
season. *Foliage* quite small and
medium green. Some excellent
baskets have been grown for
exhibition purposes. The
natural growth is very lax so it
can also be used as an upright
plant if supports are provided.
(Burns, UK, 1985)

**'Waveney Queen'**
Single H2 Bush
*Tube* short, very pale pink.
*Sepals* pale pink, tipped with
green, held just above the
horizontal. *Corolla* baby pink
with darker pink veining.
*Foliage* lightish green. Growth
is a self-branching upright
bush. A very versatile fuchsia
which is extremely floriferous.
('Border Queen' seedling)
(Burns, UK, 1984)

**'Waveney Sunrise'**
Single H2 Bush
*Tube* and *sepals* pale pink,
tipped with green, upturned.
*Corolla* bright red. The
medium-sized flowers are
very freely produced. *Foliage*
bright yellow with red veins.
Growth is upright and quite
vigorous.
(Burns, UK, 1986)

**'Waveney Unique'**
Single H2 Bush
*Tube* moderately long, pink.
*Sepals* pink on the upper side
and darker underneath almost
horizontal. *Corolla* pink with a
tinge of apricot. Each petal has
a darker margin. The medium-
sized flowers are freely
produced. *Foliage* matt green.
The growth is strongly upright.
('Margaret Roe' × 'Lye's
Unique')
(Burns, UK, 1985)

**'Waveney Valley'**
Single H2 Bush
*Tube* short, white. *Sepals* white
tipped with green, reflexing to
completely cover both tube and
ovary. *Corolla* lavender blue on
opening, maturing to baby
pink. The medium-sized
flowers are freely produced.
*Foliage* lime green with a slight
yellow flecking. Growth is
upright and bushy. ('Margaret
Roe' × 'Eden Lady')
(Burns, UK, 1984)

**'Waveney Waltz'**
Single H2 Bush
*Tube* short, baby pink. *Sepals*
baby pink, held almost at the

horizontal. *Corolla* white with
very little veining. The flowers
are medium-sized and very
freely produced. *Foliage* light
green. Growth is upright and
very bushy.
(Burns, UK, 1982)

**'Wave of Life'**
Single H2 Lax bush
*Tube* thin, scarlet. *Sepals* short,
also scarlet, broad and
upturned. *Corolla* magenta
purple, small and compact.
*Foliage* greenish-yellow and
gold. The leaves are small to
medium-sized. Growth is very
lax as a bush, not particularly
vigorous and can be used, if
desired, for hanging
containers.
(Henderson, UK, 1869)

**'Wedding Bells'**
Double H2 Bush
*Tube* white. *Sepals* white,
fading with maturity to light
pink. *Corolla* white. The
blooms are medium-sized.
*Foliage* light green. Growth is
upright and bushy.
(Dresman, UK, 1987)

**'Wee Lass'**
Single H2 Bush
*Tube* short thick, red. *Sepals*
also short and thick, cardinal
red. *Corolla* tiny, bluebird blue,
lighter at the base, passing to
spectrum violet. The flowers
are very small. *Foliage* very
small, medium green. The
growth is very dwarf but
upright. Height up to 10in
(25cm). Ideal for small pots, or
in rockeries. ('Gambit' ×
'Upward Look')
(Gadsby, UK, 1975)

**'Welsh Dragon'**
Double H2 Bush
*Tube* long, red. *Sepals* long and
broad, rose opal. *Corolla*
magenta rose, the petals falling
in layers. The large blooms are
fairly freely produced. *Foliage*
medium green, medium-sized,
leaves finely serrated. Growth
is upright, bushy and strong.
(Baker, UK, 1970)

'WAR PAINT'

'WASSERNYMPH'

'WAVENEY GEM'

'WAVENEY VALLEY'

'WEDDING BELLS'

'WELSH DRAGON'

**'Wendy'**
Double H2 Lax bush
*Tube* white. *Sepals* coral pink
on the upper surface and
tipped with green, pinkish-
orange underneath. *Corolla*
pinkish-orange splashed with
orange. The medium-sized
blooms are fairly full. *Foliage*
medium green. Growth is
rather lax so can be used for
hanging containers or for a
bush if given supports.
(Dresman, UK, 1986)

**'Wendy Atkinson'**
Semi-double H2 Bush
*Tube* longish, pale pink. *Sepals*
white, short, reflex all the way.
*Corolla* dark burgundy which
matures well and has little
fading. The blooms are small
to medium. *Foliage* dark green.
Growth is rather stiff but
short-jointed. ('Checkerboard'
× 'Northway')
(Dyos, UK, 1987)

**'Wendy Harris'**
Double H2 Bush
*Tube* short, thick white striped
neyron rose. *Sepals* pale neyron
rose, tipped with green. *Corolla*
white veined with neyron rose.
The blooms are medium-sized
with fairly short petals. Growth
is a compact bush.
(Harris, UK, 1978)

**'Wendy Leedham'**
Double H2 Bush
*Tube* delft rose. *Sepals* delft
rose on top and rose red
underneath, held horizontally
with recurving tips. *Corolla*
white flushed with rose red.
The flowers are medium-sized
and freely produced. *Foliage*
medium green on top, lighter
underneath, leaves medium-
sized with crimson veins and
serrated edges. Growth is
upright and self-branching.
(Bielby, UK, 1984)

**'Wendy's Beauty'**
Double H2 Trailer
*Tube* white. *Sepals* white tinged
with rose on the upper surface,
light rose on the lower. *Corolla*
violet maturing to pale purple.

*Foliage* dark yellowish-green on
the upper surface, lighter on the
lower. The flowers are profuse.
The growth is naturally trailing
and will make a superb basket.
('Quasar' × 'Applause')
(Garrett, USA, 1989)

**'Wennington Beck'**
Double H2 Trailer
*Tube* short, reddish-brown.
*Sepals* pink flushed with green,
the underside clear pink,
reflexing back to the tube.
*Corolla* soft violet-blue, bluish-
pink at the base of the petals.
The blooms are of medium size
and fairly freely produced.
*Foliage* medium green. Growth
is a lax bush or a trailer so can
be used for either purpose.
('Dorothea Flower' seedling)
(Thornley, UK, 1973)

**'Wentworth'**
Single H2 Trailer
*Tube* long, flesh-coloured.
*Sepals* flesh-coloured. *Corolla*
bright orange and rather short.
The flowers are produced in
profusion throughout the
season. *Foliage* medium green.
The growth naturally trails so
will make a superb basket.
(Goulding, UK, 1986)

**'Wessex Belle'**
Double H2 Lax bush
*Tube* white striped with light
pink. *Sepals* light pink with
recurved tips. *Corolla* white
flushed with light pink. *Foliage*
pale to dark yellow or
variegated from near white to
dark yellow. Growth is lax
upright so like its parent, it
could be used for either bush or
basket. (Sport from 'Annabel')
(Luther, UK, 1969)

**'Westergeest'**
Single H2 Bush
*Tube* short, thick, empire rose.
*Sepals* claret rose on top, empire
rose underneath with recurved
green tips. *Corolla* small, opens
neyron rose maturing to
crimson. The smallish flowers
are freely produced, mainly
terminally. *Foliage* light fuchsia
green, and even lighter on the

reverse. Growth is rather small
and upright.
(de Graaff, Holland, 1985)

**'Westgate'**
Triphylla type H1 Trailer
Terminal flowering. *Tube* long,
mandarin red. *Sepals* small,
red. *Corolla* red, with an
unusual white streak on the
petals. *Foliage* mid- to dark
green. Will make a good plant
for a hanging container.
(Bielby/Oxtoby, UK, 1987)

**'Westminster Chimes'**
Semi double H2 Lax bush
*Tube* deep rose. *Sepals* rose, fade
to pink, spreading but not
reflexing, tipped with green.
*Corolla* violet-blue ageing to
magenta with pink at the base of
the petals. The smallish flowers
are very prolific. *Foliage* fairly
small, spinach green. Growth is
very lax and will cascade quite
naturally; with supports,
however, it will also make an
extremely handsome bush.
(Clyne, UK, 1976)

**'Wharfedale'**
Single H3 Bush
*Tube* and *sepals* pale pink.
*Corolla* purple. *Foliage* medium
green. The natural growth is as
an upright and spreading bush.
An excellent plant for the
centre of a hardy border. H.
and S. 30–48in (75–120cm).
(Raiser and date unknown)

**'Whickham Beauty'**
Single H2 Bush
*Tube* and *sepals* white. *Corolla*
pale pinkish-mauve. *Foliage*
medium green. The strong,
upright growth is slightly lax
so it can be used to make an
excellent weeping standard.
(Bainbridge, UK, 1993)

**'Whickham Blue'**
Single H2 Bush
*Tube* white. *Sepals* white edged
with pink. *Corolla* aster violet.
*Foliage* medium green. The
natural growth is as a fairly
strong upright bush. Has
'show' potential.
(Bainbridge, UK, 1990)

'WENDY ATKINSON'

'WENDY LEEDHAM'

'WENDY'S BEAUTY'

'WHICKHAM BLUE'

**'Whirlaway'**
Semi-double H2 Lax bush
*Tube* medium length, white.
*Sepals* long, narrow and
curling, white faintly tinged
with pink, with green tips.
*Corolla* white with a faint tinge
of pink as the bloom matures.
*Foliage* long, mid-green, the
leaves having finely serrated
edges. Growth is lax but
upright with longish willowy
branches. Growth is fairly
vigorous and the plant is free-
flowering. Early stopping is
advised to get the best shapes.
(Waltz, USA, 1961)

**'Whistling Rufus'**
Single H2 Bush
Small flower. *Tube* and *sepals*
light red. *Corolla* also light red.
*Foliage* medium green. The
natural growth is as an upright
bush.
(de Graaff, Holland, 1988)

**'White Ann'**
Double H2 Bush
*Tube* short, crimson. *Sepals*
short and broad, also crimson.
*Corolla* white with scarlet
veining. The medium-sized
bloom is a full double. *Foliage*
darkish green, small to medium-
sized. Growth is upright, self-
branching and bushy. A very
free-flowering plant. (Sport of
'Heidi Anne' and synonymous
with 'Heidi Weiss')
(Wills, UK, 1972)

**'White Bride'**
Double H2 Bush
*Tube* medium length, white.
*Sepals* slightly upturned and
tipped with green, white flushed
with pink. *Corolla* long and full,
also white. *Foliage* largish and
round, medium green. Growth
is upright, self-branching and
free-flowering. Prefers to be
grown in the shade.
(Gadsby, UK, 1970)

**'White Clove'**
*Encliandra* type H1 Bush
Very small single flowers,
typical of the *Encliandra* type
of fuchsia. *Tube* white, long
and narrow. *Sepals* white.

Corolla pink. *Foliage* small,
medium to dark green. Growth
is upright but wiry.
(Raiser and date unknown)

**'Whitefalls'**
Semi-double H2 Trailer
Medium-sized flowers. *Tube*
and *sepals* baby pink. *Corolla*
creamy white with pink veins.
*Foliage* light to medium green.
It will make an excellent
basket.
(Raiser and date unknown)

**'White Falls'**
Semi-double H2 Lax bush
*Tube* short, medium thick,
baby pink. *Sepals* short, baby
pink and have green tips.
*Corolla* creamy white with
pink veins. *Foliage* medium
green, the leaves slightly
crinkled, ovate. The growth is
self-branching and vigorous.
Will make a good plant for a
hanging container.
(Tolley, UK, 1974)

**'White Galore'**
Double H2 Trailer
Large flowers. *Tube* and *sepals*
white. *Corolla* also white with
a faint touch of pink in the
petals, a very full double.
*Foliage* medium green. The
natural growth is as a trailer.
(Fuchsia La, USA, 1968)

**'Whitehaven'**
Single H2 Bush
*Tube*, *sepals* and *corolla* of this
recent introduction are all
white. The flowers are of
medium size and are very freely
produced. *Foliage* medium to
light green. The short-jointed
growth of the plant is very
bushy. (A cross between
'Border Queen', 'Liebriez' and
'Ann H. Tripp')
(Arcadia Nurseries
Introduction, UK, 1994)

**'White Joy'**
Single H2 Bush
*Tube* white. *Sepals* white with
a faint pink flush. *Corolla* also
white. The flowers are of
medium size and are bell-
shaped. *Foliage* attractive,

medium green. The natural
growth is upright and bushy.
(Burns, UK, 1980)

**'White King'**
Double H2 Trailer
*Tube* short and fairly thick,
white. *Sepals* long and broad,
held over the corolla, also
white. *Corolla* pure white with
very large and pleated petals.
The bloom is a very full and
fluffy double. *Foliage* medium
green. The natural growth is as
a trailer. Growth is vigorous,
but early stopping will be of
assistance.
(Pennisi, USA, 1968)

**'Whiteknight's Amethyst'**
Single H2 Bush
*Tube* red-purple. *Sepals* shade
from pale red-purple at the
base through greenish-white to
yellow-green at the tips.
*Corolla* violet ageing to red-
purple, tubular with heart
shaped petals. Style and
stamens purple-red with blue
pollen. *Foliage* dark green.
Growth is upright and
vigorous. Takes full sun.
(Wright, UK, 1980)

**'Whiteknight's Blush'**
Single H2 Bush
*Tube* medium length, pale pink.
*Sepals* pale pink, spreading,
and have green tips. *Corolla*
clear pink. *Foliage* dark green
with green veining, the leaves
quite small. Growth is upright
and self-branching.
(Wright, UK, 1980)

**'Whiteknight's Cheeky'**
Single H2 Bush
*Tube* long, of the triphylla
type, dark tyrian purple. *Sepals*
small and spreading, also dark
tyrian purple. *Corolla* similar
in colour with very small
petals. The flowers are carried
in erect terminal racemes,
horizontally and clear of the
foliage. *Foliage* dark with a
velvety texture and red veins.
Growth is upright but small
and bushy. ('Whiteknight's
Ruby' × *F. procumbens*)
(Wright, UK, 1980)

'WHIRLAWAY'

'WHITE FALLS'

'WHITE ANN'

'WHITE GALORE'

'WHITE JOY'

'WHITE KING'

**'Whiteknight's Glister'**
Single H2 Bush
*Tube* medium length, red.
*Sepals* small and spreading, red
at the base shading to white at
the tips. *Corolla* red-purple
with rounded petals. *Foliage*
green with a cream border,
strongly variegated. Although
the growth is upright and fairly
vigorous it is rather slow
growing. Occasionally throws
green shoots. (Sport of *F.
magellanica* var. *molinae* × *F.
fulgens*)
(Wright, UK, 1980)

**'Whiteknight's Goblin'**
Single H2 Bush
*Tube* fairly long, crimson lake.
*Sepals* also crimson lake.
*Corolla* scarlet. *Foliage*
medium green. The natural
growth is as an upright bush. A
natural variant of *F. denticulata*
grown from imported seed.
(Wright, UK, 1981)

**'Whiteknight's Pearl'**
Single H2 Bush
*Tube* thin, medium length,
white. *Sepals* pale pink with
small green tips. *Corolla* clear
pink with roundish petals.
*Foliage* dark green and quite
small. Growth is upright and
very strong and bushy. (*F.
magellanica* var. *molinae* × (*F.
magellanica* var. *molinae* × *F.
fulgens*))
(Wright, UK, 1980)

**'Whiteknight's Ruby'**
Triphylla type H2 Bush
A true triphylla type, with
flowers carried at the ends of
branches. *Tube* long and thin,
cardinal red to tyrian purple.
*Sepals* small, tyrian purple.
*Corolla* petals quite small, of
the same colour. Foliage dark
green with a light purple
reverse, red veining. The
natural growth is upright but
not too vigorous. (*F. triphylla* ×
*F. procumbens*)
(Wright, UK, 1976)

**'White Loeki'**
Single H2 Bush
Medium-sized flower. *Tube* and

*sepals* red. *Corolla* petals
white; corolla opens flat and is
very attractive. *Foliage* medium
green. The natural growth is as
an upright, fairly small bush.
(de Graaff, Holland, 1986)

**'White Pixie'**
Single H3 Bush
*Tube* short and thin, red.
*Sepals* short, broad and
upturned, also red. *Corolla*
white, reddish-pink veins. The
flowers are fairly small and
compact. *Foliage* yellowish-
green with red veins and
serrated leaves. Growth is
upright and bushy. A free-
flowering plant for the hardy
border. H. and S. 24–30in
(60–75cm). (Sport of 'Pixie')
(Rawlins, UK, 1967; also by
Wagtails Nursery as 'Wagtails
White Pixie')

**'White Queen'**
Single H2 Lax bush
*Tube* long and fairly thick,
white. *Sepals* short, broad and
held well back from the
corolla, creamy white. *Corolla*
small and compact, salmon
orange. The blooms are fairly
long. *Foliage* medium green,
the leaves serrated. Growth is
vigorous but rather lax. Will
make a good free-flowering
bush with supports.
(Doyle, UK, 1899)

**'White Spider'**
Single H2 Bush
*Tube* long and thin, pale pink.
*Sepals* long and narrow, curl
upwards, pinkish with green
tips. *Corolla* white with pink
veins; the long petals help to
form a fairly compact flower.
*Foliage* medium green, the
leaves fairly small with serrated
edges. Growth is upright and
vigorous. A very free-flowering
cultivar and easy to grow.
(Haag, USA, 1951)

**'White Surprise'**
Double H2 Trailer
*Tube* and *sepals* white. *Corolla*
white flushed pink. The flowers
are of medium size. *Foliage*
medium green. The growth is

naturally trailing.
(Dresman, UK, 1987)

**'White Water'**
Semi-double H2 Lax bush
*Tube* creamy white. *Sepals*
reflexed, white with rose
colouring underneath. *Corolla*
white and much creamier at the
base of the petals. The
medium-sized blooms are
carried on rather lax upright
growth. *Foliage* medium
green.
(Lockerbie, Australia, 1963)

**'Wibke Becker'**
Single H2 Trailer
Medium-sized flower. *Tube* and
*sepals* salmon rose. *Corolla*
white. *Foliage* medium green.
The natural desire of the plant
is to trail.
(Strumper, Holland, 1986)

**'Wicked Queen'**
Double H3 Bush
Large flowers. *Tube* and *sepals*
dark red. *Corolla* deep purple
splashed with pink. *Foliage*
very dark green. Growth is
naturally upright, bushy and
compact. H. and S. 24–30in
(60–75cm).
(Tabraham, UK, 1985)

**'Wight Magic'**
Double H2 Bush
Large flowers. *Tube* and *sepals*
white. *Corolla* also white.
*Foliage* light to medium green.
The natural growth is upright
and bushy. (Sport from 'Blue
Veil')
(Porter, M., UK, 1988)

**'Wild and Beautiful'**
Double H2 Lax bush
*Tube* short and thick, white.
*Sepals* longish, slightly
upturned, pale neyron rose on
the outside, darker neyron rose
on the inner. *Corolla* dark
amethyst violet fading to china
rose at the base of the petals.
The blooms are of medium
size. *Foliage* light green, the
leaves large. The natural
growth is rather lax but very
vigorous and free-flowering.
(Soo Yun, USA, 1978)

'WHITEKNIGHT'S PEARL'

'WHITE PIXIE'

'WHITE SPIDER'

'WICKED QUEEN'

'WIGHT MAGIC'

**'Wild Fire'**
Semi-double H2 Lax bush
*Tube* short and thick, rose pink.
*Sepals* bright rose pink on the
top and a deeper shade of pink
underneath; long, and curl up
and over the tube. *Corolla*
cardinal red ageing to crimson
scarlet, with salmon shading at
the base of the petals. The
flowers are freely produced.
*Foliage* medium green, leaves
fairly large and have heavy
serrated edges. The lax growth
is upright and spreading.
(Handley, UK, 1972)

**'Wilf Tolley'**
Semi-double H2 Bush
*Tube* short and thick, pale
pink. *Sepals* china rose, waxy
with green tips, held well out
from the corolla. *Corolla*
purple-violet with pale pink at
the base of the petals, changing
to cyclamen purple on
maturity. *Foliage* medium green
with small serrated leaves.
Growth is upright, self-
branching and bushy, vigorous
and free-flowering.
(Gadsby, UK, 1974)

**'Willemien'**
Double H2 Bush
Medium-sized flowers. *Tube*
and *sepals* cardinal red in
colour. *Corolla* heather purple.
*Foliage* medium green. Growth
is bushy and upright.
(Veen, Holland, 1991)

**'Willemtien Aaltien'**
Single H2 Lax bush
Medium-sized flowers. *Tube*
carmine red. *Sepals* are rose,
tipped with green. *Corolla*
carmine red. *Foliage* medium
green. The natural growth is
lax, although upright.
(Veen, Holland, 1990)

**'William Caunt'**
Single H2 Bush
*Tube* creamy white. *Sepals*
horizontally held, white flushed
pink on top and slightly paler
underneath; the tips are green
and recurve slightly. *Corolla*
opens rosy to scarlet cerise
flushed white at the base, and

matures to a lightly paler
colouring. The flowers are
carried horizontally. *Foliage*
dark green. Growth is self-
branching and bushy.
(Caunt, UK, 1984)

**'Wilson's Joy'**
Single H2 Bush
*Tube* short, white. *Sepals* white
and tinged with pink, short,
broad, held well out. *Corolla* is
cerise blue shading to cerise.
The medium-sized flowers are
fairly profuse. *Foliage* medium
green, medium-sized, slightly
serrated. Growth is upright and
bushy. ('Mrs Marshall' x)
(Wilson, UK, 1974)

**'Wilson's Pearls'**
Semi-double H2 Trailer
*Tube* short, red. *Sepals* curl
back and tend to spiral, also
red. *Corolla* white veined with
pink. The medium-sized blooms
are freely produced. *Foliage* pale
green with a central red vein.
Growth is lax so will make a
good basket. A bush can be
trained if supports are used.
(Wilson, UK, 1967)

**'Wilson's Sugar Pink'**
Single H2 Lax bush
*Tube* is white, shading to pink.
*Sepals* very pale pink almost
white on the top surface, deeper
pink underneath. *Corolla*
mallow to pale pink; the small
flowers are very prolific. *Foliage*
pale green. Growth is rather lax
so could be used for either
baskets or bushes.
(Wilson, UK, 1979)

**'Wine and Roses'**
Double H2 Trailer
*Tube* short and thick, pale
pink. *Sepals* pale pink on top
and darker on the undersides,
short and broad, curl upwards
and have green tips. *Corolla*
wine purple in the centre
shading to pale pinkish-white
at the base of the petals; long
pink petaloids on the outside.
*Foliage* light green. The growth
is trailing and free-flowering.
Early stopping is advised.
(Walker, USA, 1969)

**'Wingrove's Mammoth'**
Double H2 Bush
*Tube* and *sepals* turkey red.
*Corolla* white, heavily veined
and splashed with carmine.
The blooms are huge but are
exceptionally free for their size.
*Foliage* medium to dark green.
The natural growth is upright
and bushy. Supports will be
needed to counteract the
weight of the flowers.
(Wingrove, UK, 1968)

**'Wings of Song'**
Double H2 Trailer
*Tube* medium length, rose pink.
*Sepals* long, broad and
upturned to the tube, also rose
pink. *Corolla* lavender pink
with pink veins. The medium-
sized blooms are fairly
compact. *Foliage* medium green
with reddish veins. Growth is
naturally trailing, vigorous,
self-branching and very
floriferous.
(Blackwell, UK, 1968)

**'Winifred'**
Single H2 Bush
*Tube* thick, pale pink. *Sepals*
upturned, long, deep rose pink.
*Corolla* cerise pink shading to
pale pink at the base of the
petals. The medium-sized flowers
are freely produced. *Foliage*
medium green. The natural
growth is as an upright bush.
(Chatfield, UK, 1973)

**'Winkelpicker'**
Semi-double H2 Trailer
Medium-sized flowers. *Tube* and
*sepals* white. *Corolla* carmine
red. *Foliage* medium green. The
natural tendency is to trail so
will make a good basket.
(Brouwer, Holland, 1987)

**'Win Oxtoby'**
Double H2 Trailer
Medium-sized. *Tube* pink.
*Sepals* recurve, also pink.
*Corolla* pink, petals have a
darker edge; the *sub-petals*
stand out horizontally. *Foliage*
medium green. Growth is
naturally trailing, and a super
basket can be grown very easily.
(Bielby/Oxtoby, UK, 1990)

'WILSON'S PEARLS'

'WILSON'S SUGAR PINK'

'WINE AND ROSES'

'WINGS OF SONG'

'WINIFRED'

**'Winston Churchill'**
Double H2 Bush
*Tube* medium length, pink.
*Sepals* pink on top, darker on
the underside; short, broad and
reflexing. *Corolla* lavender blue
with pinkish veins and splashed
pink on the outer petals. The
compact blooms are small to
medium-sized but are very freely
produced. *Foliage* medium green
with serrated edges. Growth is
upright, self-branching and
bushy. An excellent cultivar.
(Garson, USA, 1942)

**'Woodnook'**
Double H2 Bush
Medium-sized flower. *Tube* and
*sepals* white, flushed with
crimson and tipped with green.
*Corolla* pale violet-purple
flushed and marbled with rose
bengal. The attractively coloured
flowers are freely produced.
*Foliage* medium green. The
growth is upright and bushy.
(Pacey, UK, 1987)

**'Woodside Gem'**
Single H2 Bush
Medium-sized flowers. *Tube*
and *sepals* pink. *Corolla*
magenta. *Foliage* medium
green. The natural growth is as
an upright bush.
(Hanson, UK, 1990)

**'W.P.C. Kampionen'**
Single H2 Bush
Medium-sized flower. *Tube*
white flushed with orange.
*Sepals* white. *Corolla* petals
violet. *Foliage* medium green.
The growth is naturally upright
and very vigorous.
(Krom, Holland, 1989)

*F. wurdackii*
Species H1 Bush
The single flowers are produced
fairly prolifically, in bunches,
terminally. *Tube* long and
trumpet-shaped, orange to red.
*Sepals* quite small, of similar
colour. *Corolla* petals red.
*Foliage* fairly large, the leaves
dark green and hairy. Growth is
upright and bushy. A relatively
easy species to grow in pots.
(Northern Peru)

# Y

**'Yankee Clipper'**
Double H2 Bush
*Tube* short, medium length,
red. *Sepals* short, carmine red.
*Corolla* ruby red and carmine,
variegated. *Foliage* large,
medium green. The blooms are
fairly large and quite freely
produced. The natural growth
is as an upright bush.
(Soo Yun, USA, 1971)

**'Yolande Franck'**
Single H2 Bush
Medium-sized flowers. *Tubes*
light red in colour. *Sepals* rose.
*Corolla* light orange-red.
*Foliage* medium green. The
natural growth is as an upright
bush.
(Franck, Holland, 1988)

**'Yorkshire Rally'**
Double H2 Bush
Medium to large flowers.
*Tube* red. *Sepals* white, veined
with red at the base. *Corolla*
creamy white, veined pink at
the base. *Foliage* pale green.
Growth is naturally bushy and
upright.
(Redfern, UK, 1988)

**'Yuletide'**
Double H2 Bush
*Tube* medium length, crimson.
*Sepals* also crimson. *Corolla*
creamy white, very full and
quite large. *Foliage* medium to
darkish green. Growth is
upright, bushy, vigorous and
very free-flowering. A very
showy plant to grow.
(Tiret, USA, 1948)

# Z

**'Zaanlander'**
Single H2 Lax bush
Medium-sized flowers. *Tube*
cream in colour. *Sepals* light
rose. *Corolla* violet. *Foliage*
medium green. The natural
growth is as a rather lax, but
vigorous upright bush.
(Krom, Holland, 1989)

**'Zara'**
Single H2 Bush
*Tube* and *sepals* light rose in
colour. Corolla is flame orange.
*Foliage* medium green, quite
small. The small flowers are
produced very freely. Growth is
upright and bushy.
(Porter, UK, 1981)

**'Ziegfried Girl'**
Double H2 Trailer
*Tube* pink, medium length.
*Sepals* pink on top, fairly dark
pink underneath, green tips.
*Corolla* a slightly lighter shade
of pink. The largish blooms are
quite freely produced and
shaped like a rosette. *Foliage*
medium to dark green with
cream veins. Although the
growth is trailing it can be
disappointing when trying to
develop a basket.
(Fuchsia Forest, USA, 1966)

**'Zulu King'**
Single H2 Trailer
*Tube* and *sepals* deep carmine.
*Corolla* blackish-purple.
*Foliage* dark green. The growth
is naturally trailing. The colour
and form of the medium-sized
flower is retained right through
maturity.
(de Graaff, Holland, 1990)

**'Zulu Queen'**
Single H2 Lax upright/trailer.
Medium-sized flowers. *Tube*
and *sepals* white. *Corolla* dark
aubergine. *Foliage* medium to
dark green. The growth is
rather lax so can be used for
either bush or basket with the
necessary supports.
(de Graaff, Holland, 1987)

**'Zwaarte Snor'**
Double H2 Lax bush
Small flowers. *Tube* and *sepals*
deep carmine purple. *Corolla*
dark purple. *Foliage* medium to
dark green. Growth is rather
lax but upright.
(Weeda, Holland, 1990)

'WINSTON CHURCHILL'

'ZIEGFRIED GIRL'

'ZULU QUEEN'

'ZWAARTE SNOR'

# Glossary

**Anther** The pollen-bearing part of the stamen.

**Apetalous** A flower without petals, that is, without a corolla.

**Axil** The angle formed by the junction of the leaf and stem from which new shoots or flowers develop.

**Berry** The fleshy fruit containing the seeds; the ovary after fertilization.

**Biennial** The term used for the process of growing a plant one year to flower the following year.

**Bleeding** The loss of sap from a cut or damaged shoot of a plant.

**Break** To branch or send out new growth from dormant wood.

**Bud** Undeveloped shoot found in the axils of plants; also the developing flower.

**Callus** The scab formed during the healing process of a cut surface. It also forms at the end of a cutting before rooting commences.

**Calyx** The sepals and tube together; the outer part of the flower.

**Cambium** A layer of activity; dividing cells around the xylem or wood.

**Chlorophyll** The green colourant present in plant tissue which contains magnesium. It traps blue and red light (energy), and is responsible for photosynthesis.

**Chromosomes** Thread-like bodies consisting of a series of different genes arranged in linear fashion. They occur in the nucleus of every plant cell.

**Clear stem** The amount of stem free of all growth. It is measured from the soil, level to the first branch or leaf. It is of importance when growing standards or bushes.

**Compost** A mixture of ingredients specially prepared for the growing of cuttings, plants, or the sowing of seeds.

**Cordate** Heart-shaped.

**Corolla** The collective term for the petals; the inner part of the flower.

**Cultivar** A cultivated variety: a cross between two hybrids or species and a hybrid. Normally written cv.

**Cutting** A piece from a plant encouraged to form roots and thus produce a new plant. This is vegetative reproduction, and plants produced by this method are true to their parental type.

**Cyme** An inflorescence where the central flower opens first as in *F. arborescens*.

**Damp down** Raising the humidity of the atmosphere in the greenhouse by spraying plants, benches or paths with water.

**Damping off** The collapse and possible death of cuttings or seedlings usually due to attack at ground level by soil-borne fungi.

**Double** A fuchsia with eight or more petals.

**Elliptic** An oval shape, with pointed or rounded ends.

**Emasculation** The process of removing immature stamens from a host plant to prevent self-pollination, during the cross-pollination of two plants.

**Etiolation** The blanching of leaves and the lengthening of the stems that occurs when plants are grown in the dark or when the light intensity is not sufficient for adequate growth.

**Fasciation** The growing together, or fusion, of different parts of a plant. Leaves and flowers occasionally fuse together.

**Feeding** Applying additional plant nutrients to the compost in an effort to enhance growth or remedy compost deficiencies.

**Fertilization** The union of male and female cells.

**Fibrous roots** The white roots produced from the main fleshy roots vital for the taking up of water and nutrients essential for healthy growth.

**Filament** The stalk of the stamen.

**Final stop** The last removal of the growing tip which a plant receives before being allowed to grow to flowering stage.

**First stop** The removal of the growing tip of a rooted cutting to encourage branching into the required shape.

**Genus** The name given to a group of closely related species, for example *Fuchsia*.

**Hermaphrodite** Flowers which have both male and female parts.

**Hybrid** A cross between two species.

**Hypanthium** The correct term for the tube.

**Inflorescence** Of flowers – usually arranged around a single axis, as in *F. paniculata* or *F. arborescens*.

**Internode** The portion of the stem between two nodes. Rooting from this section is described as internodal.

**Lanceolate** Lance-, or spear-shaped.

**Mutation** Departure from the normal parent type, or sport.

**N.A.S.** The abbreviation used by show judges to indicate that an entry in a class is not according to the schedule. Exhibits so marked cannot be considered for an award within the show.

**Node** Part of the stem from which a leaf or bud arises. When taking cuttings, roots form most readily from this point.

**Nutrients** The food used by the plant from the growing medium, necessary for sustained and healthy growth.

**Ornamental** A term used to describe those plants which have decorative foliage. The foliage can be variegated or of a colour other than the usual green.

**Ovary** The part containing the ovules which, after fertilization, swells and encloses the seeds.

**Ovate** Egg-shaped.

**Overwintering** The storage of plants during the resting period, the winter months, so that the tissue remains alive though dormant.

**Panicles** A branched inflorescence consisting of a number of racemes.

**Pedicel** The flower stalk.

**Petal** A division of the corolla.

**Petaloid** Normally used to describe the smaller outer petals of the corolla.

**Petiole** The leaf stalk.

**Photosynthesis** The process carried out by the plant in the manufacture of plant food from water and carbon dioxide, using the energy absorbed by chlorophyll from sunlight.

**Pinch** To remove the growing tip.

**Pistil** The female part of the flower, consisting of the ovary, stigma and style.

**Pot-bound** When the plant container is full of roots to such an extent that the plant will become starved of nutrients.

**Pot on** To transfer the plant from one size of pot to a larger one so that there will be a continuous supply of nutrients.

**Potting up** Transferring a seedling or rooted cutting from its initial seedbox or propagator into a plant pot.

**Propagation** Increasing of stock by means of seeds or by rooting cuttings.

# Glossary

**Pruning** The shortening of laterals or roots to enhance the shape of the plant or to remove a damaged portion.

**Raceme** A flower-cluster with the separate flowers attached by short equal stalks at equal distances along a central stem.

**Rubbing out** The removal of unwanted side growths, for example on a standard stem, usually in early bud stage.

**Self-pollination** The transference of pollen from anther to stigma of the same flower or another flower on the same plant.

**Semi-double** A fuchsia with five, six or seven petals.

**Sepals** The outermost part of the flower; four sepals and the tube form the calyx.

**Shading** The exclusion of some of the rays of the sun by the use of blinds, netting or a glass colourant.

**Shaping** To grow a plant into a definite shape by means of training the laterals or by selective pinching out of the growing tips.

**Siblings** Offspring of the same female and male parents.

**Single** A fuchsia with only four petals.

**Species** The smallest unit of classification. Individuals in a species are assumed to have emanated from a single original genetic source and are sexually compatible with each other.

**Sport** A shoot differing in character from the typical growth of the parent plant, often giving rise to a new cultivar, which must be propagated vegetatively.

**Stamen** The male part of the flower comprising the filament and anther.

**Stigma** The part of the pistil to which the pollen grain adheres.

**Stop** To remove the growing tip.

**Striking a cutting** The insertion of a prepared cutting into a suitable rooting compost.

**Style** The stalk carrying the stigma.

**Sub-species** A partially differentiated group within a species.

**Systemics** Insecticides or fungicides taken up by the roots and carried into the sap of the plant, thus causing it to become poisonous to sucking insects or protected from the attack of viruses. Can also be absorbed through the foliage if applied in spray form.

**Terminal** At the extremities or ends of the branches.

**Ternate** Arranged in threes; of leaves or flowers at a joint.

**Trace elements** Nutrients required by a plant to maintain steady and healthy growth (boron, copper, manganese, molybdenum and zinc).

**Tube** The elongated part of the calyx, correctly called the hypathium.

**Turgid** The condition of the plant cells after absorption of water to full capacity.

**Turning** The term used to describe the turning of a plant daily in an effort to achieve balanced growth from all directions.

**Variety** Botanically a variant of the species, but formerly used to denote what is now more commonly called a cultivar.

**Virus** An agent causing systemic disease. It is too small to be seen other than with powerful microscopes, but is transmitted very easily.

**Whip** A term given to a single stem of a plant being grown with a view to producing a standard.

**Wilt** Drooping caused by a lack of moisture within the plants. Can also be caused by disease or toxins.